Sustainable Design of
Research Laboratories

Sustainable Design of
Research Laboratories

PLANNING, DESIGN, AND OPERATION

KLING STUBBINS

WILEY

John Wiley & Sons, Inc.

Published by John Wiley & Sons, Inc., Hoboken, New Jersey

Published simultaneously in Canada

For general information about our other products and services, please contact our Customer Care Department within the United States at (800) 762–2974, outside the United States at (317) 572–3993 or fax (317) 572–4002.

Wiley also publishes its books in a variety of electronic formats. Some content that appears in print may not be available in electronic books. For more information about Wiley products, visit our web site at www.wiley.com.

Library of Congress Cataloging-in-Publication Data:

KlingStubbins.
Sustainable design of research laboratories : planning, design, and operation/KlingStubbins.
    p. cm.
Includes index.
  ISBN 978-0-470-48564-4 (cloth : alk. paper); ISBN 978-0-470-91596-X (ebk); ISBN 978-0-470-91597-8 (ebk);
  ISBN 978-0-470-91598-6 (ebk)
1. Laboratories—Design and construction. 2. Laboratories—Environmental aspects. 3. Sustainable architecture. I. Title.
  NA6751.K58 2010
727'.5—dc22   2009051014

Printed in the United States of America

10 9 8 7 6 5 4 3 2 1

Contents

Chapter 4

Site Design: Connecting to Local and Regional Communities _____ **73**

Chapter 7

Chapter 9

FOREWORD

People have come to realize that it is buildings, not just transportation, manufacturing, and forest loss, that produce a lion's share of energy consumption, carbon concerns, and material flows. It follows that if we want to get to the heart of one of the biggest creative opportunities of our time and find the most creative solutions, our efforts can include a close examination of how buildings are designed, constructed, and maintained, and even how they are deconstructed and reconstructed over many useful lifespans.

Of all building types, research laboratories are some of the most resource-intensive. They use an enormous amount of energy to heat, cool, and power sophisticated equipment; they produce by far the largest volume of emissions in terms of exhaust air; and they use a lot of material. By finding ways to design and engineer research laboratories more efficiently, effectively, and sustainably, the lessons learned easily can be adapted to the design of other building types and other industries.

That's what makes this book, *Sustainable Design of Research Laboratories*, indispensable to understanding recent advances in the field. It's a compilation of tools and techniques from a wide variety of sources about what works, and what doesn't, in the search for sustainable lab design. It will open new doors—and change attitudes—about what's possible, and will point the way to significant reductions in energy use and carbon emissions while actually promoting a healthier workplace for staff. Because lab buildings typically operate on a 24/7 basis, every improvement can make an enormous difference.

In a way, research labs can be seen as some of the most technically sophisticated architecture that our society creates. They embody in function, style, and structure the culture of our age, symbolizing our scientific capacity to explore and discover new ways of doing things. As we enter a new age of a sustaining and self-renewing economy, it's important that we get it right and a sustaining design agenda is one of the best gifts that we can bestow upon the next generation; the consequences will be felt for decades to come. It's a long-term journey that starts with steps in the right direction, and this book will provide a valuable compass.

William McDonough, FAIA
Charlottesville, VA

ACKNOWLEDGMENTS

In the same way that a sustainably designed laboratory requires the integrated efforts of an entire team of architects and engineers, so too did this project. We'd like to acknowledge the efforts of a number of people here at KlingStubbins who were instrumental in the research, writing, and production of this book:

Text contributions by Debra Aungst, Alberto Cavallero, Nic Gurganus, Charlie Hayter, Jeffrey Kahn, Chris Leary, Jim Lindquist, Mike Lorenz, Mark Maguire, Amy Manley, John Neilson, Alberto Rios, Mike Schwarz, Scott Simpson, Veronica Viggiano, and Bruce Werfel formed the basis for much of the content of the book. Thanks are due to Melissa Bernstein, Michael Kolonauski, Eric Kuszewski, Stuart Mardeusz, Natasha Luthra, Travis Rothbloom, Abigail Sparks, and Ximena Valle for their assistance with graphics; and to Tari Maynor for her meticulously maintained benchmarking databases. We are grateful for Royce Epstein's research into various materials and Emma Corbalan for her assistance with energy analyses. Without the help of Katie Cipolla and Adam Clair, who worked tirelessly to track down required permissions, organize captions, and oversee the organization of hundreds of images, and Josie Tustin who formatted and reformatted our text, this book would not have come together.

We'd like to acknowledge all of our outside contributors who provided additional project images and, in some cases, text. They are identified in the captions of images they provided and in the bylines accompanying any text they authored. Thank you, as well, to the many clients, institutions, and building owners who kindly agreed to allow their projects to be included in this work. Finally, this list would not be complete without mentioning the support provided by everyone at John Wiley & Sons, Inc., and in particular that of John Czarnecki, Sadie Abuhoff, Nancy Cintron, and Kerstin Nasdeo. Thank you all for your patient guidance throughout the entire process.

Ellen Sisle, AIA, LEED AP
Director of Laboratory Planning, KlingStubbins

Paul Leonard, PE, LEED AP
Director of Engineering, KlingStubbins

Jonathan A Weiss, AIA, LEED AP
Director of Sustainability, KlingStubbins

1 Introduction

Courtesy of KlingStubbins.
Photography by Ron Solomon—Baltimore © 2008.

If our designs . . . are to be correct, we must at the outset take note of the countries and climates in which they are built. This is because one part of the earth is directly under the sun's course, another is far away from it, while another lies midway between these two . . .

—Vitruvius[1]

Core Principles

While the terms "green building" and "sustainability" are relatively recent, the idea of sustainable design has been an intrinsic part of building design and operation since the beginning of organized civilization. Because there were no mechanical and electrical systems, early buildings needed to be designed to carefully take advantage of the environment and climate of the places they were constructed. They needed to be sited to catch prevailing winds, and to take advantage of natural shading to stay cool in warmer months. Organizing the functions of the buildings so they would receive sunlight as it moved through the sky was important before there was easy access to electric lighting. The walls of the buildings needed to be constructed to protect against temperature changes throughout the year. Before global transportation networks, it was critical to build out of materials that could be sourced locally, would last a long time, and could be easily removed and disposed of with minimal effort. It took a great deal of effort to find clean water, and fuel for heating (wood, peat, and coal), so these resources were carefully managed. In short, there was no such thing as building "green," buildings had to be able to mitigate local environmental conditions and efficiently make use of the materials and resources close at hand.

With the advent of industrialization, another issue came into the public eye—the connection between living and working conditions and human health. Increasing occupant access to light and fresh air was proposed to alleviate these challenging conditions. The link between buildings and the occupants' health and safety has been an important part of public regulation of buildings ever since.

The connection among buildings, resources, and human health as a focus of sustainable design makes a strong case for sustainability in laboratory buildings. The scientific mission and organizational goals of most laboratory users are a natural fit for sustainability. Research scientists are striving to find out more about how things work in the world, biologically, physically, chemically, and environmentally. Sustainability is focused on maintaining a balance between what our buildings need in order to support us, and what that means for the world around us. Intrinsic to that is how we make and operate the building, and how the building affects us as we occupy it.

This book will focus on how laboratory facilities can be more sustainable in design, construction, and operation. We will look at what makes buildings more sustainable, and focus on how laboratory facilities differ from other buildings to get an overall look at how to design and operate a sustainable lab building. While lab buildings offer challenges to green building goals, there's also the potential for great impact by making these buildings perform optimally. If lab buildings use five to ten times more energy than office buildings,[2] even a modest percentage reduction means a large amount of energy saved. Over the last ten years or so, many groups have begun to refer to "green" buildings

as "high performance" buildings, to emphasize that the goal is to find a way to make these buildings perform in a highly efficient fashion. While part of green building is conservation—reducing what we need—another aspect of it involves a strong focus on optimization—making sure we deliver what we need in the most efficient manner possible. For example, a great deal of energy can be saved by changing the temperature setpoints, i.e., turning the thermostats up in the summer, and down in the winter. This is conservation—changing what we ask our buildings to do, and changing **our** behavior. Optimization means finding a more efficient way to make the building cool in the summer and warm in the winter. True high-performance building design counts on **both** conservation and optimization, and for a laboratory building, it is critical to make sure that this does not threaten the research objectives. While the process is the same for lab buildings and nonlab buildings, the decisions and results will be different.

There are many different factors involved in high-performance building design covering a broad range of different aspects of the design and operation process. In reality, the concepts are very simple; there are three main ways that a building impacts the environment: site impacts, resource use, and human factors.

Site Impacts

The broadest category is the site; this includes site selection, site design, and site connection with the community for transportation, infrastructure, and waste. Possibly the biggest impact is determined by which site the lab building will be built on. Should it be a new building, or a renovation of an existing building? Should it be in a developed area, near existing infrastructure, or an undeveloped greenfield site? Should it

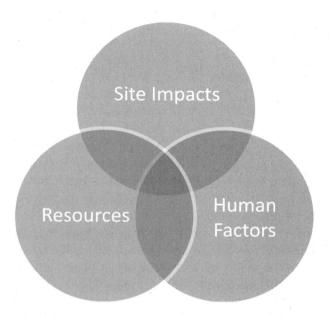

Although there are many different strategies to pursue sustainability, most can be ascribed to three main categories: minimizing site impacts, reducing resource use, and improved human factors. *Image courtesy of KlingStubbins.*

For the Novartis Institutes for Biomedical Research Global Research Headquarters in Cambridge, Massachusetts, the project team adapted an existing industrial building (the historic NECCO building) and converted it for use as a research facility. By taking advantage of the existing embodied energy inherent in this 1923 structure, as well as connecting with dense existing urban infrastructure, the environmental impact of this building was drastically minimized. *Courtesy of KlingStubbins. Photography © Jeff Goldberg/Esto.*

be near potential employees or occupants? Each of these questions has a big impact on the project, and for each, laboratories often require different answers than other types of buildings. For example, while it is relatively easy to adapt a building to office use, only certain buildings can be renovated into ventilation-driven labs, based on the infrastructure needs.

Once the project site has been selected, the integration of the building with the site can significantly reduce its impact. The project can minimize changes to the natural hydrology of the site and can work to minimize the flows of water and waste into existing ground sources and waste streams. The project can minimize the amount of impervious materials added to a site, which will reduce runoff. The project can also put in place natural controls and features to treat

runoff and waste on site rather than letting it contribute to stormwater system overloads of volume and suspended solids. Laboratories, depending on the type of research being done, are likely to have significantly more waste products, and care must be taken to manage, remediate, and treat liquid and airborne wastes to minimize impacts on the surrounding community. Care must be taken to ensure that waste stacks are modeled and monitored to prevent laboratory exhaust from reentrainment at building air intakes.

Resources

The second category of impact for a project is resources: water, energy, and materials. We'll focus on a number of different strategies, but they all really

For this detailed study of wind-wake analysis at the University of Colorado Denver's new Research 1 and 2 complexes in Aurora, Colorado, computer simulation or physical wind-tunnel testing can ensure that exhaust streams will be safely dispersed and diluted before getting to nearby buildings, outdoor occupant areas, or air intake louvers in the vicinity. *Image courtesy of RWDI.*

boil down to three main concepts: reduce the amount of resources needed, find a more efficient way to deliver the resources, and use alternative sources for these resources. Careful attention to these three aspects during design, construction, and ongoing building operation is necessary to reduce the overall "environmental footprint" of the project. For each of these three categories of resource use, the research requirements and criteria will affect which strategies are possible for each project.

Water

The supply of safe and plentiful drinking water is critical to human survival. In many parts of the world, the available supply of potable water is insufficient. The amount of energy spent to transport water from one place to another is significant. Studies have shown that in some areas, the energy used to transport water is a larger proportion of the carbon footprint than localized energy use. Water tables are dropping in many parts of the United States, and in many coastal regions saltwater levels are encroaching on former freshwater aquifers, rendering them useless as potable water sources. Laboratory facilities are significant water users for both sanitary and process uses. Sustainable strategies for water reduction have focused on two main areas—reducing the amount of water needed by using more efficient fixtures and closed-loop systems where possible, and by using nonpotable water for as many uses as pos-

At Johnson & Johnson's Pharmaceutical Research and Development (PRD) Drug Discovery Laboratory, Phase II building in La Jolla, California, several water conservation measures were undertaken. In addition to high-efficiency sanitary systems, the project employed a cooling coil condensate recovery system, reusing that water for cooling tower makeup water, and combining it with municipally provided reclaimed water to handle all irrigation needs with nonpotable water. The company has calculated that they save approximately one million gallons of water per year using this system. *Image courtesy of KlingStubbins. Photography © Tom Bonner 2007.*

sible. Highly efficient glasswash systems, closed-loop process chilled water systems, and use of water-free handwash stations are methods of reducing water use as required in labs. Reuse of reverse osmosis and deionized (RO/DI) reject water is another way to minimize the water waste in a laboratory facility.

Energy

Reducing the energy usage of a building is really achieved by three separate strategies, each of which works together to achieve optimal energy use. The first is **rightsizing loads**. Project design starts with assumptions about design criteria—what temperature and humidity is desired, what light level is needed, how much fresh air is needed for each space, and what amount of variability is acceptable for each of these criteria. Each of these criteria has an impact on the size of the systems designed, their cost, and the amount of energy they will use. When project criteria are challenged, internal loads on the systems are reduced. Another critical part of rightsizing the loads is to minimize any external gains and losses on the building—by studying the optimum orientation and the proper exterior building components, the project can reduce and mitigate exterior loads due to solar gain and exterior environmental factors. Insulation can be added, shading devices can be designed to reduce the solar loads on the glazed areas of the building.

The second strategy is **system selection and design.** Once the loads have been minimized, systems can be selected and designed. Often starting with lower assumed loads will mean there are more options possible for system selection and design.

The third strategy is **energy source efficiency.** Once the loads are minimized and optimal systems are

For the Smithsonian Tropical Research Institute Field Station Laboratory at Bocas del Toro in Panama, the design team first challenged criteria, divided functions to minimize loads, and created this large photovoltaic panel canopy that provides added shading and diffusion of light entering the occupied spaces below, as well as generating the majority of energy required for this laboratory facility. *Image courtesy of Kiss + Cathcart, Architects.*

designed, the team can look at ways to find cleaner sources of energy through onsite generation through renewables or co-generation, or through green power procurement. For a good example of successful energy-source efficiency implementation, see color images C-66 through C-73 of the Johnson & Johnson La Jolla, California site.

Materials

There are several different ways that environmentally preferable materials can be evaluated. It is necessary to consider not just the material itself, but to factor in the overall impact over the lifecycle of its use. Environmentally speaking, the ideal material is made from raw materials that are nontoxic, plentiful, and renewable; takes very little energy to extract, formulate, and

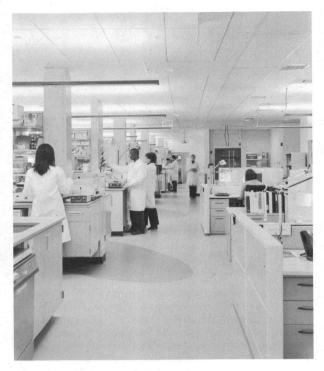

For the Novartis Institutes for Biomedical Research 100 Tech Square project in Cambridge, Massachusetts, the team evaluated the cost over the lifespan of the flooring material and determined that the rubber flooring, although more expensive to purchase and install, would last longer and require significantly less maintenance over its service life. This was a successful "rightfit" approach to finish materials for the lab. *Image courtesy of KlingStubbins. Photography © Chun Y Lai. All Rights Reserved.*

fabricate; uses very little energy to transport and install; is extremely durable and easy to maintain; and at the end of its useful life can be recycled or reused efficiently. There are several different ways to categorize materials. Laboratory materials have some added factors, depending on the type of research being done. The materials may need to be chemically resistant, or impervious to radioactive or biological agents. Cleanability and durability under more stringent cleaning and maintenance routines are required

for many lab materials. Critical to effective selection of materials is "rightsizing" the materials for the scientific requirements of the space. For example, selecting scrubbable ceiling tiles is only necessary if the ceilings are actually going to be scrubbed. For many labs, conventional office ceiling systems are perfectly acceptable, and can be made from more environmentally friendly materials.

Human Factors

People spend more than 90 percent of their time inside buildings. How the building environment impacts them plays a big part in overall satisfaction, productivity, and human health. Although sustainable materials, energy efficiency, and water consumption comprise a big part of our focus on green building, many have argued that the major way that green buildings contribute to the environment is through human factors inside the building. The major strategies that address human factors in buildings are air quality, occupant comfort, and connection with the exterior environment.

Air Quality

Although part of indoor air quality is concerned with protecting occupants from outdoor contaminants, it has been shown that contaminant levels inside buildings can be many times higher than outdoor levels. Increasing outside air quantities can help reduce contaminant levels. For lab buildings, where there are often high ventilation requirements, air quality must be controlled through careful separation of chemical uses and ventilation design. Use of low-volatile organic compound (VOC) materials is important to minimize sources of contaminants in buildings, and many conventional laboratory materials—epoxy flooring, adhesives, and epoxy paints—are now formulated with low VOC levels.

Occupant Comfort

There are several factors contributing to occupant satisfaction and productivity, including lighting, glare, acoustics, and air movement. Studies have shown that the most important factor contributing to occupant satisfaction is thermal comfort. Since different people can experience the same spaces with different reports of thermal comfort, providing some level of occupant controllability or adjustability is important. This is challenging in laboratory spaces where frequently the HVAC system is closely controlled and monitored from a central building automation system. Conventional design has focused on ensuring that systems will offer consistent and even conditions. Recent studies have borne out that providing zones for occupant control is also important for thermal comfort.

Access to Environment

Another category which has been positively correlated with occupant satisfaction and productivity is visual connection to the exterior environment. Spaces lit by natural daylight have been proven to improve occupant health and satisfaction. For space where daylight penetration is not desirable or possible, views to the exterior have also been shown to correlate to occupant productivity. Providing views to the exterior requires attention to shading, since solar gains and glare can negatively impact the research objectives.

In summary, there are some special challenges in creating a sustainable laboratory building. Many labs use a lot of energy for process loads, equipment loads,

At the University of California, San Diego's Leichtag Biomedical Research Building, the design team organized the overhead service and ductwork distribution to allow the ceiling to slope up to an increased head height at the exterior wall. This allows for added daylight penetration farther into the lab building. Note that there are exterior shading devices as well as frit patterns on the glazing to cut down on glare at the perimeter work areas—a "right-fit" approach to finish materials for the lab. *Image courtesy of ZGF Architects LLP. Photography © Anne Garrison.*

computer loads, and other "plug loads." These process loads can represent a significant majority of overall building loads, and cannot necessarily be changed with current available scientific equipment. Many labs use stronger and more toxic materials for research. This means that the finishes and systems that come in contact with these materials need to be highly resistant. Many labs require tighter control of the environment for scientific purposes. Maintaining tight control of temperature, airflow, and humidity takes far more energy than in nonlab spaces, where people can tolerate a broader range of comfort factors. When the research studies require it, the tight control can reduce the ability to optimize the energy use.

DESIGN AND OPERATION OF THE SUSTAINABLE LABORATORY BUILDING:
Considerations and Musings

Dennis M. Gross, M.S., Ph.D
Associate Dean
Jefferson College of Graduate Studies
Thomas Jefferson University
Philadelphia, Pennsylvania

As noted by the authors of essays and chapters in this new work, innovative new models for the design of the laboratory of the future have been emerging over the past few years. These models are expected to be able to create laboratory environments that can respond to the needs of the present while being flexible enough to accommodate the demands of the sciences of the future. These demands will influence not only industrial and government laboratories but also academic laboratories. The latter types of laboratories are very important in our discussions of industrial and government laboratories because the academic laboratory is where the scientist of the future not only receives their training but develops their skill sets, both scientific and social. Furthermore, they also develop their habits, expectations, scientific work ethic, acceptance, and tolerance to changes in their work environments.

When looking at trends in laboratory design that emerge from conferences, professional architectural journals, or even commentary on new architecture in the public media such as newspapers, it is hard to dissociate architectural design for something even as specific as a research laboratory from the concept of sustainable architecture. In this instance, as noted by J.J. Kim (National Pollution Prevention Center for Higher Education, 1998) the debate over the terms "sustainable," "green," or even "ecological architecture" is not terribly important. What is important is that the concept of sustainable architecture is driven by an observation patently obvious to most working scientists that there is a very important and at times intense social aspect to modern science. Even as scientific collaborations and drug discovery become virtual because of a Web 2.0 world, research laboratories will still exist. Hence, the social aspects of science will lead to the design of more social buildings to enhance and support team-based research.

However, can one go from the definition of sustainable architecture offered by the UNCED Brundtland Commission (1987)

> . . . a building "that meets the needs of contemporary society without denying future generations of the ability to meet their needs . . ."

to the design of sustainable labs? In essence, can one design a social building that is flexible in design and operations, yet fosters team-based interdisciplinary collaborative research, and is sustainable in its internal operations involving energy usage and downstream byproducts of the research process? Here, too, we need to address the byproducts and be aware of the potential downstream pollution caused by the building itself and the consequences of the science carried out in the building. Part of this concern is the ultimate awareness of the external environmental issues caused by the building and how it architecturally relates not only to the local but also to the global environment. The key to successful implementation of this concept again comes back to sustainable design.

The flexibility of the laboratory of the future is not incongruent with the above definition of sustainable architecture, and the need for social buildings that respect the local and global environment. It is how we get convergence of the two concepts that will be brought forth by the discussions herein. We need to be continuously aware of the competing logic inherent in an architectural design that is sustainable. Sustainable in that the technology we use to construct our buildings is nontoxic, participatory, and flexible. The buildings should also embody certain critical values, two of which are that they should look like the coming age and be nonhierarchical and socially cohesive (S. Moore, Univ. of Texas Center for Sustainable Development). These strategies involve many principles as outlined by J.J. Kim of the University of Michigan (1998).

One needs to think first about the economy of the resources needed to construct and operate the building. Kim thinks of a building as partly a dedicated ecosystem and as such, feels the architect should think about both the upstream flow of materials into the building during construction and the downstream flow as output from the building's ecosystem into the local and then global environment. The latter, that of downstream material flow, is perhaps one of the most nebulous to consider when thinking about sustainable design of any R&D laboratory. While we can think about designing flexibility into the laboratories, offices, and support and interaction space, it is very difficult to try to predict where the science might be directed 10 or 15 years in the future. Peter Drucker once commented, "The only thing we know about the future is that it will be different." This is, perhaps, the best way to think about strategic planning for the laboratory of the future. In essence, we must plan for events and activities to be different and be conscious of the fact that the science of the future needs to be transformational.

However, in addition to designing for science to be transformational, we also need to think even more long term. Philosophers of science in the 1960s like Thomas S. Kuhn wrote about scientific revolutions and paradigm shifts. These paradigm shifts in thought and approaches to science emerged from war efforts such as the Manhattan Project, where suddenly the government and private industry became the primary source of financial support, and at times, the primary driver for the directions pursued by science. This influenced not only the physical sciences but also the biological sciences. Almost 50 years later, modern-day philosophers of science look not just to paradigm shifts, but also to disruptive technologies that will change the pursuit of science and remap entire fields of scientific endeavor. On the consumer side, the personal computer and the iPOD are examples of disruptive technologies that have changed how we can interact with information on a personal level. Will our labs of the future be ready for similar disruptive technologies? More importantly, will the scientists in training today be ready to interact with these disruptive technologies? Is the virtual drug discovery firm enabled by the advent of the Web 2.0 world, the disruptive technology we all hope will move fields ahead?

Again, while we now think about flexibility, does it mean that we can still design for a sustainable, environmentally friendly structure—both internally and externally? We need to be mindful now that as the science changes, the downstream material flow will most assuredly change. Sometimes the internal and external impact of that changed flow will not be predictable as the technology frequently races ahead of our understanding of its long-term consequences. One movement is attempting to gain traction in industrial and university settings by attempting to address one of the largest sources of negative internal and external environmental impacts: chemistry. This new movement has been termed "Green Chemistry."

Berkeley and colleagues (*Pharmaceutical Engineering*, March/April, 2009) have asked a very relevant question: Should the biopharm industry really be interested in green chemistry? Their very well-documented and pointed argument is that, indeed, biopharm must be interested for green chemistry is the "how" in how biopharm becomes a sustainable industry with a firm

continued

commitment to building sustainable laboratories and manufacturing sites. It is only via these sustainable facilities that biopharm is part of a healthy environment. This movement has raised the awareness of industrial and university chemists because even pursuing synthetic inorganic and organic chemistry on a small scale still results in the import and export of chemicals to buildings. These materials enter laboratory buildings in the forms of solids, gasses, and liquids, presenting both defined and undefined risks to building occupants. Management of these risks internally is readily achievable via proper building design and internal material management. However, downstream there is even more of a potential risk in that long-term environmental consequences of many of these waste and defined products have yet to be fully understood. This is of special concern to the public in areas of emerging technology such as genetically modified foods and nano particles. This should really force industrial concerns and universities concerned with sustainability to a lifecycle view for all solvents and waste streams from their facilities.

Nevertheless, green chemistry is being turned to for the opportunities it affords in reducing waste that leads to reduced operating and perhaps even maintenance costs of a sustainable laboratory. It really comes down to applying paradigms of operational excellence; activities that biopharm firms have been slow to embrace let alone act upon. Obviously, the biggest impact of green chemistry is on the manufacturing side of the equation in the production of intermediates, API, and finished pharmaceuticals because of the volume of the waste stream generated by the synthesis of these materials. How much waste is actually produced is up for conjecture, as no one knows precisely what those volumes are. However, Berkeley and colleagues estimate that worldwide it might be as much as 6.6 billion pounds produced in the manufacture of API. Add to this tonnage the chemicals that do not end up in the API and, as noted by Berkeley, the industry further encounters lost opportunity costs as well as the regulatory burdens associated with waste materials handling within buildings and subsequent disposal costs of solvents and waste byproducts. As noted by the late Senator Evertt Dirksen, "A billion here, a billion there—pretty soon it adds up to real money."

However, even in the research lab, the tenets of green chemistry are important considerations in the discovery phase when synthetic processes are being explored and designed for scale-up to the manufacturing level. This is especially important as so many pharmaceutical chemical and even biological synthetic processes that are scaled-up consume large quantities of water. Water shortage is a critical issue worldwide as are the consequences of managing water usage and disposal in an environmentally responsible manner in a building. Hence, water usage as a facet of green chemistry is an important factor that must be considered in the sustainable design of a modern laboratory building and, again, putting material usage and operations in the context of a lifecycle analysis framework.

Couple the above concerns with the fact that we know that a typical research laboratory uses five times as much water and energy per square foot as a modern office building. Link that with some of the more reasonable requirements in designing research space and many opportunities and challenges present themselves:

• Many redundant systems, e.g., power, lighting, telecommunications;

• The requirement for 24-hour access by the scientists and critical support staff in areas such as vivariums and mechanical spaces;

• Modern research instrumentation such as NMR, Mass Spec, robotics, tissue culture incubators, etc., that produce significant quantities of heat and;

• Depending upon the nature of the science involved, there may also be a significant number of hoods (chemical and biological) that requires not only containment but also the necessity to exhaust either partially or totally to the outside environment;

• These hood and heat requirements create a very intense HVAC requirement that also include "once through air" for specialized labs (high containment) or vivariums.

If done correctly, assessing the operating requirements in a holistic manner can lead to better sustainable design that will conserve energy, water, and key consumables while improving productivity as a consequence of an improved laboratory environment.

Another principle, as noted by Kim, is the concept of thinking about the lifecycle of the design. The concept of lifecycle is a notion that is well engrained in software engineers and developers who always think about the:

• Planning Phase

• Design Phase

• System Development and Testing

• System Qualification and Commissioning

• System Operation

• System Retirement and Decommissioning

If one looks at the software lifecycle, it does not really take much imagination to replace the word "system" with "building" and apply the above phases to thinking about sustainable architectural design. There is indeed significant congruence in the phases and the sequence of events.

As more and more architecture and building operations approach the principle of being sustainable, one needs to think about the lifecycle process. This means addressing not only placing the building in the environment respectfully and responsibly, but also designing the building and operating it responsibly. What must also transpire is the need to address what will happen when it is no longer cost-effective to renovate the building or repurpose it. The concept of retirement and decommissioning is very important to sustainable architecture but not one usually given much thought. Have we chosen wisely in utilizing materials that can be recycled into the next project, or ultimately is the entire building consigned to a landfill? In looking specifically at an R&D laboratory, the ability to recycle building materials as part of being environmentally aware is affected by the nature of the science that goes on in the building. We can indeed create systems to contain toxic chemicals and biological substances, and protect the building occupants and the environment from them. However, does the way these containment systems are designed lead to long-term "corruption" of the building materials so that it can never be reused or repurposed? Do we create an even bigger problem in that many of the building components must now be treated as hazardous waste when the building is decommissioned, adding further to the closure costs. No pun intended, but that is not a sustainable scenario for the future.

The final principle that affects sustainable design as outlined by J.J. Kim is the idea of humane design. It is one that he considers perhaps the most important to the concept of sustainable design, especially as it applies to an R&D laboratory. As humans, we spend a significant percentage of our lives indoors. For scientists, this may be even more on a percentage basis than the average office occupant may. Architects have hypothesized for many years that the space we occupy influences our behaviors, feelings, thoughts, and ultimately our social interactions. Designing a building solely to address style and form making ignores

continued

modern research on social cohesion: something that is extremely important in science where interdisciplinary and collaborative research is necessary, again reinforcing the social nature of modern science.

Many R&D firms have approached the concept of collaborative research by designing space around "tribes" of scientists from multiple disciplines, all socially linked via common projects. This approach also involves flexible design, further enhancing and in some instances forcing interactions among scientists with different skill sets but all collaborating on the same research projects. Those interactions can be critical in advancing the science rather than waiting for chance encounters in breakrooms or hallways. Joan Meyers-Levy of the University of Minnesota has recently published studies that even show that the height of the ceilings in a room can negatively or positively affect how people think. Her observations on ceiling height stress how a high ceiling may actually lead room occupants to making connections that are more abstract. This could lead to better and more enriching interactions between scientists from differing disciplines such as biologists, chemists, statisticians, development pharmacists, and process chemists—all are physically co-located with the common goal of problem solving for dedicated projects.

Additionally, many studies over the years, especially in Europe, have shown the value of bringing more natural light into our work environment where conditions permit. Obviously, restrictions are present especially for specific needs such as darkened rooms, instrumentation impacted by changing light levels, or very specific vivarium requirements for defined light/dark cycles only controlled via artificial lighting. However, just as the animal occupants of vivariums need a defined light/dark light cycle, humans need natural light to help synchronize our circadian rhythms enabling us to stay awake during the day and sleep at night. Buildings, and especially labs of the past, were not designed to optimize the need for natural light. Rather, we maximized footprints with as much internal, and at times, windowless space as possible and maximum usage of corridors without natural light to enhance the movement of people and materials. However, the sustainable laboratory architecture of the future needs to factor in access to natural light wherever possible.

Circling back to our original focus on sustainable design and more importantly the humane connection, critical factors repeatedly noted in sustainable design also relate to the preservation of natural conditions surrounding the building, site planning, and ultimately how the design impacts human comfort. Affording natural light and settings have been shown to improve mental focus as noted previously. These and other design considerations could lead to better and more enriching interactions between scientists from differing disciplines such as biologists, chemists, and statisticians. Again, all parties are physically co-located and share a common goal of problem solving for dedicated projects. Putting all these concepts together, sustainable architecture should lead to an improvement in both qualitative and quantitative benefits by:

• Further enhancing the operation and maintenance of new laboratories;

• Putting the usage of material and the building into the contextual framework of a lifecycle paradigm;

• Ensuring the preservation of the natural conditions surrounding the site;

• Providing a better holistic fit for the structure and its activities in the surrounding community and environment; and

• Creating a work environment that enhances productivity and nurtures interdisciplinary and team interactions by fostering the creation of a social building.

Dennis M. Gross, M.S., Ph.D, Associate Dean, Jefferson College of Graduate Studies, Thomas Jefferson University, Philadelphia, Pennsylvania

Metrics/Ratings/Scorecards—Why Use Them?

The design and construction process includes many different players. The team is made up of the owner, the design professionals, and the builders. Within each of these groups there are different stakeholders. The owner usually includes organization leadership, end users, facilities planners, facility maintenance groups, and safety officers. The design professionals include engineers, architects, interior designers, and often specialized consultants for specific areas. The construction group can include estimators, schedulers, construction subcontractors, and sometimes logisticians who focus on phasing and move planning. Within all of these different groups there are usually very different points of view about what is most important. Starting out with a clear set of metrics or goals can help all of these groups to have a common language about what strategies to pursue. It provides a single clear way to communicate between different groups—how they define energy

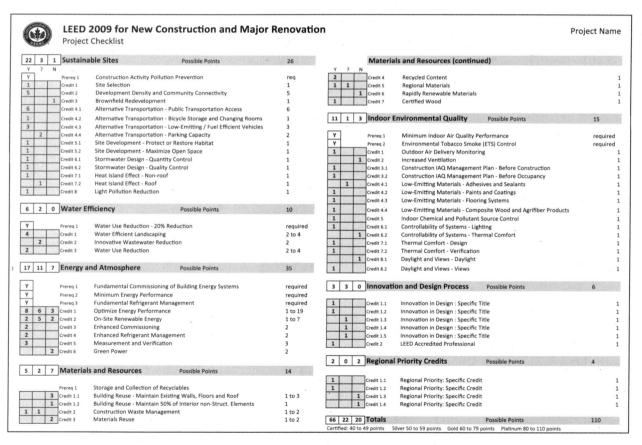

The U.S. Green Building Council's LEED rating system is currently on its third major release, called "LEED 2009." The checklist approach allows different team members to share information with a common set of assumptions and definitions. *Image courtesy of U.S. Green Building Council. Used with permission.*

efficiency and environmental performance. A number of different rating systems and guidelines have been developed for this purpose. The challenge in creating a rating system is that it needs to be simple enough that it can easily be applied to a variety of projects, but with sufficient complexity to reflect true differences in environmental performance. A number of different systems have been created in the last 20 years or so, all attempting to be easily integrated into practice to influence conventional decision-making patterns in practice. One of the earliest, in 1990, was BREEAM, developed in the United Kingdom, followed by LEED, developed in the United States. A few years later others were developed such as CASBEE in Japan, and Green Globes, which grew out of BREEAM implementation in Canada.

BREEAM

In 1990, a system was created in the United Kingdom called BREEAM, the Buildings Research Establishment Environmental Assessment Method, which breaks down building systems, components, and operations and ranks them based on the carbon impact of each decision. It includes assessment in nine different categories:

Management
Health and Well-being
Energy
Transport
Water
Materials and Waste
Land Use and Ecology
Pollution
Innovation

Each project receives a score for each category, is assigned a weighting according to the environmental

breem

BREEAM is a registered trademark owned by the BRE Group. *Image reproduced by permission of the BRE Group.*

impact of each category, and the resulting score will indicate achievement of one of five levels—Pass, Good, Very Good, Excellent, or Outstanding. Projects below a threshold will not pass. Over the last 20 years the system has been broadened to include specific systems for different types of buildings, such as offices, education, healthcare, and retail, and has other systems geared toward larger developments, core and shell development, and existing building assessment. Recognizing that some broad requirements should be applied differently to building types where conventional criteria may not be applicable, there is a process in place where specialized projects can be assessed using a customizable system, called "BREEAM Other Buildings" (formerly known as BREEAM Bespoke). This process involves working with the founding organization, the Buildings Research Establishment (BRE), to have a project-specific system developed. Although there is not a laboratory-specific system, BRE specifically notes labs as a good fit for the BREEAM Other Buildings process. One unique aspect of this system is the integration of the practices and materials of design of the building with the operation and management of the building.

LEED

Founded in 1993, the U.S. Green Building Council (USGBC) developed a rating system called "Leadership in Energy and Environmental Design (LEED),"

LEED is a registered trademark of the USGBC. *Image used with permission.*

a broad-based, consensus-driven process that included government, manufacturing, and design and construction professionals in the process, the main goal being to create a system that would transform the market. By having a system that started with modest yet important improvements over conventional practice, tying the requirements to standards that would get progressively more stringent, the system would change both conventional practice and the definition of green building. The system starts out with a set of prerequisites that all projects need to meet to start the assessment process, which sets a threshold of aspects that all "green" projects should achieve. Similar to BREEAM, there are categories of different strategies, and four different levels of certification—here the levels are called Certified, Silver, Gold, and Platinum. The first pilot rating system was introduced in 1998, and the formal issue of the program was in 2000. Over the next few years, additional systems were introduced to focus on Interior Fitout (Commercial Interiors), Core and Shell development, and a system focusing on existing building operation. An additional system has been developed for Schools, and systems are being developed for Retail, and Healthcare. Building on work developed by the Labs21 team (see below), there was a preliminary guideline for laboratories developed for LEED in 2005. This guideline is still in draft form, and it is unclear when the USGBC will finalize or issue it publicly. It is a useful document for reference, but not as helpful as the resources developed and revised by the Labs21 partnership.

Labs21

In the mid-1990s, a partnership between the U.S. Department of Energy, and the U.S. Environmental Protection Agency was formed to develop tools and resources for high-efficiency laboratory facilities. Called the "Laboratories for the 21st Century," or "Labs21" for short, this program brought together designers, engineers, and policymakers from different groups and developed resources very useful to lab owners, designers, and operators. The organization's first public conference was held in 1999, with attendance by federal agencies, public utility and service companies, along with research universities and private companies. (labs21 conferencehistory2009_508.pdf)[3]

Focusing on energy efficiency in design and operation, reduction in water consumption and emissions, protecting occupant safety, and using an integrated "whole building" approach to laboratory design, the Labs21 program offers several different types of resources that can help in lab design and operation. The core resource is the Labs21 Toolkit—a suite of tools that includes Best Practice Guides focused on laboratory-specific technologies, Case Studies of high-performance laboratories, a Design Guide, an Energy Benchmarking Tool, and several design support tools including the Labs21 Environmental Performance Criteria (EPC).

The Labs21 EPC is a rating system for use by laboratory building project stakeholders to assess the

Image courtesy of NREL, Laboratories for the 21st Century (Labs21®).

environmental performance of laboratory facilities. The EPC leverages and builds on LEED-NC, extending it to set appropriate and specific requirements for laboratories. It was developed in response to a desire by laboratory designers to have a rating system similar to LEED, but more tailored to the unique characteristics of laboratory facilities. It was developed with the expertise of over 40 volunteers, including laboratory architects, engineers, facilities, and health and safety personnel. The EPC modifies some of the LEED credit requirements, and adds several new credits and prerequisites in areas not addressed by LEED. The EPC has been used on many projects, in most cases as a complement to LEED. The EPC was also incorporated into the University of California Regents' policy on sustainable design. It is anticipated that the EPC in some form will eventually be incorporated into LEED version 3. Until that time, Labs21 recommends that projects pursing LEED also be evaluated using the EPC to ensure that laboratory-specific sustainability opportunities are addressed. The EPC credits can also be applied as innovation points under LEED.

The EPC and other Labs21 resources are all available via the Labs21 website (www.labs21century.gov/toolkit). In addition the program has developed educational coursework and an annual conference that provides opportunities for face-to-face learning about how to significantly reduce the environmental impacts of research buildings, with a clear understanding of the unique challenges posed by the requirements for air, water, and energy of laboratory buildings.

ASHRAE Standard 189

After the LEED rating system started to take hold in the United States, several states and local municipalities began to reference the LEED requirements in zoning and code language, as an effort to legislate and require new buildings to meet certain environmental goals. One of the challenges of this approach was the fact that LEED was a specific procedure, and enforcing a requirement to achieve USGBC certification was not easily done. In an effort to push this specific goal of legislated sustainable design, the USGBC partnered with ASHRAE and the IESNA (Illuminating Engineering Society of North America) to develop a minimum standard for green buildings. Different than a rating system, the standard is being created using ASHRAE's ANSI-accredited process for consensus-based code and standards development. The standard has been named *ASHRAE/IESNA/USGBC Standard 189P: Standard for the Design of High Performance Green Buildings Except Low-Rise Residential Buildings*. By having a performance-based standard in place, building codes and energy codes could adopt their requirements by reference, requiring buildings to meet certain threshold levels of sustainability without requiring a specific rating system or certification process. The standard went through several public review comment periods, and was published in 2010. It is based on prescriptive measures drawn from LEED's five categories, and adds some additional requirements as well. Like some of ASHRAE's other standards, for some of the requirements the design team can elect to comply through the prescriptive measures or can use a performance-based model approach instead. At this writing, there are several different standards being pursued by different code organizations, and it re-

Courtesy of American Society of Heating, Refrigerating and Air Conditioning Engineers (ASHRAE).

mains to be seen which, if any, will gain widespread adoption. Each of them functions similarly, offering a higher level of performance above the base building and energy code requirements for building design and operation.

Focus on Energy and Carbon

In the past five years, there has been increasing focus on energy use and reduction in fossil fuels used to generate energy. There have been industry initiatives such as the Architecture 2030 initiative, a volunteer commitment which proposes reduction in reliance on fossil fuels for energy for buildings progressively, beginning with 50 percent reductions when first published, 60 percent by 2010, and leading toward a target of zero fossil fuel use by 2030. The Energy Policy Act of 2005 put into place similar targets for all federally funded projects. Currently, projects are working to achieve these targets through three main strategies—reduction of loads, onsite renewable energy generation, and green power procurement. For most projects, no one of these strategies will get to the target, but a combination of two or more are needed. For laboratory projects, the challenges are more significant—higher energy use and more prescriptive criteria makes the task more difficult. In addition, most of the defined metrics for carbon reduction use a baseline of commercial office buildings. There is currently no baseline in either the EPA Energy Star Target Finder program[4] for laboratory buildings or in the Commercial Building Energy Consumption Survey (CBECS) for lab buildings.[5] The EPA has surveyed all of its own lab facilities for energy use intensity, and the Labs21 program has developed a benchmarking database that can be used to compare individual facilities against other facilities for many different environmental metrics.[6] This database allows searches for different laboratory types, and different climate types, recognizing that these factors have a big impact on the potential performance of the labs.

While carbon reduction is an admirable pursuit, it should be noted that this is a significant conceptual departure from current practice, and will require some revision to standard methods of calculation and strategizing. As an effort to equalize between different types of energy and sources of raw materials for energy, ASHRAE, and LEED use a cost-basis to compare, for example, gas-fired equipment with electrically operated equipment. Energy calculations depend on energy cost, which can lead to strategies that save energy cost while using the same or more actual energy. For example, ice storage systems use more energy, but use them at night, when energy is less costly. This doesn't save energy use, but it helps reduce peak loads, which has a different benefit. Carbon-based calculations would not differentiate between these two, so different conclusions may be reached depending on the metrics employed. Refer to Chapter 6 for additional information about carbon reduction strategies.

Laboratory Types

Sustainable design strategies cannot be applied indiscriminately to all laboratory types; the suitability of each solution must be evaluated on a case-by-case basis given the laboratory type.

There are many different types of laboratories and even different ways to characterize the typology. One method is by client type. The result is a rather short list, typically denoted as private, academic, and government. The private sector is predominately composed

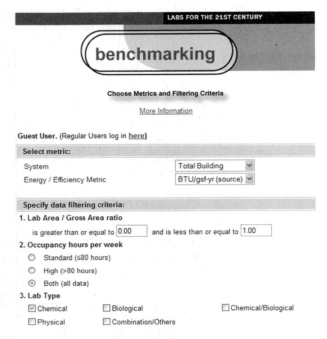

The Labs21® Benchmark database is useful to evaluate different energy and environmental metrics between similar laboratory types. *Image courtesy of NREL, Labs21®. Used with permission. (http://labs21.lbl.gov/CompareData.php)*

of pharmaceutical research and development laboratories. The academic sector may be further broken down into teaching and research laboratories, and, of course within the category of teaching, one could focus on secondary schools, collegiate, or graduate. Another way to classify laboratories is by the science occurring within them. Gone are the days when the division was as simple as biology and chemistry. New science fields emerge rapidly now and the lines between the sciences are blurred. A list based on science types would include not just biology and chemistry, but biochemistry, biophysics, electronics, electrophysiology, genetics, metrology, nanotechnology, pharmacokinetics, pharmacology, physics, and so on. Finally, a classification system could be based on the function of the laboratory—analytical, quality assessment, stability testing, or more simply, whether

the laboratory is defined as wet (using fume hoods or biosafety cabinets, water, and piped gasses) or dry (an electronics- or computer-based laboratory.)

There is no one approach to the design of a sustainable laboratory that is right for any one particular laboratory type, but consideration of the typology is necessary to evaluate the appropriateness of a design strategy. The client type might influence the tolerance for lengths of payback periods on various energy saving initiatives. The type of science might impact the suitability of a particular "green" material for inclusion in a project. For instance, a recycled flooring material might not have the required static dissipative properties required for an electronics laboratory. The function of a laboratory might drive lighting requirements that render occupancy sensors impractical and necessitate manual switching. A carefully considered sustainable design approach will in no way negatively impact the performance of science; ideally it should enhance the user's ability to conduct his or her experimental study within the laboratory environment.

Sustainability Categories

Although there are many different nuances to sustainability, and many ways that different approaches can be considered sustainable, all of them can be distilled into five basic ideas:

• Reducing demand for resources

• Delivering those resources you need more efficiently

• Finding an alternative source for those resources

• Finding ways to collect and dispose of waste with less environmental impact

• Providing a safe and healthy place to live and work

Although the topics discussed in this book are wide ranging and span many disciplines, they can all be connected to one or more of these ideas. To assist the reader, icons corresponding to these categories appear in the margins at the beginning of each chapter. These icons are as follows:

Reduce demand

Deliver Efficiently

Alternative Source

Minimize Waste

Improve Health and Productivity

As an example, changing lighting level criteria from 85 foot candles to 35 foot candles, would be one method of reducing demand. Finding a high-efficiency light fixture to provide the light would be delivering efficiently, and using photovoltaics to generate the electricity would be an alternative source. This same logic can be applied to other resources (water, materials) as well.

Summary

In many ways, designing sustainable laboratory buildings is the same as designing other green buildings— the most important part is to understand how each

aspect of sustainability is linked. Starting with a clear definition of what the right programmatic requirements are, how the local environment and site can contribute to a sustainable solution, selecting the right materials and systems to answer technical and scientific needs, and balancing flexibility, safety, and efficiency can lead to a building that significantly reduces the resources needed to construct and operate the lab facility.

Like nonlab buildings, the most important part of the process is understanding how each of the different aspects of sustainability are linked. Starting with an integrated process that helps work with interplay of disciplinary requirements will lead to buildings where the sustainable strategies reinforce the design intentions of the project team.

Key Concepts

- Sustainability can be distilled into three main concepts: minimizing site impacts, resource reduction, and improved human factors.

  - Site Impacts are minimized through selecting which site to use, designing on that site, and maximizing connections to existing infrastructure.

  - Resource reduction applies to water, building materials, and energy. Carbon reduction is connected to each.

  - For each of these three they consist of three methods of reduction:

    - Setting loads, criteria, and needs carefully to minimize how much you need.
    - Designing the most efficient way to deliver the resource to the building.
    - Finding alternative greener sources for the resource.

- Human factors include air quality, occupant comfort and safety, and designing a connection to the outdoor environment.

- Rating systems and benchmarks have been developed to help project teams make design decisions.

- Rating systems: BREEAM, LEED.

- Guidelines/benchmarks: Laboratories for the 21st Century (Labs21), ASHRAE Standard 189.1.

- Different laboratory types mean different design solutions; each design must address different needs for different types of research, as well as consider potential for change.

REFERENCES

1. Vitruvius, *The Ten Books on Architecture,* Tr. Morris Hicky Morgan, New York, Dover Publications, 1960, p. 170. Originally published Harvard University Press, 1914.
2. Labs21 Laboratory Design Guide, Overview, http://ateam.lbl.gov/Design-Guide/DGHtm/abstract.energy.efficientresearchlaboratories.htm.
3. labs21 conferencehistory2009_508.pdf.
4. www.energystar.gov/index.cfm?cew_bldg_design.bus_target_finder.
5. www.eia.doe.gov/emeu/cbecs/contents.html.
6. The database of EPA's own facility energy use is posted online, at http://epa.gov/greeningepa/facilities/index.htm#labs. The Labs21 database can accommodate reporting both text-based and graphical data, and allows the user to filter based on region, laboratory type, and other criteria. http://labs21.lbl.gov/CompareData.php.

chapter **2** # Integrated Design
Working Collaboratively to Achieve Sustainability

Courtesy of the Smithsonian Institution.
Image courtesy of Kiss + Cathcart, Architects.

Introduction to Integrated Design

Like many other professions, scientific research has grown ever more complex, sophisticated, and technologically demanding over time. As a result, laboratory facilities need to accommodate new technological demands. In response to this escalating complexity, specialists have emerged. Their deep specific knowledge results from a full-time focus on a particular subject. However, while specific expertise is essential to research efforts, a general overview of the problem under investigation, as well as the orchestration, coordination, and collaboration—or integration—of many specialists is also critical to a successful research program.

In recent years, there has been a significant shift in organizational structures from isolated research efforts driven primarily by individual initiative to interdisciplinary team-based research. Research is now routinely conducted in larger teams, and sometimes

This chapter focuses on all five of the sustainability categories discussed in Chapter 1. See page 18 for more information.

even in multiple locations linked by electronic media. As a result, laboratory planning has also evolved in response to the needs of this "integrated" approach. Laboratories have become more open, with office spaces and wet lab areas physically and visually accessible to one another to enable interaction and collaboration. Similarly, strategically located formal and informal social interaction spaces ranging from meeting rooms to interaction areas encourage serendipitous encounters and more casual meetings outside of the laboratory.

This evolution in research sociology, orchestrating teams of experts in an interdisciplinary study, provides a good metaphor for the integrated design approach necessary to design and build technically demanding, high-performance laboratory building and spaces. The term "integrated design" is used to describe a team-based approach where deep expert knowledge in specific aspects of the design process is strategically applied at the right time and in the right venue to promote synergies among the various aspects of the design, with the goal of achieving innovation that would otherwise remain undiscovered using a traditional "sequential" design approach.

In a traditional design process, each individual discipline focuses on a narrow scope of design and engineering. The structural engineer would have limited input on the design of the mechanical system, whereas with integrated design, the structural engineer and the mechanical engineer would jointly explore the relationship between the thermal mass and air conditioning, and a different structural and mechanical system might result. In another example, the architect would conceive a conventional exterior building envelope, and the mechanical engineer would respond with an appropriate mechanical system solution. With integrated design, the mechanical engineer and the architect would work together in shaping the fenestration, shading, and insulation with respect to climate and orientation. The resulting design solution would not only be more energy efficient, but also allow the team to better manage the budget, both in terms of capital cost and long-term operational cost. Architecturally interesting features such as sun shades and light shelves can be incorporated in the design, but they really only make sense in the design if they are coordinated and optimized to reduce envelope loads.

Integrated design seems like an obvious improvement. However, due to well-intentioned efforts to save consulting fees, oversimplified top-down project management structures, or general lack of project planning and organization, the appropriate voices are not always heard at the right time in the design process to realize the maximum value. Integrated design is a different approach that requires careful planning and, even more importantly, willingness to engage a team of experts in a new kind of planning process. It is not easy to implement, but it may bring compelling benefits. This chapter describes the strategies and the essential components of an integrated design process.

Planning an Integrated Design Process

Successful integrated design results from careful project planning, a willingness to engage a team of

Image courtesy of KlingStubbins.

NORTH SIDE

SOUTH SIDE

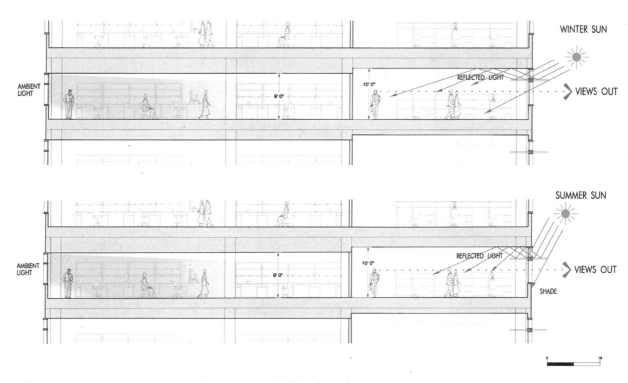

Schematic design of a solar access diagram, useful for massing and shading device design.

experts in an interactive process, and an expectation that this process will lead to a more beneficial outcome. When planning an integrated design process, consider the following:

Assembling the Team

Assemble the project team early in the project process when their input will be most meaningful. In a conventional design process, team members are included on an as-needed basis which often means that their input is offered after key decisions have already been made. With integrated design, all the key stakeholders (owner, architect, engineers, con-

sultants, construction manager, plus subcontractors and suppliers) participate from day one. This is the best way to take advantage of all the available knowledge and experience.

Communicating Expectations

A team-wide kick-off meeting offers the opportunity for the project team to begin the job with shared expectations, unfiltered and uninterrupted. This meeting also offers each team member a chance to share how their individual expertise can contribute to the overall project success. Large meetings require careful planning and facilitation to make the most of

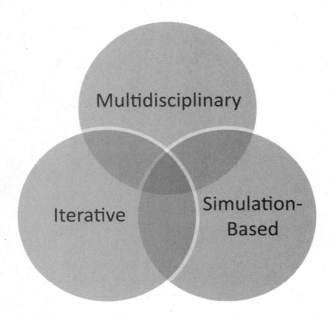

Key concepts to a successful integrated design process. *Image courtesy of KlingStubbins.*

create opportunities, structured and serendipitous, for meaningful exchange among these experts. The work plan must maximize the potential of the team by reinforcing this cross-pollination among experts, thus increasing overall team synergy.

Traditional Sequential Design versus Integrated Simultaneous Design

The traditional approach has been based on making decisions in an orderly sequence. Once the program is confirmed, design proceeds in phases, starting with Schematic Design (SD), followed by Design Development (DD), Construction Documentation (CD), Bidding & Negotiation (B/N), and finally Construction

the time invested. The agenda for the kick-off meeting should include an introduction of all the participants, explaining their roles and responsibilities; a statement of the project goals; a discussion of how success will be measured and reported; and an opportunity for each participant to share what they can offer to the project. The overall goal of this meeting is to set clear expectations for the project, with shared vision and goals, with an appreciation for the resources available to the team and how these resources will collaborate to archive exceptional results.

Ongoing Interactions

Most experts will naturally be more comfortable working within their individual fields, and conventional design practice has only reinforced this behavior. It is the role and the challenge of the project leadership to

Integrated design charette efforts take on a new look in the digital age—for this project in Waltham, Massachusetts, the architects, engineers, construction managers, and subcontractors meet together and work on conceptual design and coordination before the construction phase begins. By bringing different viewpoints to the table early, synergies and tradeoffs can be weighed and resolved electronically rather than through reconstruction. *Courtesy of KlingStubbins and Virtual Construction Manager, Tocci Building Corporation.*

Administration (CA). These steps are codifed in standard AIA contract language and are commonly understood throughout the industry. At each stage, more experts and additional detail are brought to the table. Design options are developed, tested against the program criteria, and modified and refined as needed. Hence, the process is "iterative" in nature.

Generally speaking, it is the architect who takes the lead during the SD process, establishing the orientation and the overall form, footprint, and massing of the building. These are key decisions which in large measure will predetermine the subsequent performance of the lab in terms of both operational efficiency and energy consumption. For example, buildings with long, slender footprints will admit natural light deeper into the interior of the space. But long and slender geometries also increase the ratio of perimeter wall to enclosed area. A high ratio will generate higher capital cost (because more exterior wall is needed to enclose the same amount of interior space), with correspondingly higher heat loss and/or heat gain, which in turn will define the required size of the MEP systems. The orientation of the building also has a substantial effect. If the main axis is north/south versus east/west, there will be significantly different characteristics with regard to energy consumption. It is easy to see that decisions made early on in the process will have a profound effect on the engineered systems.

As the design process moves from the SD to the DD phase, structural and MEP engineers become more involved. Detailed decisions are made about column grids and floor-to-floor heights and the equipment is sized for the expected loads. However, key decisions about the overall architectural envelope have already been made, too often without meaningful input from the relevant engineering experts. During the construction documentation phase, the process of adding increasingly detailed information continues, often aided by specialty consultants for items like vertical transportation, vibration, wind/wake analysis, specialty lighting, and so forth. Once again, however, the key parameters have been set, and so these newly arrived experts are able to contribute their knowledge only at the margin.

The ultimate irony is that the entity which will spend the vast majority of the client's money—the construction manager (CM)—does not arrive on the scene until the CDs have been completed, and therefore has no opportunity to provide advice or guidance about the cost, constructability, or logistics of the project. Nonetheless, the CM is forced to make an educated guess about design intent, capital cost, and schedule, based on documents which are frequently far from complete and/or fully coordinated. The lack of early knowledge of the design intent coupled with potential errors or omissions in the design documents often lead to bids which are higher than necessary, and/or significant change orders during the course of construction.

It's clear that the traditional "sequential" method of laboratory design leads to suboptimal results. Because labs are so inherently complex, the architecture, structural engineering, and MEP engineering are highly intertwined and mutually dependent; each affects the other in very significant ways. It follows that during design, the key stakeholders should be at the table contributing to the overall effort as the project evolves. For obvious reasons, this includes the CM. This integrated design approach changes the basic paradigm from one of sequential decision-making to simultaneous decision-making, whereby all key issues are considered from a variety of perspectives at the same time before the team commits to a preferred alternative. A team that uses the principles of integrated design understands the power of coming to the table with "decision-ready information," so that the options for design, engineering, cost, and schedule can be fully vetted, each in terms of the other. Once the team commits to decisions, this significantly reduces backtracking and redesign, which saves both time and money, as well as improving the overall quality of communication and documentation. With integrated design, the design process tends to be richer, and the design outcomes of higher quality, because more brainpower from different perspectives is engaged in making key decisions. Most importantly, by inviting meaningful engagement by key experts early in the process, the design team can create more functional, flexible, and efficient lab buildings, which perform far better than conventional projects. Capital cost can be contained while long-term maintenance and energy consumption are reduced.

Project Tasks in an Integrated Design Process

With integrated design, it's important to recognize that many of the design tasks that were previously pursued by a single discipline or entity will now be done in collaboration with multiple stakeholders. This means that the typical workflow and planning associated with a conventional project will need to be modified. In addition, there are different types of tasks that need to happen. For example, energy modeling is normally completed during design development to confirm that the systems as designed will meet the loads. This is too late for the model to have any impact on the overall energy performance of the building, except at the margin. With integrated design, simulations and modeling will happen much

earlier, so that the results can inform the design decisions about the building. Other examples are discussed below.

Research/Evaluation

Research is a critical step in successful design. For example, weather and wind data; the potential to use renewable energy such as solar, wind, or ground sources; or the possibility for night-purge or natural ventilation strategies can be evaluated as possible strategies during the early stages of design. Other items include utility rate programs, peak-shaving options, and overall utility management. By starting with a clear understanding of these potentials, the design team can look into different approaches that might otherwise have been left unexplored.

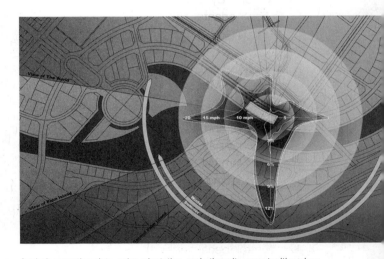

Analyzing weather data, solar orientation, and other site opportunities plays a large part in determining what design response is most appropriate for the project. Often the decisions made early on regarding site selection, orientation, and massing can play a major role in the capability of the project to realize energy and resource savings. For this project in the Middle East, analysis of major view corridors, prevailing winds, and solar access was critical to an early understanding of the potentials and challenges of the design phase. *Image courtesy of KlingStubbins.*

Criteria/Loads

Hand in hand with an understanding of the existing site conditions is an evaluation of what the loads will be. Determining the loads will affect what the engineering systems will need to be. "Rightsizing" the loads, both internal and external, will result in smaller MEP equipment and reduced long-term operating costs. External loads are primarily solar and wind loads, and protection of the interior environment from these factors is critical to an efficient building. Depending heavily on the climate throughout the year, the external loads need to be controlled and mitigated. In moderate climates that experience both heating and cooling seasons, the challenge is to reduce solar loads during the cooling season, admit solar energy in the heating season, and allow visible light to enter throughout the year. This can only be effectively done by careful design of the building's configuration, orientation, massing, and envelope design.

Orientation and Massing

In order to balance cooling load reductions, heat gain when desirable, and daylight harvesting, most projects need to have an orientation in which solar gains and daylight glare can be controlled through external and internal shading devices. Optimal orientation will depend on the latitude and longitude of the building plus the assumed hours of operation. In most parts of the world, eastern and western glazing is more difficult to control (because the morning and afternoon sun gets very low in the sky). That said, each project must balance optimal orientation for energy and daylight with other site-driven factors such as circulation, zoning regulations, topography, setbacks, landscaping, underground utilities, and other contextual issues. Buildings in climates where natural ventilation is feasible for part of the year may employ natural stack effects to induce ventilation during the "shoulder seasons" between heating and cooling. This also requires zoning of the different building functions so that any special areas that are not suitable for natural ventilation can be segregated without adversely affecting the naturally ventilated spaces.

Envelope Optimization

The building envelope, consisting of opaque areas of walls and roofs, glazed areas of windows and skylights, and underground areas, plays a big part of building loads. External loads can be reduced through improvements to these different areas. Strategies to reduce the cooling load due to conduction through the opaque assemblies include using higher resistance assemblies for walls, roofs, and windows. This can be done through insulation, thermal mass, and reflectivity. Increasing the insulation value of the walls (R-value) will reduce the amount of heat that will pass through the walls. Depending on the load driver for the building, increased insulation values can help with energy costs. There is a practical limit for increased insulation, and it is important to coordinate the cost and complexity of higher insulated systems with the energy savings predicted.

If the building has heavy exterior envelope and structural materials—masonry or concrete, for example—the solar heat will be absorbed during the day and reradiated at night. Depending on the climate conditions of the site, this can be an effective way to dampen the effects of daytime swings in temperature. Absorption of solar radiation by the roofing material is a function of color. A darker material has a higher absorptivity; since this absorbed solar energy eventually becomes a cooling load in the floor below, conduction heat transfer is reduced if lighter-colored

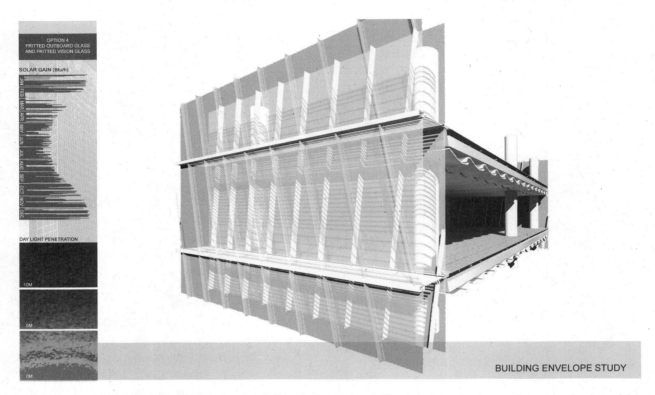

OPTION 4
FRITTED OUTBOARD GLASS
AND FRITTED VISION GLASS

SOLAR GAIN (Btu/h)

JAN FEB MAR APR MAY JUN JUL AUG SEP OCT NOV DEC

DAY LIGHT PENETRATION

10M

5M

0M

BUILDING ENVELOPE STUDY

For Poly Group Real Estate's Pearl River Towers in Guanghzhou, China, the team reviewed different shading and enclosure options, and analyzed annual daylight penetration (lower left shows a plan view light-level graph), as well as annual solar gain (left side thermal load graph)—vertical axis is months, horizontal axis is load. By graphing annual solar gain for different envelope options, the team could optimize maximum daylight admission relative to heat gain. This study was repeated for each of the exterior wall configurations of the building. *Image courtesy of KlingStubbins.*

roofing materials are specified. Incorporating a vegetated roof also raises the Solar Reflectance Index (SRI). For example, Johnson & Johnson installed a new 400,000-square-foot white roof at the Health Care System site in Memphis, Tennessee and realized a 13 percent internal rate of return on its $660,000 investment.

Glazed Areas

Depending on the building massing, the glazed areas often play a large role in the envelope's overall performance. As noted above, the amount of glazing needs to balance the need for visual connection with the exterior with the building's thermal performance. In the last few years, new technologies have been developed that improve glazing assemblies' performance, yet it is still true that an opaque wall offers better thermal performance than the best unprotected glazed window. Of course the window does a much better job of letting light in and views out! There are a number of different methods for improving the performance of glazed systems in buildings.

Project envelope_orientation_NFRC100--VIRACON.cck - COMcheck 3.6.0   Code: 90.1 (2004) Standard

File Edit View Options Code Help

Project | Envelope | Interior Lighting | Exterior Lighting | Mechanical

Roof | Skylight | Ext. Wall | Int. Wall | Window | Door | Basement | Floor

#	Component	Orientation	Assembly	Construction Details	Gross Area		Cavity Insulation R-Value	Continuous Insulation R-Value	U-Factor	SHGC	Projection Factor	Heat Capacity	Comments/Description (Optional)
	Building												
1	⊟Roof 1		Insulation Entirely Above... ▾		67488	ft2		17.12	0.056				
2	—Skylight 1		Metal Frame with Therma... ▾	Glazing: Cl... ▾	350	ft2			0.220	0.27			
3	⊟CW - North	North ▾	Other ▾		20831	ft2			0.288			1.00	
4	—CW 1 - SPANDF	North	Metal Frame with Therma... ▾	Glazing: Cl... ▾	2295	ft2			0.058	0.01	0.00		Placard, Cantilever & Ameni...
5	—CW 1 - FRIT	North	Metal Frame with Therma... ▾	Glazing: Cl... ▾	4764	ft2			0.310	0.19	0.00		
6	—CW 1 - SHADE	North	Metal Frame with Therma... ▾	Glazing: Cl... ▾	9527	ft2			0.310	0.28	0.15		Vertical Shades
7	—CW 1 & 2	North	Metal Frame with Therma... ▾	Glazing: Cl... ▾	2075	ft2			0.288	0.28	0.00		Cantilever & Amenities, Not ...
8	—CW 2	North	Metal Frame with Therma... ▾	Glazing: Cl... ▾	2170	ft2			0.288	0.28	0.38		Below Placard & Entrance
9	—Masonry Type 1	North ▾	Steel-Framed, 16" o.c. ▾		379	ft2	0.0	16.73	0.051				Brick
10	—Masonry Type 2	North ▾	Steel-Framed, 16" o.c. ▾		694	ft2	0.0	16.64	0.051				Stone
11	—Metal Panel	North ▾	Steel-Framed, 16" o.c. ▾		8541	ft2	0.0	18.05	0.048				
12	⊟CW - South	South ▾	Other ▾		17733	ft2			0.288			1.00	
13	—CW 1 - SPANDF	South	Metal Frame with Therma... ▾	Glazing: Cl... ▾	2628	ft2			0.058	0.01	0.00		Placard
14	—CW 1 - FRIT	South	Metal Frame with Therma... ▾	Glazing: Cl... ▾	3858	ft2			0.303	0.19	0.00		
15	—CW 1 - SHADE	South	Metal Frame with Therma... ▾	Glazing: Cl... ▾	3858	ft2			0.310	0.28	0.58		Horizontal Shades
16	—CW 1	South	Metal Frame with Therma... ▾	Glazing: Cl... ▾	3825	ft2			0.310	0.28	0.00		
17	—CW 2	South	Metal Frame with Therma... ▾	Glazing: Cl... ▾	3531	ft2			0.288	0.28	0.10		Below Placard
18	—Masonry Type 1	South ▾	Steel-Framed, 16" o.c. ▾		1965	ft2	0.0	16.73	0.051				Brick
19	—Masonry Type 2	South ▾	Steel-Framed, 16" o.c. ▾		978	ft2	0.0	16.64	0.051				Stone
20	—Metal Panel	South ▾	Steel-Framed, 16" o.c. ▾		8321	ft2	0.0	18.05	0.048				
21	⊟CW - East	East ▾	Other ▾		10308	ft2			0.288			1.00	
22	—CW 1 - SHADE	East	Metal Frame with Therma... ▾	Glazing: Cl... ▾	473	ft2			0.310	0.28	0.58		
23	—CW 1 - FRIT	East	Metal Frame with Therma... ▾	Glazing: Cl... ▾	473	ft2			0.310	0.19	0.00		
24	—CW 1 & 2	East	Metal Frame with Therma... ▾	Glazing: Cl... ▾	2656	ft2			0.288	0.28	0.00		
25	—CW 2	East	Metal Frame with Therma... ▾	Glazing: Cl... ▾	352	ft2			0.288	0.28	0.24		Below Cantilever
26	—CW 2 - SPANDF	East	Metal Frame with Therma... ▾	Glazing: Cl... ▾	2050	ft2			0.058	0.01	0.00		Cantilever and Amenities
27	—CW 2 - SHADE	East	Metal Frame with Therma... ▾	Glazing: Cl... ▾	4304	ft2			0.281	0.27	0.19		Cantilever and Amenities
28	—Masonry Type 1	East ▾	Steel-Framed, 16" o.c. ▾		1541	ft2	0.0	16.73	0.051				Brick
29	—Metal Panel	East ▾	Steel-Framed, 16" o.c. ▾		3743	ft2	0.0	18.05	0.048				
30	⊟CW - West	West ▾	Other ▾		749	ft2			0.288			1.00	
31	—CW 3	West	Metal Frame with Therma... ▾	Glazing: Cl... ▾	700	ft2			0.379	0.28	0.00		
32	—CW 3 - SPANDF	West	Metal Frame with Therma... ▾	Glazing: Cl... ▾	49	ft2			0.058	0.01	0.00		
33	—Masonry Type 1	West ▾	Steel-Framed, 16" o.c. ▾		5433	ft2	0.0	16.73	0.051				Brick
34	—Metal Panel	West ▾	Steel-Framed, 16" o.c. ▾		12200	ft2	0.0	18.05	0.048				
35	—Floor 1		Slab-On-Grade:Unheated ▾	Insulation:... ▾	67488	ft		5.0					

Although it was developed as a way to determine code compliance, the COMCHECK software is a tool that allows teams to evaluate their building envelope configurations against the code minimum requirements. Where conventional projects would complete this checklist to make sure the minimum was met, the tool also gives rough estimates of what percentage better than the code minimum each design demonstrates. This tool allows the team to look at what the impact would be for increased insulation value or different performance values for each envelope component. *Image courtesy of KlingStubbins.*

External Solar Controls

External solar control measures (overhangs, vegetation) can be used to minimize solar heat gain. Depending on the climate, these can be configured to allow for winter solar gains if desired. For many lab buildings, however, internal equipment provides enough heat that added solar gain is not necessary; this will need to be studied for each specific project and climate, as well as the ratio of wall to enclosed area of the lab.

By incorporating skylight monitors to the green roof at the U.S. Food and Drug Administration's Engineering & Physics Laboratory in White Oak, Maryland, lower-level spaces can receive natural daylight and the exterior landscaping can continue up to the building entry. Benefits include stormwater management, local habitat and microclimate, and energy benefits from this one strategy. *Image courtesy of KlingStubbins. Photography by Ron Solomon—Baltimore © 2008.*

High-Performance Glazing

In addition to shading the glazed areas, several different strategies of what types of glazing to specify are critical to this overall balance of vision glazing and daylight with thermal performance of the wall. Spectrally selective and low-emissivity ("low-e") glass allows visible light to enter the building, and also reflects energy in the wavelengths associated with room heat gains. For some areas, patterned glazing preserves the views to the outside but reduces the cooling load entering the room. In some conditions, photovoltaic systems can be integrated into the glazing to provide a pattern, and the spaces between individual cells can allow for light and views.

Double-Wall Facades

One strategy that has been used in some situations is the double-wall facade—two glazed facades sep-

arated by a deep cavity or airspace. The performance of these walls is based on using the air space as an insulator, with controls that allow for venting the air when appropriate. By incorporating shading devices in the cavity, these walls can act to allow for more glazed area while minimizing thermal losses due to the glazed areas. Double-wall facades can be

For Johnson & Johnson's Pharmaceutical Research and Development (PRD) Drug Discovery Laboratory, Phase II building in La Jolla, California, the team used a combination of patterned glass, spectrally selective vision glazing, and external shading devices to reduce solar gain on the south-facing laboratory spaces. Balancing the need for daylight penetration with a need to minimize external loads, the shading devices cut out direct solar gain while allowing for ambient light penetration. *Image courtesy of KlingStubbins. Photography © Tom Bonner 2007.*

designed to act as a "solar chimney" in which heated air is forced through a vent at the top of the double wall. The driving force is the difference in buoyancy between the solar-heated air and the cooler room air. By controlling openings at the top and bottom of the cavity, the performance of the wall can be modulated to different seasonal and diurnal conditions. For many lab buildings, this technology is too expensive to be feasible—especially in buildings dominated by internal loads rather than external skin loads.

Demand-Responsive Facades

For some buildings, fixed exterior shading devices add complexity—they can provide a perch for birds or a place for snow and ice to accumulate. For this type of situation, project designers can look toward an active system that responds to external signals. In addition, for certain orientations, fixed shading devices are still not completely effective. Active systems allow for operable shades, louvers, or blinds that retract to allow for daylight and views, but close up when there is excessive solar gain or vision glare. One system consists of 4-inch slats mounted 35° from the horizontal on the outside of a building. Based on the expected solar position available, a programmable controller positions the slats to minimize solar gain incident on the glass. For a government laboratory project in Maryland, the analysis shown in the following figure demonstrates that the glass on the south side of the building rarely receives direct solar radiation (or insolation) with the operable louvers. Without shading devices, the glass receives direct insolation during the majority of occupied hours.

Dynamic Glazing

Electrochromic glass darkens in the summer when cooling is required but lightens the glass in the winter when heating is needed. Two technologies in use are suspended-particle devices and polymer-dispersed liquid crystal display (PDLCD) devices. Suspended-particle technology energizes a laminate to darken glass. PDLCD devices apply voltage to a liquid crystal display (similar to a calculator display) to darken glass. This technology has been used in some limited applications, and currently it is usually too expensive to consider for exterior enclosure systems, but it has potential to provide a dynamically changeable level of light transmittance in response to exterior conditions.

Internal Loads

External load reduction strategies require interdisciplinary cooperation, and a conventional design process would result in missed opportunities for efficiency and synergies between architectural and engineering decisions. For internal loads, there are a number of possibilities for more savings through interdisciplinary design. During the programming and criteria-setting stage, many different assumptions and decisions are made about how the facility will function which all too often are based on preexisting standards and common practices. It is important to ensure that the adopted criteria will meet the functional requirements of the researchers, including the appropriate amount of flexibility for change. At the same time it is critical to examine and challenge the criteria to avoid creating designs that are overpowered and overventilated. These criteria include temperature and humidity, lighting levels, air change rates, and systems diversity. Rightsizing each of these criteria to the different space types can make a big difference in the overall performance of the building. Allowing wider temperature swings in transitional spaces or less stringent humidity control in spaces with operable windows are a few ways to save energy. Although lighting levels are typically set by space type, there are several ways to reduce energy use. By

Without automated exterior blinds:

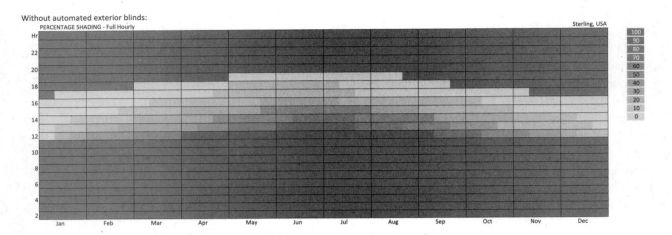

With automated exterior blinds:

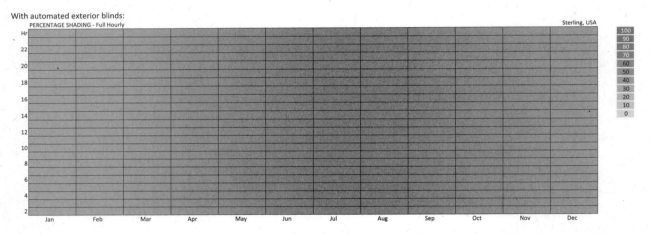

An automated dynamic shading system will close exterior blinds during times of peak solar gain. This graph shows potential for energy savings and glare reduction. *Image courtesy of Nysan Shading Systems, LP.*

specifying finish materials with lighter colors, the same light levels can be achieved with less electricity. By selecting and controlling fixtures to dim when there is sufficient natural light, the energy can be saved when the lights are off. In both cases, this reduces both the electricity and the heat rejected by the fixtures, so these strategies save both electricity and cooling load simultaneously.

Integrated Design and Building Information Modeling

Integrated design is greatly aided by Building Information Modeling (BIM) technology, which is sophisticated software that incorporates information from a variety of sources into a single integrated database. Simply put, BIM can cross-reference input from the architect, engineers, consultants, and CM simultaneously, and the results can be displayed in 3D and 4D format so that they are easily accessible to clients, who are often not familiar with reading the abstract language of plans, sections, and elevations.

In the last few years, the term BIM has been used as a catch-all term to represent what are in fact four distinct but related branches of digital simulation techniques that touch different aspects of the design and construction industry, all of which have profound consequences for how buildings are designed and constructed. These four branches of BIM are: Comprehensive 3D Modeling, Design Optimization, Construction Implementation, and Building Operation and Performance Monitoring.

1. *3D Modeling:* At its most basic level, BIM provides the foundation for integrated practice in how it displays comprehensive spatial information. Changes are tracked and coordinated continuously, so that an adjustment in plan is also simultaneously noted in section. For lab buildings, it is critical that this spatial information include all design disciplines. "Clash detection" identifies inconsistencies in advance, greatly enhancing coordination in the field. BIM is also useful in tracking materials counts, so that it is possible to know in advance, with a high degree of certainty, what building components will actually be needed, right down to the desks and chairs.

Building information modeling has been helpful in integrated coordination during the design process for the Moore Building Addition and Renovation project at The Pennsylvania State University's main campus in University Park, Pennsylvania. *Image courtesy of KlingStubbins.*

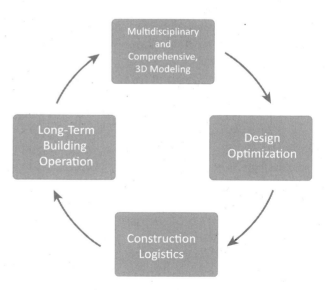

Four distinct components of a BIM project. *Image courtesy of KlingStubbins.*

2. *Design Optimization:* BIM also provides the ability to perform simulation studies in order to help analyze and refine design options. For example, it is possible to create a series of alternative wall sections and then compare them objectively in terms of solar orientation, shading, heat gain/heat loss, and capital cost all at the same time. Other simulation techniques such as energy modeling can be performed much earlier in the design process compared to a pre-BIM workflow. The key here is providing early, performance-driven information that enables the team to make good design decisions.

3. *Construction Logistics:* Simulation studies can also be used to analyze such things as site logistics—tracking not only the materials arriving at the site, but also managing the waste stream. This is especially powerful in an industry that traditionally wastes 30 percent of the materials used. BIM gives the design team a level of information that was not previously available, and it greatly helps the owner compare options with regard to aesthetics, cost, and constructability. Better informed teams make better, faster decisions, with a higher degree of predictability. This, in turn, leads directly to buildings that are more flexible, efficient, and cost-effective. One of the most powerful aspects of BIM is that it encourages early engagement of suppliers and subcontractors, who can now become intimately involved in the design process. As their input is added to the BIM model, it's actually possible to reduce or eliminate the time-consuming and error-prone shop drawing process, as the BIM model can be used directly for fabrication and installation. This has huge potential to reduce waste, both in the shop and in the field.

4. *Long-Term Building Operation and Performance Monitoring:* BIM has the potential to provide a realistic and meaningful linkage between the design process and ongoing building operations and management. It is critical that we take careful stock of actual building performance in order to inform the modeling and optimization of the design. Although the model can be used effectively for managing and operating the building, detailed building design simulations and building automation systems must be calibrated as part of a Measurement and Verification (M&V) process. By definition, simulations are based on assumptions about occupancies, behaviors, and building operation. Calibrating the simulation model with the actual performance data is a necessary step to optimize the way the building is being run.

The combination of integrated design with BIM technology is extremely powerful in how it affects team dynamics on complex projects such as laboratories. The level of information is highly detailed and sophisticated, and equally available to all, since the BIM model operates on the principle of "shared authorship." This, in turn, helps to eliminate the "silo thinking" that too often undermines true team collaboration, something that is especially important in early formative stages of design. With integrated design and BIM, the traditional sequential thought process is replaced by high-functioning teams, working closely in concert with one another, making decisions simultaneously. The conventional steps of SD/DD/CD/CA are no longer needed, as information usually provided in later phases is now available much earlier in the process. Each participant provides expert input, with overall leadership provided by the architect.

The accompanying diagram illustrates the new process. Design concepts are created and then critiqued in a team setting, with input from all key team

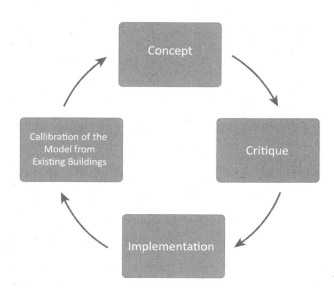

The iterative nature of a BIM process benefits from a feedback loop from actual performance. *Image courtesy of KlingStubbins.*

breaking down the silos that have too often created barriers between design and construction experts, traditional notions of professional liability need to be reexamined and recast. The architect must retain both responsibility and authority for code-compliant design, and the CM must do the same with regard to means and methods as well as construction site safety. As decision-making and the associated risk are shared, it becomes increasingly difficult to focus blame on individual performance. The success of indi-

members. Options are vetted in terms of form, function, aesthetics, constructability, and cost with a high degree of predictability. Evolving design decisions are entered into the BIM model, which automatically updates *and coordinates* the inputs. Information can be extracted as needed for comparison, simulation, or further analysis. Adjustments can be made at any time during the process, and no data gets lost. This process *both encourages and requires* open communication and a higher level of creativity among all involved, since *everyone now knows* precisely how their efforts will affect (and be affected by) the work of the other experts on the team. In a sense, nobody "owns" the BIM model, since it's clearly a joint effort, and this is perhaps the biggest psychological change, since it requires new terms of engagement.

Integrated design will surely require new forms of contract language and a creative response from the risk management industry. By sharing information openly and transparently, by making decisions jointly, and

Although the premise of BIM is a single model with all information, for larger complex models, different components of the building are modeled separately and then linked together for coordination and design resolution. This project for the U.S. Food and Drug Administration's Southeast Quadrant project in White Oak, Maryland is modeling several linked buildings using BIM. *Image courtesy of KlingStubbins.*

View at entry of Smithsonian Tropical Research Institute Field Station Laboratory in Bocas del Toro, Panama, completed October 2003. *Image courtesy of Kiss + Cathcart, Architects.*

vidual team members depends absolutely on the success of the entire team. In essence, everybody wins, or nobody wins.

The following case study shows a successful example of design integration. Corresponding color images are shown in Figures C-6 through C-10. Only through a careful iterative process was the project able to incorporate significant sustainable strategies into a laboratory in a sensitive environment with significant climate challenges and aggressive energy targets.

Smithsonian Tropical Research Institute Field Station

A Field Station Laboratory in Bocas del Toro, Panama
Kiss + Cathcart, Architects
Arup, Engineers

The Smithsonian Tropical Research Institute (STRI) is a bureau of the Smithsonian Institution, and one of the world's leading centers for basic research on the ecology, behavior, and the evolution of tropical organisms. STRI retained Kiss + Cathcart with Arup Consulting Engineers USA to design the main laboratory building at its new marine research facility on land on Isla Colon, an island in the province of Bocas del Toro, Panama. The province of Bocas del Toro has coasts only on the Caribbean shoreline, and Isla Colon is one of more than 50 barrier islands which form the archipelago of Bocas del Toro. Bocas del Toro has a unique fauna and flora cover and contains the most complete record of the marine environment in the southernmost end of the Caribbean.

The site location of the Smithsonian Tropical Research Institute (STRI) Field Station Laboratory in Bocas del Toro, Panama. *Image courtesy of Smithsonian Institution.*

View of STRI Field Station Laboratory site from north, at the narrowest part of Bocas del Toro island, Panama. An existing sawmill building is visible onsite; the Caribbean Sea is on the left, Matambal Bay is on the right. *Image courtesy of Kiss + Cathcart, Architects.*

Site

The project site is a narrow strip of low-lying land between a mangrove swamp on Matambal Bay and the beach of the Caribbean Sea. Since STRI's mission is the study of marine biology and environmental science onsite, it was imperative to minimize the new building's impact while providing an exemplary scientific facility. Research performed at STRI helped prevent the building of an electricity-generating station less than a mile along the coast, because concerns arose about warming and pollution of the marine environment.

Kiss + Cathcart Architects, with Arup Engineers, designed the main laboratory building to be as close to "net zero" environmental impact as possible. The building collects all of its own water, treats all of its own waste, and generates all of its own energy, the PV roof generating 75 percent of the building's energy needs.

Density and Community Connection

Lot size: 26,000 square miles
Building footprint: 30,800 square feet (2,860 square meters)

The building design takes cues from the local vernacular in its raised wood frame, siding, and large overhanging roofs. Its combination of high-tech and low-tech solutions suits its location as a remote research station with sophisticated scientific equipment.

The majority of the building's users are visiting scientists who stay either onsite in the dormitories or in the village of Bocas del Toro. Many of these offsite visitors use a bicycle, taxi, or local bus to get to the site. The amount of parking provided onsite is minimal, accommodating approximately eight cars.

continued

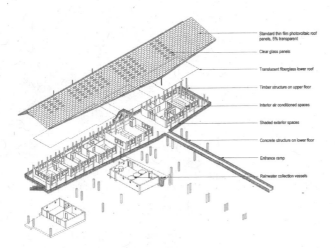

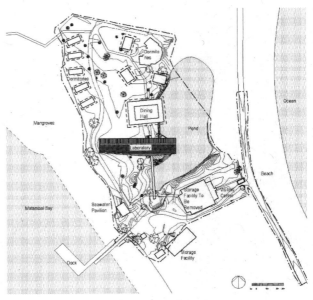

Raising the entire STRI Field Station Laboratory on concrete piers helps to catch prevailing breezes for passive cooling, and also provides a measure of flood protection and minimizes the lab's impact on the site. Air conditioning is zoned so that individual rooms can be cooled separately. *Image courtesy of Kiss + Cathcart, Architects.*

Site plan for STRI Field Station Laboratory in Bocas del Toro, Panama. Lot size: 26,000 square meters; building footprint: 30,800 square feet (2,860 square meters). *Image courtesy of Smithsonian Institution.*

Ecological Issues

The site is a former sawmill with landfill from the sawmill's waste. Adjacent land is lightly inhabited with a radio antenna on municipal land to the north, and small, inhabited shacks on the land to the south. Master planning of the site included protecting the mangrove swamp to the west and allowing views to both the bay and ocean sides of the site. Impervious area was minimized with gravel roads and paths. This was especially important, since the site is already often waterlogged. The concrete floor slab of the former sawmill building was reused for visitor parking. The location of the laboratory was influenced by large tree locations, the conditions of the fill, and the relationship of the building to the pond, the dock, and the seawater tank pavilion. The former pond, which had been filled with sawmill waste, was restored to provide habitat for local species. Six crocodiles now reside there. A future phase will add a constructed wetland system adjacent to the pond to treat waste from the building.

Climate and Bioclimatic Design

The basic strategy was to maximize airflow and minimize solar heat gain. The form of the building developed out of passive solar concerns. The double roof, which has an overhang large enough to prevent the sun from hitting the exterior walls, shades the enclosed, conditioned spaces. This substantially lowers solar heat gain, and ventilation of the large space between the two roofs (with louvers at the apex of the roof) prevents the build-up of hot air. The translucent lower roof, together with the partially transparent photovoltaic roof, allows an optimum 5 percent of daylight into the interior rooms for daylighting.

The building-integrated photovoltaic (BIPV) roof faces south with a shallow 17-degree pitch, designed for an optimal combination of energy generation and water capture at this latitude. The photovoltaic system provides up to 30 kilowatts (kW) of

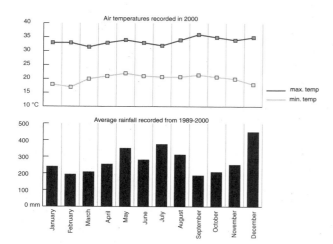

Bocas del Toro has a very humid, tropical climate with average temperatures of 31.5°C in the summer and 26°C in the winter with an average relative humidity of 80 to 85 percent. Diurnal temperature difference is minimal. Average monthly rainfall varies from 160 to 450 millimeters. The ground on the site is often waterlogged, and there are many insects, especially low to the ground. *Image courtesy of Kiss + Cathcart, Architects.*

Building configuration of the STRI Field Station Laboratory, Bocas Del Toro, Panama: raised on piers, open circulation, and double-roof construction contribute to maximize airflow and minimize solar gains. *Image courtesy of Kiss + Cathcart, Architects.*

actual instantaneous output and a yearly total of close to 70,000 kilowatt-hours (kWh). As designed, the BIPV roof supplies approximately 75 percent of the base building energy use of the facility. Because the grid power on the island is a diesel-generated, very dirty, and unreliable source of power (compared to the average U.S. grid supply), the environmental benefits of the BIPV system are significantly greater than they would be in the mainland United States.

The air conditioning system was designed to lower relative humidity to 35 to 65 percent, while providing an internal temperature of 75°F ± 4°F. Ceiling fans are provided in each room to allow occupants to be comfortable at higher temperatures. The air-conditioning units are zoned to adjust to use patterns. A separate fresh-air heat pump supercools the air to reduce humidity before supplying makeup air to the labs. The system was designed as a two-stage heat pump cooling with sea water heat rejection. The water-source aspect of the system was changed during construction to be a conventional air-cooled system, due to concerns of first cost and a lack of familiarity with maintenance issues. As a result, the system installed is less efficient than the one designed, and the percentage of PV energy production is lower.

Efficient lighting strategies include 100 percent daylighting during daylight hours and the exclusive use of fluorescent light bulbs at other times. Nighttime light pollution is minimized by using low-level exterior path lighting and minimizing light trespass through the PV roof.

Energy Security

As mentioned, the unreliability of the local power grid was a major impetus behind the design. To compensate for this unreliability, there is daylight in every room; the main photovoltaic system has been configured so that, when the grid shuts

continued

Photovoltaic array at the double roof of STRI Field Station Laboratory provides approximately 75 percent of the base building energy, plus provides a
consistent energy source, which is a benefit in this location, where utility-
based power is inconsistently delivered. *Image courtesy of Kiss + Cathcart, Architects.*

STRI Field Station Laboratory's modular wood structure at double-roof construction. *Image courtesy of Kiss + Cathcart, Architects.*

down, the PV system turns off for only a few seconds, coming back on when the onsite generator activates. A secondary PV-
UPS subsystem dedicates 6 kW PV to a 16-kWh battery bank serving one or two outlets in each lab for sensitive electronic
equipment so that experiments never have to be interrupted due to power fluctuations. Onsite photovoltaic generation provides
the most electricity at similar times to peak air-conditioning loads. Because of these energy security measures, all parts of the
building could continue to operate even during a blackout that affects the surrounding locality.

WATER AND WASTE

Water Supply

In an area with abundant rainfall and a nonpotable municipal supply, the decision to collect rainwater was an easy one. The form
of the roof directs rainfall into centrally located tanks on the lower level, where it will be stored in 4,000-gallon storage containers,
filtered, and treated with ultraviolet light before being used as the building's water supply and for other campus buildings. Since
the site is already hooked up to the municipal water supply, emergency back-up is easily provided. Fixtures are of the lowest
water consumption locally available. Potable water is supplied via bottled-water coolers. No water is used for landscaping
purposes.

Waste

STRI is currently designing a constructed wetland, to include the existing onsite pond, to treat both graywater and blackwater
from the facility. The laboratory is a marine research field station, and STRI does not allow hazardous chemicals to be used in the
laboratories since they would be difficult or impossible to treat in the wetland. Currently, waste is treated with a conventional
onsite septic system.

Materials

Materials were chosen for environmental reasons, and, where possible, were left without additional finish. Sustainably harvested local hardwood was used for the upper structure and siding of the building.

Extensive research was done to find the most suitable type of wood for the upper frame and siding. The wood chosen, canafistula, is naturally very resistant to termites and fungi. FSC-certified wood is not produced in Panama, but the Panamanian environmental agency, ANAM, has its own sustainable forestry regulations, and the wood used was locally harvested and certified by ANAM.

The foundation had to be a reinforced concrete mat, because the bearing capacity of the soil was extremely low. The site is also often waterlogged, and the concrete lower level helps minimize termite and fungi damage to the upper wood structure. The same hardwood was also used for windows, doors, exterior siding, and siding in the lobby.

Wherever possible, the structure became the finish, and there are minimal other finishes; interior walls are water-resistant gypsum wallboard, and the lower roof is translucent fiberglass. Specified paints are low-VOC, and the interior floor finish is ceramic tile.

Design for Adaptability to Future Uses

The double-roof construction of the STRI Field Station Laboratory allows light to filter through the PV and the inner roof of translucent panels, providing an even daylighting effect through the majority of spaces in the facility. *Image courtesy of Kiss + Cathcart, Architects.*

By maximizing the open-air spaces used for circulation, the STRI Field Station Laboratory in Bocas del Toro, Panama, could minimize the areas that require mechanical conditioning, which reduces the overall energy demand of the project. Shelter is required to accommodate the significant rainfall in this region. *Image courtesy of Kiss + Cathcart, Architects.*

Within this structure, the interior volumes are not structural and, therefore, can be easily reconfigured for adaptive reuse. Space can be enclosed on the ground floor for additional storage and service use. The wood frame is bolted together for possible disassembly. However, as it stands right now, the building could be easily reused to serve as a hotel or school.

Indoor Environment

The building's main functions—labs for resident and visiting scientists, teaching labs, a conference room, and support spaces—occupy a string of volumes on a raised platform shaded by an overhanging pitched roof. Interior volumes are shaded by the large photovoltaic roof, which minimizes direct heat gains. The narrow plan, together with the space between the two roofs,

continued

allows cross-ventilation to keep the building cool while providing daylight and views. The translucent lower roof, along with the partially transparent photovoltaic roof, admits an optimum 5 percent of daylight into the interior rooms for daylighting. Since the exterior areas are shaded, users' eyes will have time to adjust to the lower interior light levels, and they will not immediately turn the lights on before their eyes have time to adjust.

All working spaces have translucent, daylit ceilings and are within 5 meters of a window, affording good views and daylighting. Individual occupants in all spaces have the choice of air conditioning, ceiling fans, or natural ventilation from operable windows.

Low-VOC paints were used throughout, and wood that did not need to be treated was chosen. Detailing of water runoff, along with good ventilation of all spaces, was designed to avoid conditions favorable to mildew growth.

Conclusion

Like lab design itself, the process of architectural and engineering design is undergoing profound changes, both in terms of process (integrated design) and technology (BIM). In today's complex world, it is simply not possible to create state-of-the-art facilities for research without using the most sophisticated tools and methods for design. The result will be better buildings: facilities that are more flexible, more adaptable, more cost-efficient, and better able to support the evolving needs of the research community.

Key Concepts

- Integrated design means simultaneous decision-making, broad groups of architects, engineers, construction groups, and owner groups. This is in contrast to a conventional "sequential" process where the architect makes some decisions, then passes it to an engineer who makes other modifications, and then passes it to a construction group who builds it.

- In an integrated process, tradeoffs are possible to get the most sustainable building possible.

- The integrated process includes the following tasks.

  - Research/Evaluation—Studying what is possible; what the site and climate afford

  - Criteria/Load-setting—Taking a close look at what is needed to serve the building spaces and occupants. External loads can be mitigated through design, internal loads are developed from the criteria and program. Challenging these setpoints and criteria can have a very large impact

  - Design—Including massing, orientation, envelope optimization, shading, and system design

- Building information modeling is a methodology that allows for much of the coordination that used to take place in the field to be simulated and tested in computer model form.

- Key components of BIM include :

  - 3D Modeling

  - Design Optimization

  - Construction Logistics

  - Building Operation and ongoing Performance Modeling

chapter **3** # Programming
Laying the Groundwork for a Sustainable Project

Introduction

Image Courtesy of KlingStubbins. Photography © Sam Fentress.

A widely repeated statistic is that laboratories use five to ten times more energy than equivalently sized office buildings. Laboratories for the 21st Century (Labs21®): An Introduction to Low-Energy Design (http://labs21.lbl.gov/) elaborates further and states that figure increases to as much as 100 times when specialty labs like clean rooms and process-driven facilities are compared to other commercial facilities. They go on to say, "Assuming that half of all American laboratories can reduce their energy use by 30 percent, the U.S. Environmental Protection Agency (EPA) estimates that the nation could reduce its annual energy consumption by 84 trillion Btu"—or 840,000 households worth of energy. Given figures like these, the impact of a sustainably designed laboratory building cannot be disputed.

At the core of all strategies for improving a laboratory's sustainability lies the most basic, yet the most

This chapter focuses on several of the sustainability categories discussed in Chapter 1. See page 18 for more information.

significant strategy—sustainable laboratory programming. However, when considering the design of a sustainable laboratory building, it is not possible to discuss laboratory programming in a vacuum. Because the individual laboratories themselves are the building blocks of the facility, programming them must be viewed as a component of the holistic programming and planning effort for the entire project. Of course, in theory this statement rings true for any laboratory project, but the success of the project from a sustainable standpoint specifically rests on a holistic, iterative approach to its design. (See Chapter 2 for a discussion of integrated design.) What is intended to occur inside the laboratory establishes the criteria that drive the need for engineering systems to support mechanical and utility needs. The amount of space these engineering systems take up, how and where that mechanical space is accommodated, and how the laboratories, laboratory support spaces, offices, and other program pieces are sized and arranged all impact the sustainability of the project.

Every decision made during the programming phase influences how much space the laboratory building takes up (its physical efficiency) and how much energy it uses (its operational efficiency). The more efficient a laboratory is and the fewer resources it uses during operation, the more sustainable it becomes. Whether a project is begun with a previously determined program or only a few parameters (the number of scientists, types of processes to be accommodated, and a site) an opportunity exists to influence the impact a project makes on the environment through careful and well considered decisions made during the programming process. Following is a discussion of strategies and considerations for using the laboratory programming process to maximize a facility's sustainability. It supposes that overall goal setting

sessions for the entire project have been conducted already, and that critical information such as lengths of payback periods that are acceptable to the owner have been discussed. This chapter focuses on programming at the scientist/user level.

Macroprogramming

There are two pieces of the overall laboratory programming effort: macroprogramming and microprogramming. Macroprogramming is the phase of information gathering during which large-scale issues are evaluated—the **program**, the **laboratory module**, and the **overall building organization**. The program chronicles what space types and how many of each the building will accommodate; it also lists the size of each space, the square footage for all spaces of that type, and frequently provides information on personnel and additional comments. The basic laboratory module itself is defined, and often a "kit of parts" to be used as the basis for developing individual laboratories is identified. Building organization characteristics (appropriate relationship between laboratories, support spaces, corridors, and offices; flow of people, materials and waste through the building; functional relationships between major components—required adjacencies and blocking/stacking) are defined. Strategies are developed for building-wide issues such as flexibility and adaptability, openness, and integration with engineering systems.

The Program

The smaller the laboratory building is, the fewer resources required to construct and to operate it; a smaller laboratory building is a more sustainable facility. To reduce the size of the facility, the design team and the client should start by examining the program from a master planning perspective. During early planning sessions, the team should consider whether it makes sense to house every part of the program in this particular facility. Some spaces might be accommodated more efficiently elsewhere on an existing campus. Major equipment to be used by occupants might exist in a nearby facility.

There are opportunities outside of the laboratory space itself for reducing the overall size of the facility. Challenge the requirements for private offices. Corporate facilities of all types have been designed around an effective model that creates team-oriented, collaborative environments. An open office model with fewer private offices and more teaming areas could function well for many research facilities too, and would help to increase lab efficiency and foster interaction between scientists. Conference room space could be ganged together and divided by operable partitions so that it might function as training room space. More frequent deliveries of supplies or removal of waste might decrease storage requirements within the facility. The opportunities are wide ranging and vary with each project. The important point is that the overall program should be scrutinized for spaces that might be made smaller or eliminated altogether.

When the program is first defined, space assignments are often determined based on head count. That is, a certain net square feet (NSF) of lab and lab support space is allocated per scientist. If the NSF assigned to a scientist is reduced, the size of the building can be reduced or more scientists can be placed into one laboratory building. Sometimes clients come to the table with this figure defined already, but sometimes this figure is determined during macroprogramming. Regardless of how it is derived, this metric should be compared to other similar facilities. This process of comparing metrics is called **benchmarking**.

KlingStubbins embarked on an extensive benchmarking effort in 1999 to compare design concepts, data, and costs of research and development facilities in the biopharma industry; over 20 biopharma companies have contributed multiple projects to the effort, and information is updated annually. Since the initial undertaking, the benchmarking database has expanded to include many different project types—quality laboratories, process development laboratories, undergraduate teaching laboratories, and graduate research facilities. The intent of this bench-

Biology Department Program

Staff	No. of Rms	Title/Room Name	Unit NSF Area	Total NSF Area	Comments
Office					
3	3	Executive Director	250	750	
6	6	Director	165	990	
10	10	Administrative Assist. Workstation	80	800	
57	57	Senior Scientist Office	110	6,270	
118	59	Junior Scientist Office	55	6,490	Shared Office
194				15,300	
Office Support					
	3	Conference Room 10 Person	350	1,050	
	4	Break Room/Coffee	265	1,060	
	4	Copy / Fax Rooms	160	640	
	7	Team Area	220	1,540	
				4,290	
Biology Laboratories:					
	13	3 Module Biology Labs	2650	34,450	Incl. En-Suite Tissue Culture
	1	2 Module Biology Lab	1842	1,842	
	1	BL3 Lab	1092	1,092	Incl. Vestibules & Mech. Room
	1	Double Tissue Culture Suite	822	822	Incl. Air Lock and Cold Storage
	2	Single Tissue Culture Suite	474	948	Incl. Air Lock and Cold Storage
	7	Cold Lab	118	826	Prefabricated Environmental Room
	2	Warm Lab	112	224	Prefabricated Environmental Room
				40,204	
Biology Support:					
	7	Equipment Room	362	2,534	
	4	Camera Rooms	56	224	
	4	Film Processing Room	124	496	
	3	Autoclave Rooms	118	354	
	1	Confocal Microscopy Room	258	258	
	2	Cold Storage	322	644	Prefabricated Environmental Room
				4,510	
Subtotal NSF Biology Department:				64,304	

Sample program for Biology department. The program lists each space type, how many of that space type are included in the facility, the area of one unit of the space, and the resultant overall area. Information on personnel per space and comments is sometimes provided as well. *Image courtesy of KlingStubbins.*

marking effort is to provide data to help each client examine facility needs of their own organization in light of design concepts and criteria the industry is currently using. Many trends, figures, and charts included in this and other chapters are derived from this database.

Historic data indicate that NSF of laboratory and laboratory support per scientist have reduced over the past decade. Although benchmarked metrics are not prescriptive, they are useful as a reality check against which newly gathered requirements may be compared. If specific project metrics are significantly higher, the design team should reexamine project data to determine what is driving the larger numbers and whether the drivers are legitimate or not. Regardless of where new project metrics fall, the design team should consider all strategies for reducing the NSF per scientist. One key strategy for doing so is reducing the size of the laboratory module.

Laboratory Module and NSF/Scientist

The laboratory module is the primary building block of the laboratory building. Linear feet of bench, hood, and equipment space per scientist determine how many scientists will fit into one laboratory module, and in turn the laboratory module itself establishes the size of the building. Bench depth and aisle width establish the module width. Compare the two modules shown in the figure: Module B on the right shows an 11-foot-0-inch-wide module as described in the *NIH Design Requirements Manual for Biomedical Laboratories and Animal Research Facilities*. Module A, on the left, illustrates a typical 10-foot-6-inch-wide module. If the width of a module is reduced by just 6 inches, an entire module is saved for every 22 laboratory modules required.

Consideration should be given to whether the client can function in the narrower module. If 3-foot-deep benches are to be used primarily, and most modules will be enclosed by partitions on either side, then 10 feet-6-inches might be too narrow, since the resulting aisle width in a single module laboratory is only 4 feet-0 inches wide. However, if most modules are planned to be open with 5-feet-0-inch-deep double-

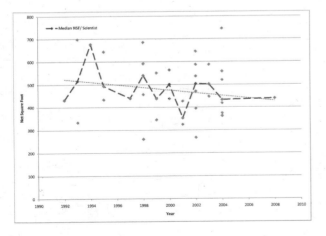

The dashed line represents the trendline showing the decline in average net square foot of laboratory and laboratory support space assignment per scientist over the past decade. *Image courtesy of KlingStubbins.*

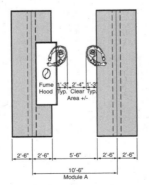
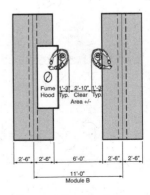

Module B shows an 11-foot-0-inch-wide module. Module A shows a typical 10-foot-6-inch-wide module. *Image courtesy of KlingStubbins.*

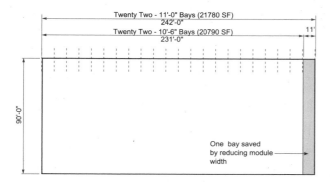

Reducing the module width by just 6 inches saves an entire module for every 22 modules required. *Image courtesy of KlingStubbins.*

Less frequently used or shared equipment is placed on mobile tables that may be moved from lab to lab at this research facility. Courtesy of KlingStubbins. *Image courtesy of KlingStubbins. Photography © Sam Fentress.*

sided island or peninsula benches, or if enclosed modules are planned with benches that are only 2 feet-6 inches deep, then the 10-foot-6-inch module width is adequate.

The NSF per scientist can be reduced by challenging the space requirement drivers themselves. Assignment of linear feet of bench, hood, and equipment space (sometimes collectively referred to as "equivalent linear feet of bench," or ELF) that impacts module length is another major factor setting space requirements. The ELF assignment should always be questioned and examined, even if the client has an established standard. Less bench space might be required if the laboratory casework system to be used is better suited to the work than what the scientists currently are using. Equipment can be stacked more efficiently on specially designed shelving. Infrequently used or shared equipment can be kept on racks that are wheeled from laboratory to laboratory as needed. For more information about this project, see color images C-51 through C-55.

Careful observation of the actual use of the space may inspire more efficient, alternative lay-outs that

can be suggested to the client. Or, the observations may lead to the conclusion that an institution's standard ELF assignment is too high based on how the scientists truly are using the space. It is not uncommon to see that in an academic graduate level research lab only half as much space is dedicated to each researcher compared to the amount allotted in a pharmaceutical laboratory. However, some private pharmaceutical laboratories function more like academic laboratories, with scientists spending little time in their labs. If scientists are only setting up experiments, leaving, and working in their offices all day, it is possible they might require no more than 6 linear feet of bench top for set up, plus equipment space. Coming to a conclusion during the programming stage involves interviewing scientists about their work habits and even observing the scientists at work in their spaces. The drawback to the "rightsize" approach to lab design is that space can be econo-

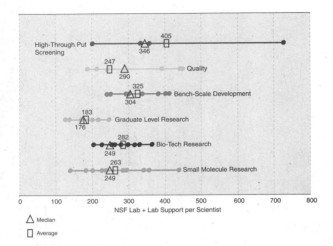

Median and average NSF assignment of laboratory and laboratory support space per scientist for a number of different laboratory types. *Image courtesy of KlingStubbins.*

mized to where it is perfect for now, but will not have the flexibility to adapt to changing protocols in the future.

Bench top and above bench top shelving is sometimes used for storage of items that could be accommodated outside of the laboratory more efficiently and economically, since storage space can use recirculated, conditioned air rather than the once-through air (at six air changes an hour) typically provided to labs. If there is a high enough demand for storage, there is a potential for merging the various storage spaces into a single high-density storage space. By addressing the misplaced storage and relocating it outside the laboratory, the once unusable bench space is now available for the scientist, thus allowing a reduction of lineal feet of bench per scientist while still maintaining an adequate work surface. Lab managers should consider a just-in-time delivery system so that scientists are less inclined to hoard supplies and materials inside the laboratory at the bench. In

addition to the sustainable advantages, a well-planned, clutter-free lab space will provide a much more pleasant work environment.

Along with the assignment of bench space per scientist, hood space is also assigned on a per scientist

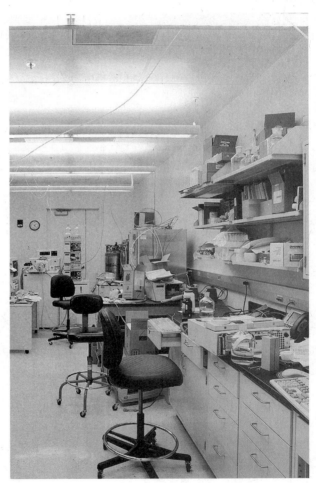

At this laboratory facility, relocating consumable supplies to a central storage location and removing unused equipment would free up space for lab work here. Storage rooms require fewer air changes than laboratories; organizing and allocating space for these functions saves energy, since less lab space is required for the same number of scientists. *Image courtesy of KlingStubbins. Photography by Ron Solomon—Baltimore © 2008.*

basis and often can be reduced. Fume hoods should be used efficiently for procedures—not as storage units for solvents or infrequently used equipment. Explaining to scientists the environmental penalty for high fume hood density and suggesting during programming viable options for solvent and equipment storage most often results in a re-evaluation of fume hood requirements.

Building Organization

The first opportunity to work with engineers in an integrated fashion to plan efficiently occurs during macroplanning when overall building organization is studied. As program elements are blocked and stacked, the entire design team should consider mechanical distribution, both to optimize efficiency and to allot space as needed. Certain energy saving engineering solutions such as heat wheels and heat recovery systems require additional space. Discussions with engineers must occur at the beginning of the project, so that possible strategies are not eliminated simply because space is no longer available to incorporate a desired technology.

There is no single "right" solution for organizing a laboratory building's mechanical distribution system. Different solutions make sense for different projects. Some might require an interstitial floor—that is, an accessible level above the occupied level for ductwork and service distribution. Other projects might incorporate multiple smaller duct and service distribution shafts spaced intermittently along the floor. Still others might have larger mechanical shafts located at third points in the floor plan. In any of these scenarios, coordination with the engineering team is required to develop a distribution strategy that works optimally for the particular project. It might make more sense to locate a mechanical room on an inter-

mediate floor in a multilevel laboratory so that ductwork never has too long of a vertical run. Not only does less ductwork mean less material on the project, but less energy is needed to propel the air through the system. Armed with this information early on, a project team can incorporate it into the overall project planning strategy.

The engineers' input on the floor plate goes beyond just looking at the ideal location for the mechanical spaces. Early on in planning, engineers should share information with the design team on the arrangement of program pieces too. Engineers might see opportunities for utilizing transfer air from positively pressurized clean spaces in the laboratory

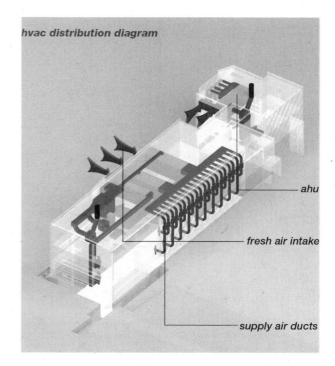

hvac distribution diagram

ahu

fresh air intake

supply air ducts

Studying mechanical distribution options during early blocking and stacking exercises allows for an integrated design that minimizes ductwork runs. *Image courtesy of KlingStubbins.*

building if those spaces are located where this can be done effectively. Or, they might point out that while relocating dry workspaces from the laboratory module to an area outside of it will not reduce the overall NSF of a floor plate of a building, the move still reduces the overall size of the building by reducing the amount of space that must be conditioned as laboratory space. By using recirculated versus once-through air in dry labs, the amount of ductwork can be reduced and the floor-to-floor height of the building can be lowered. Less air being moved through the building results in smaller mechanical equipment and less space required in which to house the equipment.

In some newer laboratory buildings, offices are segregated from the laboratories so completely that they are on a dedicated mechanical system and can have operable windows or even their own local heating and cooling. There is always lively discussion regarding where offices should be located. Not only does an arrangement with offices located outside the laboratory allow for the energy efficiencies described above, but also it enables researchers to enjoy a cup of coffee while working, something they cannot do inside the laboratory. This arrangement might even encourage more interaction, as nobody winds up isolated in a laboratory all day, and there are greater opportunities for casual discussions en route between the office and laboratory. Benchmarking data shows us that scientists spend more time in their offices than they used to, and in general, more of the laboratory floor plate is dedicated to office space than in the past.

The operable windows in the office wing of The Donald Bren School of Environmental Science and Management at the University of California, Santa Barbara, have a mechanical interlock (a small sensor in the frame) so that, upon opening, the heaters in the offices are automatically turned off. The ventilation system for the laboratories is the most efficient available. *Image courtesy of University of California, Santa Barbara and ZGF Architects, LLP.*

Offices located outside of but with full visual access to laboratory at AstraZeneca's R&D Expansion in Waltham, Massachusetts. *Image courtesy of KlingStubbins. Photography © Robert Benson Photography.*

On the other hand, with the unpredictability of science, the most flexible type of space (and thus the type of space requiring fewer resource-intensive renovations) might actually be a laboratory with everything inside it—a warehouse of sorts combining laboratory, laboratory support, and office workspace—sometimes referred to as a "cellular" arrangement. To do this in an energy efficient manner, the processes driving the need for once-through air must be enclosed in effective ventilated enclosures. Regardless of whether the ventilated enclosure enables recirculated air in the laboratory or not, it most definitely improves energy efficiency as air change rates in the space outside of it can be reduced. Also helping to make the vision of the cellular laboratory more viable is the trend toward dryer laboratory spaces with more work being done on computers or remotely monitored. "Lab-on-a-Chip" technologies might have been the stuff of science fiction years ago but exist now and most likely will be commonplace in the near future.

Building and Floor Plate Efficiency

After looking at ways to reduce the net square feet assigned to each scientist, one of the next steps is to evaluate the space from an efficiency standpoint. Gross square feet (GSF) assigned to each scientist must be assessed in order to determine efficiency. The ratio of net to gross square feet is defined as the building efficiency, and the higher this number, the more efficient the building. This number is increased by reducing space that is not part of the building net

Ventilated enclosure around equipment limits the area requiring higher air change rates. *Image courtesy of KlingStubbins.*

Lab support space, informal conference space, and write-up areas are included within the laboratory module in this design. The "all-in" cellular scheme can be quite flexible, since space is not limited to a single function. *Image courtesy of KlingStubbins.*

square feet. An efficient floor plan is also a compact floor plan, and the more compact a floor plan becomes, the shorter the duct and utility runs. Shorter duct runs also reduce the duct depth and in turn lead to a reduction of the floor-to-floor height of the building.

Benchmarking data shows that, generally speaking, over time, laboratories are becoming more efficient. There are many approaches to laying out an efficient, flexible building. The three floor plates depicted in the figure show very different answers to the same problem. Scheme 1 consists of a single row of offices on the perimeter of the building. With borrowed lights, the labs get daylight. A service corridor in the center allows for lab material flow, cylinder space, and some equipment such as ice machines and freezers. Scientists involved in the lab planning for this project were able to choose from a "kit of parts" that allowed flexible lay-outs based on their need for support spaces and number of lab modules per space. A drawback of this lay-out is that while it was an ulti-

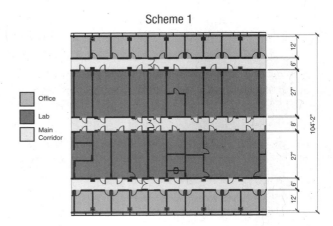

Scheme 1

Scheme 1 has a central service corridor that allows for material flow, cylinder space, and some equipment. Labs have borrowed lights to allow in some daylight that passes through perimeter offices. *Image courtesy of KlingStubbins.*

mately flexible space in the planning stages, with all of the enclosed lab space, future revisions to laboratory sizes will require that lab partitions be demolished. Utilizing demountable partitions or partitions formed by removable panels integrated with the

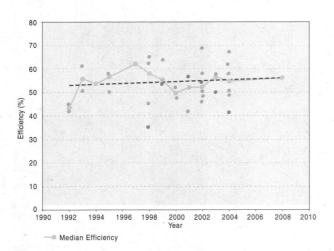

This chart compares laboratory efficiency ratios over the last decade and shows that, in general, laboratories are becoming more efficient. *Image courtesy of KlingStubbins.*

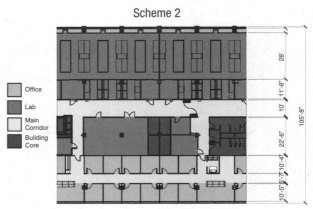

Scheme 2

Scheme 2 is more flexible with a lab zone at the top of the plan and a ghost corridor between labs and general support. Specialized support labs are located in the center of the floor plate and offices are on the opposite side. *Image courtesy of KlingStubbins.*

Scheme 3

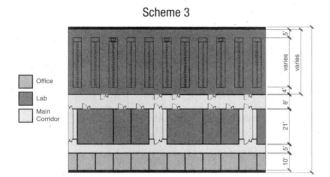

Scheme 3 has distinct zones for open labs, support, and single-loaded offices. *Image courtesy of KlingStubbins.*

Mechanical equipment in an enclosed penthouse. The enclosed space is included in the building's gross square. *Image courtesy of KlingStubbins. Photography © Sam Fentress.*

casework would minimize that disruption and waste of materials.

The second scheme is very flexible in plan. In the lab zone (at the top of the plan), the ghost corridors allow for multiple egress paths from the labs and can accommodate equipment when divided lab modules are required. The ghost corridors also allow for a direct connection to the lab support zone. An additional support zone in the center of the building allows for any specialized labs that can't or don't want to be in the open lab zone. Scheme 3 shows a lab that is very utilitarian. It has distinct zones that serve specific functions. It consists of a large open lab, a distinct lab support zone, and an office zone.

Mechanical equipment housed behind a screen on the rooftop versus within an enclosed penthouse provides yet another possible reduction of building gross square footage.

Equipment Requirements

The amount of equipment required in a laboratory, the location of that equipment, and the equipment selection itself all impact the amount of energy required. The first two equipment issues are examined here in this discussion of macroprogramming, as they are related to building organization. Equipment selection is addressed later in the microprogramming section of this chapter.

Laboratory lay-outs should be arranged to facilitate sharing of equipment. The less duplication of equipment at individual benches, the less bench top each scientist will require. Benches can be arranged so that the end portion of each bench is available for shared equipment or shared equipment can be segregated in separate rooms. Of course, when the

Rooftop mechanical equipment does not contribute to the building's gross square footage at University of Colorado Denver Research 1 in Aurora, Colorado. *Image courtesy of KlingStubbins. Photography © Ron Johnson Photography.*

the heat that is rejected dealt with more efficiently. Instead of cooling requirements for an entire laboratory being increased, only the smaller equipment room must be addressed, and often this can be accomplished with a small fan coil unit versus an increase in major equipment size. Most likely, the locally cooled air in the equipment room can be recirculated, unlike the air in the laboratory that is more likely once-through, in which case cool air is provided to the laboratory and then wastefully discharged to

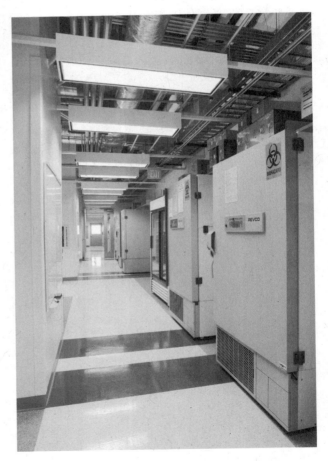

At the University of Colorado Denver Research 1, noisy, heat-producing, shared equipment is located in a linear equipment corridor. *Image courtesy of KlingStubbins. Photography © Ron Johnson Photography.*

quantity of pieces of equipment is reduced, there is a corresponding reduction in utilities to service the equipment and environmental conditioning to remove heat produced by the equipment. Therefore, less equipment equates to lower energy consumption. Stated requirements for individually owned equipment might be based on a different laboratory configuration than the one being considered, so the laboratory planner should challenge the scientist being interviewed to consider whether a different layout would enable him or her to share more pieces.

Shared equipment rooms and linear equipment corridors offer multiple advantages. Like bench arrangements, they enable equipment sharing so less is required. Also, noisy, heat-producing equipment is removed from the laboratory and relocated to a space where the acoustics can be addressed and the outside environment. Finally, if specialized equipment is confined to equipment rooms or alcoves, more of the main laboratory space can be generic and thus will require fewer renovations over time.

Program Space for Sustainable Operations

When the program is being developed, the design team should not overlook dedicated spaces that facilitate sustainable operations within the laboratory facility. Space must be allotted at the dock to accommodate multiple dumpsters for waste stream separation. Depending on how waste is to be picked up on the floors, dedicated alcoves or small rooms for recycling paper from laboratory offices and other material from break spaces might be required. Recycling and appropriate separation of waste should be encouraged within individual laboratories too; this should be accounted for in module size and casework lay-out. Waste containers and collection vessels might be accommodated within a recessed niche or perhaps in open areas below bench tops. The easier the activity is for researchers, the higher the compliance level will be. If there is no space dedicated and aisles become cluttered with various containers, not only is safety compromised, but also within time the containers will be pushed out of the way and not used.

Reduce the Frequency and Scope of Renovations

The sustainability of a lab may also be influenced by planning a space that minimizes the frequency and scope of renovations. Computer sizes have been becoming increasingly smaller, but this increase in computing power brings with it a constant stream of spectacular new equipment with new requirements in laboratory spaces. Research methods change. Team sizes change. Projects stop and start. The Greek philosopher, Heraclitus, identified the trend in 500 BC, when he posited that the only constant is change! Labs are no exception and now, more than ever, must be planned to allow for an ever-changing environment and ultimate flexibility.

One common method of achieving an adaptable laboratory (one that can accommodate change without major renovation) is to use flexible casework, which of course leads to less replacement and change out of casework. There are many systems on the market. In general, the systems allow for the addition or removal of base and upper cabinets or shelving. Base units might be suspended from the bench top or loose on the floor, with or without casters, not unlike an office file cabinet pedestal. The bench top above likewise might be suspended from a frame or might simply be table-like and easily removed. Certain systems allow for height adjustments—either manually or hydraulically. Services are either supplied

Flexible casework with overhead services creates an adaptable laboratory where change can be accommodated without major renovations. *Image courtesy of KlingStubbins. Photography © Sam Fentress.*

from overhead, integrated in vertical supports, or run through the casework core. The advantage of these systems, in addition to the flexibility they provide, is that they facilitate the installation of only as much casework as needed. Lab users are more comfortable deferring requests for base or wall cabinets if they know that these can be added later. Many laboratories are filled with empty or underutilized cabinets or drawer units; opening a drawer and finding only an outdated manual for a piece of long-gone equipment is all too common. The most sustainable option for casework, of course, is having less of it.

There are other ways to achieve flexibility that do not involve specialized casework systems. By locating sinks along perimeter walls versus at the ends of island bays, removal of entire benches is possible when needed. Standard moveable tables with utilities supplied overhead can be arranged and rearranged to suit changing requirements and needs within the space.

Having a modular lay-out of utilities and easy access to major runs minimizes the impact of renovations and the amount of finished construction to be torn out. Another option is to run a 10-inch-wide "utility ledge" along the inside face of the rear partition of every lab to provide flexibility and ensure that almost

At University of Colorado Denver Research 1, locating sinks along perimeter walls means that drains and vents are here versus in center casework islands. Thus, the islands can be removed if needed. *Image courtesy of KlingStubbins. Photography © Ron Johnson Photography.*

At the University of Arizona's Medical Research Building and Thomas W. Keating Bioresearch Building in Tucson, Arizona, standard moveable tables with overhead utilities can be rearranged easily. *Image courtesy of ZGF Architects, LLP. Photography © Robert Canfield.*

any reconfiguration in the future will be possible with minimal impact to the existing infrastructure. The temptation to create flexibility by providing every service in every location must be avoided; this only leads to larger systems and the subsequent chain reaction of nonsustainable outcomes related to the increase in space and materials tied to those larger systems. A thoughtful response to this dilemma is illustrated at AstraZeneca in Waltham, Massachusetts, where services are run down a central spine but only branched out to feed service carriers above individual benches as required. Refer to color images C-1 through C-5 for additional information on this site.

Careful selection of materials that are appropriate and durable enough for the work being conducted at that facility reduces the frequency of renovations. These materials will wear better, last longer, and require less frequent replacement. This alone could have more impact on sustainability than the recycled content of material in the first place.

Weighing the impact of a material's short- and long-term maintenance requirements is important, too. Certain linoleum manufacturers have enhanced the sustainability of their laboratory flooring offerings by adding an integral top coat that minimizes care. Some sustainable products might not work at all in a research facility, even outside the laboratory space itself, due to maintenance considerations. For example, bamboo flooring might at first seem like a reasonable sustainable selection in lab office space; but when it is time to refinish the flooring, the entire building might need to be shut down because of the fumes. Therefore, this material, despite its environmental benefits, might not be the most suitable choice for offices within laboratories if downtime is a consideration. (See Chapter 8 in this book for more information about material selection.)

Services located along a central spine are brought to benches via overhead carriers only as required at AstraZeneca's R&D Expansion in Waltham, Massachusetts. *Image courtesy of KlingStubbins. Photography © Robert Benson Photography.*

Microprogramming

In contrast to the large-scale vision with which macroprogramming is approached, during microprogramming the specific criteria for each individual laboratory space is identified. Individual laboratory requirements for casework, utilities, and environmental conditions are examined based on, or in tandem with, the macroplanning process. This information is recorded on a lab card that is referred to throughout the entire design process. At the early stages during programming, engineers use this information to establish block loads for the building to determine a general sense of the size (and thus space) for systems. This information is then used to develop the design documents for the building. During construction, these lab cards are referenced frequently to make sure that on the day the scientist walks into his or her lab, it looks like what was agreed to early on in programming.

Visualization tools such as three-dimensional computer models enable the users to see what his or her space will look like and to explore options early on in the process. This, in itself, cuts down on physical waste. If all details are worked out electronically in "cyberspace," there are fewer instances of installed work ripped out in the field because it does not meet

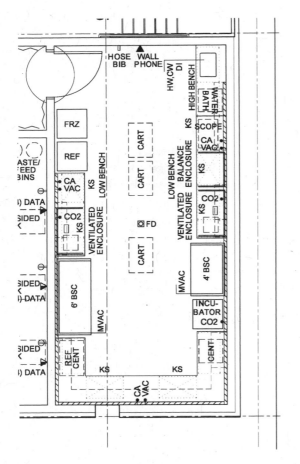

Casework, finish, and utility requirements as well as criteria for environmental conditions are recorded on lab cards that are developed during the programming process. *Image courtesy of KlingStubbins.*

the individual scientist's expectations. The models range from fairly simple, static representations of the lab to interactive models that allow the user to navigate his or her way around the space. Modeling is also used to facilitate the coordination of the engineering and structural systems throughout the building.

Once microplanning conclusions have been documented, users are asked to review and confirm that information is shown accurately on lab cards. At predetermined points along the way, there should be a signing off process by the individual scientists and their leaders to make sure that all stakeholders agree with the criteria gathered, and that it is a sound basis upon which to move forward with the project. This simple act not only obviates the need to revisit decisions repeatedly during design, but also it minimizes wasteful and costly rework during construction.

A 3D model of a customized rack arrangement with gas purification panels and solvent collection on one end was developed for review by scientists early in the design process. *Image courtesy of KlingStubbins.*

The discussion regarding energy efficiency and increased utilization of a building or lab needs to be initiated in the early stages of its conception. Once the building's design progresses beyond the initial programming, implementing change becomes increasingly difficult and affects more space as structural bays and runs of ductwork are set. Although a late-blossoming environmental awareness is nicer than none at all, it does not serve the project well. During one-on-one microprogramming meetings with scientists, the connection between what happens in the laboratory and the overall sustainability of the project should be explained. Scientists are more likely to let go of the old attitude frequently encountered during microprogramming in the past—that is, "I can do more with more"—once the connection between doing with less when possible and an overall reduction of material and energy usage is explained.

When first sitting down with a scientist during microprogramming, start by asking the most basic question: What is he doing in his laboratory? Then ask more detailed questions: How does his work fit into the overall picture of the building that is emerging? Are his needs fairly consistent with the requirements for typical spaces, or is a greater degree of specialization needed? Are there any processes occurring within his laboratory and support spaces or products housed there that are more critical than the standards and criteria established for the building itself? Whenever possible, attempt to house scientists in open, flexible laboratories and avoid customization, as this makes for a facility that will require less change in the future. Initially, it is common to encounter scientists with long equipment lists and "wish" lists accompanied by requests for workspaces within separate rooms for specific procedures. However, it is likely that most of the equipment can be placed and procedures performed in an open lab with minor modifications. Of course, an institution's environmental health and safety group and the scientists ultimately make this determination, but laboratory planners should do their part to challenge the thinking and share experiences from similar projects that might have taken different approaches. In some cases uniquely designed, closed laboratories in place of flexible open laboratories are more of an entrenched cultural inheritance and not science based. These are the situations with the most potential for an updated approach.

Microprogramming is rich with opportunities to challenge criteria. Once the criteria are gathered, the design team develops strategies to fulfill it in the most efficient way possible. In this section of the chapter the type of criteria gathered during microprogramming is identified, and those opportunities for challenges and second looks are pointed out. Sus-

tainable design strategies themselves are examined in following chapters. The criteria gathered relates to lab environment (temperature and relative humidity), operations (air changes, hours of operation, redundancy, filtering), utilities (plumbing, process piping, power, lighting, exhaust devices), code classification, and structural requirements (loading and vibration). Finally, laboratory equipment (already discussed in the macroprogramming section of this chapter) is revisited, this time looking at it from a microprogramming perspective.

Laboratories are much more likely to meet energy efficiency goals if quantitative metrics and benchmarks are explicitly identified and tracked during the course of design, delivery, and operation. Energy benchmarking should be an integral element of the microprogramming process. See the sidebar discussion for more information on energy benchmarking and its application in laboratories.

Energy Benchmarking

Paul A. Mathew, Ph.D
Staff Scientist, Lawrence Berkeley National Laboratory

Energy benchmarking can be used to compare the performance of new designs (using modeled data) as well as existing buildings (using measured data) to a peer group of similar facilities. Energy benchmarking is typically done at the whole-building level using metrics such as overall energy use per unit area (e.g., BTU/sf). Whole-building energy benchmarking has been effectively used for evaluating the energy efficiency of offices, schools, and other commercial facilities, most notably in the EnergyStar™ program. Whole-building metrics are useful for identifying the overall level of efficiency, but do not provide any information on system-level factors that contribute to a particular level of efficiency. Action-oriented benchmarking extends whole-building benchmarking to the system and component level, which allows designers and operators to assess the relative level of efficiency of each system and thereby identify potential efficiency opportunities.

Labs21® recommends using a suite of metrics to track efficiency during the design and operation of laboratory buildings. Lawrence Berkeley National Laboratory has developed an action-oriented benchmarking guide that could be used to assist in this process (*http://labs21benchmarking.lbl.gov/*). The template of metrics is shown in the accompanying table. Additionally, the Labs21® benchmarking tool has benchmarking data from about 200 facilities (http://labs21.lbl.gov/).

Laboratory Benchmarking: Data Collection Worksheet

Project: <Name>

Notes:
* Assign priority for each datum based on priorities of metrics that utilize it
* This list includes some data that are not directly used for metrics, but may be needed for diagnostics
* Default units and priorities are provided - change as needed
* Priority levels: 1 - Must have; 2 - Important, subject to ease of data collection; 3 - nice to have if easy to collect

ID	Data	Unit	Priority	Value	Source / Measurement	Responsible Party	Notes
General Building Data							
dB1	Building Gross Area	gsf	1				
dB2	Laboratory Area	nsf	1				
dB3	Laboratory Volume	cuft	1				
dB4	Building Occupant Count	#	2				
dB5	Laboratory Occupant Count	#	2				
dB6	Fumehood Count	#	2				
dB7	Fumehood Total Length	ft	2				
dB8	Typical Daily Occupied Hours (weekday)	hrs	2				
dB9	Year of Construction (or major renovation)	-	3				
Building Energy Data							
dE1	Annual Electrical Energy Use	kWh	1				
dE2	Annual Natural Gas Energy Use	MMBTU	1				
dE3	Annual Fuel Oil Energy Use	MMBTU	1				
dE4	Annual Other Fuel Energy Use	MMBTU	1				
dE5	Annual District Steam Energy Use	MMBTU	1				
dE6	Annual District Hot Water Energy Use	MMBTU	1				
dE7	Annual District Chilled Water Energy Use	MMBTU	1				
dE8	Annual Energy Cost	$	2				
dE9	Peak Electrical Demand	kW	2				
Ventilation Data							
dV1	Laboratory Supply Airflow Min	cfm	1				
dV2	Supply Side Fan Peak Power	kW	1				
dV3	Exhaust Side Fan Peak Power	kW	1				
dV4	Supply Side Fan Peak Airflow	cfm	1				
dV5	Exhaust Side Fan Peak Airflow	cfm	1				
dV6	Supply-side Pressure Drop	in. w.g.	1				
dV7	Exhaust-side Pressure Drop	in. w.g.	1				
dV8	Fumehood Average Airflow	cfm	1				
dV9	Fumehood Minimum Airflow	cfm	1				
dV10	Ventilation Annual Energy Use	kWh	2				
Cooling & Heating Data							
dT1	Heating Setpoint	F	1				
dT2	Cooling Setpoint	F	1				
dT3	Minimum Humidity Setpoint	%RH	1				
dT4	Maximum Humidity Setpoint	%RH	1				
dT5	Cooling Plant Annual Energy Use	kWh	1				
dT6	Cooling Plant Annual Load Served	Ton-Hrs	1				
dT7	Chiller System Minimum Turndown Ratio	-	1				
dT8	Installed Chiller Capacity (w/o backup)	Tons	2				
dT9	Peak Chiller Load	Tons	2				
dT10	Chilled Water Supply Temperature	F	2				
dT11	Chilled Water Return Temperature	F	2				
dT12	Heating Plant Annual Energy Use	MMBTU	1				
dT13	Heating Plant Annual Load Served	MMBTU	1				
dT14	Reheat Annual Energy Load	MMBTU	1				
Plug Load Data							
dP1	Laboratory Plug Load: Actual Peak	kW	1				
dP2	Laboratory Plug Load: Design Peak	kW	1				
dP3	Plug Load Annual Energy Use	kWh	3				
Lighting Data							
dL1	Laboratory Task Illuminance	fc	1				
dL2	Laboratory Ambient Illuminance	fc	1				
dL3	Laboratory Lighting Installed Power	kW	1				
dL4	Laboratory Lighting Zone Size	sf	2				
dL5	Lighting Annual Energy Use	kWh	3				

A template for whole-building and system level metrics to track laboratory energy efficiency during design and construction.
Source: http://labs21benchmarking.lbl.gov/

continued

Laboratory Benchmarking: Metrics Calculation Worksheet

Project: <Name>

Notes
* *Default units and priorities are shown - change as needed*
* *Priority levels: 1 - Must have; 2 - Important, subject to ease of data collection; 3 - nice to have if easy to collect*
* *Most 'Value' cells have built-in formulas referencing data items - assuming default units indicated*

ID	Name	Unit	Priority	Value	Notes
Building					
B1	Building Site Energy Use Intensity	kBTU/gsf.yr	1		
B2	Building Source Energy Use Intensity	kBTU/gsf.yr	1		
B3	Building Energy Cost Intensity	$/gsf.yr	2		
B4	Building Peak Electrical Demand Intensity	W/gsf	2		
Ventilation System					
V1	Min Laboratory Ventilation Rate: Area-based	cfm/nsf	1		
V2	Min Laboratory Ventilation Rate: Volume-based	ACH	1		
V3	Fumehood Density	#hoods/1000 nsf	2		
V4	Overall Airflow Efficiency (sup&exh W/ sup&exh cfm)	W/cfm	1		
V5	Total System Pressure Drop	in. w.g.	1		
V6	Fume hood Airflow Management Ratio (avg cfm/min cfm)	-	1		
V7	Ventilation Energy Use Intensity	kWh/gsf.yr	3		
Cooling & Heating					
T1	Lab Temperature Setpoint Range	F	1		
T2	Lab Humidity Setpoint Range	%	1		
T3	Cooling System Efficiency	kW/ton	1		
T4	Chiller System Minimum Turndown Ratio	-	1		
T5	Peak Cooling Load	gsf/ton	2		
T6	Cooling System Sizing Factor (Installed vs. Peak tons)		2		
T7	Chilled Water Loop Temp Differential	F	2		
T8	Cooling System Energy Use Intensity	kWh/gsf-yr	3		
T9	Heating System Efficiency	%	1		
T10	Reheat Energy Use Factor	%	1		
T11	Heating System Energy Use Intensity	kBTU/gsf-yr	3		
Process Loads					
P1	Laboratory Design Plug-Load Intensity	W/nsf	1		
P2	Laboratory Actual Plug-Load Intensity	W/nsf	1		
P3	Laboratory Plug-Load Sizing Factor (design/measured)	-	1		
P4	Total Plug Load Energy Intensity	kWh/gsf-yr	3		
Lighting System					
L1	Laboratory Task Illuminance	fc	1		
L2	Laboratory Ambient Illuminance	fc	1		
L3	Laboratory Lighting Installed Power Intensity	W/nsf	1		
L4	Laboratory Lighting Zone Size	sf	2		
L5	Lighting Energy Use Intensity	kWh/gsf-yr	3		

Key Considerations

- While ASHRAE Standard 90.1 can effectively be used as a basis for evaluating whole-building performance, it is important to ensure that the modeling properly addresses lab-specific issues such as equipment load diversity and fan power limitations.

- It is strongly recommended that whole-building targets be evaluated against empirical benchmarks, that are based on the measured energy use of peer facilities.

- Key ventilation system metrics include: minimum air change rate (ACH, cfm/sf), hood density (hoods/nsf), hood airflow efficiency, and system airflow efficiency (W/cfm).

- Heating, cooling, and lighting system efficiency metrics for laboratories are not significantly different from those used for other commercial buildings, although there are some special considerations for laboratories, such as reheat energy use and temperature and humidity requirements.

- Design assumptions for plug loads should be benchmarked against measured values in comparable laboratories.

Key Process Steps

1. *Identify metrics and set targets with stakeholder team.* Metrics and targets are, in effect, key performance indicators for the quality of design and operation, and therefore should have the buy-in of all the key stakeholders (owners, designers, and operators). This could be done at project conception, and refined during the early stages of the project.

2. *Incorporate key metrics and targets in programming documents.* Designers and operators are much more likely to ensure that targets are met if they are officially incorporated into the programming documents.

3. *Identify individual(s) responsible for tracking metrics.* Ideally, the commissioning authority would have overall responsibility, since metrics are integral to the performance tracking and assurance process. However, various design professionals may have responsibility for computing individual metrics and providing these to the commissioning authority (e.g., lab planner for hoods/nsf, HVAC engineer for W/cfm, etc.)

4. *Determine process and format for tracking and documenting metrics.* Project teams may develop their own formats based on the Labs21® template.

Paul A. Mathew, Staff Scientist, Lawrence Berkeley National Laboratory

---

Temperature and Relative Humidity

During scientist interviews, requests for specific temperature and humidity requirements should not be taken at face value. Sometimes these requests are overstated, as scientists might be coming from a poorly operating, older facility and tend to build in a safety net when asking for certain criteria in a new facility. Temperature fluctuations due to poorly performing air systems might have been the norm in an older building; so in the new building, the lead researcher might ask for such tight criteria that supplemental cooling is needed. However, the true motivation behind this request is that she is only trying to protect her research from extreme, unanticipated rises in temperature—a situation that will not occur in a new facility. Spaces that do require more stringent temperature values or particularly tight humidity criteria should be zoned together so that they can be handled efficiently and locally.

Air Changes

Not every laboratory requires once-through air, and it is not required by building codes; however, it is recommended. This model should be discussed with the facilities safety officer and challenged when appropriate. The evaluation should be done on a specific lab-by-lab basis. With the advent of reliable air monitoring, there are more situations in which recirculated air might be considered acceptable. Air changes per hour (ACPH) is generally not criteria

Multiple enclosures provide local ventilation for bench top work for Fairfield University's Rudolph Bannow Science Center Addition in Fairfield, Connecticut. *Image courtesy of KlingStubbins. Photography © Robert Benson Photography.*

stated by the individual scientist but rather by a safety officer. If air change rates are requested that are higher than the code-required minimums, this request should be justified. If there is one offending procedure, perhaps it can be contained within a custom ventilated enclosure to allow for recirculated air in the laboratory itself, or if not that, then at least to allow for reduced ACPH.

Hours of Operation

More laboratories operate on a 24/7 basis as collaboration becomes global or as shift work is introduced to maximize facility usage. Nonetheless, hours of operation should be discussed to confirm that assumptions are correct. If systems are designed for 24/7 operation but only used eight hours per day in reality, then they are oversized.

Redundancy

Scrutinizing redundancy for any mechanical system will lead to the reduction of mechanical systems, which decreases the overall facility size. However, in some cases such as BSL-3 spaces, the redundancy cannot be avoided. During microprogramming, researchers and management from the client side, along with the laboratory planners, should meet to assess the ramifications of system failures. Compromising life safety is not an option, but loss of research materials, data, and experimental results must be evaluated on a case-by-case basis in terms of lost time and money. By encouraging the client to set up objective criteria against which individual requests can be compared, the programming process is more efficient and not subject to an individual's emotions regarding the "importance" of his work.

Filtering

Frequently, a scientist might request HEPA filtered supply air in a new facility based more on her experience in an older facility than on scientific need. Ductwork in the older facility might have been dirty, and to remedy this, a resourceful researcher might have installed a filter at the supply register to capture particles. To avoid this in her next lab, she might ask for HEPA filtration. Instead of merely noting the requirement, the laboratory planner should investigate the request; adding HEPA filtration increases the static pressure that the HVAC system must overcome, and thus increases the amount of supply air required; this in turn, increases system size. If the work done in this laboratory is not different than work done in similar laboratories without HEPA filtered supply air, chances are good that the request will be withdrawn once cleanliness of the supply air system planned for the new facility is explained. Criteria for HEPA filtration on the exhaust side should be aligned with the Center for Disease Control's Biosafety in Microbiological and Biomedical Laboratories (BMBL) and risk analyses conducted by the client's health and safety officers.

Plumbing and Process Piping

Challenging requests for lab gas outlets and cup sinks typically leads to a reassessment of the quantity that actually is required. Not only should laboratory planners point out that as the number of outlets is reduced, calculated loads are decreased and systems size reduced, but they should also point out that facility costs go down as well. Identifying locations on a conceptual laboratory plan where outlets are desired is simple, and it is all too easy to forget about the resource and cost ramifications of these "dots on paper." In the same way that observing

actual laboratory usage can be used to track where researchers spend their time, it also can be used to track the frequency of outlet use. The results are often surprising. Reducing or eliminating cup sinks minimizes or eliminates the possibility of hazardous waste being dumped down the drain at a laboratory bench or fume hood. Additionally, this discourages researchers from dumping cooling water to a drain versus utilizing a process cooling water loop.

Power

There are two approaches from which power requirements for a laboratory can be reduced—one approach is from the user side and has to do with the user's requests for standby (emergency) power; the second approach has to do with how the design engineers address the project from a load standpoint. The strategy for addressing users' requests for standby power is similar to addressing requests for mechanical redundancy. Every researcher has emotional attachments to his work, but objective criteria must be set ahead of time to evaluate the time and financial threshold below which a loss of work or products can be tolerated. If not, the result is a facility where much of the equipment is requested to be on standby power. This leads to larger generators requiring more space and more resources. Examples from the other end of the spectrum should be cited. Some researchers live in "lean" facilities where a request for a refrigerator or freezer on standby power must be accompanied by a form stating the scientific need for this request.

From a design standpoint, properly sizing the electrical loads based on actual connected equipment loads versus equipment nameplate load can save substantially on infrastructure costs. The National

Electric Code (NEC) allows a reduction to loads based on these actual demand factors. A reduction of the electrical loads allows for the potential reduction in both feeders and switchgear sizes and for a significant cost savings on both the initial first costs and lifecycle costs. However, there still remains a need to carefully allocate enough capacity to allow for flexibility in future use.

Another method for rightsizing electrical loads is examining the client's own usage data. KlingStubbins had the opportunity to do this while designing the second phase of a research and development facility for Johnson & Johnson PRD in La Jolla, California. The first phase of this complex was designed to 15 W/SF for laboratory equipment loads in most laboratory areas. The client provided power trending data from the first phase labs. The peak equipment power draw was 8 W/SF for chemistry and 10 W/SF for biology. (This included labs, support labs, adjacent lab offices, and lab corridors; the overall combined lab and nonlab measured peak building-wide value was 4.7 W/SF.) For the design of the second phase, systems were rightsized based on the phase one operating data. Downsizing based on W/SF affected the space airflows and cooling load, which meant smaller ducts, fans, and chillers for the second phase. This translated to energy savings and increased efficiency since the second phase system operates closer to its design points more frequently. Metering facilitated gathering this data. Refer to Chapter 5 for further discussion of measuring and metering.

Lighting

As described in more detail in Chapter 7, the Illuminating Engineering Society of North America (IESNA) recommendations for laboratory lighting levels have come down in recent years. However, many institutions still cling on to rather outdated criteria of 90 foot candles at 3 feet above the floor. Clients should be schooled in why the lower lighting levels are typically adequate, and how higher levels are no longer compatible with current energy codes. Sometimes, clients are reacting to an older space that might have been dim due to tired finishes, poor lighting design, and even dusty lamps. Perhaps their older laboratories did not have task lighting. Very few procedures in laboratories truly require higher lighting levels. Most work is not done on open bench tops. The most frequent visual task is reading a computer monitor. Work done in biosafety cabinets or fume hoods is done under the supplemental light provided by the fixtures within these units.

Exhaust Devices

Exhaust devices in the laboratory consist of chemical fume hoods, biosafety cabinets, point exhausts

Point exhausts with snorkel attachments (articulated exhaust arms) in a flexible, modularly designed laboratory at the University of Arizona's Medical Research Building and Thomas W. Keating Bioresearch Building. *Image courtesy of ZGF Architects, LLP. Photography © Robert Canfield.*

(and the related snorkel attachments) and ventilated enclosures. Of these listed, chemical fume hoods have the most impact on building systems (air requirements and ductwork sizing). See further discussions on this topic in Chapter 6. Minimizing the number of fume hoods increases the sustainability of the laboratory. As noted earlier in the chapter, one must make sure that the requirements are being driven by truly efficient use of them, and not because they are being used for solvent or equipment storage.

In addition to the number of hoods, face velocity requirements (both code and facility based) must be addressed. Institutions typically have requirements of 90 to 100 feet per minute, but newer, low-flow hoods on the market are able to capture fumes effectively while operating at an average of 60 feet per minute.

Active monitoring and control at chemical fume hoods are also becoming prevalent in lab design. The active controls increase the exhaust rates when the sash is raised during set up, and once the sash is closed the controls throttle the exhaust rates down. Also, proximity sensors are available to close sashes when they sense that nobody is in front of the hood. While interconnection to the exhaust fan and the sash increase the up-front costs of the hoods, facility owners will inevitably see a decrease in operating costs with no compromise in safety. Sash configurations impact energy usage as well. A horizontally operating sash with two sashes can only ever be 50 percent open, while a vertically operating sash can be opened 100 percent. The smaller the opening, the less air required. A combination sash can be opened completely for set up, but during operation, can function like a horizontal sash. (Again, see Chapter 6 for further explanation.)

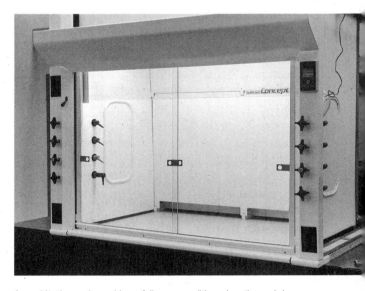

A fume hood with a vertically operating sash (left) adjacent to a fume hood with a horizontally operating sash (right). Sash configurations impact energy use by allowing for different opening sizes. *Image courtesy of Thermo Fisher Scientific.*

A combination sash provides a full open condition when the sash is operated vertically for experiment set up. During operation, it functions horizontally to only allow a smaller opening. *Image courtesy of Thermo Fisher Scientific.*

A critical evaluation of the size of exhausted biosafety cabinets can also lead to reductions in energy and floor space. A scientist requesting a 6-foot unit should be asked whether his operations could be performed safely in a 4-foot unit, for example. This not only saves utility costs, but it also saves initial equipment costs and lab square footage costs. Requests for exhausted versus recirculated biosafety cabinets should be scrutinized. The BMBL allows for recirculated biosafety cabinets even in BSL-3 laboratories.

Code Classification

Safety must always be the first priority. That being said, most laboratories can be classified as B (business) occupancies, as long as the amount of hazardous materials stored and used within control zones is within the exempt amounts allowed by code in B occupancy. If the users of a laboratory cannot work within those parameters, then the laboratory must be given a more stringent H (hazardous) classification. Along with this classification though, are construction and ventilation requirements that call for more material and more energy. Lab planners should strategize with the users to minimize the areas that must be classified as H occupancies. At Johnson & Johnson PRD in La Jolla, California, dedicated H occupancy rooms were created on each floor for solvent storage and dispensing so that the entire floor would not have to be classified as an "H" occupancy. Whether the concern is chemical or biological, with the help of the users and the client's safety officers, the agents being studied and the specific procedures that will be performed in a laboratory must be identified to make sure that in an effort to produce a sustainable lab, nobody is put at risk.

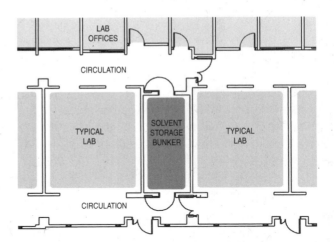

Dedicated "H" occupancy bunkers on each floor provide space for localized solvent storage and dispensing at Johnson & Johnson PRD Drug Discovery Laboratory, Phase II project in La Jolla, California. *Image courtesy of KlingStubbins.*

Solvent stations are located in each dedicated "H" occupancy bunker for localized dispensing and storage at Johnson & Johnson PRD Drug Discovery Laboratory, Phase II project in La Jolla, California. *Image courtesy of KlingStubbins.*

Structural

A heavier structure, and thus more concrete or steel, is needed to achieve tighter vibration criteria. The more material on a project, the less sustainable it is. Material equals resources—to produce, deliver, and ultimately dispose of. Unusually high structural criteria should be challenged. If a particular piece of equipment has more stringent requirements, the lab programmer should inquire about whether a vibration dampening table would be sufficient. Or, the equipment could be located in an area of the facility that is naturally stiffer—either the slab on grade, or closer to column lines, since stiffness across a typical column bay varies. Isolation joints can be added to minimize vibration from adjacent spaces to the areas where sensitive equipment is located.

Equipment

During microprogramming, lab planners should specify the most efficient available models of the large equipment that they typically specify, such as glass washers and sterilizers. Most companies now offer energy efficient models that make use of various technologies to conserve. Although lab planners do not typically specify individual pieces of scientific equipment, there are still valuable contributions to make around this topic. First, to simply coax out during programming all information regarding all equipment intended for the laboratory is beneficial, so that planning for cooling requirements can be executed efficiently and centrally. If addressed on a building-wide basis, a chilled water cooling loop can be incorporated into the design so that scientists are not purchasing multiple small chillers for their own equipment that either expel heat to the lab environment (adding to the building cooling load) or worse, use water for cooling that is then dumped down the drain. An engineer would never design a once-through cooling water system, but on a case-by-case basis, it is nearly impossible to prevent individual scientists from setting them up, unless there is a workable alternate in place. During conversations about scientific equipment, lab planners can share information resources, such as the laboratory equipment WIKI that is accessible on the Labs21® website: *http://labs21.lbl.gov/wiki/ equipment/index.php/Energy_Efficient_Laboratory_ Equipment_Wiki.* This WIKI serves as a repository for the rating of equipments' energy efficiency. There is valuable information here too on actual versus name-

The design and engineering of equipment such as the 1600 LXP Washer has been improved so that the operation is more sustainable. Not only has water consumption per load been decreased, but capacity has been increased so that fewer loads are required. *Image courtesy of LANCER.*

plate plug loads, so that planning for electrical requirements may be done more accurately.

Many times during the initial planning stages of the facilities not all users have been identified and general assumptions are made that potentially increase the size of both the facility and the utility requirements. Since utility and equipment assumptions are made based on estimates rather than actual equipment, a thorough reevaluation that might lead to further reductions should be conducted as better information is obtained.

Conclusion

Designing a laboratory means dealing with complex problems and finding balanced solutions on multiple levels. When considering the sustainable impacts of reducing energy consumption and wasted space through careful macro and microprogramming, the "softer" issues associated with sustainable design must not be overlooked. Acknowledging that this facility is a workplace for people informs the macro and microlab programming process. See Chapter 7 for further discussion. Addressing the human needs for a healthy environment, clean air, access to daylight, comfortable spots for interaction and relaxation, ergonomically considered workspaces, and aesthetically pleasing surroundings is just as important as addressing the scientific and technical needs of the processes that will occur within. The art is in combining the two. Nonetheless, the three frequently repeated basic tenets—reduce, reuse, and recycle—provide a simple guide for sustainable laboratory programming: Reduce—focus on reducing the physical size of and utilities consumed within the laboratory. Reuse—provide spaces that are flexible enough to change with the times. Recycle—carefully select the

appropriate materials while balancing sustainability and durability.

Key Concepts

- Individual laboratories are the building blocks of a research facility. Programming them must not be conducted in a vacuum, but rather as part of the integrated design of the project.

- Decisions made during programming impact the facility's physical and operational efficiency and therefore its sustainability.

- Many strategies exist for using macroprogramming—when the program, lab module, and building are defined—and microprogramming—when criteria for casework, utility, and environmental conditions are set—to maximize a facility's sustainability.

- Challenge all assumptions and criteria. Use benchmarking data as a metric against which to compare facility requirements. Although not prescriptive, the data might reveal requirements that should be revisited.

- Tools such as three-dimensional models and lab cards make the programming process more efficient and impact sustainability as well. Options can be explored early in model form before real-world resources are required; programming decisions should be recorded on lab cards to minimize wasteful rework of built conditions.

REFERENCES

Biosafety in Microbiological and Biomedical Laboratories, U.S. Department of Health and Human Services, Public Health Service, Centers for Disease Control and Prevention and National Institutes of Health, Fifth Edition, 2007, U.S. Government Printing Office, Washington, 2007 (www.cdc.gov/OD/ohs/biosfty/bmbl5/)

Laboratories for the 21st Century: An Introduction to Low-Energy Design (http://labs21.lbl.gov/)

2008 National Institutes of Health (NIH) Design Requirements Manual for Biomedical Laboratories and Animal Research Facilities, Division of Technical Resources, Office of Research Facilities, The National Institutes of Health, (http://orf.od.nih.gov/PoliciesAndGuidelines/)

chapter 4

Site Design
Connecting to Local and Regional Communities

Image courtesy of KlingStubbins.

Introduction

Successfully defining and implementing a sustainable site development strategy starts at the very beginning of the project planning process. Developing a new lab building on either a greenfield site, a previously developed site, or redeveloping an existing building, will involve the use of a certain amount of land. That land could be an undeveloped property in the suburbs zoned for research use, or part of a new medical technology park located in a redeveloped abandoned urban rail yard. Built sites can no longer be looked upon as isolated properties disconnected from the world around them. How can the land be responsibly developed to provide a stimulating work environment, an efficiently operating facility, and also maintain or enhance the ecological benefits that the land currently provides or could provide again? This is now the overriding challenge when developing a sustainable site design strategy. Incorporating a philosophy of increased stewardship of the land into our

This chapter focuses on several of the sustainability categories discussed in Chapter 1. See page 18 for more information.

73

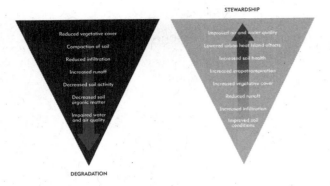

collective design processes will result in reversing the bad habits of the past, reducing the degradation of the environment, and ultimately establishing a regenerative process for the benefit of all future generations.

General Principals of Sustainable Site Design

There is an evolving understanding that all sites have a certain potential to provide positive benefits to the buildings and people who inhabit them, the region they are located in, and to preserve or restore habitat for a variety of native or migratory animals. Restoring the connection of people to the natural world has been proven to be beneficial to our daily lives and sense of well-being. A collaborative effort between the United States Botanic Garden, The American Society of Landscape Architects, and The Lady Bird Johnson Wildflower Center to develop a more comprehensive sustainable site development guideline has resulted in the 2008 draft version of the "Sustainable Sites Initiative, Standards & Guidelines." This guideline is being developed with the joint cooperation of the United States Green Building Council

(USGBC). The guideline acknowledges the growing trend to value sites for the "eco services" they provide. Ecosystem services (as described in the guideline) are considered to be either goods or services that provide a direct or indirect benefit to humans that are produced by the interaction of living elements such as soil organisms and vegetation and nonliving elements such as bedrock, water, and air. These services range from water supply and regulation, air and water cleaning, local climate regulation, to hazard mitigation, human health and well-being, plant pollination, and cultural benefits. The USGBC has already committed to incorporating a final version of this initiative into future versions of the LEED™ rating system.

All sites have different degrees of topography, vegetation, solar exposure, prevailing winds, soil variability, and water resources that can be beneficial to the development of that site. Proper orientation of the building combined with appropriate architectural design elements such as sun screens can aid significantly in reducing the energy needed for heating and cooling. Local, state, and federal agencies have established stormwater management regulations such as the Clean Water Act, The EPA General Stormwater Permit, and The National Pollution Discharge Elimination System (NPDES) that are now the standard that must be met in order to comply with LEED™ rating systems. Labs typically use a significant amount of water in their normal operation. Capturing stormwater on a vegetated green roof, or in on-grade or buried chambers, can provide a significant source of nonpotable water for a variety of uses such as irrigation, or gray-water flushing of toilets, significantly reducing the demand for potable water.

Maintaining existing vegetation and landscaped open spaces, and minimizing impervious surfaces, reduces the impact on existing stormwater manage-

This exterior view of the Johnson & Johnson PRD Drug Discovery Laboratory, Phase II project in La Jolla, California, shows the sun screens and native plantings. Drought-tolerant native plantings are irrigated using a high-efficiency system that uses a municipal gray-water system. *Courtesy of KlingStubbins. Photography ©Tom Bonner 2007.*

ment infrastructure, and minimizes the need for new systems by providing the eco service of naturally infiltrating stormwater into the local groundwater system. Restoring pervious open spaces to a previously developed impervious site is part of a regenerative approach that will help restore the eco services that the site once provided. Preservation of these features should always be a prime consideration.

Communities also benefit from a sustainable approach to development. Guidelines such as LEED™ ND (for Neighborhood Development) encourage locating new facilities in areas already served by public transportation such as established neighborhoods or in large-scale urban sites targeted for new neighborhood development. This results in providing new job opportunities near available transportation, hous-

ing, and support services such as schools, banks, churches, restaurants, and retail. This approach helps to maintain and restore the vitality of existing and new urban neighborhoods while taking advantage of the existing utility infrastructure and mass transit services already in place, reducing the dependence on private cars. Carefully locating new plantings to provide shading on pavements will help reduce the impact of the heat island effect. This can be particularly important in urban sites were this problem is compounded by the density of development. Proper water management onsite leads to reduced demand on the local stormwater infrastructure, and increased levels of groundwater recharge, improving the health of local streams, rivers, and animal habitat.

Choosing an Appropriate Site

The process of selecting a site is based on a variety of factors. The potential for sustainable development is just one of those factors and the opportunities to successfully implement the project will vary depending on the site ultimately chosen. Does the organization wish to have an urban presence located close to other research facilities and organizations, or do they prefer a suburban location along a major highway with a more private location?

These are key questions that will immediately impact many decisions and opportunities to create a sustainable site design strategy. Does the client need to add a new building to existing facilities on a campus or will it be a standalone project? Are employees being relocated from another location or will the building be staffed will all new employees? How will employees travel to the site? What is the availability of mass transit? What is the availability of needed research materials? What is the corporate culture? Municipalities may offer financial incentives for locating at one

Selecting an urban site can make construction logistics, site security, and other issues more complicated, but from an environmental viewpoint it takes advantage of existing infrastructure, transportation networks, and the embodied energy of all the amenities. It is arguably the highest impact decision a project team can make as was the case for Merck Research Laboratories (MRL) in Boston. *Courtesy of KlingStubbins.*

location versus another which will also influence the decision. These are only some of the issues that to varying degrees will influence the decision of where to locate a new facility. Each location—urban, suburban, and campus settings—will have unique characteristics and opportunities that will require a focused investigation to identify the strengths and weaknesses. This investigation is part of a comprehensive approach to sustainable site design.

It is vitally important for the owner to develop a comprehensive space allocation program prior to undertaking the site investigation effort. Understanding the building needs and massing is critical to assessing the ability of a site to meet those needs. For example, can the building footprint be minimized to reduce the

site disturbance by adding additional floors or is there a need for large footprints for manufacturing processes? Will the local zoning allow taller buildings, or should the project pursue a variance? Once the general building program is understood, the first step is to form a Site Selection Committee. The makeup of the committee is flexible but should include at a minimum the owner, a representative from the user group, and a team of independent sustainable design professionals, LEED™ certified with proven experience. This team of professionals should include, at the very least, an architect, a building systems engineer, a landscape architect, and a civil engineer. A Site Assessment Study should be prepared by this committee for each site under consideration to preliminarily evaluate the sustainable design potential and should be based on comparable and objective criteria. The current LEED™ rating system checklist is a very good measuring tool. The experience of this team of design professionals should allow them to make an educated initial assessment of each site's potential to earn LEED™ certification.

Site Assessment Study—Part 1

The site assessment should be a two-part study. The first part of the site assessment should be an environmental analysis of the site. What are the unique features of the site? Are these features a potential benefit to a sustainable design development strategy or are they a weakness?

• Acquire a complete topographic and boundary survey of the site if possible.

• Identify the slope characteristics.

• Identify the change in elevation.

• Identify environmental limitations.

- Perform a zoning analysis.

  - Confirm zoning district and allowable use for the site.

- Inventory the existing vegetation including species, size, type, health, and potential sustainable benefits.

  - Large mature vegetation provides shade to reduce heat island effect.

  - Does it contribute to the removal of air-borne particulates.

  - What is the aesthetic benefit to the project?

  - If removed, and depending on species, trees can potentially be reused for wood products in interior fit-up of the building, which contributes to recycled content.

  - Root systems aid in water management and erosion control.

- Identify any environmentally sensitive areas or endangered species habitat.

  - Wetlands provide beneficial habitat and are a key part of stormwater control.

  - Do they contribute to the open space requirements with limited expense to the owner?

  - Can it be part of an educational experience for employees or visitors?

- Are there any soil contamination issues?

  - Will mitigation improve the viability of the site?

  - Is the mitigation too costly?

  - Is the site classified as a brownfield?

  - Perform ASTM Phase 1 and 2 investigations as part of LEED requirements.

- Locate rock outcroppings.

  - If removed, can the rock potentially be crushed and reused as aggregate for concrete, or for base course of foundations or roads?

- Investigate the soils.

  - The investigation must be performed by a qualified professional geotechnical engineer.

  - Are soils suitable for incorporating pervious pavements and easily migrate water to subgrade levels providing recharge of groundwater?

- Does the site have appropriate solar orientation?

  - Is the site shadowed by adjacent structures?

  - What are the potential new shadow patterns across the site?

- Does the site lend itself to a variety of potential building configurations?

  - Consider North/South versus East/West.

- What are the prevailing wind patterns?

  - Will the dispersal of building exhaust impact abutters?

  - Will winds aid in building ventilation?

- What is the annual rainfall?

  - What are the potential volumes of rainwater that could be collected?

  - What techniques would be appropriate for rainfall collection and storage?

- What are the natural water drainage patterns across the site?

  - Does the site have structured control of stormwater or natural infiltration and vegetated basins?

- Review the history of the site.
  - What's it agricultural use?
  - Is it a greenfield?
  - Is it a grayfield?
  - Is it a brownfield?
- What are the potential opportunities to restore eco services to the site?

Site Assessment Study—Part 2

The second part of the site assessment study should focus on the regulatory and regional context of the site.

- Identify the agencies and regulations that will have jurisdiction.
  - Consider local, state, and federal.
- Does the site have good access to mass transit?
  - Consider all means: commuter rail, bus, subway, private shuttle service.
- Are there existing parking facilities?
  - Is there potential for shared parking?
- What are the neighborhood characteristics?
  - What are the demographics?
  - Is it rural versus urban?
  - Is it residential versus commercial?
- Prepare a detailed zoning summary.
  - What is the allowable building envelope?
  - What is the allowable floor area ratio?
  - Consider the allowable impervious coverage.

- Include requirements for open space.
- What are the required parking ratios (auto and bicycle)?
- Include loading and service requirements.
- Consider site lighting requirements.

Designing a Project to Fit Sustainably on a Site

After a site has been selected, a more detailed analysis should be completed. The preliminary site assessment study prepared as part of the site selection process will be the basis for this continued analysis. Additional consideration includes issues such as

- Detailed soil borings.
  - Define soil permeability for groundwater recharge.
- Consider building configuration alternatives.
  - Perform conceptual orientation and massing studies for best solar and wind benefits.
- Outline vehicular and pedestrian movements.
  - Minimize impervious pavements.
- Is the site limited to service areas and roads?
- Determine sizing and routing of utilities.
  - Consider existing vegetation.
- Establish plant lists of indigenous plant materials.
- Develop a comprehensive water management strategy.
  - Consider amount of stormwater.
    - Quantity and quality
    - Pervious pavements
    - Bioretention basins

- Vegetated filter strips
- Below-grade infiltration chambers

- Consider rainwater capture and reuse.

  - Storage
  - Coordinate with MEP for water recovery and possible areas for reuse.
  - AC condensate recovery
  - Irrigation supply

- Develop an integrated pest management program.

  - Include both interior and exterior areas.

  - Establish controls to limit points of access to the building.

  - Avoid plants susceptible to infestation.

  - Consider choice of lighting fixtures.

    - Certain fixture types attract bugs.
    - Location of fixtures at loading areas

Lab-Specific Site Design Considerations

Lab buildings do have special site design considerations that should be given additional focus during this initial site evaluation. Labs are very energy-intensive. Available utility capacities and how these utilities can be routed to the building will significantly influence the siting of the building and consequently the opportunity to implement sustainable site design strategies. Urban sites typically have significant infrastructure in place. Undeveloped suburban sites may need to have utilities brought to the site from significantly greater distances. This is an area of assessment that needs close coordination between the site design professional and the building systems engineer. Understanding both the conceptual needs for vehicular and pedestrian circulation as well as the owner's security

needs will significantly influence the initial site assessment. Depending on the type of research being performed, there may be a need for regular deliveries of various lab materials. Some materials may be small samples of highly controlled substances; some may be large tanks of flammable or inert gases. Adequate areas of pavements for vehicular deliveries, loading operations, foundations for large gas tanks, and potential spill containment facilities must be accommodated within a sustainable design strategy of limiting impervious surfaces. Safety precautions must be implemented in order to comply with regulatory standards. Many labs have security requirements that include controlled access and camera monitoring of the grounds. Line of sight requirements for video cameras can interfere with the placement of trees intended to provide shading on paved surfaces to mitigate the heat island effect at building entries. Limited access to a building will control the movements of staff, visitors, and service deliveries. It will also influence the location of parking facilities. Security lighting demands can also present a challenge to controlling light pollution.

Developing on a brownfield site can often provide tax advantages to an owner. The degree of contamination and the cost of the necessary remediation efforts are an obvious consideration. When considering a brownfield site a geo-technical soils expert should be added to the Site Assessment Committee. In many cases brownfield sites are located in older industrial zones that have been underutilized for a long time. Many brownfield sites are located near major downtown centers, and have access to mass transit and a potential population base. Brownfield sites by their nature are significantly environmentally challenged but also provide a tremendous opportunity to create good community relations by regenerating a damaged property back to an environmentally contributing and economically vibrant part of the community.

If the opportunity presents itself when redeveloping an existing site, the option to reuse an existing building should also be given consideration when searching for a site for a new lab facility. Chapter 9 goes into much more detail regarding assessing the needs of the building but there are certain site design-related issues that should be given proper consideration. Does the property present the opportunity to develop sustainable design features? Does the site allow development of a water management strategy that will effectively reduce the volume of stormwater and increase groundwater recharge? Can the project develop vegetated open space at grade or is the existing roof structure capable of supporting a vegetative green roof? Is the building orientation on the site conducive to improved energy performance and enhanced daylighting infiltration?

The energy used to construct a building is also part of the overall environmental impact that should be considered when selecting a site. This includes the manufacture and delivery of materials to the construction site. Certain LEED™ credits require that materials be sourced from a location within a specific distance from the site. Locally supplied materials will require less energy to transport. Labs typically have more specialized construction needs so the availability of skilled local construction labor should also be factored in.

Stormwater Management Techniques

It is widely recognized that environmentally responsible stormwater management is critical for the return to health of many damaged urban waterways, and the future health and viability of all waterways and habitat subject to impact by development. Many federal, state, and local regulations for managing stormwater have become more restrictive in recent years and it is likely that this trend will continue. Programs such as the EPA's National Pollution Discharge Elimination System (NPDES) are the back bone of the effort to clean our water ways, and are the reference standards for complying with LEED certification programs. In most cases, NPDES is administered by individual states. As a response to this trend, stormwater management technologies have advanced significantly in recent years, developing new techniques to reduce the volume of stormwater runoff, increase the volume of groundwater recharge, improve the quality of the water released to receiving water systems, reduce the development costs to the property owner, and reduce demands on local municipal stormwater infrastructure. Many civil engineers, landscape architects, and land development professionals have become well skilled at these techniques and continue to advance the state-of-the-art.

Pervious pavements, both asphalt and concrete, are becoming more commonly used, and the expertise needed for proper design and installation of these pavements is becoming more widely available. Interlocking pervious unit concrete pavers are another technique commonly used to create a pervious pavement. All these types of pervious pavements have been successfully installed in cold weather climates. The State of Vermont recently installed a new, 85-space Park & Ride in Randolph just off Interstate Route 89, replacing a 20-space gravel lot. All of the parking spaces are made of porous concrete.

Below-Grade Stormwater Storage Chambers

Underground storage chambers can be located below pavements to provide temporary storage, filtration, and delayed release of stormwater runoff.

This approach to stormwater management is particularly effective on constrained sites that do not have enough room to incorporate more aesthetically appealing solutions such as vegetated swales or constructed wetlands. This type of storage system is appropriate for commercial, industrial, municipal, recreational, or residential applications and when properly designed will provide significant vehicle loading.

All these systems when correctly designed provide removal of surface pollutants and sediments leading to dramatic improvements in the quality of stormwater. Organizations such as the National Ready Mix Concrete Association, the National Asphalt Pavement Association, and the Interlocking Concrete

Below-grade stormwater chambers. *Image courtesy of StormTech, LLC, Wethersfield, Connecticut.*

Paver Institute, maintain databases of publications with the latest technical information, and lists of contractors certified in pervious pavements.

These techniques are not intended to be specifically detailed in this book. Each development situation is unique. Rainfall patterns, soil conditions, climate zone, and regulatory standards will all need consideration. It's advisable to include the authorities having jurisdiction over stormwater management permitting in the design process, to ensure a level of comfort with the performance of a pervious pavement. New technologies are not always readily accepted by those who have a tried and true approach to dealing with certain development issues like stormwater management. A professional, comprehensive, collaborative, and thoughtful stormwater management strategy should be prepared for any development site.

Pervious Pavements in Action

The parking lot shown here was designed by KlingStubbins to support the parking demand for a new lab building located in a suburban development. It combines multiple stormwater management techniques. Pervious asphalt pavement was placed in the rows of parking spaces with standard impervious asphalt placed in the drive lanes. This provides the opportunity for groundwater infiltration while providing the long-term strength and stability of the more heavily used drive lanes. In the unlikely event that the pervious pavement becomes clogged, regularly spaced curb cut-outs in the parking islands allow stormwater to flow into the island area and be recharged into the ground. Overflow drains are provided in the islands as an emergency backup. Proper maintenance of these systems such as yearly vacuuming of the pervious pavement is essential for successful long-term operation.

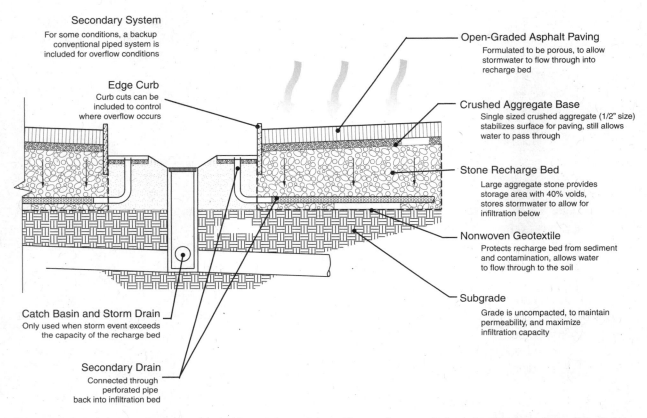

Secondary System
For some conditions, a backup conventional piped system is included for overflow conditions

Edge Curb
Curb cuts can be included to control where overflow occurs

Catch Basin and Storm Drain
Only used when storm event exceeds the capacity of the recharge bed

Secondary Drain
Connected through perforated pipe back into infiltration bed

Open-Graded Asphalt Paving
Formulated to be porous, to allow stormwater to flow through into recharge bed

Crushed Aggregate Base
Single sized crushed aggregate (1/2" size) stabilizes surface for paving, still allows water to pass through

Stone Recharge Bed
Large aggregate stone provides storage area with 40% voids, stores stormwater to allow for infiltration below

Nonwoven Geotextile
Protects recharge bed from sediment and contamination, allows water to flow through to the soil

Subgrade
Grade is uncompacted, to maintain permeability, and maximize infiltration capacity

This detail shows both the general components required for a pervious asphalt condition as well as some details employed. *Image courtesy of KlingStubbins.*

As the example in the accompanying images shows, parking lot islands can be effectively used as areas to help manage stormwater and to provide opportunities for groundwater recharge and filtering of sediments while maintaining an aesthetically appealing appearance. In this example, stone was used as the surface material. Vegetated swales, basins, and constructed wetlands are also techniques to temporarily store and filter sediments from stormwater runoff.

The courtyard shown in the following photograph was designed by KlingStubbins for a multibuilding suburban lab development. The original design, by a different architect, called for an extensive impervious asphalt parking lot within the limits of the building facades with minimal open space for employees or visitors. Views from all the buildings were to a parking lot. As part of the design solution, the active parking that had been planned for the courtyard area was relocated to the perimeter of the site development, to an area that had been originally designated as land-banked parking. The courtyard area could now be designed as a significant landscaped space providing both a visual and physical amenity to the building occupants and visitors. The courtyard was designated to accommodate the displaced land-banked

For this project, porous asphalt is used in the parking spaces; standard asphalt at the drive aisle. The island spaces are vegetated overflow drainage, also illustrated in the section detail. *Image courtesy of KlingStubbins.*

parking and to be held in reserve to meet municipally required parking counts. Additional parking would only be constructed if the actual future parking demand increased due to a change in building use. (Typically, lab buildings require fewer parking spaces than office buildings.) Minimal active parking was accommodated in the courtyard with pervious concrete pavers providing for reduced stormwater runoff, increases in groundwater recharge, and reducing the amount of conventional piped stormwater infrastructure. The landscaped courtyard reduces the heat island effect adjacent to the buildings and increases groundwater infiltration. Standard asphalt pavement was provided for the circulation drives and fire truck access.

Landscaping Considerations

In recent years there has been tremendous growth in the availability of ornamental landscape plants for use in commercial developments. Many of these materials are not native to the region where the particular site is being developed. They may have significant water needs, be prone to infestations of insects, or require special soil conditions for proper growth. Insect contamination can be a significant concern in the operation of a lab building and minimizing the exposure is

Pervious concrete pavers used for parking spaces. *Image courtesy of Joanne Deyo.*

critical. Indigenous plant materials are naturally adapted to their local climate and are generally hardy under normal weather conditions of sunlight and rainfall. They can be maintained with minimal supplemental irrigation. They are locally available, reducing energy use for transportation to the site. LEED™ compliance requires the use of indigenous or adapted plant materials. In addition, many states are now implementing bans on plant materials that are considered invasive to the local environment. Plants such as the Burning Bush (*Euonymus Alatus Compactus*), a

very dependable, long-used deciduous shrub, once a staple of most commercial and residential projects, is now considered an invasive species and is no longer allowed in Massachusetts. The Highbush Blueberry (*Vaccinium Corymbosum*), a Massachusetts native plant with similar characteristics, is now considered a good substitute for the Burning Bush. Ironically, the substitute plant has been underused, available all along and provides the additional eco services benefits of edible fruit for people, birds, and small animals, enhancing the local ecosystem.

Hawaii Institute for Marine Biology, New Dry Labs Complex, Coconut Island, Hawaii

FERRARO CHOI AND ASSOCIATES
William D. Brooks, AIA, LEED AP
Mark E. Ayers, AIA, LEED AP
With Waste Stream Management Text Contributed by:
ENGINEERING SOLUTIONS, INC.
June Nakamura, P.E.
Kyle Okino, P.E.

For some laboratory projects more than others, the site influences which sustainable design goals are pursued as well as decisions about design and construction. The Hawaii Institute of Marine Biology (HIMB) is an example of one such project. Corresponding color images are shown in figures C-46 through C-50.

HIMB Background

The Hawai'i Institute of Marine Biology (HIMB) conducts research on Coastal and Pelagic Ecosystem Processes involving Coral Reefs, Marine Animal Sensory Processes & Ecology, Marine Evolutionary Genetics, and Physiology & Diseases of Fish and Corals. HIMB is a research institute of the School of Ocean and Earth Science and Technology (SOEST) at the University of Hawai'i (UH) at Manoa, and a member of the National Association of Marine Laboratories

Aerial view of the Hawaii Institute of Marine Biology New Dry Labs Complex at Coconut Island, Hawaii *Courtesy of Ferraro Choi and Associates. Aerial photo by Brian Daniel.*

(NAML). The HIMB facilities are primarily for research by UH faculty and students, but collaborative projects with visiting national and international researchers is accommodated and encouraged.

Located on Coconut Island (*Moku O Loe*, in Hawaiian) in Kaneohe Bay, Oahu, the institute is surrounded by 64 acres of coral reef designated by the State of Hawaii as the Hawaii Marine Laboratory Refuge. Coconut Island is approximately 1,500 feet off the eastern shore of Oahu in Kaneohe Bay. The island was once a luxurious, private residential retreat with elaborate decor and fancy ponds to entertain the rich and famous. Abandoned and in disrepair from years of neglect, many of the old buildings and eloquent features from its former life are still present. However, today, the entire island is used exclusively by the HIMB as a research center with laboratories and dormitories for its visiting professors and research assistants. Currently, the island consists of 28.8 acres of which 6.15 acres are submerged. The original island was 12.5 acres. Since the 1930s it has been modified and artificially enlarged to create multiple lagoons and peninsulas. The inhabited area is approximately 500 feet across at its widest point and 1,400 feet long, not including its lagoons, peninsulas, and spits. The HIMB mission pays literal tribute to its unique setting by " . . . promoting stewardship of the living oceans; restoring, preserving, and sustaining marine ecosystems in Hawai'i and the Pacific Rim through integrated scientific research, community involvement, education and example . . ."

The resources surrounding HIMB afford it opportunities to advance the understanding of the coral reef ecosystem, in developing and managing coastal resources, and in conserving these resources so that they are available for Hawaii and beyond. These resources include:

• Proximity to living reefs and the open ocean.

• Location with an estuary bounded by a coastal watershed.

• Access to a dependable supply of high-quality seawater.

• Logistical and legal means to collect and safely maintain marine organisms.

• Animal and plant holding facilities for short- and longterm projects.

Existing facilities at HIMB include the 1965 Hawaii Marine Lab constructed at sea level on the east lagoon; the Pauley Marine Laboratory constructed in the late 1990s on the south knoll; numerous fish holding facilities; six controlled tidal ponds; three piers; a boat house; a Boston Whaler fleet; and one 14-meter passenger/cargo vessel.

Client Goals and Objectives

To maintain existing programs and expand into new areas of needed research, HIMB determined the need for additional laboratories. The envisioned design would serve as a model for sustainable research laboratories in tropical environments with all the attendant problems of humidity, cooling, laboratory safety, storage, and air conditioning. In addition, the design strategies were seen as being applicable to other countries that need sustainable marine laboratories such as Palau, Pohnpei, Federated States of Micronesia, and Saipan.

In 2001, the Hawaii legislature passed an Appropriations Bill that included a provision for a new Dry Labs Complex at HIMB. The intent of the new laboratory is to communicate the Institute's mission while providing needed additional space within the context of sustainability so that lifecycle costs, energy consumption, and facility impact on the environment are minimized.

continued

The client's stated sustainable design goals for the new dry labs included:

• Exceed Labs for the 21st Century (Labs21®) standards.

• Achieve LEED NC v2 Gold Certification or higher.

• Achieve international recognition as a sustainable laboratory leader.

• Establish and maintain a world-class marine research facility.

• Strive for energy and potable water independence from the main island of Oahu.

• Establish a "Center for Sustainability" that attracts and accommodates international research partnerships, education, and demonstration of sustainable laboratory facilities.

Master Planning Considerations

The laboratory project sets a new direction for the facilities at Coconut Island. It embodies new levels of laboratory efficiencies and is an example of high-performing, low-impact facilities that demonstrate energy and resource conservation and incorporate renewable energy technologies. Because of its unique location, the importance of developing a facility within the reasonable opportunities and constraints of Coconut Island was seen as a fundamental design driver.

As a first step therefore, the design team reviewed and updated the existing master plan for the expanded research facility, which included upgrading and interconnecting existing laboratories and support buildings with the new dry laboratories. An integrated energy-efficient and environmentally responsive infrastructure was also envisioned to protect the local ecosystem with the goal of developing the island into a self-sustaining site.

Primary master planning considerations included:

• Refining and building upon the sustainable goals and objectives outlined in the existing Long Range Development Plan.

• Assessing reasonable access and shoreline parking.

• Determining potential locations for onsite renewable energy production including solar water heating, photovoltaic (PV) arrays, wind turbines, and ocean thermal energy conversion.

• Assessing existing infrastructure limitations and parameters (power, water, and sewer).

• Analyzing alternative building sites.

The process above resulted in a location for the new laboratory that would enhance interrelationships with, and circulation between, the new dry labs complex and the

Rendered view of the HIMB New Dry Labs Complex's centralized open-air main entrance canopy and visitor receiving area. Visitors are oriented in this area before proceeding to any areas at the HIMB. Featured in the receiving area is a seawater aquarium, shown on the left. *Image courtesy of Ferraro Choi and Associates.*

existing Hawaii Marine Lab and Pauley Marine Lab; be well-suited for the primary point of entry to HIMB; and avoid conflicts with future land use for ancillary facilities and renewable energy farms.

The new 14,880-square-foot laboratory complex is designed as a scientific "village" of self-contained laboratory modules. Each laboratory is designed with individual control of air conditioning, lighting, and ventilation to respond to differing occupant requirements and research platforms.

The design team conducted studies on numerous traditional and nontraditional construction methods.

While many modular panel-type construction methods might seem applicable to the design concept, Hawaii's remote location and lack of manufacturing facilities has proven to be a real-life cost constraint. The additional design challenge of getting materials from the main island of Oahu to Coconut Island required thoughtful consideration. The design team felt compelled to examine a number of available options to either validate or reject the local paradigm of using traditional building elements.

The following partial list of criteria was used to analyze the products:

- Is there a local product representative?
- How does the material arrive onsite?
- Is it inherently structural?
- Is it fire rated? If not, how can it be made to be rated?
- What is the resistance to corrosion/salt environment and termites?
- Does it require additional sheathing?
- What is the thermal resistance "R" value?
- Does it require special installer training?
- How are building services integrated with the material?
- How can building services be modified in the future?
- What are additional advantages and/or disadvantages over stick-frame construction?

The design team ultimately explored products ranging from typical concrete masonry (CMU) which is locally fabricated, to insulated concrete forms (ICF) and various types of structural insulated panels (SIP). The final determination was to design the facility in light-frame steel construction on stepped building pads which would minimize the construction impacts on the island and provide an opportunity for offsite prefabrication and small-scale material transportation. The decision was additionally based on factors involving material cost and availability, flexibility in a laboratory for building services, and local labor skills to allow for the best possible cost to the owner.

Single-sloped curving roofs on the labs provide high-bay ceilings with clerestory windows facing north for effective daylight without glare. External pedestrian circulation walkways will connect the labs in the complex effectively decreasing the need for conditioned space.

continued

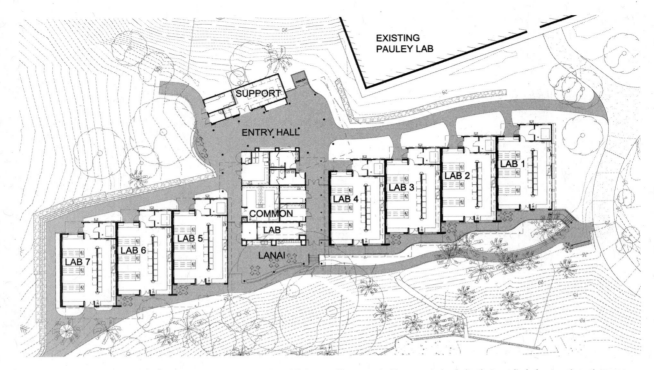

Floor plan of the HIMB Dry Labs Complex, highlighting the modular lab lay-out. To contend with a constrained site that results in long east-west exposures, the lab roof forms are also modular allowing each to have a north-facing clerestory for effective indirect daylight without glare. To control direct solar heat gain, the east- and west-facing portions of the labs have very small and protected windows. *Image courtesy of Ferraro Choi and Associates.*

Energy Conservation

The design of the new HIMB Dry Labs Complex approaches energy conservation in accordance with best practice, but also differentiates itself from many "energy efficient" laboratories in one very important aspect. Most laboratory guidelines place the primary emphasis on minimizing internal process loads. While this is appropriate given the proportionally dominate amounts of energy consumed by laboratory hoods and air conditioning, the new HIMB labs go a further step to achieve maximum energy conservation by application of passive architectural building envelope design strategies coupled with the concept of individual laboratory "suites" to minimize the energy that would need to be provided from the grid or renewable sources.

Passive Energy Conservation Strategies

• Building orientation for best daylighting (reduce electric lighting load and interior heat gain load).

• High ceilings and curved roof-form for best daylighting (reduce electric lighting load and interior heat gain load).

• Building insulation and shading (reduce exterior heat gain load).

- Laboratory "suites" to allow HVAC for single or multiple lab configurations (maximize system efficiency, and minimize load at a given time).

- Laboratory "suites" to allow for individual control (allows labs to shut off when not in use, except for minimum code-required ventilation at hoods).

- Externalized circulation to minimize the conditioned building footprint (Hawaii has a nice climate).

Active energy conservation strategies were implemented to complement and increase the energy conservation initiated by passive strategies.

Active Energy Conservation Strategies

- Whole-systems building design (idealize system functionality).

- Lifecycle cost analysis (allows selection of system based upon lifetime performance and savings).

- Computer modeling to verify building performance (ensures design functionality meets objectives).

- Variable flow chilled water system with high-efficiency magnetic bearing chillers.

- Variable condenser water system with seawater heat rejection and back-up cooling tower with variable speed fans.

- Hood ventilation rates of 6 ACH (occupied) and 3 ACH (unoccupied).

- Displacement air conditioning in high-bay portion of laboratories, delivered low between benches and exhausted high on opposite wall.

- Run-around coil to capture waste heat from the exhaust air stream for supply air reheat.

- High-efficiency lighting fixtures for both ambient and task lighting.

- Renewable energy production via solar hot water panels and a 30-kilowatt, thin-film photovoltaic (PV) array (assists to stabilize the cost of energy, and reduce dependence upon fossil fuel–based grid energy).

- Measurement and verification (maintain lifetime performance).

- Full systems commissioning (maintain lifetime performance).

The most energy-intensive equipment requiring the highest cooling loads are concentrated in one central room so the loads can be treated independently of the individual laboratory loads.

A unique aspect of the HIMB labs is that the researchers and staff are typically at sea for three to four months out of the year. This absence enhances the benefits of individually controlled labs while also offering the opportunity for monitoring and accountability within a researcher's own funding capacities. The new labs are anticipated to reduce energy consumption by 40 percent in comparison to a code-compliant base case.

Water Conservation

Water conservation was prioritized as a sustainable strategy at the new dry labs complex as a matter of environmental stewardship that recognizes the need to conserve limited precious resources. In addition, water conservation was considered of

continued

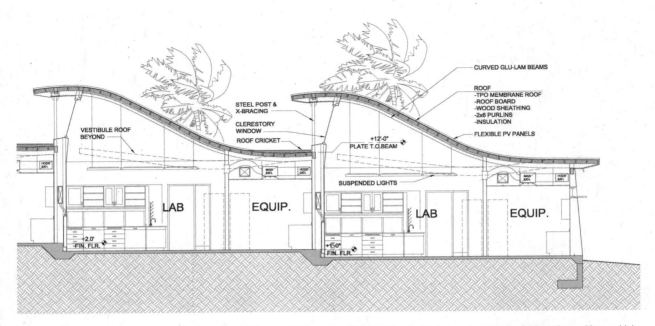

Longitudinal section through two typical laboratories, looking east. This section highlights the basic design strategies implemented to achieve a high-performance building envelope including high north-facing clerestories, a curved roof form to evenly diffuse daylight, and the use of the south-facing slope of the roof for thin-film photovoltaics. The section of the HIMB Dry Labs Complex also highlights the advantage of a modular lab approach for dealing with a sloping site, as each lab is stepped relative to the next, minimizing the need for grading. *Image courtesy of Ferraro Choi and Associates.*

high importance relative to the facility's role as a model sustainable laboratory located in a remote or pristine location, where potable water is typically very limited. In the case of Coconut Island, the existing potable supply is minimal. To avoid the significant cost of increasing the service to the island, the tact taken was to design within the constraints of the existing capacity.

Applied water conservation strategies include:

- Rainwater harvesting.
- Gray-water irrigation coupled with drought-tolerant native coastal landscaping.
- Use of seawater storage for the fire water supply.
- Low-flow fixtures.
- Waterless urinals.

Waste Stream Management

Onsite waste water treatment was prioritized as a sustainable strategy at the new dry labs complex to deal with an aged existing system near capacity and because of the role of the new facility as a model sustainable laboratory located in a remote location where municipal waste treatment is not available and environmental concerns are high. According to data from the University of Hawaii's Long Range Development Plan for the research island, less than 10 percent of the 167,000 gallons per day (gpd) of potable water supplied to the island by an 8-inch pipeline from Oahu, is returned to the wastewater system. The wastewater generated from the existing laboratories and residences is collected through an 8-inch gravity sewer pipe and manhole system to a central pump station, where it is then discharged through 3,100 linear feet of 4-inch sewer force main that returns the wastewater back to Oahu for treatment. The Environmental Impact Statement and Long Range Plan both indicate that the capacity of the existing City system is insufficient.

A due diligence report published in 2004 noted that there were serious maintenance problems and deficiencies with the existing sewage pump station and standby generator and recommended these issues be addressed before additional flows are added to the existing wastewater pump station.

As a first step to implementing and supporting the vision of a totally self-sustainable island concept, an independent Individual Wastewater System (IWS) was proposed to handle the domestic wastewater generated by the new marine laboratories. This would take the new laboratory building "off-grid," serve as a pilot project for future developments, and eliminate overtaxing the existing wastewater system. The proposed IWS system includes a preloader, aerobic units, chlorination, and a pressurized irrigation system.

To calculate wastewater flows, engineers assumed that each lab unit could be occupied by as many as 16 persons over the course of the day. Since there are no restrooms within these laboratories, the domestic wastewater generated will be minimal, similar to that of a school classroom. Using the State of Hawaii Department of Health (DOH) standards and the assumed population per day per lab unit, the anticipated future population is 128 persons, and the maximum wastewater flow is estimated to be about 1,920 gallons per day (at 15 gallons per day per person).

Anticipated wastewater quality from the dry marine laboratories is not expected to be any stronger than domestic wastewater, since no chemical or animal waste will be drained down the sinks. Based on the anticipated wastewater, a preloader sized to provide a two-hour detention time is provided to settle larger solids out of the wastewater stream.

Because the site is near the groundwater and the effluent will be reused, an aerobic unit was selected over a septic tank to provide added treatment. Typically, aerobic units are used to provide some biological treatment of the wastewater. Aerobic and anoxic environments are created within an underground enclosure, promoting the growth of microorganisms and therefore oxidation of organic compounds. Biological solids and liquid separation occur within the same enclosure. The wastewater treatment system is located adjacent to the existing pump station to handle emergency situations. In the case of equipment failure or inability to meet water quality requirements, the wastewater would be discharged to the City system.

To avoid straining the capacity of the existing sanitary sewer, the new dry labs waste stream gravity flows to a nonleaching aerobic treatment unit that functions on the principle of pressurized irrigation and evaporation-transpiration. Primary consideration was given to providing a safe and reliable disposal system. Other considerations included the costs and effects on the receiving environment. Two disposal systems were considered. The first option was a plastic leaching chamber system. This system is similar to a leaching field except instead of using perforated pipe within a gravel bed, it utilizes open-bottomed, arched leaching chambers. Each chamber is approximately 1 foot high, 3 feet wide, and 6 feet long. The chambers are interlocking in a

continued

train pattern and require an area of 1,700 square feet. The chambers offer more storage capacity than a stone and pipe system and are less prone to clogging. A gravel bed is not required. However, this option would have required chlorination.

Instead, a second option, a nonleaching system that does not require chlorination, was selected. This second option is a pressurized irrigation system, similar to a drip irrigation system, that disposes of the wastewater through evapotranspiration. The pressurized irrigation system is composed of a network of "irrigation blocks" of perforated poly-tubing, buried 4 to 12 inches below the surface, varying with the needs of the irrigation demand. A moisture sensor located within each irrigation block determines the quantity of water required to satisfy the irrigation demand, and the subsequent need to alternate to a different irrigation block. Effluent is introduced into the network of irrigation blocks via a pump and filter system. The pressurized irrigation system has the ability to back flush its piping and tubing reducing the tendency for the small perforations to become plugged. One such system marketed as the "Perc-Rite" wastewater disposal system, by Wastewater Systems, Inc., has been approved by the State Department of Health and has been used before in low-lying areas subject to groundwater infiltration.

The extent and feasibility of using recycled/reclaimed water beyond subsurface irrigation is always an interesting topic when designing for sustainability. The risks associated with health and safety as well as public perceptions sometimes prevents taking further steps. However, the potential benefits of reducing impacts and demands on our valuable potable water resource can be significant. As the flows anticipated from this laboratory are minimal, it would not be advantageous, in this case, to treat the wastewater to a high quality for other uses.

Biosolids and chemicals are separated and containerized at the source for retrograde and proper disposal off-island. Solid waste will be separated and recycled according to current HIMB practice.

Boston University Medical Center, BioSquare III, Boston, Massachusetts

BioSquare at the Boston University Medical Center is a successful example of strategically locating new biomedical research lab facilities adjacent to an urban neighborhood on a significantly underutilized property. The site of the BioSquare research park historically has been used for numerous functions. The site was formed by filling operations over the years and had an old drainage canal buried and boxed within a concrete culvert still flowing below grade. The site required certain levels of soil remediation to mitigate some contamination. Most recently the entire 15-acre site had been used as a surface parking lot for the adjacent Boston Medical Center. The surface was a mixture of densely packed gravel and bituminous pave-

ments. Impervious cover was significant and the amount of stormwater runoff had been a neighborhood problem for many years. The site was a visual eyesore for the community.

KlingStubbins was selected as the architect for the second and third buildings of this research park in formulating the design of two 8-story, 180,000-gross-square-feet lab buildings known as BioSquare II and III, respectively. BioSquare III was successfully awarded LEED™ certification under the Core and Shell Pilot program for lab buildings. See Chapter 9 for more information about this project and for a discussion of leased laboratories as a delivery method for research space.

The site design was challenged by a number of factors. The location of the buildings had been established by a master plan completed several years earlier. The site had numerous existing

Master plan for BioSquare at Boston University Medical Center in Boston, Masschusetts. *Image courtesy of KlingStubbins.*

Predevelopment site conditions at Boston University Medical Center's BioSquare III consists of a nearly 100 percent impervious bituminous parking lot. *Courtesy of Google Earth.*

Structured parking at BioSquare III allowed for denser development while still meeting zoning requirements for automobile parking, and resulted in nearly 38 percent of the site area to be restored to pervious open space. *Image courtesy of KlingStubbins.*

utilities to relocate within the newly defined streets and utility corridors. The utility demands of the new lab buildings added to the coordination efforts. These efforts coupled with new street lighting, street trees, and landscape plantings, open spaces, pedestrian walks, and bike paths set high standards for sustainability. In some respects starting with such a challenging site increased the opportunities to create a sustainable development strategy and to meet the desired LEED™ objectives.

The master plan called for the creation of new parking structures to accommodate the projected demand for the new technology campus and the loss of the on-grade parking. Each building would be apportioned parking within the new multistory garages. This provided the opportunity to reduce the imperious footprint of each development project and to restore open space. The BioSquare III project was able to restore 38 percent of the designated site to open space with indigenous or adapted plant materials.

Site Design Strategy

- Redevelop underutilized urban brownfield site.
- Locate site to be accessible to existing public transportation.

8	Sustainable Sites	Possible Points	15
Y	Prereq 1	Construction Activity Pollution Prevention	req
	Credit 1	Site Selection	1
1	Credit 2	Development Density and Community Connectivity	1
1	Credit 3	Brownfield Redevelopment	1
1	Credit 4.1	Alternative Transportation - Public Transportation Access	1
	Credit 4.2	Alternative Transportation - Bicycle Storage and Changing Rooms	1
1	Credit 4.3	Alternative Transportation - Low-Emitting / Fuel Efficient Vehicles	1
	Credit 4.4	Alternative Transportation - Parking Capacity	1
1	Credit 5.1	Site Development - Protect or Restore Habitat	1
	Credit 5.2	Site Development - Maximize Open Space	1
	Credit 6.1	Stormwater Design - Quantity Control	1
	Credit 6.2	Stormwater Design - Quality Control	1
1	Credit 7.1	Heat Island Effect - Non-roof	1
1	Credit 7.2	Heat Island Effect - Roof	1
	Credit 8	Light Pollution Reduction	1
1	Credit 9	Tenant Design and Construction Guidelines	1

3	Water Efficiency	Possible Points	5
1	Credit 1.1	Water Efficient Landscaping - Reduce by 50%	1
	Credit 1.2	Water Efficient Landscaping - No Potable Use or No Irrigation	1

Final LEED Score Card: Sustainable Sites and Water Efficiency for BioSquare III. *Image courtesy of KlingStubbins.*

- Restore open space.
- Reduce impervious cover and stormwater runoff.
- Use indigenous plant materials.
- Design a high-performance irrigation system.
- Provide parking for alternative fuel vehicles.
- Locate parking in campus garage.

AstraZeneca, R&D Expansion, Waltham, Massachusetts

AstraZeneca has developed a research campus in Waltham, Massachusetts. The project was master planned as two clusters of three lab buildings in a bent fork configuration with a remotely located parking garage. KlingStubbins was commissioned to design the first building in the second cluster of three lab buildings. This project was targeted for LEED™ certification. The site presented a number of significant challenges to implement a successful sustainable design solution. On this project KlingStubbins teamed with consultant Vanasse Hangen Brustlin, Inc. (VHB), who specializes in transportation, land development, and environmental projects.

Site Design Strategy

The research being performed in lab buildings can require the use of various materials with special handling and protection needs. In the case of AstraZeneca, the site was located near a municipal drinking water supply, so it was critical to design the

Carefully placing AstraZeneca's R&D expansion in Waltham, Massachusetts, on a sensitive site required bridges and setbacks from existing and restored wetlands. Landscape design was primarily natural native plantings, to eliminate the need for irrigation or extensive landscape maintenance programs. *Image courtesy of KlingStubbins.*

AstraZeneca's Waltham employee bridge connection elevated above wetlands. *Image courtesy of KlingStubbins.*

site drainage systems to provide absolute protection from any potential hazardous material spills. The BMPs (Best Management Practices) employed included vegetated bioswales, wet basins or ponds with an aeration system, oversized detention basins to accommodate the 100-year storm volumes, and a manually operated control valve to capture any material spills before they enter into the drainage system. These techniques help limit the use of municipal potable water. All the BMPs employed were sized above and beyond the current regulations in anticipation of new, more restrictive stormwater management regulations currently proposed by the Massachusetts Department of Environmental Protection. These new regulations propose to establish a statewide general permit program aimed at controlling the discharge of stormwater runoff from certain privately owned properties containing large impervious surfaces.

A pedestrian bridge was incorporated into the building design to avoid impacting on an existing wetland area between two of the buildings. All new plantings incorporated native plant materials. A palette of several dozen different species of native plant materials was used, including Bank Restoration and Wetland Mitigation planting.

In many site development projects the desired location for the building ultimately determines the vehicular access and circulation on the site. In this situation the environmental constraints combined with the needed vehicular access and parking requirements ultimately determined the building site. The garage, which houses 87 percent of the required parking, was located somewhat remotely from the buildings, but within easy walking distance on fully ADA-compliant walks. On-grade parking was also conveniently located near the buildings for handicap and visitor needs. Transportation studies were prepared to identify opportunities for providing access to public transit services and to minimize the vehicular impact of the development. AstraZeneca now operates two shuttle services. One route provides regular access to the center of the nearby town Waltham, 4 miles away, where employees can access the regional commuter rail system. The second route connects to a multimodal transit station 8 miles away in Cambridge, providing direct connection to city buses, the subway system, and bicycle trails.

Required fire department access to the exterior of the building was provided in certain areas with the use of open-cell, pervious pavers planted with native grasses to limit the amount of pervious pavements and to limit stormwater runoff. A preengineered vehicular bridge was employed to span over a wetland area to maintain the existing natural water flow across the site.

continued

Environmental information programs for the employees and visitors were developed to raise awareness of the importance of developing and maintaining a sustainable philosophy. Prior to starting the master planning process, members of the design team toured other AstraZeneca facilities in Sweden and England to gain an understanding of the company philosophy toward sustainable design. This project was awarded LEED Gold Certification by the USGBC in September, 2009, making it the third LEED-certified project within AstraZeneca. A number of other sustainable features such as chilled beams, heat recovery, variable frequency drives, high-performing envelope and shading devices, energy-efficient lighting and construction waste management were some of the strategies contributing to the LEED Gold Certification.

Vehicular bridge spanning wetlands at AstraZeneca's Waltham site. *Image courtesy of KlingStubbins.*

The Arnold Arboretum at Harvard University, Weld Hill Research and Administration Building, Jamaica Plain, Massachusetts

Working with the Arnold Arboretum and the Faculty of Arts and Sciences at Harvard University, KlingStubbins master planned an enhancement of facilities at the Arboretum and was commissioned to design a new 45,000-square-foot research and administrative building on the 14.2-acre parcel of land at the Weld Hill site.

This project was targeted for LEED™ Gold certification. The site presented a number of significant challenges to implementing a successful sustainable design solution. On this project KlingStubbins teamed with Reed–Hilderbrand, Landscape Architects.

The Research and Administration Building enhances the Arboretum's botanical research capabilities through the cre-

ation of new, state-of-the-art greenhouse and laboratory facilities. The major priority of the overall sustainable site design strategy was to strategically locate the new facility to respect the historic Arboretum landscape; expand the community benefits of its research, collections, and educational programs; and create new benefits through landscape and public enhancements to the Weld Hill parcel. The overall effect of the proposed siting is to have minimal impact on the pastoral character of the site, which is comprised of undulating meadow with scattered specimen trees bordered by woodlands. The hillside location for the Research and Administration Building employs the mass of the hill to visually screen the building from neighbors on Weld Street. The building was held back from the northern edge of the parcel to preserve the mature trees along the border with the neighboring residences. The hilltop and woodlands visible from the north, south, and east were also preserved.

The project site, adjacent to such a significant property as the Arnold Arboretum, required that the entire construction process take significant steps to protect soils from erosion, and impacts to existing significant mature vegetation. Com-

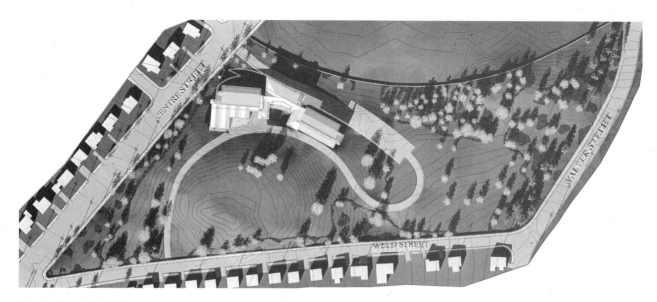

Site plan for the Weld Hill Research and Administration Building at the Arnold Arboretum at Harvard University in Jamaica Plain, Massachusetts. *Rendering courtesy of Mongkol Tansantisuk.*

Building entry drive for Arnold Arboretum's Weld Hill Research and Administration Building. *Rendering courtesy of Mongkol Tansantisuk.*

Using building information modeling (BIM), the team was able to carefully coordinate with the construction groups so that this major construction could be accomplished with a minimum of site disturbance on this environmentally sensitive site. The Weld Hill Research and Administration Building model was arranged to show scheduling impact of different components over the course of construction. *Image courtesy of Skanska USA Building, Inc., who provided preconstruction planning on project.*

puter models developed as part of the design process were used to develop construction staging strategies to minimize these impacts.

Geo-Thermal Well Field Design Challenges

The mechanical systems design for the Research and Administration Building included a geo-thermal well field as part of the overall approach to the heating and cooling of the facility.

There were a number of significant challenges encountered during the site design process.

• The well field would have to be located on the top of a hill above the elevation of the building. This would require the need for pitched piping and a valve to purge any trapped air in the system.

• Drilling the wells on a slope required the need to temporarily grade the earth to create a series of steps to set up the drilling rig at each change of elevation. The grade was returned back to slope after the wells were completed.

• Erosion and sediment control was critical during the drilling operation as a significant amount of groundwater and sediment was extracted, ranging from 0 to a couple hundred gallons per minute. This groundwater was channeled through a gravel-lined swale from the drilling site to a clarifying basin at the bottom of the hill where the sediment was allowed to settle and the water was then recharged back into the ground.

• Noise abatement and control were also a significant issue. An acoustical consultant was commissioned to test ambient noise levels at the neighbor's property to ensure that construction noise did not exceed regulated levels. The air compressor for operating the drilling rig was located remotely at the bottom of the hill to mitigate the sound. Temporary fences with sound attenuation panels were used to further buffer noises.

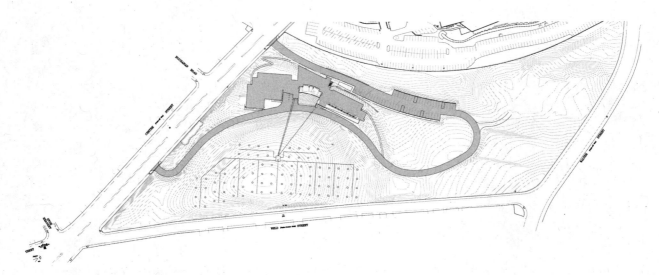

Geo-thermal well field for Weld Hill Research and Administration Building. *Image courtesy of KlingStubbins.*

Clarifying basin for Weld Hill Research and Administration Building. *Image courtesy of KlingStubbins.*

Gravel swale for Weld Hill Research and Administration Building. *Image courtesy of KlingStubbins*

Conclusion

In many ways the approach to sustainably developing a site doesn't change from one building type to another. There are many issues that apply to all sites and building types. Unique situations will occur. Establishing a logical, systematic, and collaborative approach at the beginning of the project provides the best opportunity for successfully completing that project.

Key Concepts

- Fully understand the client's needs and building program.
- Establish what level of sustainability the project will attain. The LEED checklist is an excellent guide.

- Identify any specific development or operational issues unique to the project.
- Create a Site Selection Committee.
- Prepare a thorough site assessment study for each site under consideration.
- Review studies and select the most appropriate site.
- Prepare alternate schematic site development plans.
- Review plans to determine the most advantageous sustainable development strategies including:
  - Orient the building(s) to take best advantage of solar and ventilation opportunities.
  - Minimize the amount of impervious cover.
  - Consider pervious pavements.

- Retain existing vegetation and open space when appropriate.

- Limit the amount of site disturbance.

- Reuse and recycle existing materials where possible (i.e., crush old pavements for aggregate).

- Consider parking decks to minimize on-grade impervious pavements.

- Use indigenous plants.

- Recycled water or high-performance irrigation systems.

- Manage stormwater quantity and quality.

- Capture stormwater for reuse—it's a resource not a problem.

- Use full cut-off light fixtures to limit light pollution.

- Implement appropriate sustainable development strategies during the design process.

If the project team implements this type of development strategy, and faithfully follows it through to conclusion, the result should be a successful project that meets the client's needs, has a positive impact on the local environment, and enhances the stewardship of our fragile environment.

REFERENCES

LEED Building Design + Construction Reference Guide, USGBC, 2009.
The Sustainable Sites Initiative—Guidelines and Performance Benchmarks, Draft 2008, by American Society of Landscape Architects, Lady Bird Johnson Wildflower Center, University of Texas at Austin, United States Botanic Garden.

chapter 5 Laboratory Performance
Simulation, Measurement, and Operation Characteristics

Image courtesy of KlingStubbins.

Introduction

Although in many ways laboratory buildings are similar to other facilities, they are typically much larger consumers of utilities and natural resources. This chapter will focus on laboratory building operating characteristics and techniques to quantify energy, water usage, and savings realized by sustainability measures.

The overall approach to minimizing energy usage in a new lab facility begins with the development of a baseline energy model. This model may be used to forecast annual energy consumption of a typical code-compliant building and benchmarked against similar facilities to verify the results. The first section of this chapter provides information regarding the construction and analysis of energy models. Processes to meter and measure performance of constructed buildings and verify that performance goals are being met also will be discussed. Lastly, com-

This chapter focuses on several of the sustainability categories discussed in Chapter 1. See page 18 for more information.

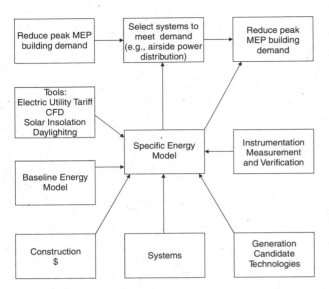

The building energy reduction and optimization process. *Image courtesy of KlingStubbins.*

missioning procedures for existing and new laboratory buildings and their systems are outlined at the end of this chapter.

Energy Modeling

Laboratory Energy Estimation Basics

As noted elsewhere in this book, energy usage in laboratory buildings is typically five to ten times higher than ordinary commercial building stock such as office or institutional buildings. Cleanroom-type facilities with a controlled level of particle filtration or biosafety level can consume up to ten or more times the energy of such typical buildings. However, the difference in energy usage is not limited to total building consumption. Common energy use (and resulting operating cost) values used for comparative design purposes are typically reported by end use in annual-

ized terms so that a full year's worth of weather and operational data is included. This data may then be extrapolated to provide future projections.

It is evident by comparing energy use figures for different building types, such as those indicated in the accompanying graphs, that certain differences may be expected between office and laboratory buildings. These represent models of buildings situated in different climatic regions and differences solely due to weather may also be expected. Office buildings generally have more homogeneous end-use consumption than laboratories—the pieces of the pie tend to be more similar in size when building energy use is displayed in this format. As the internal and ventilation loads in a building increase, as is the case in the laboratory building models displayed in the figures, plug loads rise as a percentage, but the various cooling equipment energies actually drop on a percentage basis. This is not because those systems use less total energy than the office building, but rather use less energy as a percentage of the building total. Laboratory systems also operate beyond standard building operating hours so their performance is inherently different than those in offices, and have greater opportunities for features such as heating, ventilation, and air conditioning (HVAC) economization and increases in system efficiency. The bulk effect of heating and humidification energy due to higher ventilation rates is also evident in these simplified results. Note that the laboratory building in Tucson, Arizona, a geographic location with a relatively mild heating season and heavy cooling, utilizes evaporative systems for cooling and humidification which use much more water than conventional systems, but less energy. The impact of other systems, such as lighting, on the building energy total may also be quantified in this manner. One can see how the percentage of energy consumption due to lighting

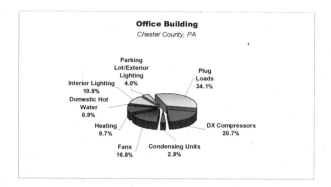

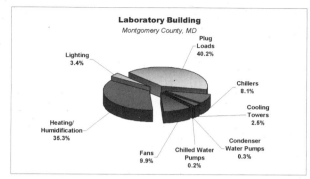

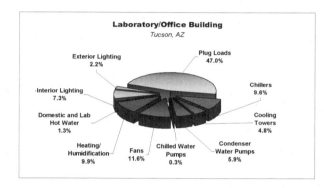

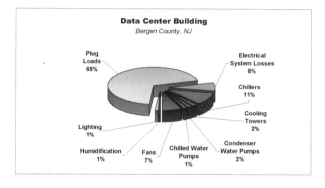

Annual building energy usage percentages classified by end use for various building design types. *Image courtesy of KlingStubbins.*

systems decreases as their relative consumption becomes smaller when all the building energies are considered. Lastly, the effect of miscellaneous loads such as domestic hot water and exterior lighting can be significant in any building type, and should be considered during meaningful energy analysis and design efforts.

All of these energy end uses translate into building operational expenses, and while easy to overlook during design, they will be scrutinized in detail when the building is in operation. Such whole-building analysis is a growing industry trend and is critical to lifecycle cost evaluation and financial analysis of sustainability efforts. This will be discussed in more detail

later in this chapter. Laboratory-specific details regarding modeling protocols and standards used in rating the energy efficiency of building designs will also be discussed.

On the extreme end of the building energy distribution examples is a data center facility, which consumes the highest percentage of plug load energy and lowest heating and humidification energy expenditures. As one might expect, this is due to a relatively constant computing electrical load. In general, such a property of an internal cooling load–driven building tends to neutralize the effects of climate on building energy consumption when compared to lab or office buildings.

Energy usage in a laboratory building is largely driven by the (1) functional activities within the building and (2) the infrastructure required to maintain its environmental conditions. This second driving force is commonly referred to as *process energy* and is usually attributable to many different end uses and activities in the building, making it difficult to quantify. However, once the process energy is quantified, a building designer can model and simulate the functional internal activities. Performance may vary widely because of variables ranging from building construction to weather conditions to system characteristics. For example, heating and cooling energy use attributable to a manifolded laboratory fume hood exhaust system may be calculated if the relevant details about the building and affected systems are known. So in the case of an existing building where retrofit measures are being considered, this system may be surveyed and the typical usage pattern may be quantified through trending. However, during energy estimation of new building construction, the design professional is tasked with making projections about how the fume hoods connected to the exhaust system are going to be used (i.e., schedules and diversity), since the building and systems do not yet physically exist. This will result in assumptions being factored into the calculation. Data such as the architectural program, the type of research being performed, and characteristics of the scientists' existing laboratories may help to inform such assumptions about the operation of a laboratory building, which in turn drive the energy use of the mechanical and electrical infrastructure.

Process energy due to miscellaneous electricity-consuming equipment, or *plug load*, is much more difficult to estimate since the building does not yet physically exist and its occupancy, usage patterns, and peak load density only can be estimated. This is similar to the fume hood example described above, and it is likely that the design professional will rely on a combination of measurement of existing buildings similar to that of the proposed design, criteria assumptions provided by end users, and industry benchmarking data to estimate the process loads and energy consumption.

It is important to note that plug load has two primary components—load density (watts per square foot) and hourly operating percentage of that load. Although load density has a major impact on system size, and thus what efficiency systems will operate at during part load conditions occurring throughout most of the year, the latter component of hourly operating profiles has an even greater impact on energy consumption projections. As a result, these profiles need to be defined on a per day basis for Monday through Friday of a typical week, weekends, and holidays in an energy model. The "24/7" loads, such as computing or manufacturing energy end uses, may warrant separate profiling. Specialty lab equipment and systems, such as process chilled water systems, high-purity water systems, glasswashing and autoclave equipment, robotics, and other types of process equipment also may require separate estimates and scheduling, especially if there are known properties which are unique. Such loads also have the effect of heating building spaces not only during the cooling season, but during the heating season, and will offset related HVAC energy to balance the overall building thermal mass. Care must be taken not to overstate these loads and thus underestimate heating energy and misstate comparative savings achieved by the building systems.

Building Information Technology (IT) plug loads due to data centers, server rooms, or other 24/7 mission-critical computing uses and their support infrastruc-

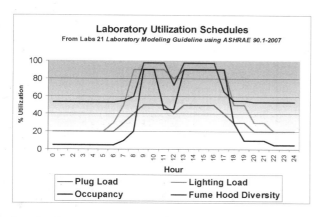

Example of utilization schedules for laboratory buildings developed by Labs21®. They assume heavier loads during typical working hours, 8 AM to 5 PM. The fume hood diversity schedule is based on the premise that fume hood use is directly related to occupancy of the laboratories and turndown is 50 percent of maximum airflow during unoccupied periods. If variations are expected, schedules should be modified to suit particular operating conditions as well as holiday and individual weekday types. *Image courtesy of KlingStubbins.*

ture usually can be found in some form in most modern laboratory buildings. The presence of these 24/7 plug loads in existing and new laboratory buildings is expected to increase steadily in the future due to the growth of computing capacity. Data centers frequently are provided with very high future capacities in terms of reliable electrical power supply and cooling. However, experience has shown that it can take years for a design load–density to be achieved in a data center. During this period of IT growth, the data center may operate at relatively low utilization and is typically not as energy efficient as the design intended. Adding to this is the operation of redundant equipment and its effect on infrastructure efficiency. For example, Uninterruptible Power Supply (UPS) systems may operate in pairs at 50 percent maximum operating load until there is a failure event in the system, and this event only may last for an extremely small percentage of the system's total operational lifetime. This means that the equipment never regu-

larly will operate at its peak efficiency, which like many systems typically occurs when operating closer to its design capacity. Other examples of this phenomenon can be found in IT cooling airflow rates as well as refrigeration systems and equipment. Special consideration also should be given to possible implementation plans for IT, and whether the capacity will be installed in phases or if equipment will be operated in phases according to load thresholds. The metric of Power Utilization Effectiveness (PUE), and its reciprocal, Data Center Infrastructure Efficiency (DCiE), is the ratio of total facility power to IT power, and is becoming the industry-standard terminology for reporting data center system efficiency. PUE can be used to quantify differences in power demand and annual energy consumption of related building systems, and the basis for its calculation or measurement should be clarified by the design professional.

Energy Modeling Protocols

Energy modeling protocols, or definitions about how to quantify the relative energy performance of building designs, have become the most commonly accepted method of energy estimation in the building design and construction industry due to their flexibility. Site-specific energy models, which are calibrated to actual reported utility meter data, remain very powerful tools to quantify retrofit measures and energy-savings initiatives. These models have the benefit of proven accuracy and are used regularly in performance contracting, but ultimately an energy modeling protocol may be required in parallel with a model of an existing building to provide additional energy-efficiency metrics. Also, system-specific energy models are useful in isolating individual energy-efficiency measures without the added complexity of modeling other unrelated parts of the building and its systems, for which data necessarily may not be desired. For example, the performance of a chiller or boiler plant can be modeled and analyzed without specifically modeling the hour-by-hour thermal performance of the building(s) it serves, so long as cooling or heating load profiles are known or assumed. The performance of a photovoltaic generation system is another example where the modeling protocol may differ from the one used for the rest of the building and its systems, since its net energy flow may be independent. The purpose and type of the energy model and corresponding protocols used in sustainability efforts ultimately depend on the specific project goals.

The ASHRAE Performance Rating Method (PRM) contained within Appendix G of ASHRAE Standard 90.1 has become the most common building energy modeling protocol in the United States. It is the recognized method for determining theoretical energy cost savings for LEED Energy and Atmosphere (EA) Credit 1 points in the U.S. Green Building Council's LEED NC (New Construction) Green Building Rating System(tm). Standard 90.1 has contained the PRM since its 2004 release, and in 2007 the required efficiencies of some systems increased and some calculation parameters specific to laboratories were revised. Historically, very little deviation from the parameters contained within the PRM modeling protocol has been permitted by the U.S. Green Building Council in calculations used to determine LEED credit points.

A full explanation of the ASHRAE PRM is beyond the technical scope of this chapter; however, some laboratory-specific guidance will be provided. The PRM is a more flexible version of the Energy Cost Budget (ECB) method, also contained within Standard 90.1. The ECB method is a set of building energy modeling rules intended to provide an alternative energy code compliance path for buildings that do not meet the code's prescriptive or envelope tradeoff requirements, but will have an energy cost equivalent to a building that meets those requirements. The equivalent energy cost is achieved by electrical and mechanical system efficiencies designed into the building. The ECB method is not as flexible as the PRM, and many sustainability features are not allowed to be modeled using the ECB method, but are allowed in the PRM. The PRM allows the *proposed design* energy cost, determined from a "computer representation of the actual proposed building design or portion thereof" to be compared to the *baseline design* energy cost, which is "a computer representation of a hypothetical design based on the proposed building project." Therefore, the PRM allows energy and resultant energy cost savings to be calculated for buildings that are designed to substantially exceed the minimum requirements of the ASHRAE Standard 90.1 Energy Code (ASHRAE 2007, 173).

In addition to the LEED green building rating system™, other current energy-efficiency programs are requiring use of the PRM. The United States *Energy Policy Act of 2005* (EPAct 2005) included new federal tax incentives for owners of energy-efficient commercial buildings. Calculation of the tax deduction requires use of the PRM in order to calculate tax deductions available for an energy-efficient building, with the efficiency values found in ASHRAE Standard 90.1–2001 substituted where applicable in the baseline design. In addition, for government-owned buildings, the tax deduction may be taken by the party primarily responsible for designing the property for the year in which the property is placed in service. Various utility incentive programs also utilize forms of the PRM as an energy-efficiency measurement tool. In addition, the Federal Government has recently mandated that new federal buildings must be designed to exceed ASHRAE 90.1–2004 by at least 30 percent solely on a *regulated* energy basis using the PRM, as well as other initiatives set forth by the Department of Energy's Federal Energy Management Program. The mandate, contained within *10 CFR Part 433*, defines regulated energy consumption for the purposes of calculating the 30 percent savings to include space heating, space cooling, ventilation, service water heating, lighting, and all other energy-consuming systems normally specified as part of the building design, except for plug and process loads. So while plug and process loads need to be included in any energy model for thermal load simulation, the energy consumption associated with those loads should be deducted from the building energy totals when determining percentage savings attributable to regulated loads. In this specific case, the added step of aligning the energy data to utility rate structures and costs is not required in the modeling protocol. Experience has shown that the basis of such percentage values related to energy protocols may be easily confused. The various types of benchmark targets should be established early in a project and during any energy modeling efforts, so that goals are clearly quantified and may be verified. In general, professionals designing modern, sustainable laboratories are often confronted with somewhat divergent demands—meet safety requirements with sufficient ventilation, conserve energy, make the building operation automated, and limit capital first costs. For this reason, energy modeling efforts must be employed early in projects to take advantage of the benefits and truly achieve integrated architectural and engineering design.

Several items deserve special consideration when the PRM is applied to laboratory buildings. First and foremost is the methodology for baseline fan power calculation, as this energy end use in laboratories can be significantly higher than the broad array of building types that the protocol was intended to address. In Standard 90.1–2007, additional baseline fan power credits are provided for various HVAC system devices and components frequently required in laboratory air systems, such as fume hoods, ducted exhaust and return air, high-efficiency filtration, and heat recovery. This allows the design to gain additional calculated savings through measures such as low pressure-drop building air distribution and high-efficiency fans and motors. There is also an exception in the baseline building system type definitions found in Appendix G that allows the use of constant-volume direct expansion systems for spaces that have peak thermal loads that differ by roughly 3 watts per square foot when compared to the rest of the building, have operating schedules that differ by more than 40 equivalent full-load hours per week, or have special pressurization relationships, cross-contamination requirements, or code-required minimum circulation rates. Laboratory buildings frequently have many spaces that meet this exception and appropriate credit should be taken in the baseline building model. Note that this exception may not be allowed depending on the quantity of ventilation outdoor air required in the system, and an economizer may be required on the baseline system according to its geographic location. For laboratory spaces with a minimum of 5,000 CFM of exhaust, Appendix G in Standard 90.1–2007 clarifies that they should be modeled with a baseline variable volume system that reduces exhaust and makeup air volumes to 50 percent of design values during unoccupied hours. Exhaust air heat recovery in this baseline laboratory system is not required when following Standard 90.1–2007 Appendix G. Therefore, any level of heat recovery in systems with exhaust rates of 5,000 CFM or greater will be rewarded in the proposed building energy comparison, as will turndown of air systems below 50 percent of design airflow rates. Note that if a VAV system is not employed, exhaust air heat recovery with a minimum 50 percent level of total effectiveness remains a requirement for high outdoor air percentage systems in order to prescriptively comply with Standard 90.1–2007 as an energy code. Another lab-based modification to Appendix G incorporated in Standard 90.1–2007 is that the chiller plant selection for the baseline model is a function of building peak cooling load and not building conditioned floor area.

Special attention should be paid to the site's utility rate structure, especially if percentage energy cost savings of the proposed design is a benchmark of interest. Detailed analysis may be performed in a spreadsheet once monthly energy demand and consumption data are available. Since cooling requirements are typically a driving factor in laboratory HVAC system design, detailed part and full load performance data should be obtained for the cooling equipment under consideration, since the energy consumption of these systems can vary widely according to ambient weather conditions. In addition, many laboratory buildings are located in a complex or on a campus where central district thermal energy such as chilled water or steam is used. In many cases, utility rate data may be obtained from the central plant and used in a cost-neutral manner among the various energy models. For purchased heat such as campus steam, the PRM requires that those costs be factored into both the baseline and proposed models. Purchased cooling, such as campus chilled water, is only modeled in terms of cost in the proposed design, and the baseline cooling plant characteristics are defined according to tonnage capacity or air-conditioned floor area (depending on the version of Standard 90.1). If more than two LEED EA Credit 1 points are sought for a project, the USGBC requires

two sets of energy model comparison scenarios for district thermal energy systems, the first step being a building standalone scenario where district energy is held cost-neutral to prove that the building itself (building and equipment downstream of the central plant) is providing energy savings. The second step is an aggregate building scenario where the central plant is explicitly modeled and compared to minimally efficient heating and cooling plants defined by Appendix G to account for the additional energy savings provided by the central plant. This prevents projects from attaching a building with poor energy characteristics to an efficient central heating and cooling plant and achieving LEED certification.

Many new lab buildings are designed with shell space intended for fit-out after the building has been occupied, and this is recognized in the PRM. If the properties of those spaces are known and equipment capacity is being installed in the base building project to support those spaces, they should be modeled according to those assumed future conditions. However, if the future use of the space is undetermined, it should be modeled as office space with features identical in the baseline and proposed models. Finally, the PRM also includes a provision for *exceptional calculation methods* that may be used to directly discount the proposed building annual energy costs due to measures such as equipment and appliances that may be more efficient than the standard, "business as usual" stock. Also, the exceptional calculation method may be used where a simulation program cannot explicitly model a performance feature of the building, allowing that item to be modeled and estimated separately and the results integrated with those of the model representing the rest of the building project. One measure that may involve such a calculation is natural or hybrid ventilation of certain spaces. Of course, when measures are

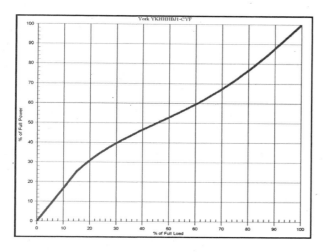 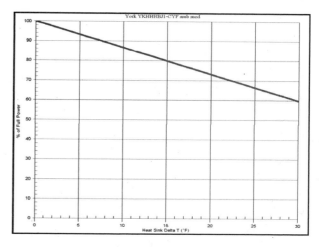

Example of detailed part-load performance data for a centrifugal water-cooled chiller. For a given chilled water load, the input power is calculated from the curve on the left and then modified using the curve on the right based on the ambient wet-bulb temperature experienced by the cooling tower. This calculation is performed in an energy model with the building load profile on an hourly basis to determine the annual energy consumption of chiller compressors. *Image courtesy of KlingStubbins.*

used that essentially change the plug (unregulated) load profile assumed between the baseline and proposed models, documentation may be required along with any PRM calculations that demonstrates that the systems to be installed in the proposed design represent a "significant verifiable departure from documented conventional practice." Proposing a building automation system or specific building appliances that limit standby or "parasitic" energy consumption during unoccupied periods is an example where a lower internal load profile would need to be modeled to calculate savings and supporting documentation would need to be produced.

Energy Analytics

Once energy modeling protocols and goals have been determined for a project, consideration should be given to the phasing of the building energy modeling. It may be desirable to first complete an early schematic model of the project with a relatively low

number of thermal zones and simplified systems but with enough detail to capture the average characteristics of the different building spaces and bulk square footage. Also, reduced-year building schedules and weather data in lieu of full 8,760-hour-per-year simulation may be used to capture a typical day of each month and then scaled-up to get annual data. This will allow the model to be more workable so that relative energy reductions due to individual strategies, such as differences in building massing and materials, HVAC systems, lighting, or onsite generation, may be tested with the corresponding building energy baseline and process components. Then a menu of candidate measures and technologies may be identified and considered for integration into the building as the design progresses. Analysis of the building consumption by end use as discussed earlier may help to target the largest energy-consumers and specific areas for efficiency measures. For example, if lighting systems are determined to account for a relatively small percentage of the overall building energy, efficiency increases in those systems may not provide significant overall building energy savings and therefore may not be strong candidates for improvement. An ASHRAE baseline model and relative testing of efficiency measures can be performed even if only schematic information is available for a project. Such modeling usually provides the most value and benefits to the overall project design considering the labor required to produce the models. Once a building and its systems are fully designed, the degree of energy savings may be difficult to manipulate without significant design changes, which may be scrutinized from a cost and schedule standpoint.

One such test of an individual energy-efficiency measure is simulation of the proposed building envelope to determine what percentage energy savings it provides relative to the baseline building. If the PRM is used to define the baseline building envelope construction and the corresponding systems and equipment is modeled identically in both the baseline and proposed models, the relative contribution or penalty of the proposed envelope to the overall building energy and cost savings may be quantified. For example, it may be determined that paying a slight penalty in the thermal performance of a more transparent envelope system is offset by greater savings through daylight harvesting, and interactively they may present a more efficient design.

During the schematic phase of an energy modeling effort, the results should be verified by checking them against comparable data, which may consist of data from models of similar buildings in the area, actual utility bill data, or industry averages. The Commercial Buildings Energy Consumption Survey (CBECS), published by the U.S. Energy Information Administration, is useful for verifying energy model data for certain building types and locations. This data is also

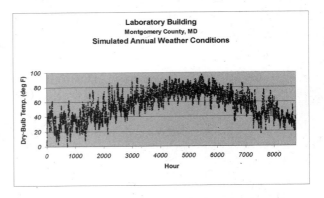

Example of hourly dry-bulb temperature data extracted from an annual TMY2 (Typical Meteorological Year) data set provided by the National Renewable Energy Laboratory. *Image courtesy of KlingStubbins.*

used in benchmarking tools such as the EPA's Target Finder. At some point further into a project the model will be updated, or an entirely new model built to reflect the actual proposed building characteristics and thus determine if the project will meet the energy or operating cost goals defined earlier on. A final step in the energy modeling process may include verifying that the building is operating at or below the energy consumption simulated during design, and will be discussed in more detail later in this chapter. Verification can be problematic since certain differences in the data will become apparent—actual building energy consumption will differ from simulated results due to variations in occupancy, building operation and maintenance, weather, process loads, utility rates, as well as the precision of the energy calculation itself.

Domestic water usage due to plumbing fixtures, process uses, or irrigation in a building project is typically calculated separately from a building energy model, and reduction strategies for those systems are discussed in the next chapter. Although energy modeling protocols such as the PRM do not currently require specific accounting of HVAC water consump-

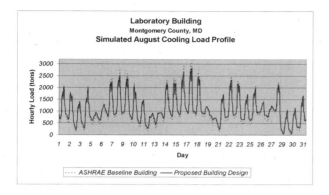

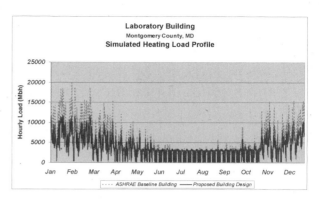

Energy simulation results indicating a building cooling load profile for August. Note the decrease in total cooling load at peak times due to more effective heat recovery utilized in the proposed building design model. Also illustrated are the lower cooling loads during unoccupied periods in the proposed building model, which are attributable to greater system airflow turndown. *Image courtesy of KlingStubbins.*

Building simulation results indicating an annual heating load profile. Note the building base reheat load during the summer months, as well as the hourly load reductions due to more effective heat recovery in the proposed building design. Since the laboratory airflow is load-driven, the reheat load decreases during each weekday and remains relatively constant during summer weekends and other unoccupied periods—control of operation during these times is therefore critical to energy conservation. *Image courtesy of KlingStubbins.*

tion, buildings that use evaporative cooling equipment such as cooling towers may require treated makeup water volumes several orders of magnitude higher than the building's plumbing fixtures and systems. The consumption of cooling tower makeup water and water used for humidification and direct evaporative cooling consumption can be extracted from energy models and used to create an overall yearly "water balance" model for the building, which may help to determine the performance of sustainable systems such as rainwater capture or building gray-water recycling. Such models may also be coupled with average rainfall data for the site location.

An extension of the energy analysis process may be calculation of a project's greenhouse gas emissions. Once energy simulation data has been produced, the annual emissions, or "carbon footprint," of the project and any associated reductions may be calculated in terms of carbon dioxide and other greenhouse gases. Indirect, or "source" carbon emissions related to remote energy plants, power plants, or central util-

ity plants may be determined by using average data for the region (in terms of pounds CO_2 per kilowatt-hour, for example) and resource utilization factors, then scaled-up according to the site energy consumption. Local emissions due to combustion in the building related to boilers, absorption chillers, or other direct-fired equipment or generators can be calculated in parallel using the known combustion efficiency of the equipment. Many measures intended to reduce total carbon emissions, such as onsite electricity generation, actually increase net site energy consumption, but reduce the total amount of carbon dioxide related to the building emitted into the atmosphere. The carbon reduction depends on the amount of carbon dioxide emitted from the energy-producing source per kilowatt-hour of electricity used in the building. This is mostly due to the fuel type used in generating electricity for the building and the inefficiency of transferring this energy through the grid to the site. Carbon footprints and emissions will be discussed more in the next chapter.

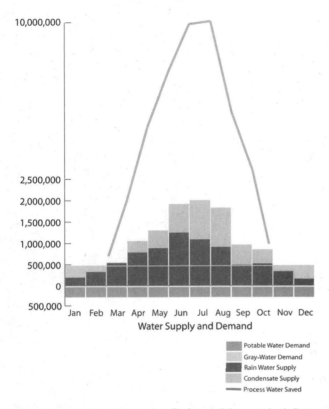

Annual water supply and demand profile for a building complex indicating scale of savings provided by gray-water collection relative to evaporative cooling equipment process water consumption. *Image courtesy of KlingStubbins.*

Energy savings and reduced carbon emissions due to improvements in buildings may also be quantified in terms of equivalencies such as passenger vehicle emissions, barrels of oil consumed, quantity of average homes powered, acres of forest needed for carbon sequestration, and other similar terms. Since it is difficult to visualize what a pound of carbon dioxide actually looks and feels like, these types of equivalencies may be useful in communicating to people what building energy actually means in more tangible terms.

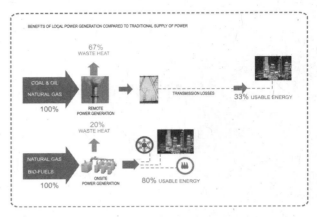

Source-to-site efficiencies and energy generation impact on carbon emissions related to the building. *Image courtesy of KlingStubbins.*

Of course every building project will have different features and energy sources, and the degree of energy use, energy cost, and carbon emissions, as well as any savings achieved in these different categories will be different and the interrelationship among the values should be understood by the project team. Another factor in understanding building energy consumption is that various alternatives may perform differently when combined in an interactive manner due to rightsizing of systems or when peak loads are shifted to times when weather conditions are different and the systems therefore operate at different efficiencies.

Lifecycle Cost Analysis

Once energy simulation data and first-year energy costs are determined a number of economic analyses may be performed. A simple payback may be calculated using the additional construction cost of the energy-efficiency measures as an input. Some businesses and building owners have established target internal rates of return that need to be achieved with the investment of additional capital in efficiency measures.

Many energy-efficiency measures carry an additional capital expense which should be scrutinized. The lifecycle cost method of economic analysis is the best way to determine the cost-effectiveness of a particular measure or set of measures. It consists of accounting for all present and future costs associated with operating a facility—acquisition and installation of the building and its systems, energy costs, repair and maintenance, equipment replacement, inflation, and discount rates. "Soft" costs, such as those associated with the building occupants or processes that may not be affected by the building design and specification process, are seldom included in such calculations. After the decision to build a new facility or renovate is made by an organization, lifecycle cost analysis is the most appropriate method for building-related and cost-focused decisions.

Lifecycle cost analysis takes all the present and future costs of the building and converts them into a cumulative net present value, or "total cost of ownership." The net present value of different design alternatives may then be compared, and the alternative with the highest net present value therefore has the lowest lifecycle cost and provides more overall value to the building owner. A major assumption in lifecycle cost analysis is the building or system lifespan (in years) that is assumed—a longer lifecycle will tend to justify greater expenditure in energy-efficiency measures. The estimation of construction cost, especially during the schematic phases of a building's design, also adds complexity to such analysis.

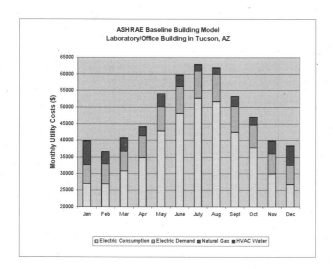

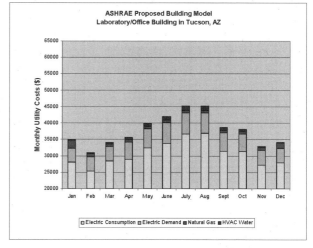

Monthly building energy cost results from a performance rating method simulation used in determining the number of qualifying LEED Optimize Energy Performance credit points for a project in Tucson, Arizona. A total annual energy cost reduction of 22 percent below the ASHRAE baseline building budget was projected. Note the increased consumption of HVAC makeup water in the proposed building mode due to evaporative cooling systems, but lower natural gas and electric consumption due to the efficiencies gained in humidification and cooling. Other measures such as chilled beams and daylighting controls also contribute to the calculated energy cost savings. *Image courtesy of KlingStubbins.*

Metering for the Sustainable Laboratory Building

Introduction to Metering

Building utilities metering is the foundation for establishing a program to reduce energy and water consumption in sustainable laboratory buildings. Without a metering system, it is difficult to ascertain how the building is currently being operated or how it has been in the past, as well as to predict future trends. There is an old business adage "you can't manage what you don't measure." In the world of engineering, this same sentiment is often restated as "you can't control what you don't measure." These sayings are equally valid when it comes to energy management and control for laboratory buildings. Measurement of building energy and other utility use, more commonly referred to as metering, is a critical component of sustainable laboratory building design and operation. For existing laboratory buildings without adequate metering, installing a more comprehensive metering system is an important step in improving the sustainability of operations. There are many commercially available utilities metering designs that lend themselves to retrofit, with minimal impact on continuous building operations. This section provides some background on metering for sustainable laboratory buildings, and examines guidelines for metering applications and the associated benefits.

What to Meter?

The most common metering applications in laboratory buildings are for those utilities that are paid for by the building owner, namely reading electricity, natural gas, and water meters. Sometimes utility bills from the suppliers of these services only provide a sum-mary and historical data from the previous billing period, which may be monthly or quarterly. However, it is generally possible to obtain a signal, such as an electrical pulse, from a utility meter to provide real-time input to the laboratory building's Building Automation System (BAS—sometimes referred to as BMS, for Building Management System), which records the pulses over a fixed time interval so trends and deviations in building performance may be observed and investigated.

Standalone laboratory buildings often have meters provided by the utility companies at the building service entrance, but utilities distributed in a campus setting may have utility company meters at a common service point, such as an electric substation transformer, rather than at each building. If utilities are only metered at the building service entrance the task of analyzing the building utility to end users to determine which system or equipment is contributing to unexpected poor performance can be difficult, and the true source of performance problems will often be masked for some time, resulting in wasted resources. Metering is more effective as a diagnostic and investigative tool to guide building operators in running the building equipment and systems efficiently if large loads are separately classified and metered rather than being lumped together on a single meter reading. A modern sustainable laboratory should include separate metering of the following components:

- All energy/utility sources, including electricity, natural gas, potable water, gray water, steam, heating hot water, chilled water, and condenser water

- Electric metering of large air handling unit motors and other major HVAC equipment such as chillers

- Natural gas and fuel oil metering of building boilers

- Cooling tower makeup water or other HVAC systems and equipment requiring significant water volumes

- Makeup water metering for purified water systems

- Electric metering of lighting loads, preferably on a floor or area basis

- Water metering of glassware washers or other laboratory equipment

The detailed selection of metering points should be developed specifically for each laboratory building and should provide adequate information to support measurement and verification of sustainable design features, which will be discussed later in the chapter. Metering is also an essential element of LEED certification. The USGBC's LEED for Existing Buildings (LEED-EB) Rating System specifically recognizes the value of metering in Water Efficiency credits for Water Performance Measurement (Credits 1.1 Whole Building Metering and 1.2 Submetering) and Energy and Environment credits for Performance Measurement (Credits 3 System Level Metering).

Components of a Metering System

A standard metering system minimally consists of three distinct subsystem elements: (1) meters, (2) meter data transport, and (3) the meter data management system, or MDMS. There are several types of electrical meters including socket meters, which are typically installed on the exterior of a building at the service entrance, and panel meters, which are typically installed in a building substation, switchboard, or panelboard by the electrical equipment manufacturer. Another type is standalone "tenant" meters, which are typically installed in wall-mounted enclosures in an electrical room within the building. The socket-type meters and panel meters generally

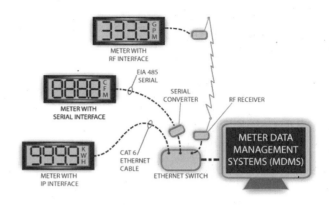

Components of a metering system. *Image courtesy of KlingStubbins.*

use solid core current transformers for isolation from the electrical service feeders. Tenant meters are often installed after the building is constructed, and commonly include split core current transducers (CTs) or current sensors, which can be installed around the service conductors without the need to disconnect them. Some manufacturers provide meter electronics integrated in a set of split core CTs, providing an economical justification for a larger number of strategically located meters.

The MDMS is normally based on a personal computer (PC) workstation running specialized software to retrieve data from the meters, store it in a database, and provide specialized energy consumption reporting and analysis. An MDMS may be a standalone system or integrated into the BAS that controls building HVAC systems. It may be installed in the laboratory building and maintained by the building owner, or managed offsite by a metering service provider.

There are numerous options for data transport and many systems use a combination of methods. The most common data transport methods within

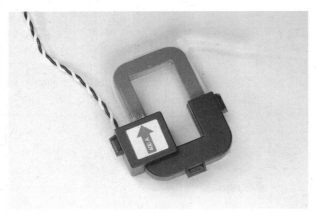

A variety of electrical meters: standalone tenant meter (courtesy of E-Mon, LLC); panel meter (Shark® 200 Multifunction Power and Energy Meter, courtesy of Electro Industries/GaugeTech 2008); and meter electronics integrated in split core CTs (courtesy of E-Mon, LLC).

laboratory buildings are hardwired signals (pulses or serial data stream such as MODBUS) and Ethernet network connections, such as MODBUS IP. However, for communication between buildings on a campus, additional options include a radio frequency mesh network operating in the unlicensed 900-MHz spectrum, or using power line carrier signals that transport the data through building electrical distribution feeder cables. Both of these approaches have

the advantage of not requiring additional cabling infrastructure.

Many electric metering systems provide the capability to incorporate natural gas and water metering by using pulse inputs to either the standalone electric meter or a companion device that conditions the meter pulse data and stores it for processing by the MDMS.

Metering for the Multitenant Laboratory Building

Examples of a multitenant laboratory building are developer-owned laboratories with space leased to several different corporations and university or Federal Government laboratories with autonomous departments occupying different spaces. Regardless of whether occupants or tenants are paying for their own energy and utility use, they should be accountable for their resource consumption and should be provided with monitoring tools and data to contribute to overall resource use reduction.

Metering in Federal Government Laboratories

All U.S. Government facilities, including sustainable laboratory buildings, must comply with the *Energy Policy Act of 2005* (EPAct 2005). Section 103 of EPAct 2005, *Energy Use Measurement and Accountability*, requires that all federal buildings be metered for electricity, using to the extent feasible advanced meters that measure consumption on at least an hourly basis, and provide data to a meter data management system at least daily. The U.S. Department of Energy (DOE) has published guidelines for electric metering in federal buildings. In addition, the *Energy Independence and Security Act of 2007* (EISA 2007) includes requirements to meter natural gas and steam. The designer or operator of a sustainable laboratory must remember that these are only the minimum standards required by law for federal facilities. High-performance, sustainable design practice will in most cases require submetering of different loads and load categories within the laboratory building.

Advanced Metering

Many electrical metering applications, including those in U.S. Federal Government laboratories, require the use of advanced meters that are able to measure and record interval data. Intervals are at least hourly, but

BioSquare III's extensive utility submetering helped establish the feasibility of this LEED Certified multitenant building for Boston University Medical Center. *Image courtesy of © Trustees of Boston University and KlingStubbins. Photography © Robert Benson Photography.*

U.S. Department of Energy published these guideline documents for electric metering in U.S. federal buildings. *Image provided by the U.S. Department of Energy, Federal Energy Management Program.*

more commonly they span every 15 or 30 minutes to correspond with the electrical utility provider's demand charge interval. These advanced meters communicate the data to a remote location (such as the MDMS discussed above) on at least a daily basis, although many systems communicate the data more frequently. The meters can provide information on consumption and demand by interval for a specific time of day. This capability corresponds to time-of-use or time-of-day pricing adopted by some utility service providers for many of their larger customers, since the cost of producing each kilowatt-hour of electricity is typically much higher during times of peak demand (when less economical generating resources must be used) compared to off-peak periods (when the most economical resources can be used). The added intelligence gained from an advanced metering system supports better decision-making regarding the facility, and in some cases, real-time control decisions that reduce utility costs and promote efforts targeted at reducing consumption.

The Laboratory Building Dashboard

Experience has shown that scientists in a laboratory are more sensitive to using building resources when information is available to them regarding how much energy and water they are consuming. This can be accomplished by educational tools such as display dashboards.

A dashboard in an automobile provides convenient access to the most commonly required driving information, such as speed and fuel remaining. This information is displayed in a convenient fashion so that the driver can easily process it and make appropriate decisions. In the same manner, sustainable laboratories should include laboratory building dashboards providing convenient access to important informa-

Building Dashboard®. *Image courtesy of Hamilton College and Lucid Design Group, Inc. © 2004–09 Lucid Design Group, Inc. All rights reserved. Patents pending.*

tion regarding building performance. The dashboard should be designed to be a user-friendly software display which is accessible to building managers and occupants. It should indicate cumulative metered information in a graphically powerful fashion to quickly convey basic information on building performance and resource consumption. In addition to automatically displaying metered information, the dashboard may also be designed to display other sustainability metrics, such as material use, based on manual input. Building dashboards are generally web-based, so they may be accessed through a corporate intranet or remotely, but it is advisable to also provide a large display screen mounted in a prominent position within the laboratory building, such as an employee entry lobby or other common area, to promote occupant education and foster "water-cooler" interaction.

Scientists also are more sensitive to using building resources when they are shown simple yet effective measures to reduce energy and material consumption in their own lab spaces. Many organizations have in-house groups that work to educate the scientists about these issues. One such group is LabRATS, from the University of California.

LabRATS Sustainable Laboratory Operations ·

Allen Doyle, M.S. Chemical Oceanography
Sustainability Manager, University of California, Davis
Katie Maynard, B.A. CCS Biology
Sustainability Coordinator, University of California, Santa Barbara

Have you ever noticed light switches taped on, ovens burning all night, and thermostats blocked by boxes in a lab? The occupants of the buildings you design may have a big effect on its energy and resource efficiency over the long run. In addition, some of them will tell you just how well your building works, or doesn't. Designers and building managers need to keep the occupants in mind and work with them for maximum efficiency. Occupants need to pay attention and understand how to use the smart building you built.

The focus in laboratory operations has always been the science, since the science is the purpose for the existence of the facility. Typically, all personnel dedicate themselves to a safe and stable environment to minimize interruptions to the workflow. To that end, researchers and technicians often overstock supplies and equipment in or near the laboratory, request high light levels, and build in planning for "possible future" requirements to ensure they are never in need. This model is no longer necessary, effective, or sustainable in a time of joint lab spaces, collaborative research and teaching models, and a strongly connected community of scientists. (See Evan Mills, Env Sci Technology http://eetd.lbl.gov/EMills/pubs/pdf/sustainable-scientists.pdf.)

A holistic approach to sustainable laboratory design is more than just the design of the building itself. Use and care of the building and its resources can play a vital role in cost savings and energy savings over the long term.

A group at the University of California, Santa Barbara (UCSB) founded a program called Laboratory Research and Technical Staff (LabRATS) Network that connects laboratory researchers between labs and with safety and operations staff. Their goal is to increase resource efficiency and quality of research while making the smallest environmental footprint possible. A culture of collaboration is fostered that values sustainable practices as a top priority in laboratory settings. This program has expanded to several other campuses including Harvard, UCLA, and UC Davis where one of the co-founders, Allen Doyle, is campus Sustainability Manager.

Current programs include: formal laboratory assessments; a surplus equipment website with built-in campus approval system; exchange of clean surplus chemicals through an easy-to-use web interface; exchanging spirit thermometers for hazardous mercury thermometers; creation of a campus listserve feedback forum; occupancy surveys to reduce ventilation when safe; downtime for fume hoods not in use; metering of laboratory equipment; searches for the most efficient models (in conjunction with Labs21's Energy Efficient Laboratory Equipment Wiki: http://labs21.lbl.gov/wiki/equipment/index.php/Energy_Efficient_Laboratory_Equipment_Wiki); facilitating the exchange of old, inefficient freezers using utility company rebates; and removing unnecessary fluorescent lamps in overhead light fixtures.

When a team of students and staff assess a lab, it stimulates researcher participation, both through direct laboratory analysis and through exposure to a campus network that allows researchers to share technical ideas, equipment needs, and surplus. The assessment sometimes connects researchers to repair and support staff they didn't know were available, such as glassblowers, or electronics and refrigeration technicians. The LabRATS team collects data on equipment energy use and

continued

The LabRATS team at a collaborative planning session. *Image courtesy of The Regents of the University of California, Davis and Santa Barbara campuses. Used by permission. All Rights Reserved. For more information contact copyright@ucdavis.edu.*

Chemical exchange program minimizes the amount of each specialized chemical required for inventory. *Image courtesy of The Regents of the University of California, Davis and Santa Barbara campuses. Used by permission. All Rights Reserved. For more information contact copyright@ucdavis.edu.*

general observations about the laboratory, and they interview the lab manager. Experienced assessment personnel can sometimes play matchmaker with unexpected bonuses, such as a spare $12,000 autosampler, with unmet analytical needs that are available in the next building, or by alerting maintenance staff to leaky water systems. Finally, the team compiles an assessment database and reviews their evaluation with the lab staff. They commend the researchers' good habits and practices, discuss opportunities for conservation, and help set self-determined goals. An overview of the program and the assessment protocols are readily accessible to researchers on the extensive website: *www.sustainability.ucsb.edu/LARS*.

During the design of a new lab, LabRATS will meet with campus facilities staff and the architect to review and offer advice on programming or blueprints, and will help facilitate interactions between researchers, faculty, and the design team. The Department of Facilities Management at UC Santa Barbara, like most campuses, engages faculty members through the departmental building committees and the Academic Senate. Facilities management also hosts energy and resource-focused design charrettes for most new buildings. LabRATS supplements this interaction by seeking advice from other faculty and researchers who will use the building but might not have the time or inclination to commit to a committee. This presents an opportunity to merge lab functional requirements with accurate research needs and building lifecycle savings early on during the design process.

The Surplus Chemical Program reduces chemical waste streams and saves money on the purchase of new supplies. Chemical use is essential to the operations of many labs, and disposal can be very costly. LabRATS co-designed a website with UCSB's Environmental Health & Safety which displays available surplus chemicals, complete with pictures and descriptions of reagent quality for campus labs interested in getting free chemicals. Familiarity with the program has encouraged the return of unused chemicals that can accumulate in labs, thereby increasing safety and decreasing waste. The website can be viewed at: http://sustainability.ucsb.edu/LARS/programs/adopt.php.

Fume hoods are integral to the operation of many types of labs and represent a significant source of energy use. Because a large quantity of air must be exhausted through a fume hood while the sash is left open, air supply to the lab needs to be able to compensate for that exhaust. A sash management campaign and improved signage reduced wasted energy by getting researchers to close fume hoods. In addition, LabRATS determined through user surveys that 10 to 12 hoods were not used in one building. Consultation with their Environmental Health & Safety department, and a professional engineering analysis showed that they could be turned off without altering negative air balances. The result was a cost savings of $20,000 to $30,000 per year.

Auditing existing spaces and removing lamps for energy savings is a retro-fit project of LabRATS. Signage indicates to facilities staff that the lamps are removed intentionally. This is a good interim measure for projects where redesigning lighting systems is not financially feasible; newer more efficient designs would be a next step. *Image courtesy of The Regents of the University of California, Davis and Santa Barbara campuses. Used by permission. All Rights Reserved. For more information contact copyright@ucdavis.edu.*

Lighting makes up 10 to 20 percent of laboratory energy. Many labs are lit throughout the entire space, even when only a small area of the lab is in use. This can be addressed by only turning on light switches that are needed, utilizing task lighting, and removing bulbs in overlit areas of the lab. LabRATS and their facilities maintenance department initiated the BulbFree campaign that encourages researchers to evaluate how much light they need and to intentionally remove bulbs in overlit areas. Two lamps use 50 to 60 watts and, once removed, will save about $20 per fixture per year. Lighting demand can be cut by as much as 10 to 20 percent, saving 1 to 4 percent of total laboratory energy needs.

LabRATS also provides a list of "best practices" to the lab users, making them aware of daily activities that can promote energy and water conservation, reducing, reusing, and recycling opportunities, use and care of electronics and apparatus, research efficiency and communications, and chemical exchange. It is a fundamental belief of LabRATS participants that most scientists want to connect with the sustainability movement and use the most proactive conservation measures possible. "Conservation in the lab; it's good science," is one of their mottos.

Measurement and Verification

Introduction

Earlier sections of this chapter dealt with energy modeling and metering of laboratory buildings and their systems. Measurement and verification (M&V) is a means to test the validity of the projections and estimates modeled during the design phase of the constructed laboratory building using metering technology. M&V provides a formalized approach to evaluating how effectively a building's water- and energy-consuming systems perform when compared to their design intent.

Where there are performance-contracting incentives in place for a project, such as in a U.S. Government Energy Savings Performance Contract (ESPC), third-party M&V is usually required. Detailed technical information and best practices recommendations regarding M&V may be found in the *International Performance Measurement and Verification Protocol* (IPMVP), published by the Efficiency Valuation Organization (EVO). For U.S. government laboratory buildings, supplemental guidance is provided in *FEMP M&V Guidelines: Measurement and Verification for Federal Energy Projects*.

The M&V Plan

M&V requirements need to be developed for each laboratory building and documented in an M&V plan. The plan is required to implement M&V and achieve LEED Energy and Atmosphere Credit 5. Just as all laboratory buildings are unique but have some elements in common, all M&V plans are unique but also usually have some common elements. This section presents the typical requirements for developing an energy use M&V plan for a sustainable laboratory building. Where M&V of water-consuming systems is desired, a comparable plan would also be developed. The objectives of the plan should include the following:

- Determine the energy used by the laboratory building for heating, cooling, receptacle, lab equipment, and lighting loads

- Estimate as-built energy savings of the whole building relative to the baseline energy model under actual operating conditions

- Confirm that energy-efficiency measures continue to function as intended

- Assess and validate the simulation methodologies used in the baseline model for their accuracy

- Test the validity of operating and occupancy assumptions used in the design-phase simulation

A review period must also be established in the M&V plan. A typical length is one year, which allows for results from all seasons to be incorporated into the review. The M&V review period should coincide with the annual calibration cycle of the associated sensors in the building.

The annual building energy consumption is forecasted in the analysis and design phases by a computerized energy model as described earlier in this chapter. The M&V plan should indicate what software and methodology were used to develop the energy model. The original, design-phase energy model assumes typical yearly meteorological data. Because no year ever matches this average weather data set exactly, the design-phase model will be simulated with actual weather data recorded during the M&V review period. This data may be obtained from federal government weather services or local metered data.

M&V Analysis Approach

The M&V plan must identify the analysis approach by option and method, as defined in the IPMVP document *Concepts and Options for Determining Energy Savings in New Construction, Volume 3*. For laboratory buildings seeking LEED certification, LEED EA Credit 5 permits the use of either Option B or D:

• Option B (retrofit isolation) is used to determine savings by fully measuring the energy use of a system which has been modified (e.g., adding variable speed control to a fan)

• Option D (calibrated simulation) is used to determine savings by measuring energy use at meters or performing whole-building simulation calibrated to measured energy use data

Option D is most appropriate for new construction with fluid, lighting, and power submeters, and enables savings to be estimated by one of two possible methods:

• Method 1—Subtract the energy use of the calibrated as-built model from the energy use of the calibrated baseline model

• Method 2—Subtract the metered postconstruction energy use from the energy use of the calibrated baseline model

Method 2 is preferred when metering is available. While savings estimation is typically of interest for a limited M&V period (as defined in the M&V plan), it may be desirable to forecast long-term savings. This can be accomplished by adjusting the baseline simulation to reflect operational and weather conditions for each subsequent M&V period, since significant equipment or performance degradation can result in a reduction in energy savings.

Metering to Support M&V

Metering all energy-consuming components in a building using the methods discussed earlier in this chapter is critical to successfully determining energy use under actual operating conditions. The following elements should typically be measured in a sustainable laboratory building, and trended over time by the building automation system (BAS):

• Chilled water supply and return temperatures (°F)

• Chilled water flow rate (gpm)

• Steam consumption (lb/hr)

• Electrical power use (kW)

• Lighting use (kW)

As stated earlier in this chapter, building operational schedules and conditions will influence the annual energy consumption. Therefore, the following conditions should be monitored:

• Occupied-time profile

• Type of functions occurring in the building

• Changes to building mechanical or electrical systems

Once the trended meter data has been collected, the calculations described next will determine the building energy consumption.

Chilled Water Energy Use

Cooling in a typical laboratory building might be provided by chilled water generated in a central utility plant. The following formula calculates instantaneous cooling load:

Cooling Load (Btu/hour) = 500 × [Chilled Water Flow Rate (gpm)] × [Chilled Water Return minus Supply Temperature Difference (°F)]

or

$$LOAD = 500 \times GPM \times (T_{RET} - T_{SUP})$$

The calculation will typically be programmed in the BAS unless a direct reading thermal energy meter (Btu meter) is installed. The instantaneous cooling load will be integrated over time by the BAS to calculate the annual cooling energy (in 10^6 Btu/year).

Steam Energy Use

A typical laboratory may utilize steam for heating, humidification, or process end uses. If steam is provided from a central utility plant, instantaneous steam demand by each building (in pounds per hour) will be metered by the building automation system and converted to energy units (in Btu/hour) if the latent enthalpy of vaporization at the distribution pressure is known. The following formula calculates instantaneous steam heating load:

Heating Load (Btu/hour) = [Steam Flow Rate (pounds/hour)] × [Latent Enthalpy of Vaporization (Btu/pound)]

For example, for 60 psig steam, LOAD = FLOW × 905.3

This calculation will typically be programmed into the BAS. The instantaneous steam load will be integrated over time by the BAS to determine the annual heating energy (in 10^6 Btu/year).

Electrical Energy Use

Power for lighting and receptacles (in kW) should be metered directly. The power demand will be integrated over time by the BAS and units converted to

determine the annual electricity usage (in 10^6 Btu/year).

Comparison of Measured and Forecasted Loads

The annualized cooling, steam, and power usage during the M&V review period should be summed and compared to the value forecasted by the design-phase energy model. The calculation methodology described above relies on the BAS to trend the metered data continuously over the M&V period and save it to a robust server system that is backed up to prevent loss of data. Extrapolation from one or two months of data from each season provides some prediction of energy consumption, although this will be less accurate compared to full-year data.

Dealing with Uncertainty in M&V

The major sources of uncertainty using Option D are:

• Operational changes to the building systems

• Occupancy or schedule changes

• The ability of the simulation software used for the design-phase energy model to accurately forecast energy consumption

• Accuracy of the metering systems

• Physical similarity between the as-built and simulated building

• Interpretation of metered or simulated results

These sources of uncertainty should be clarified during the M&V process. Changes to the building systems or occupancy patterns will influence the energy consumption, which will cause a difference in results from one year to the next. However, this effect can be estimated, and if it is temporary then the excursion can be added as an explanation between the predicted and actual energy consumption. If the effect is permanent, the energy model can be recalibrated to include the energy consumption related to this effect.

Computerized building energy simulation software programs have some inherent uncertainty, particularly if the baseline simulation occurs during the design phase. Effects due to program inputs and methodologies can be resolved by calibrating the design-phase baseline model against the energy consumption of the actual building. Analysis results should be compared to the design-phase baseline energy model, and variations should be justified. More common calculation methodologies, such as spreadsheet-based bin weather data analyses, may also be performed from year to year to confirm the order of magnitude of computer simulation results.

The annual building energy consumption data is calculated from trending data and is therefore sensitive to the sensors used to create the data. Temperature, pressure, flow, and current sensors should be calibrated annually. Performing calibration against traceable values minimizes error related to these calculations and also regulates the error to be somewhat constant year to year. Dissimilarity between the as-built conditions and the building envisioned in the design-phase simulation introduces uncertainty into the model. However, as the building operation becomes stable and the design-phase model is calibrated against actual operating results

and building modifications, this error can be reduced to an acceptable level. Uncertainty due to the human error in manipulating and interpreting raw data can be minimized by using standardized spreadsheets, which also help to regulate error to be constant year to year.

Preparation of the M&V Report

The results of the M&V process should be summarized in an M&V report. A typical M&V report will present the following information:

- Executive Summary, including a comparison of results to the design-phase baseline model and results from previous years

- Identification of modifications to the building systems or occupancy which would influence energy usage

- Results of any previous M&V reviews including corrective actions recommended and degree of implementation

- Current M&V review and detailed comparison to previous years and design-phase baseline model

- Recommended corrective actions

- Appendices containing detailed technical analyses, plots of trended data, and other supporting information

Laboratory Building Commissioning

In addition to simulation techniques and different methods to measure and analyze building energy and resource consumption, commissioning (Cx) is a process that is also highly beneficial for creating a sustainable laboratory building. Commissioning is a primary means to confirming, among other things, that the owner's requirements for the laboratory and sustainable design goals are clearly documented, that the laboratory building design is consistent with the owner's requirements, and that the construction of the laboratory building is complete and in accordance with the design. "Fundamental Building Systems Commissioning" is required as a prerequisite to LEED certification under the Energy and Atmosphere category (EA Prerequisite 1). An additional credit point is available under the rating system for "Additional Commissioning" (EA Credit 3).

Some of the fundamental requirements for commissioning are identified in ASHRAE Guideline 0–2005, *The Commissioning Process and* ASHRAE Guideline 1.1, *HVAC&R Technical Requirements for the Commissioning Process.* In addition, commissioning requirements unique to sustainable laboratory buildings are provided in Laboratories for the 21st Century's *Design Guide for Energy-Efficient Laboratories* and *Best Practice Guide—Commissioning Ventilated Containment Systems in the Laboratory.*

The sustainable operation of an existing laboratory building can be improved through a process commonly known as retrocommissioning (RCx). Retrocommissioning is a systematic process for investigating, improving, and optimizing a building's operation and maintenance, and generally focuses on energy- or resource-consuming equipment, systems, and operations. The USGBC's LEED for Existing Buildings (LEED-EB) Rating System specifically recognizes the value of the retrocommissioning process in Energy and Atmosphere credits for Existing Building Commissioning (Credits 2.1 Investigation and Analysis, 2.2 Implementation, and 2.3 Ongoing Commissioning). Comprehensive information on retrocommissioning buildings is provided in a DOE document called *A Practical Guide for Commissioning Existing Buildings.* Additional guidance specific to laboratory buildings can be found in Laboratories for the 21st Century Technical Bulletin *Retro-Commissioning Laboratories for Energy Efficiency.*

The major activities that need to be included in the RCx process are:

- Planning phase, which includes gathering information regarding the laboratory building and its systems (design information such as laboratory ventilation rates and operating information such as utility bills), and initial meetings with important stakeholders such as facility managers, laboratory users, and laboratory safety managers.

- Preliminary investigation phase, which includes more in-depth interviews with operations and maintenance personnel, review of design data and verification of built-in metering and instrumentation versus measurements that will be required to evaluate energy performance of the laboratory building. Energy benchmarking is an effective way to identify and prioritize potential opportunities during this phase and is a good application for the techniques highlighted in this chapter.

- Detailed investigation phase, which includes specific measurements and performance tests of laboratory systems operation, and preparation of a report of findings and recommendations.

- Implementation phase, which includes selection and prioritization of improvements, implementation of selected improvements, and verification that performance has improved.

Retrocommissioning

Paul A. Mathew, Ph.D
Staff Scientist, Lawrence Berkeley National Laboratory

Monitoring-based commissioning (MBCx) combines ongoing building energy system monitoring with standard retrocommissioning practices with the goal of providing substantial and persistent energy savings (Brown et al. 2006, 3:27–40). There are three primary sources of additional energy savings from MBCx relative to traditional RCx: (1) Savings from persistence and optimization of savings from RCx thanks to early identification of deficiencies through metering and trending; (2) savings from measures identified through metering and trending during the initial commissioning effort (i.e., measures unlikely to be found from RCx alone); and (3) savings from continually identifying new measures. By virtue of the continuous nature of the monitoring, MBCx can identify new problems that emerge after the initial retrocommissioning investigation stage, such as equipment cycling and excessive simultaneous heating and cooling.

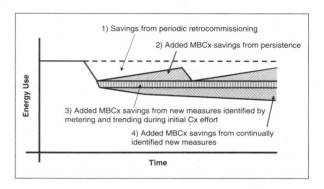

A research study by Lawrence Berkeley National Laboratory (Mills and Mathew 2009) documented the savings and costs of a range of MBCx projects on university campuses. In addition to the savings from periodic retrocommissioning, the three streams of additional energy savings relative to RCx are illustrated.

Conclusion

Since laboratory buildings typically consume significant quantities of resources, a comprehensive understanding of building energy and water usage is required to create truly sustainable environments. Load and energy performance related to building features, systems, and processes should be quantified and compared to relevant industry baseline models and benchmarking data during investigation and design activities. This allows the laboratory designer or facility owner to optimize the design in terms of different performance metrics of interest. Perhaps most importantly, building or system lifecycle costs may be developed, which helps to justify the economics of energy-efficiency measures. In addition to the simulation tools and techniques discussed in this chapter, implementation of building metering technology and procedures such as measurement and verification plans and various types of commissioning are equally valuable in physically delivering and maintaining high-performance buildings and systems.

Key Concepts

- Whole-building energy modeling should be commenced early in projects to analyze and understand energy and water consumption.

- A baseline energy model should be developed to compare the performance of building features and systems using appropriate laboratory industry standards and benchmarks—this measurement will inform whether design measures achieve sustainability goals (i.e., to save X% energy cost, etc.)

- "Bottom-line" energy metrics, such as heating and cooling energy savings, energy cost savings, energy use intensity, and achievable LEED credits are useful in conveying meaningful results to the building team.

- Lifecycle cost analysis should be performed using projected energy consumption and construction cost data to determine and optimize the cost-effectiveness of energy-efficiency measures.

- Metering devices and a comprehensive measurement and verification plan are essential for understanding and confirming the predicted performance of building systems.

- Commissioning procedures are beneficial processes for validating and maintaining the energy efficiency of new laboratory buildings or retrofit measures.

REFERENCES

ASHRAE. 2007. *Energy Standard for Buildings Except Low-Rise Residential Buildings*. American Society of Heating, Refrigerating and Air-Conditioning Engineers, Inc.

Brown, K. et al. 2006. "How Monitoring-Based Commissioning Contributes to Energy Efficiency for Commercial Buildings," in *Proceedings of the 2006 ACEEE Summer Study of Energy Efficiency in Buildings*, 3:27–40. Washington, D.C.: American Council for an Energy-Efficient Economy.

Mills, E. and P. Mathew. 2009. "Monitoring-Based Commissioning: Benchmarking Analysis of 24 UC/CSU/IOU Projects." *Lawrence Berkeley National Laboratory Report 1972E*, http://cx.lbl.gov/MBCx.html.

6 Engineering Systems
Reducing What Goes In and What Comes Out

Image courtesy of KlingStubbins.

Introduction

This chapter focuses on how to effectively design energy- and water-efficient mechanical systems for sustainable laboratories. First, some background is provided on the basis of design loads and airflows for different types of laboratory facilities. Individual strategies to reduce building heating and cooling demands, as well as system concepts to serve the mechanical and electrical demands in the most energy-efficient manner are described next. This chapter then explores ideas about implementing low-energy heating and cooling, power generation, and renewable energy strategies as well as increasing efficiency and reducing the environmental impact of laboratory plumbing systems. The concepts presented should be approached with a mindset that each laboratory building has very specific functional, operational, and safety requirements that must be satisfied, and where applicable, some background about these requirements is included.

This chapter focuses on several of the sustainability categories discussed in Chapter 1. See page 18 for more information

Mechanical and Electrical Demand Reduction

After development of a baseline energy model as described in the previous chapter, the next step in creating an energy-reduction strategy is to minimize the heating and cooling loads of the lab facility. The load and system strategies should be then developed and tested against baseline performance to forecast annual energy and cost savings. This section provides some background on the basis of laboratory design loads and some ways to reduce and optimize them.

Heating and Cooling Load Profiling

In a typical office or classroom HVAC system, air handling units supply approximately 55°F air, which is routed to individual zones to offset heat gains and then returned to the air handling units at room temperature (e.g., 74°F) to be processed again. This air recirculation conserves energy since the air handling unit is cooling a high percentage of air at room temperature. However, as mentioned in the previous chapter, HVAC systems for laboratories are different than offices or classrooms because they typically use 100 percent outside air. All air is exhausted from the lab—no air is returned from labs to air handling units. This "once-through," or "single-pass," concept minimizes cross-contamination across labs and reduces the consequences of chemical spills. For example, if air was returned from a lab to the air handling unit, solvent from a spill in one lab would be recirculated to other labs supplied by that air handling unit. Exhausting air from the labs helps to ensure that only the lab with the solvent spill is affected.

For labs with 100 percent outside air systems, reducing the demand correlates to reducing the airflow supplied to the labs. Lab HVAC supply air systems are sized to meet the largest of three criteria: (1) supply air required to offset the lab cooling load, (2) supply air needed to dilute the concentration of indoor air pollutants (e.g., solvents or odor-producing compounds), and (3) makeup air exhausted by fume hoods and other elements. For each lab, the supply airflow associated with each of the three elements is calculated, the three are compared, and the largest component is selected as the design supply airflow rate for that room.

Most labs are negatively pressurized—when the door is closed, air flows from the adjacent space (often a corridor) into the lab. This reduces the probability of odors from lab operations migrating into the corridor. The air brought into the lab from the corridor is termed "transfer air." Since transfer air also carries dust and contaminants from the adjacent space (e.g., corridor), labs that have a priority of cleanliness are sometimes positively pressurized. Examples include optics labs requiring a classified clean room environment, or procedure labs using immunosuppressed rodents.

Labs may be classified by three categories:

• *"Load-driven"* if the airflow to offset the peak cooling load is greater than the other two airflows. A dry lab with no fume hoods and a high density of heat-producing electronic equipment is load-driven.

• *"Air change-driven"* if the air needed to dilute the concentration of indoor air pollutants dominates. A holding room in a vivarium is sometimes air change-driven since the governing standard includes a minimum air change requirement.

• *"Hood-driven"* if the supply air required to makeup exhaust air removed from the lab through fume hoods and other exhaust elements, minus transfer

Room Name	Room Number	Room Type	Area (ft²)	Total Sensible Load (Btu/hr)	Airflow due to Load (cfm)	Dilution (Air Change Rate) (ACPH)	Airflow due to Dilution (cfm)	Transfer Airflow (In) (cfm)	Transfer Airflow (Out) (cfm)	Airflow due to Exhaust Elements (cfm)	Supply Airflow (cfm)	Exhaust Airflow (cfm)	Unit Supply Airflow cfm/sf
Level 01													
Typical Lab 1 Perimeter		Lab	441	14,598	795	6	441	0	0	100	800	800	1.8
Typical Lab 2 Perimeter		Lab	441	14,598	795	6	441	0	0	100	800	800	1.8
Typical Lab 3 Perimeter		Lab	441	14,598	795	6	441	0	0	100	800	800	1.8
Typical Lab 4 Perimeter		Lab	441	14,598	795	6	441	0	0	100	800	800	1.8
Typical Lab 5 Perimeter		Lab	441	14,598	795	6	441	0	0	100	800	800	1.8
Typical Lab 6 Perimeter		Lab	441	14,598	795	6	441	0	0	100	800	800	1.8
Typical Lab 7 Perimeter		Lab	441	14,598	795	6	441	0	0	100	800	800	1.8
Typical Lab 8 Perimeter		Lab	441	14,598	795	6	441	0	0	100	800	800	1.8
Typical Lab 1 Interior		Lab	221	7,299	398	6	221	150	0	100	400	550	1.8
Typical Lab 2 Interior		Lab	221	7,299	398	6	221	150	0	100	400	550	1.8
Typical Lab 3 Interior		Lab	221	7,299	398	6	221	150	0	100	400	550	1.8
Typical Lab 4 Interior		Lab	221	7,299	398	6	221	150	0	100	400	550	1.8
Typical Lab 5 Interior		Lab	221	7,299	398	6	221	0	0	100	400	400	1.8
Typical Lab 6 Interior		Lab	221	7,299	398	6	221	0	0	900	900	900	4.1
Typical Lab 7 Interior		Lab	221	7,299	398	6	221	0	0	900	900	900	4.1
Typical Lab 8 Interior		Lab	221	7,299	398	6	221	0	0	900	900	900	4.1
Typical Lab 1 Equipment Zone		Lab	221	7,299	398	6	221	150	0	900	750	900	3.4
Typical Lab 2 Equipment Zone		Lab	221	7,299	398	6	221	150	0	100	400	550	1.8
Typical Lab 3 Equipment Zone		Lab	221	7,299	398	6	221	150	0	100	400	550	1.8
Typical Lab 1 Flex Zone		Lab	221	7,299	398	6	221	150	0	900	750	900	3.4
Typical Lab 2 Flex Zone		Lab	221	7,299	398	6	221	150	0	100	400	550	1.8
Corridor		Corridor	1,344	11,004	599	6	1,277	0	1,350		1,350	0	1.0

An example of an air balance spreadsheet. *Image courtesy of KlingStubbins.*

air, dominates. A medicinal chemistry lab with a high density of fume hoods is hood-driven.

Understanding these characterizations provides insight into how the lab airflows may be reduced. The following paragraphs describe the potential drivers of lab airflows. However, these may change dynamically—for example, in a lab with variable-volume air distribution, if the fume hood sashes are closed, then the cooling load may become the driver. If the sashes are closed and the cooling load is low, then the dilution rate may become the driver. Fume hood design requirements and control strategies are discussed in more detail later in this chapter.

Supply Airflow Required to Offset the Cooling Load

To determine the supply airflow rate needed to offset the room cooling load, the following steps are sequentially performed for each zone at its peak condition.

First, each cooling load component must be understood and assessed. Next, the cooling load components for each room are added together. The supply airflow rate required to offset the cooling load can then be calculated. The cooling load components fall into two categories, envelope and interior. Envelope heat gains are caused by forces outside the building:

• Solar energy entering through transparent surfaces such as windows and skylights. This cooling load component is a function of solar energy, window area, shading coefficient, and building mass. Solar energy incident on a window is a function of time, latitude, and orientation. The shading coefficient is a measure of how much solar insolation enters the room as heat gain and roughly indicates the window "tint." For example, deeply tinted and reflective windows have a low shading coefficient. Advanced window technologies allow spectral selection so that visible light wavelengths enter the room, but heat-producing infrared wavelengths are reflected and do not enter the room. This allows occupants to perceive the room as being naturally lit without incurring an energy penalty due to the cooling load.

- Conduction heat transfer through opaque surfaces such as walls and roofs, in addition to the transparent surfaces mentioned above. For each wall or window assembly, this cooling load component is a function of the resistance to heat transfer ("R-value"), area, and outside-to-inside temperature difference at design conditions. For example, highly insulated walls have a high R-value and therefore cause less conduction heat transfer. The temperature difference is corrected for lag effects and the effect of solar energy incident on the surface—the adjustment is a function of color, mass, time of day, latitude, and orientation.

Interior heat gains result from forces inside the building:

- Occupants—a function of the number of occupants and their activity level

- Lights—driven by the input power

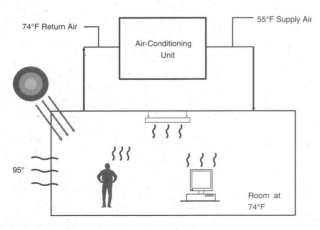

Room cooling load components. *Image courtesy of KlingStubbins.*

- Equipment such as computer workstations and analytical equipment—a function of input power and frequency of use

After the peak cooling loads are summed, the supply air required to offset those cooling loads and maintain room temperature is derived from a heat transfer balance of the zone. Because thermal equilibrium is assumed, the heat gains must equal the energy removed from the lab by the supply air. At sea level, this relationship is: Supply Air Flow Rate (cfm) = Sensible Cooling Load (Btu/hr) / 1.08 × (Room Temperature—Supply Air Temperature). Supply airflow is expressed as a volumetric flow rate, cubic feet of air per minute, abbreviated as cfm. Because air density is embedded in the equation, the constant in the denominator (1.08 at sea level) varies as a function of altitude.

Supply Air Required for Lab Dilution

Although the process for calculating the supply air required to offset the cooling load (described above) is the same as other building types, one unique requirement of labs is that the supply air flow rate may be increased to account for dilution of indoor air pollutants. Lab operations frequently include using solvents and other odor-forming compounds. Typically, activities using these chemicals are performed in a containment device such as a chemical fume hood. However, the concentration (and therefore odor) of solvents in a lab is diluted by the supply air.

Often, the supply air flow rate needed for dilution is expressed as "air changes per hour." This is the number of times per hour that air is turned over in the lab, and may be converted to flow rate by the following equation: Air Flow Rate (cfm) = Room Area (ft^2) ×

Ceiling Height (feet) × Air Change Rate (air changes per hour) / (60 minutes/hour). For negatively pressurized labs, transfer air (e.g., from the corridor into the lab) contributes to the room dilution effect and is often counted as part of the dilution-criteria airflow rate.

Supply Air Needed to Makeup Air to Exhaust Elements

Exhaust elements such as chemical fume hoods, point exhausts, and biosafety cabinets are used in labs to enhance worker safety, remove escaped odors, and capture sources of heat. To maintain the air balance in negatively pressurized labs, the supply airflow to each lab plus the transfer air equals the amount of air exhausted from the lab.

Lab Driver Characterization

The three airflows (load, dilution, and exhaust makeup) are then compared and the largest value is selected. That component is said to "drive" the lab airflow—for example a lab is "load-driven" if the airflow required to offset the heat gain dominates. This characterization guides the process of reducing the supply airflow.

Perimeter Lab Calculation Example (Interior and Envelope Loads)

Consider a 22-foot by 22-foot lab module with 6-foot-tall windows and one 6-foot chemical fume hood, which exhausts 800 cfm. Using a power density of 5.5 watts per square foot for equipment and 1.5 watts per square foot for lighting, the room heat gain is 24,100 Btu/hr. Therefore, 1,200 cfm is required to offset heat gain, 435 cfm to meet dilution criteria, and 650 cfm for fume hood makeup (800 cfm exhaust air minus 150 cfm transfer air into the lab).

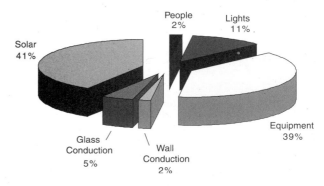

Exterior lab cooling load components. *Image courtesy of KlingStubbins.*

This lab would be characterized as "load-driven" since the airflow required to offset the room heat gains is larger than the other two airflows.

Interior Lab Calculation Example (Internal Heat Gains Only)

Often lab modules are located in interior portions of the facility. If the preceding example was recalculated using only the internal heat sources, then the airflow values would be 630 cfm to offset heat gains, 435 cfm to meet dilution criteria, and 650 cfm for fume hood makeup.

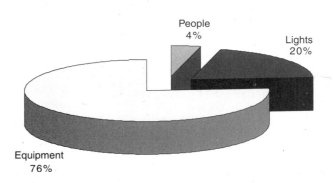

Interior lab cooling load components. *Image courtesy of KlingStubbins.*

This lab would be characterized as "hood-driven" since the airflow required for fume hood makeup is larger than the other two airflows.

Reducing Airflow Demand in Load-Driven Labs

Reducing the peak airflow demand in load-driven labs means that either the cooling loads must be reduced, or the supply-to-room temperature difference must be increased. A discussion of working with scientists to program rightsized systems is included in Chapter 3. In general, chemistry and biology labs are often supported by areas which house equipment that emit noise, such as incubators, autoclaves, and centrifuges. Locating this equipment in a dedicated room away from the chemistry or biology labs isolates noise and odors from the labs. However, the equipment also has elevated heat gains, and this layout allows the room to be cooled by a local fan coil unit which recirculates air within the equipment lab. Nominal supply and exhaust air to these rooms maintains negative pressurization. Although the equipment heat gain is much higher in these labs (relative to biology and chemistry labs), application of the local-cooling equipment means that energy-intensive, 100 percent outside-air central systems are not used to cool analytical equipment and fan energy reduction is also possible.

Reducing Demand with Envelope Improvement

In climatic zones such as the northeastern United States that experience both heating and cooling seasons, the challenge is to reduce solar energy entering the building in the summer when it represents a cooling load, admit solar energy in the winter when it assists in heating the building, and allow visible light to enter the building, so that occupants perceive a connection to the outside and daylighting controls

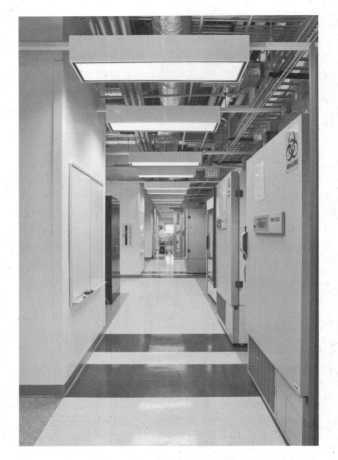

This photograph, taken at University of Colorado Denver Research 2 in Aurora, Colorado, is an example of a lab area with equipment that may be cooled with local recirculating fan coil units in lieu of 100 percent outside air central systems. *Courtesy of KlingStubbins. Photography © Ron Johnson Photography.*

may be implemented. Refer to Chapter 2 for some specific strategies for building envelope solar and conductive load reduction.

Reducing Demand Caused by Equipment Heat Gain

Electrical power used by scientific equipment results in heat dissipation into the laboratory, which in an all-air system is offset by supply air. As shown in the examples above, the equipment heat gain has the potential to be the largest cooling load component in a laboratory. As previously discussed, it is also the most difficult to forecast—scientific research is the exploration of the unknown, so the properties of analytical equipment supporting future discovery processes is also unknown. Therefore, an interactive and hands-on process is required to properly align equipment load criteria and "rightsize" systems.

Reducing Demand in Hood-Driven Labs

Maintaining worker safety, providing comfort, and reducing energy consumption are key goals when designing or operating sustainable laboratory buildings. These three goals often appear divergent, especially in laboratory buildings with large numbers of chemical fume hoods and other containment devices that are exhausted and require significant volumes of conditioned makeup air. After safety and comfort are addressed, laboratory airflow, pressurization, and fume hood systems and their controls are crucial issues when aligning these goals with energy efficiency. Achieving the three goals together requires well-planned and executed fume hood operational and control strategies. Some background on fume hood system design criteria and rightsizing is provided below—refer to the next section for further discussion about fume hood system controls.

A fume hood protects scientists by limiting their exposure to hazardous chemical vapors. Ducted fume hoods are the most prevalent type of fume hood in chemical laboratories. Exhaust airflow from each fume hood is a function of the design face area and the design face velocity, plus an allowance for leakage at the bottom airfoil and around the glass sashes. For example, a 6-foot-wide bench-top chemical fume hood exhausts approximately 800

cubic feet per minute of air if the design open sash area is 50 percent and the design face velocity is 100 feet per minute (fpm).

The fully open sash area is established by the fume hood dimensions. However, the working sash height is often prescribed by the laboratory's environmental health and safety officer with an understanding of how the researchers use their fume hoods. For example, researchers may agree that the working sash height is 50 percent of full height—this is driven by the sash providing a level of protection against debris resulting from an event occurring inside the fume hood. In this scenario, the sash would only be raised to its full height when equipment is being lifted into the fume hood to start an experiment, or in set-up mode when solvents and other chemicals are not open and the exposure risk is less. However, some laboratory owners argue that scientists are at risk of spilling chemicals when experiments are being started. With this assumption, the design sash position is the area corresponding to the full height—therefore increasing the design exhaust airflow.

The other component of the fume hood design exhaust airflow is face velocity—airflow increases with increasing face velocity. There is general consensus that while face velocity is not the only relevant containment metric, 100 fpm provides adequate worker protection. Although increasing air velocities are generally thought to increase worker protection, velocities entering the fume hood above 125 fpm can create turbulence and a low-pressure zone in front of the fume hood, pulling vapors out of the hood and ironically providing less protection to the worker in front of the fume hood. Proper design requires determination of the lowest face velocity that provides worker safety. This optimum face velocity is one that meets safety objectives while allowing a reduced exhaust airflow rate as an energy-efficiency measure.

One concept is to experimentally determine the optimum face velocity. ASHRAE Standard 110 identifies a method to test the ability of a fume hood to contain a tracer gas by placing a mannequin in front of the fume hood and monitoring the concentration of the tracer gas that reaches the mannequin. Better containment is achieved as the measured tracer gas concentration is lower. In order to determine the optimum face velocity, this test would be conducted for face velocities in 10 fpm increments, starting at 100 fpm. Testing would occur under as-built conditions, since the containment capability of fume hoods is sensitive to location—staff walking past the fume hood may create enough turbulence to cause vapors to be entrained outside the fume hood. The lowest face velocity that provides worker protection, with

some factor of safety, would be selected as the target face velocity.

To incorporate flexibility in the design of laboratories, an assumption is often made about the number of fume hoods and other exhaust elements to be used in the future. The number of fume hoods used in the building may change as the scientific research changes. For example, university labs are often renovated to support grant-related research opportunities. Private sector labs are sometimes renovated to allow labs to adapt to changing market opportunities. One concept is to design for an ultimate future condition—a certain number of fume hoods might be assumed per structural bay. The ultimate fume hood count would be a function of the research mission and the initial program. Also, assumptions may be made such as a biology lab will never be converted to a chemistry lab with a high fume hood density.

Bench-top laboratory fume hood at Johnson & Johnson PRD Drug Discovery Laboratory, Phase II in La Jolla, California. *Courtesy of KlingStubbins. Photography © Tom Bonner 2007.*

Consider a recent chemistry lab that was designed to have eight fume hoods per lab module, each occupied by four researchers. There were a large number of modules, and preliminary calculation of the air handling system size indicated a huge amount of air required to accommodate the hoods in a fully open position. The team was alerted to the considerable capital costs of the air handling systems, as well as ductwork distribution, space for the equipment, and supporting chilled water, steam, and electric infrastructure. Challenging the criteria that all fume hoods could operate simultaneously initially received some disapproval from the scientists, who were concerned about limiting their research flexibility. However, review of operations in similar existing labs indicated that no more than four of the eight hoods were ever simultaneously open. Adjusting the criteria from eight hoods per module at full flow to four hoods at full flow resulted in a 35 percent reduction in peak building airflow. This reduction in peak airflow resulted in capital cost savings in the supply air handling units, exhaust fans, boilers, chillers, ductwork and piping distribution systems, size of outside air intake louvers, and floor-to-floor heights, as well as energy savings attributable to rightsized systems.

Reducing Demand in Air Change–Driven Labs

There is no generally agreed-upon air change rate to dilute the concentration of indoor air pollutants in labs. This criteria is usually established by the client's environmental health and safety officer. The air change rate rarely establishes the peak supply airflow—typically the cooling load or exhaust-makeup requirements are greater. However, in a variable-volume application, the lab air control system dynamically calculates the three lab air drivers—for example, as the fume hood sashes are closed and the cooling load declines, then the air change rate dominates.

Toxic and biologically active compounds are typically handled in exhausted containment devices such as fume hoods or biosafety cabinets. These devices and the lab operating protocols are the first two levels of worker protection. This supports an argument to reduce the dilution rate—solvents are in a container until they are used in a fume hood. However, solvents must be carried through the lab on their way to the fume hood and may be dropped, resulting in container damage and a solvent spill in the open lab. The concentration of a spill as a function of the airflow becomes asymptotic after 15 minutes—twice as much dilution air does not reduce the spill concentration twice as fast.

Often, a different dilution rate is specified for occupied and unoccupied modes, with the occupied mode being higher. Historically, the argument has been that when the lab is unoccupied (as indicated by a light switch or other means), the probability of a spill is much less. With the increase of robotic processes that operate continuously, there is now a higher (although still small) probability of a spill in an unoccupied lab.

Energy-Efficient Systems to Meet the Demand

After the building loads have been reduced and optimized, the energy efficiency of building-level systems should be investigated. Candidate technologies for heating and cooling in the facility with minimum energy use are discussed next.

University of Colorado Denver, Research 2, Aurora, Colorado

The Fitzsimons campus' primary heating and cooling systems use centralized steam and chilled water generation. Campus distribution capitalizes on building diversities to make equipment selections at higher efficiencies and lower operating costs than a Research 2 building dedicated system could provide.

continued

Eight 80,000 cfm custom variable volume air handlers provide conditioning and ventilation for the laboratory, support, and office spaces. These units are positioned on the second level where manifold connections provide enhanced reliability through redundancy. Although all units are active, failure of one air handling unit results in a relatively small loss of capacity (12.5 percent), which can be offset by curtailment or diversity.

Supply air is ducted vertically to horizontal manifolds on each floor; airflow to each lab and office is regulated by variable air volume (VAV) boxes. Each VAV box controls a damper to allow enough air into the lab to maintain the room temperature or makeup to exhaust elements such as fume hoods. The VAV boxes have integral hot water reheat coils which are controlled to maintain room temperature during periods of minimum supply airflow.

Wet laboratory criteria often uses 12 to 16 air changes per hour of 100 percent outside air—this design set a typical VAV lab environment of 6 to 15 air changes per hour with flexibility for chemical fume hood, equipment, or biosafety cabinet loading. In order to minimize energy use, air from offices is ducted back to the air handling units. Air from laboratories is exhausted.

The air handling units are configured with evaporative cooling sections and heat recovery coils to reduce heating and cooling loads by approximately 15 percent. The hot and arid climate of the southwestern United States allows use of this technology. A glycol runaround heat recovery system recovers energy from the exhaust air stream to preheat or precool the outside airstream.

The University of Colorado Denver's Research 2 in Aurora, Colorado. *Image courtesy of KlingStubbins.*

Mathematical modeling of the potential for re-entrainment of exhaust air into Level 2 outside air intakes at University of Colorado Denver Research 2 drove the location of the vertical exhaust stacks on the roof. *Image courtesy of KlingStubbins.*

Variable Air Volume Operation

As described above, peak supply and exhaust airflows to labs are calculated as a function of three parameters (cooling load, dilution, and makeup to exhaust elements). However, labs operate under peak conditions for a relatively small number of hours per year. Since labs operate under off-peak conditions the majority of the time, an efficient off-peak operating strategy is critical to minimizing building energy usage.

One concept to meet this efficient off-peak operational goal is to vary the supply and exhaust airflows dynamically to track the three drivers—this is termed a dynamic variable air volume (VAV) air distribution system. Under this control method, a control system continuously calculates the three airflow drivers:

- Supply air to offset cooling loads—as in other building types, the airflow to offset the room heat gain is modulated by the VAV box to maintain the room temperature setpoint.

- Dilution (measured in air changes per hour)—since the airflow required for dilution is a function of the room volume and air change rate, this is a constant. The air change rate is often reset downward during unoccupied periods, as previously discussed.

- Makeup to exhaust elements—for fume hoods, the exhaust air flow rate is the product of the face velocity setpoint and the open sash area. The control system incorporates a sash position sensor, which calculates the open sash area. The face velocity setpoint is a constant (e.g., 100 fpm). The control system then multiplies the sash area and face velocity setpoint to calculate the exhaust airflow for each fume hood in the room. Adding in airflow to constant-volume elements (point exhausts, biosafety cabinets, etc.) and subtracting the transfer

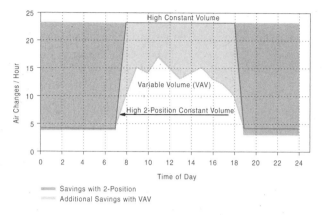

Daily lab airflow profiles illustrate savings of VAV and two-position systems over constant volume. *Image courtesy of KlingStubbins.*

air (for negatively pressurized labs) yields the supply air required for makeup to exhaust elements in a lab.

With this concept each lab has a supply and exhaust VAV box, with a flow meter and damper. The lab airflow control system continuously calculates the largest of the three drivers and positions the VAV box damper to maintain the required airflow setpoint. The flow meters allow the supply and exhaust VAV boxes to track each other to maintain room pressurization—the difference between supply and exhaust equals transfer airflow.

A form of variable volume operation is a stepwise variable volume system (two-position constant-volume system). In this model, the VAV boxes maintain constant supply and exhaust airflow during occupied periods, then are indexed to a lower airflow setpoint during unoccupied times. Since a typical laboratory is unoccupied for about 60 percent of the time, this step represents significant savings at low installed cost. The accompanying diagram illustrates typical savings available from stepwise variable-volume and dynamic variable-volume operation.

GlaxoSmithKline, Research Facility, Stevenage, United Kingdom

This 1-million-square-foot pharmaceutical research establishment is located approximately 30 miles north of London and incorporates the following sustainable features:

• Glycol runaround exhaust air energy recovery;

• Variable volume lab air distribution;

• Ozone treatment of cooling tower water;

• Minimized (6 to10) air change rate in labs;

• Heat recovery from boiler flue gases to preheat makeup water

The payback associated with glycol runaround heat recovery is climate-sensitive, and while not entirely favorable in this case, the decision to apply energy recovery was based more on good corporate citizenship and environmental stewardship.

A research facility for GlaxoSmithKline in Stevenage, United Kingdom. *Image courtesy of KlingStubbins.*

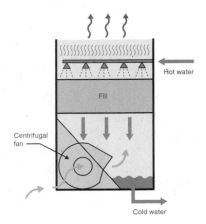

Schematic of evaporative cooling tower operation at GlaxoSmithKline's Research Facility in Stevenage, United Kingdom. *Image courtesy of KlingStubbins.*

Cooling towers are evaporative cooling devices used for heat rejection from condensers. However, the cooling tower basin collects cooled (e.g., 85°F) water in a still, low-velocity environment. This causes the potential for sediment and biological growth, which would result in condenser water tube fouling. Often, water is chemically treated to minimize growth of sediment and biological material. An alternative to chemical treatment is to inject ozone into the cooling tower water, which reacts to minimize biogrowth.

As the VAV boxes modulate, a sensor in the supply ductwork measures static pressure as an indicator of the position of VAV boxes—as more VAV boxes close, the duct static pressure will increase, since the fan is trying to move air through a closed damper. A variable frequency drive (VFD) is often used to change fan motor speed. As duct static pressure increases (i.e., fewer VAV boxes are open), the building automation system signals the VFD to decelerate the fan motor, reducing energy use. Changing the fan speed has a significant effect on fan power, since fan power demand is a function of the fan speed cubed.

Laboratory Air System Control Technology

Control of laboratory airflow is a major challenge faced in the design of laboratory facilities. Fume hoods must provide scientists with a safe working environment that minimizes their exposure, as well as the public's, to harmful gases, aerosols, and particulates while maintaining comfort and minimizing energy consumption. Once the cooling loads and laboratory exhaust air rates have been optimized as discussed earlier, the selection of control strategies and equipment is made. The following narrative provides an overview of the basic concepts of laboratory equipment controls and some innovative approaches to applying state-of-the art controls to efficiently maintain a safe and comfortable working environment.

The selection of fume hoods must consider the characteristics of the airflow control equipment to be used, including exhaust air terminal air valves and associated control devices—full coordination of these devices is possible when designing new laboratory facilities. However, when renovating existing facilities, a designer is limited by the characteristics of the existing HVAC system. The fume hood performance will be restricted by the performance of the existing HVAC airflow control devices, and the con-

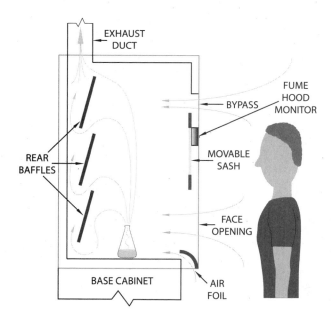

Diagram illustrating the components of a typical ducted fume hood. *Image courtesy of KlingStubbins.*

trol system may be restricted by the type and performance of existing fume hoods. These limitations may be overcome if all fume hood components, including HVAC controls, are viewed as an integrated system, and the design solutions are coordinated to achieve the greatest overall performance.

The primary containment barrier in a laboratory is typically the fume hood. Consequently, the laboratory room itself becomes the secondary containment barrier by maintaining the lab pressure negative to its surrounding spaces. The concept of multiple containment barriers is not normally applied to laboratories unless they are functionally specialized, such as with biosafety issues. The primary guidelines in the United States for laboratory ventilation are OSHA regulations (*Code of Federal Regulations Volume 29 Part 1910.1450*) and ANSI/AIHA Z9.5 (*The American National Standard for Laboratory Ventilation*). However, these guidelines, as well as other related standards such as NFPA 45 (*Standard on Fire Protection for Laboratories Using Chemicals*) and ASHRAE Standard 110 (*Method of Testing Performance of Laboratory Fume Hoods*), do not address the concepts of fume hood and room containment barriers. Nonetheless, when selecting the appropriate fume hood airflow control devices, a designer should first consider the containment requirements and then address all other control system elements required for containment, beginning with the fume hood itself.

Fume hood designs vary, and may include full bypass (for constant volume), partial bypass, or minimum airfoil bypass (for variable volume) airflow configurations. The characteristics of the fume hood airflow configurations will determine the type of control used for containment. The official definition of a fume hood, as defined by OSHA, is "a device located in a laboratory, enclosed on five sides, with a moveable sash or fixed partial enclosure on the remaining side; constructed and maintained to draw air from the laboratory and to prevent or minimize the escape of air contaminants into the laboratory." The position of the baffle plates at the rear of a fume hood is the primary method used by fume hood designers to achieve the required containment. An airfoil area in the front of the hood and below the sash is used to ensure minimum ventilation when the sashes are closed.

The simplest fume hood containment control scenario is constant exhaust airflow with a constant average face velocity across the open sash area, requiring the fume hood to have provisions for full bypass of the open area. Constant exhaust airflow control is a very expensive proposition in facilities with high densities of fume hoods—as a result it is preferable to vary the airflow quantity through variable air volume systems. With VAV control, as the fume hood sash position changes, the controlled variable is the fume hood average face velocity and the controlled element is the exhaust terminal box airflow. VAV operation requires the fume hood exhaust terminal box controller to modulate the exhaust airflow quantity in response to variations in the sash opening of the fume hood to maintain a constant face velocity set point.

Regardless of whether constant volume or VAV fume hood exhaust control methods are used, the minimum exhaust air volume requirements must be established. NFPA 45 defines this minimum exhaust volume to be 40 to 50 cfm per foot of the interior fume hood width. Typical fume hood average face velocities used today range from 80 to 120 feet per minute. Because VAV systems vary the airflow quantity distributed, they do not require a full bypass of the fume hood open sash area. VAV fume hoods still require a partial (restricted) bypass because below a certain minimum sash position, hood airflows cannot only be a function of face velocity—a bypass is still required to prevent excessive slot or airfoil area velocity. Once the fume hood exhaust air requirements are established, the designer should select the laboratory room minimum and maximum airflow ventilation rates (including both supply and transfer airflows) using a room air balance spreadsheet mentioned earlier. Limiting total building exhaust airflows to the minimum values and therefore reducing the associated fan energy consumption becomes the motivation to use terminal VAV systems.

ANSI/AIHI Z9.5 requires that fume hoods be provided with a flow-measuring device, and all fume hood control system manufacturers provide a means for local indication and alarming of airflow. Typically, the fume hood controllers operate in a standalone mode to maintain the average face velocity setpoint. Although they operate independently, the fume hood controllers must share information with a central laboratory airflow control panel, including instantaneous fume hood airflow and alarms. Based on external overrides such as building occupancy setback and emergency modes of central air handling systems, the fume hood controllers can also drive the lab's general exhaust airflow. With VAV applications, the fume hood controls can also be utilized to allow users to drive the fume hood terminal box into full flow under emergency exhaust conditions. This emergency, or "purge," mode airflow should be set to the maximum design airflow quantity, and not to the maximum available system airflow. This is particularly important for large facilities with multiple VAV fume hoods, and labs where the maximum design airflow quantity is lower than the terminal box capacity (which is quite common when terminal box sizes are selected with airflow ranges that can be provided by multiple manufacturers), since driving terminal air valves with airflows larger than the design airflow requirement may divert airflow from other fume hoods during building maximum load conditions.

Fume hood control system suppliers frequently emphasize the competitive advantages associated with their specific products and identify issues such as control system speed of response, linearity, and actual airflow feedback in their marketing differentiation strategies. Although all of these issues are important and contribute to laboratory performance, the core requirement is contained in ASHRAE Standard 110, which defines the performance testing of laboratory fume hoods. A common rule of thumb for lab designers is that any combination of fume hoods, control systems, and terminal boxes that has not previously passed the ASHRAE 110 test should not be considered. Even if precedence has been established for a particular fume hood type, it should be specified that each fume hood type demonstrate ASHRAE 110 performance criteria.

A major question facing designers of laboratory control systems is whether to measure sash position or face velocity. Depending on the type, size, and complexity of the fume hood configuration, both may be required, and most fume hoods will allow the use of either method. The most prevailing method for fume hood containment control is sash position measurement to control average face velocity. However, some control system suppliers use sash position sensors exclusively, and have optimized the control system response to match the intrinsic characteristics of their control devices. The same is true for some systems which measure face velocity, which is typically performed using thermal dispersion sensors. One control system supplier uses an airflow sensor bar located along the length of the fume hood airfoil area in conjunction with a very low draft differential pressure transmitter to measure hood face velocity. A fume hood manufacturer, in partnership with another control equipment supplier, maintains that face velocity is not crucial—their position is that since fume hood containment is the issue, it can be controlled by measuring the pressure inside the fume hood cavity to maintain a vortex in the cavity. This vortex is maintained by adjusting the position of the baffle plates at the rear of the fume hood. Also, automatic fume hood sash closing systems have been developed to close the fume hood sashes when no user presence is detected in front of the fume hood sash. When the sash is closed, the fume hood average face velocity setpoint can be lowered as a means of reducing airflow and fan energy consumption while still maintaining containment.

Most potential weaknesses of laboratory control systems concern accuracy, response, and turndown, especially during very dynamic conditions. These issues must be addressed in every design. However, regardless of whether measuring sash position, face velocity, or vortex—with either feedback or feedforward control techniques, or with directly measured or derived airflow—the ASHRAE 110 test is certain to confirm fume hood system performance.

Once the need for VAV operation is established, a process of selecting the appropriate laboratory and fume hood airflow control system must include many technical as well as nontechnical issues. User bias to specific control suppliers and lack of clear information about alternatives may place significant constraints in the technical evaluation of available control system alternatives. Consequently, everyone involved in the control system design must be in agreement regarding all issues driving the design criteria.

After fume hood controls, the next issue of importance is laboratory pressurization control, which the ASHRAE 110 performance test does not address. For example, the laboratory supply terminal boxes may be controlled in response to changes in lab exhaust airflow in order to maintain the space at a negative pressure relative to its surroundings. The selection of materials for terminal air valves and associated sensors will have an effect on the durability and, consequently, the long-term accuracy of the control components. Terminal controls for chemical fume hoods should be made of stainless steel or have a corrosion-resistant coating. To reduce exhaust air corrosion effects, one control system supplier has replaced the standard pitot tube airflow-measuring device with a square edge orifice plate and a matching sensor and transmitter in all exhaust terminal air valves for laboratory applications.

The damper fail positions for laboratory terminal air valves during emergency scenarios, such as loss of damper pneumatic or electrical power, must be established to maximize the exhaust through fume hoods and to minimize the air supply in an effort to maintain room negative pressurization. Electrically operated terminal air valve damper actuators should fail in their last position, but when pneumatic damper actuators are used supply terminal air valves should fail to their minimum position. Exhaust-driven laboratory airflow controls, such as those for chemistry labs, will modulate a general exhaust damper to its minimum design airflow in response to changes in fume hood airflow. If general exhaust terminal air valves are used, they should fail to their closed or minimum position to allow all the exhaust airflow to go through the fume hood. It is advisable to close these dampers instead of attempting to control them below their minimally accurate airflow limit, which is dependent on the type of airflow sensor used. However, before the general exhaust can be closed, the supply airflow must be reduced by the same amount to maintain the room's pressure relationship, thereby compromising temperature control but not safety. The speed of response of supply and exhaust terminal air valve actuators will be based on whether the lab is air change-, hood-, or load-driven. Air change- and hood-driven labs require fast-acting actuators (three to six-second travel from minimum to maximum design airflow) and load-driven labs can operate with standard speed (60-second travel) actuators.

Once the minimum ventilation is provided for a lab, the supply air and possibly the general lab exhaust can be separately modulated above their established minimum airflows to maintain room temperature. The use of general exhaust terminal air valves is required

Example of a walk-in fume hood with airflow controls integrated with room-level pressurization at Johnson & Johnson PRD La Jolla, California site. *Courtesy of KlingStubbins. Photography © Tom Bonner 2007.*

if the thermal load is greater than the fume hood exhaust load. Although they are comfort-related and not a primary safety concern, general exhaust should be fully integrated into the laboratory control scheme due to the ever-increasing use of heat-generating electronic instrumentation in laboratories. The control of space temperature for comfort should remain important, particularly in large lab spaces with multiple thermostatic zones and nonhomogeneous airflow distribution.

The ideal laboratory control system design process occurs in a noncompetitive procurement environment in which the control system selected is matched to laboratory exhaust and ventilation requirements. Control system selection with competitive bidding will be driven by a single common denominator, which for properly designed projects is the minimum repeatable airflow measurement achievable by the airflow measuring devices provided with the laboratory air terminal air valves. This minimum airflow defines the terminal box turndown. This is critical because if airflow cannot be accurately measured across the full range of likely operation (or calculated or derived from damper position as in some control systems), the fume hood average face velocity and laboratory room pressurization cannot be reliably maintained.

The greatest limitations in airflow turndown are inherent in the pitot tube airflow stations provided with typical butterfly-type terminal air valves—their airflow turndown is limited to five to one. The use of more accurate airflow sensors with butterfly-type terminal boxes is also limited by the availability of sufficient straight length of upstream and downstream ductwork. The placement of some sensors in close proximity to butterfly dampers or duct fittings may cause measurement errors due to air turbulence. Other terminal boxes used for laboratory airflow and fume hood applications include venturi-type air valves and bladder damper-type terminal boxes. These terminal boxes provide greater airflow turndown than butterfly-type dampers, and permit the use of different airflow sensor types or provide airflow-related feedback signals if no sensors are used.

The turndown and control accuracy of the laboratory supply and general exhaust boxes should be similar to the turndown of the selected fume hood terminal box and controller. Even though a laboratory controller can be operated having supply and exhaust terminal exhaust controls with different turndowns, it will be simpler to determine the accuracy of the overall flow signals for laboratory airflow tracking, and to calculate the minimum ventilation requirements to maintain the laboratory space pressurization, if the same turndown is used for all terminal air valves.

The above description implies the use of volumetric airflow tracking between laboratory supply and exhaust. Volumetric flow tracking possesses certain limitations because it usually accounts for the transfer air from surrounding lab spaces with the doors closed. Opening of lab doors is usually considered a transient occurrence, and will affect the lab airflow dynamics unless it is addressed in the design. If room pressure measurements are not used, the laboratory control panel can monitor door status to adjust the lab airflow balance. Volumetric flow tracking presumes (1) the ability to reasonably characterize the laboratory room envelope, (2) the ability to determine the corresponding requirements to meet containment (through negative pressurization), and (3) that the laboratory envelope remains sufficiently stable with essentially constant leakage potential. If any of these assumptions become suspect, the rationale for airflow tracking to maintain pressurization for containment becomes severely flawed, and possibly inappropriate.

Although volumetric flow tracking is the most popular control technique used today in VAV laboratories, some control system suppliers employ another technique to maintain laboratory pressurization. This technique involves actively measuring and controlling the pressure differential between the lab and its surrounding spaces. However, active pressurization control of VAV labs should only be considered in concert with control system suppliers with extensive experience in pressure control and with those suppliers who have optimized their control algorithms to account for unexpected pressure fluctuations due to opening and closing of lab doors. Active pressure control can also be used to enhance flow tracking controls and for alarming and trending purposes.

The single most important safety and energy conservation activity that may be performed by lab occupants is keeping fume hood sashes closed when not in use, particularly during unoccupied periods in the laboratory. Lab designers should specify that fume hood monitoring controls include local alarms for when the hoods are left open. Some control system suppliers have related control features available, such as face velocity setback through the use of motion sensors or from lab occupancy signals. However, the setback setpoint should not place the fume hood airflow below the minimum required for containment, without generating a local alarm at the hood. Some laboratory controllers determine occupancy by the status of the room lighting circuits or by means of occupancy sensors—when room lights are off, or an unoccupied mode is detected, the airflow rates are set to the minimum limits. Understanding the safety issues and capabilities of the available control technology mentioned earlier and applying this information to the laboratory HVAC design is the key to providing a safe and energy-efficient laboratory environment.

U.S. Food and Drug Administration, Life Sciences Laboratory, White Oak, Maryland

Chilled water supply temperature from the central utility plant will reset from 39°F in warm or humid weather conditions to 45°F when the outdoor wet-bulb temperature drops below 42°F. This not only allows the chillers to operate at higher efficiencies in the winter, but also allows the chilled water coils in 100 percent outside-air units to be used as preheat coils for the building and for free cooling for the central plant. By controlling the chilled water control valves to a 100 percent open position, and using the 45°F chilled water, the coil can serve as a preheat coil and deliver a leaving air temperature of 43°F, even when the outside air temperature is as low as 0°F. Once the air temperature rises several degrees, as a result of heat from the draw-through supply

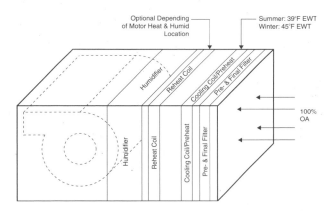

Schematic of the U.S. Food and Drug Administration (U.S. FDA) Life Sciences Laboratory air handling unit design, at the White Oak, Maryland site, utilizing one water coil for cooling and preheating, reducing fan energy consumption and capital costs. *Image courtesy of KlingStubbins.*

The U.S. Food and Drug Administration Life Sciences Laboratory in White Oak, Maryland. *Courtesy of KlingStubbins. Photography by Ron Solomon—Baltimore ©2008.*

Lay-out of utilities from a central plant to the U.S. FDA campus in White Oak, Maryland. *Image courtesy of KlingStubbins.*

continued

fans, the air handling unit supply temperature is within a few degrees of the normal summer leaving air temperature. A hot water reheat coil mounted in the air handling unit trims the temperature up to the winter leaving air temperature.

During winter operation the lower chilled water return temperature (as low as 35°F) is mixed with the higher chilled water return temperature (typically 59°F) from recirculated air handling units in the lab building and from other buildings to provide a mixed return temperature to the central plant that at times requires no chillers to run to maintain the 45°F chilled water supply temperature.

Air Distribution Efficiency

Minimization of fan energy consumption is important because it is a large component of the total energy use in laboratories. Some strategies to reduce air distribution energy are low pressure drop system design, efficient fan and belt drive selection, specifying high-efficiency motors, and minimizing duct air leakage.

Fan efficiency is defined as the ratio of the power beneficially used to increase the air pressure to the fan motor power demand. Using the highest efficiency fan causes the lowest annual fan energy usage. Several fan selections are available to meet a given airflow and pressure requirement. Selection of the fan can be made on the basis of lowest initial cost, optimum point on the performance curve, or highest efficiency. The selection process should include assessing the initial cost of the highest-efficiency fan (to ensure there is a reasonable payback period for this selection) and ensuring that the highest-efficiency fan resides in a stable region of the performance curve, both at peak and off-peak operating conditions. Better aerodynamic performance of the fan causes the higher efficiency and also generally results in a fan with a lower sound power level, which translates to a lower sound pressure level in the lab. Fan efficiency is defined in terms of "brake horsepower," which is the amount of work required just to turn the fan shaft. Another multiplicative efficiency component is the power transmission loss—

the amount of energy lost by motor inefficiency and belt losses. Methods to reduce this energy loss are described next.

For belt-driven fans, there are two popular types of belt drives—flat and synchronous. A flat belt has a trapezoidal bottom shape and sits in a groove in a pulley—friction between the belt and the bottom and sides of the pulley causes power to be transmitted from the motor to the fan. A synchronous belt improves on this concept by incorporating teeth in the bottom of the belt that engage mating teeth in the pulley. Power is transmitted through this tooth system more efficiently because belt slip, which uses energy but does not transmit power, is reduced. Although synchronous belts and pulleys have a higher initial cost than flat belts, a payback is generated because of elevated efficiency and longer life.

Direct-drive fan technology couples the motor and fan directly, without using a belt. Power transmission loss is reduced because there is no belt-related energy loss. Selection is sometimes limited in larger fan sizes—one alternative is to use multiple small direct-drive fans in lieu of one large fan. As noted above, a variable-speed drive reduces fan speed under off-peak operating conditions. Selecting the fan speed to match the actual system pressure is desirable. If the system pressure is higher than calculated, the fan speed should be increased to meet the airflow requirement. For a belt-driven fan, this is accomplished by replacing either the fan or motor pulley. This step is more difficult for direct-drive fans.

Motors convert electrical energy into mechanical energy in the form of a rotating shaft, which then rotates the fan shaft (either through a belt or directly). The motor's conversion process has some inefficiency, which should be minimized. The National Electrical Manufacturers' Association (NEMA) has generated a rating standard that allows member companies to label motors as "premium efficiency"—this standard is defined in Standard MG-1–2006 and efficiency values are contained in Tables 12–12 and 12–13NEMA Standard MG-1 2006.

Except under very special circumstances, duct systems that convey air through buildings are not designed to be leak-tight. The rate at which air leaks out of ductwork should be controlled under the design process, because the fan is sized for the amount of air required at the room level ("sum of terminals" airflow), plus the amount of air that leaks out of the duct into the ceiling space or mechanical room. The amount of leaked air is not used beneficially by the lab, but has used cooling, heating, and fan energy. Although duct leakage is an issue across all building types, it is more significant in labs because of the higher airflow volumes, the use of 100 percent outside air, and because of the higher system pressures (deeper cooling coils and higher-

efficiency filters). The Sheet Metal and Air-Conditioning Contractors' National Association (SMACNA) has developed the *HVAC Air Duct Leakage Test Manual* to assist engineers and contractors in specifying duct leakage rates and conducting duct leak tests. Duct leakage can be specified either by percentage of leakage (e.g., the duct system can leak up to 3 percent of the design airflow) or by a specific leakage rate, which is a leakage rate per unit duct surface area, multiplied by the pressure to the power of 0.65.

Independent of the specified duct leakage allowance, ducts should be leak-tested after installation. This process consists of pressurizing the duct section under testing to the specified design pressure that corresponds to the pressure that the duct section will see under operation. Because duct systems in lab facilities are typically large, they are often tested in sections, and the duct leakage airflow is prorated for the duct section being tested. In addition to the air leakage from ductwork, air is similarly wasted through air handling units, variable volume terminal boxes, reheat coils, dampers, and other devices. This leakage is generally not part of the duct leakage test, since the mechanical contractor has no control over it. This equipment leakage allowance should be specified and added to the duct leakage allowance to form a system duct leakage allowance, which is added to the fan airflow requirement.

U.S. Food and Drug Administration, Engineering & Physics Laboratory, White Oak, Maryland

The U.S. FDA Engineering Physics provides FDA researchers a facility to study and approve radiological devices. The design of the air handling units and air distribution systems balances flexibility and energy efficiency. Distribution systems (supply, return, and exhaust) were designed as variable air volume to afford flexibility for future redesign of labs primarily by providing accessibility to the duct systems throughout the facilities.

continued

Air handling systems provide additional fan capacity to accommodate changing 10 percent of the lab area in the building currently designed with recirculated air to 100 percent exhausted labs in the future, and to accommodate changing 10 percent of the 100 percent exhausted labs to recirculated air labs in the future. The branch ductwork coming out of the shaft at each floor was sized to accommodate making any floor either 100 percent exhausted or 100 percent recirculated air.

A modular lay-out of air distribution devices and uniformity to the branch duct lay-out was provided, with each laboratory module provided with a dedicated supply and exhaust or return terminal box. Wet labs or biology labs were provided with exhaust boxes while electronics labs were provided with return boxes.

The manifolded fume hood exhaust fan system was designed to accommodate an average of two additional fume hoods per floor, with the ductwork on each floor designed to accommodate an additional four fume hoods per floor.

Four 50,000-cfm custom air handling units supply laboratory and office spaces on the ground through the fourth floor. Each unit was sized at 50 percent of peak load capacity for the half of the building it serves. The two units serving each half of the building are manifolded together and distribute to supply, return air, and general exhaust air risers serving all spaces on the ground through the fourth floors.

Each air handling unit has four fans: supply air, return air, outside air fan, and general exhaust air. Each unit is provided with a 0.3-nm molecular sieve desiccant-coated energy recovery wheel.

The U.S. Food and Drug Administration Engineering & Physics Laboratory in White Oak, Maryland. *Courtesy of KlingStubbins. Photography by Ron Solomon—Baltimore.* © 2008.

Underfloor Air Distribution

As an alternative to more conventional overhead air delivery systems, underfloor air distribution (UFAD) can be used to reduce the fan power required to deliver air to occupied zones. This technology routes supply air through the cavity space created between an access tile floor and the concrete slab. Relative to overhead air distribution, UFAD decreases supply fan energy for two reasons: (1) Less air is used because convective cooling loads that occur higher than 8 feet above the floor are not offset by supply air, and (2) the pressure drop through the underfloor plenum is less than the pressure drop through an equivalent amount of ductwork in an overhead-type system.

Air is delivered to the room through floor-mounted diffusers at 63°F; since supply air is close to occupants, the temperature is elevated to minimize drafts, resulting in cooling compressor energy savings and increased usage of airside economizer controls. Internal heat gains heat air from its supply temperature, making the air more buoyant and driving it passively

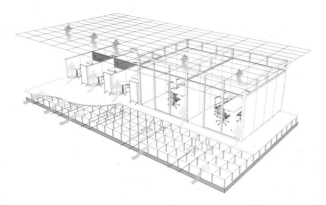

Room stratification with UFAD systems. *Image courtesy of KlingStubbins.*

into the return air system. The room volume higher than 8 feet above the floor is not directly conditioned—the room temperature setpoint is only maintained in the occupied zone. The heat gains that occur above 8 feet are not counted in the room load calculation, since air does not have to be supplied to the room to offset that gain. For tall rooms, this represents a significant airflow reduction.

UFAD technology has not been applied to research labs because there is a concern that air delivered at the floor will drive contaminants into workers' breath-

ing zones—the optimum air pattern moves contaminants into containment devices and away from workers. However, separate office portions of lab buildings may make good candidates for UFAD systems.

Chilled Beams

Ceiling-mounted chilled beams are a decentralized method of offsetting the cooling load. Passive chilled beams create a convection current due to the difference in density between the cooled air and room air, which forces air across a chilled water coil. Active chilled beams use supply air to assist in creating the convection current which forces air across a chilled water coil.

Chilled water supplied to chilled beams is reset to a higher temperature (e.g., 60°F). Often, this occurs by mixing return chilled water back into the supply chilled water line with a pump to create the higher-temperature water. A more efficient concept is to select chillers to produce the higher-temperature water. One approach is to apply two chillers in series. The first chiller cools chilled water from its return temperature to the chilled beam temperature—this chilled water is then dedicated to chilled beams. The

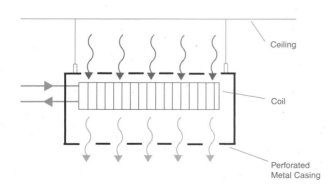
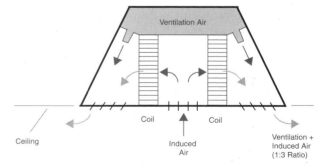

Passive (left) and active (right) chilled beams. *Courtesy of © ASHRAE Journal Vol. 49, Jan. 2006.*

second chiller in series cools chilled water from the chilled beam supply temperature (e.g., 60°F) to the chilled water supply temperature required by the cooling coil for dehumidification (e.g., 44°F) and is pumped to cooling coils in air handling units. The economic viability of this concept depends on the distance from the chilled water plant to the laboratory. If the central plant is remote from the laboratory, the economics are less favorable because two pairs of chilled water lines (one for chilled beams, one for air handling units) are required.

The higher chilled water supply temperature (above room dew point temperature) maintains the chilled beams as sensible heat transfer devices, preventing condensation above occupied areas. A feedback loop controls the room temperature in each zone with a temperature sensor modulating a control valve in each chilled beam.

Because chilled beams use chilled water to locally cool spaces, the airflow is significantly reduced relative to an all-air system. The construction cost considerations are:

- Because the chilled beam system uses less airflow, the air handling unit, ductwork quantity, and variable-volume box count is reduced.

- A chilled water piping system must be extended throughout the building to supply the chilled beams.

- The building automation system (BAS) point count rises somewhat for the chilled beam technology, although the VAV box count is reduced, each chilled beam has a modulating control valve, which requires analog signals for room temperature input and signal output.

- Potentially, the floor-to-floor height can be reduced, corresponding to a reduction in ductwork.

The energy cost considerations are:

- Less airflow requires less fan power.

- If a chilled water system dedicated to chilled beams can be used, then there is potentially a net reduction in chilled water energy.

- For office areas, the air economizer mode is not available (since the ductwork is only sized for ventilation needs). Mechanical refrigeration must be used in the shoulder seasons to cool the building (instead of using outside air directly). However, a water-side

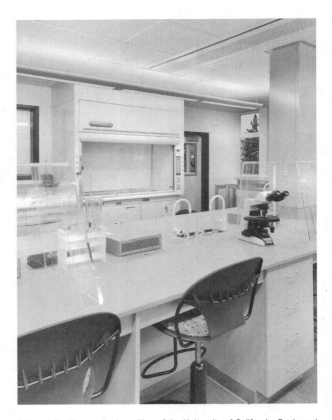

Active chilled beams in the ceiling of the University of California, Davis and Sierra Nevada College's Tahoe Center for Environmental Sciences (TCES) at Incline Village, Nevada. *Image courtesy of Collaborative Design Studio, Architects and © ASHRAE Journal Vol. 49, Jan. 2006.*

economizer may be used more frequently because of the elevated chilled water supply temperature.

Other issues associated with chilled beams are:

- Because less airflow is supplied in the chilled beam model, the rooms are more easily able to achieve a lower sound pressure level (relative to an all-air system). If an all-air system was modified to achieve the same sound pressure level as that achieved by a chilled beam system, then the building cost would increase to account for additional sound attenuation features.

- Chilled beams are lower-maintenance devices than VAV boxes; there are no flow meters to calibrate or dampers to service. Although an advantage, it is difficult to quantify this effect in an owner-maintained facility because the staff count remains the same.

One of the first laboratories in the United States to use chilled beams was the Tahoe Center for Environmental Sciences (TCES) in Incline Village, Nevada. TCES was designed by Collaborative Design Studio, Architects and Rumsey Engineers and opened in August 2006. The 47,000-square-foot facility is a joint venture between the University of California, Davis, and Sierra Nevada College. The LEED Platinum building houses research and teaching laboratories for studying the Lake Tahoe environment as well as classrooms, seminar rooms, and faculty offices for the Environmental Sciences curriculum offered by Sierra Nevada College.

Active chilled beams are used in all labs except for two of the most cooling-intensive labs, which supplement with fan coil units for peak periods. Ventilation air is supplied at 68°F when outside air temperatures

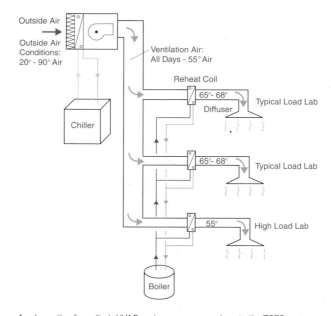

A schematic of the installed TCES system indicating major design criteria and components. *Image courtesy of Collaborative Design Studio, Architects and © ASHRAE Journal Vol. 49, Jan. 2006.*

A schematic of an all-air HVAC system as a comparison to the TCES system. *Image courtesy of Collaborative Design Studio, Architects and © ASHRAE Journal Vol. 49, Jan. 2006.*

are above 68°F. The active chilled beams use 55 to 60°F chilled water generated by a free-cooling system. When the outside air temperature is below 55°F, outside air is heated to 55°F and ventilation air is reheated at each lab. When outside air temperatures are between 55 and 70°F, outside air is not treated and chilled beams provide heating or cooling as needed by each individual lab.

This strategy of decoupling the ventilation and heating/cooling requirements reduced the air handling units and ductwork by 33 percent. Although there was a significant reduction in ducting, shafts, and air handling unit costs, the chilled beam costs were high (they had never been used in Nevada, and contractors and regulatory agencies were unfamiliar with the product). The net effect was that the installed system cost was comparable to a conventional all-air solution.

Several other strategies were integrated into the building design, including:

• Energy recovery from the exhaust air stream;

• Co-generation system which reclaims waste heat to preheat outside air;

• 100 percent free-cooling chilled water system that manufactures and then stores chilled water in tanks in cool evening hours;

• 30 kW photovoltaic system that covers 10 percent of the electricity demand of the building.

The Tahoe climate does not require as much cooling as many other climates, as the building is located at an elevation of 6,600 feet. In climates with more hours of heating and cooling, the reduction in outside air will result in further heating and cooling savings. In climates where more cooling hours are present, savings from reheat reduction will be greater. Where significant dehumidification is required, savings from reducing reheat can be maintained by a runaround coil that provides precooling and free reheat in the ventilation air handling unit (Rumsey and Weale 2007, 18–25). The fact that the project achieved LEED Platinum certification indicates that there were many other sustainable strategies involved in this design. These strategies included extensive daylighting, hydronic heating, incorporation of photovoltaic panels, site and landscape strategies, and water reclamation. For additional information about the project, see Color Insert Figures C-37 through C-40.

	Standard System Design	Active Chilled Beam Design
OA Air Handler Sizing	27,000 cfm	18,000 cfm
Ductwork	37,500 lb	30,000 lb
Exhaust Fan Capacity	27,000 cfm	18,000 cfm
Cooling System Capacity	35 tons	20 tons
Floor to Ceiling Height[1]	9 ft	10 ft
Mechanical System[2] Cost	$741,000	$722,000

1. Floor-to-floor height kept constant; active chilled beam allowed for ceiling to be raised 1 foot.

2. Laboratory portion of the building is 10,000 square feet or 25 percent of the building. HVAC costs include laboratory system

Table comparing the capacities of a conventional all-air system and the installed system at the TCES lab in Incline Village, Nevada. *Image courtesy of Collaborative Design Studio, Architects and © ASHRAE Journal Vol. 49, Jan. 2006.*

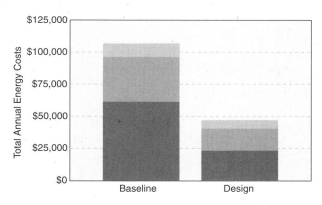

Comparison of the TCES energy consumption with the baseline building defined in Appendix G of ASHRAE Standard 90.1. *Image courtesy of Collaborative Design Studio, Architects and © ASHRAE Journal Vol. 49, Jan. 2006.*

The runaround heat recovery system conserves energy and reduces operating costs by reducing the load on the preheat coil (winter) and cooling coil (summer). *Image courtesy of KlingStubbins.*

Glycol Runaround Exhaust Air Energy Recovery

This technology consists of heat transfer coils mounted in the outside air and exhaust air streams, with a glycol/water mixture pumped between the two coils. The exhaust air heats the glycol during the winter and cools the glycol during the summer, then transfers that energy to the outside air stream.

The room-temperature (e.g., 74°F) exhaust air heats the glycol/water mixture in the exhaust heat transfer coil to 45°F. The glycol/water mixture is then pumped to a coil in the air handling unit, where the glycol/water mixture preheats outside air to 20°F. In the process, the glycol/water mixture is cooled from 45 to 35°F and returns to the exhaust coil to repeat the process. The reverse process occurs in the summer—the glycol/water mixture is cooled by the exhaust air stream and then cools the outside air stream.

The feasibility of glycol runaround heat recovery systems is dependent upon current electricity and fuel costs, forecasted inflation rates of electricity and fuel, system expense, and climate. Also, some mature

laboratory sites want to maintain annual boiler emissions at or under current levels in order to comply with state and federal regulations. One strategy to reduce emissions levels is to reduce the amount of steam used by the site, which reduces the amount of fuel burned (and therefore emissions created). Implementing heat recovery technology can be part of this strategy. An owner may even want to install an energy recovery system to demonstrate good corporate citizenship even if the project does not meet a hurdle rate.

Glycol runaround heat recovery systems are sensitive to current and forecasted electricity and fuel costs because the majority of savings (except in hot climates) is derived from preheating outside air, thereby reducing the preheat coil demand. This results in a thermal savings tied to the fuel used at the site (e.g., natural gas or oil). Cooling savings also occur, thereby reducing the chiller demand (which is typically electrically driven). The typical effectiveness of a glycol runaround heat recovery system is in the range of 45 to 55 percent. However, there is an operating cost associated with the additional resistance of the outside air and exhaust air coils—fan power increases to overcome the resistance to airflow presented by the outside air and exhaust air coils.

Heat recovery systems are efficient at extreme outside air temperatures (i.e., very hot or very cold), since the log mean temperature difference (LMTD) is higher and causes more heat transfer per coil surface area. This results in these systems being more cost-effective in climates where there is a longer duration of hot or cold outside air temperatures (e.g., Canada). In more temperate climates (e.g., the northeastern United States), there are relatively few hours when it is very hot or cold, and many hours when the temperature is between 40 and 60°F. The heat exchange process is less efficient in that range of outside air temperatures, which makes the economics of heat recovery less promising—the beneficial heat recovery rate is low, but the parasitic losses (glycol/water mixture pumping and fan power increase) remain virtually constant. In colder climates, there are more hours at

the lower end of the distribution, which causes more energy to be recovered.

There are several strategies to enhance heat recovery economics in shoulder seasons. Air may be bypassed around the outside air and exhaust air coils when the heat recovery rate is low. This reduces the resistance to airflow associated with the coils, but has the downside of being more space-intensive. Also, the glycol/water mixture pump can be de-energized when the beneficial cost of recovering energy is less than the electricity cost to pump the glycol/water mixture.

Another concept to improve the economics of heat recovery is to evaporatively cool the exhaust air stream by spraying water into the exhaust air before it enters the coil during the summer. Water sprayed into the air stream will evaporate, and the energy to

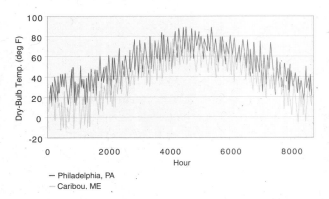

Temperature data for two climates for comparing the economics of heat recovery. *Image courtesy of KlingStubbins.*

Rooftop-mounted exhaust air runaround heat recovery units atop a research facility. *Image courtesy of KlingStubbins. Photography © Sam Fentress.*

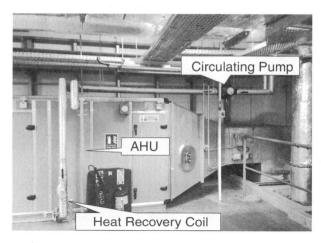

The Alza Corporation manufacturing site in Cashel, Ireland installed a glycol runaround heat recovery system which has demonstrated a 42 percent internal rate of return on its $220,000 investment. *Image courtesy of Johnson & Johnson.*

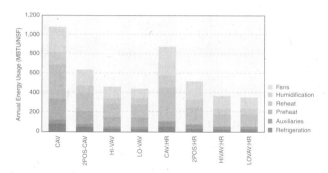

The savings available from a combination of airflow reduction and energy recovery technologies. *Image courtesy of KlingStubbins.*

cause this liquid-to-vapor phase change comes from the air itself. This has the net effect of suppressing the exhaust air temperature when it arrives at the coil. The lower exhaust air temperature increases the log mean temperature difference and increases the heat

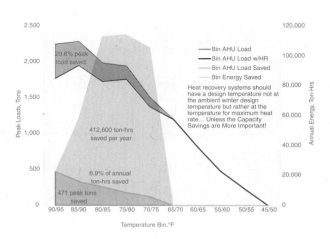

The peak demand reduction and annual energy savings available from a glycol runaround heat recovery system. *Image courtesy of KlingStubbins.*

recovery rate. Evaporative cooling also extends the number of hours when heat recovery is economically feasible.

Heat Pipe Exhaust Air Energy Recovery

Heat pipes consist of sealed copper tubes, filled with refrigerant that span the exhaust and outside air streams. The room temperature exhaust air vaporizes the refrigerant, which then flows to the opposite end of the tube (in the outside air stream) due to the vapor pressure difference between the liquid and vapor phases. The outside air then condenses the refrigerant from a vapor to a liquid, which then flows by gravity back to the evaporator. The vapor-to-liquid phase change causes the refrigerant to lose energy, which is transferred to the outside air stream. The reverse process occurs in the summer. The heat pipe heat transfer process is more efficient (relative to glycol runaround) and is passive because there is no pump or piping system, as in the glycol runaround system. The typical effectiveness of a heat pipe system ranges from 45 to 60 percent.

Because the heat pipe system uses gravity to drive refrigerant flow, the heat pipe must be installed

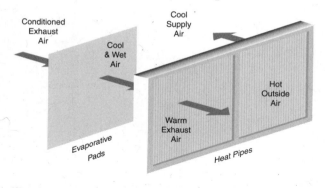

Heat pipe energy recovery concept with evaporative precooling of exhaust air. *Image courtesy of NREL, Labs21®.*

Heat transfer process within heat pipe refrigerant tubes. *Image courtesy of KlingStubbins.*

horizontally, and the distance between the supply and exhaust air streams is limited to 3 feet. If the distance exceeds 3 feet the refrigerant must be pumped between the coils—this approach has a history of service problems.

Heat pipes can be used as indirect evaporative coolers, in which water is sprayed on the exhaust side of the heat pipe to cool the outside air. This application has been successful at the Process and Environmental Technology Laboratory at Sandia National Laboratories in Albuquerque, New Mexico. At the 120,000-square-foot Fox Chase Cancer Center in Philadelphia, Pennsylvania, heat pipes with bypass sections were installed in two 30,000-cfm air handling units. The incremental cost for heat pipes with the indirect evaporative cooling option on the exhaust was $300,000. Anticipated energy cost savings were $72,510, resulting in a simple payback of four years.

One goal of the design of mechanical systems for laboratory facilities is to minimize the probability of reentrainment of exhaust air fumes into the outside air intakes. One strategy used to achieve this goal is

to provide separation between the exhaust stack and the outside air intake louver (this will be discussed in more detail at the end of this section). However, the heat pipe requires the exhaust and outside air streams to be adjacent to each other, which does not allow the separation technique.

Exhaust Air Energy Recovery by Energy Wheels

This technology consists of a desiccant material built into a segmented wheel shape that rotates at a low speed (15 rpm) through the outside air and exhaust air streams. As exhaust air passes through the energy wheel in the winter, the desiccant material is heated and adsorbs water vapor—as the wheel rotates through the outside air stream, heat and water vapor are transferred to the outside air. This preheats and prehumidifies outside air, therefore saving energy. The reverse process occurs in the summer. The system is more efficient (relative to other heat recovery technologies), since both sensible (temperature-related) and latent (moisture-related) heat transfer occur. The effectiveness of an energy wheel is generally around 55 to 70 percent.

Energy wheels rotate between the exhaust and outside air streams, and therefore have a potential issue of cross-contamination in lab applications. A few techniques have been developed to minimize the probability of travel of material from the exhaust air into the outside air. First, a coating with 0.3 nanometer (nm) pores is applied over the dessicant, using molecular sieve technology. Molecules with kinetic diameters larger than the pore size cannot penetrate into the honeycomb-shaped dessicant material and pass through the energy wheel. The 0.3-nm pore size was selected to allow water molecules (0.25 nm) through, but to exclude virus and bacteria, which have a diameter several orders of magnitude higher. High molecular-weight molecules such as solvents also have a higher diameter and cannot penetrate the pore into the dessicant. Because ammonia molecules have a diameter less than 0.3 nm, special labs with a high concentration of ammonia are at higher risk of cross-contamination. Second, labyrinth seals close off the opening in the casing between the outside and exhaust air streams. Labyrinth seals present a circuitous route to the air that could travel from the exhaust air to the outside air stream. This route presents a high pressure drop to the air, making airflow through the seal difficult. Because the labyrinth seal does not physically touch the rotating wheel, wear is reduced. Air is also directed to each "wedge" of the wheel just as it is ready to pass into the outside air stream to purge contaminants from the wheel segment. Lastly, supply and exhaust fans may be arranged so that the exhaust air pressure is lower than the outside air pressure at the wheel, causing air to flow from the cleaner outside air stream to the more contaminated exhaust air stream.

Testing by Georgia Tech Research Institute sponsored by energy wheel manufacturer Semco shows zero contamination for 0.3 nm energy wheels for compounds typically found in R&D facilities— isopropanol, methanol, acetaldehyde, methyl isobutyl, ketone, xylene, carbon dioxide, propane, and sulfur hexafluoride.

The Ross Research Institute at Johns Hopkins University in Baltimore, Maryland, installed energy wheels to precondition 300,000 cfm of outside air. The chiller and boiler loads have been reduced by 50 percent and 75 percent, respectively, relative to the demand required if energy wheels were not used. No air quality issues have been identified, even though a mercaptoethanol spill occurred. Although mercaptoethanol can be perceived at a concentration of 3 parts per trillion, the odor was eliminated from the building in about 20 minutes. The system annual maintenance requirement consists of semi-annual bearing lubrication and inspection. The Whitehead Biomedical Research Building at Emory University in Atlanta, Georgia, uses energy recovery wheels: The installation cost for the wheels was reported at $425,000, with annual energy savings estimated at $125,000.

Comparison of Energy Recovery Technologies

In 2002, an analysis of energy recovery wheels, heat pipes, and runaround loops was performed for Laboratories for the 21st Century. It analyzed a typical 100,000-square-foot laboratory in four locations: Minneapolis, Denver, Seattle, and Atlanta. The simulation assumed a constant-volume air distribution system. Electricity rates included an energy charge of 3 cents per kWh, a peak demand charge of $7/kW, and an off-peak demand charge of $4/kW. Natural gas cost was $6/million Btu. The most significant findings were (EPA 2003, 6):

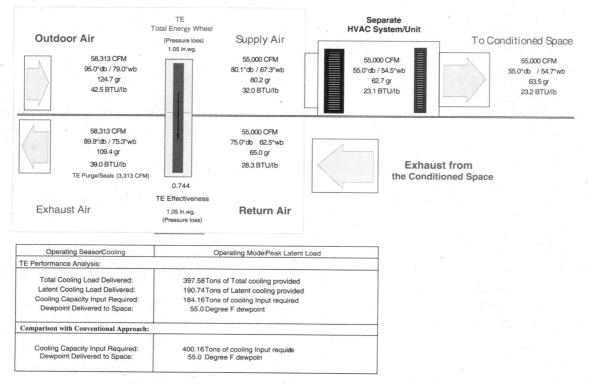

Cooling (left) and heating (right) desiccant energy recovery wheel performance data. *Image courtesy of © SEMCO Incorporated.*

- Air-to-air energy recovery reduces natural gas consumption for space heating and dehumidification reheat by more than 35 percent in all climates.

- Savings in peak electricity demand associated with an energy recovery wheel depend on climate—no demand savings were predicted for heat pipes and glycol runaround systems.

- Annual energy cost savings are $0.27 to $1.95/cfm of fan airflow. Energy recovery wheels, with sensible and latent heat recovery, appeared cost-effective in

all climates. The cost savings obtained with heat pipes and runaround loops are relatively small in warm, humid climates.

- Only in the hot, humid climate of Atlanta did annual electricity savings occur with the energy recovery wheel; in other climates, the increase in annual fan energy offset the annual electricity savings.

- The greatest reduction (approximately 20 percent) in chiller size occurs with energy recovery wheels in humid climates; the savings are approximately half

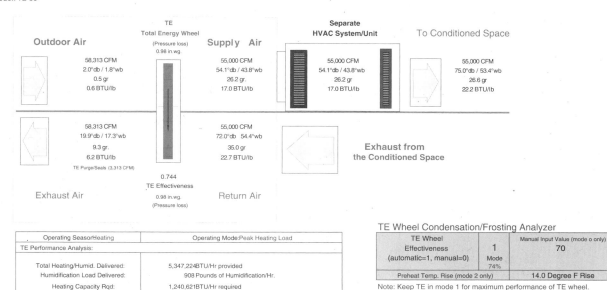

Model: TE-56

TE Wheel Condensation/Frosting Analyzer		
TE Wheel Effectiveness (automatic=1, manual=0)	1 Mode 74%	Manual Input Value (mode o only) 70
Preheat Temp. Rise (mode 2 only)		14.0 Degree F Rise

Note: Keep TE in mode 1 for maximum performance of TE wheel.
Use mode 0 to modulate performance to avoid condensation/frost
Use mode 2, providing maximum performance with preheat, to avoid
condensation/frost when extreme conditions are encountered

Operating Season:Heating	Operating Mode:Peak Heating Load
TE Performance Analysis:	
Total Heating/Humid. Delivered:	5,347,224 BTU/Hr provided
Humidification Load Delivered:	908 Pounds of Humidification/Hr.
Heating Capacity Rqd:	1,240,621 BTU/Hr required
Humidification Capacity Rqd:	15,526 BTU/Hr required
Comparison with Conventional Approach:	
Heating/Humid. Capacity Required:	5,347,224 BTU/Hr required

this amount with sensible-only recovery devices. In the dry Denver climate, the potential reduction is 10 percent with all three devices.

- The minimum reduction in boiler size is 15 percent with any of the devices. If the building is also being humidified in the winter, the additional latent energy recovery with energy recovery wheels results in up to a 50 percent reduction in heating and humidification requirements.

Low Pressure Drop Air Distribution

The supply fan in a laboratory application is sized to overcome many resistances, such as outside air intake louvers, filtration, preheat, heat recovery, and

cooling coils, supply ductwork, variable air volume (VAV) terminal boxes, and diffusers. Designing a low pressure drop air distribution system offers considerable savings, since fan energy is a large component of the total energy use in an R&D facility. The two largest

	Minneapolis	Denver	Seattle	Atlanta
Enthalpy Wheel	65%	58%	49%	48%
Enthalpy Wheel w/VAV	75%	64%	62%	68%
Heat pipe	41%	36%	41%	36%
Run-around loop	44%	36%	42%	38%
Enthalpy Wheel	3 W/sf	1 W/sf	0	3 W/sf
Enthalpy Wheel w/VAV	3 W/sf	1 W/sf	0	4 W/sf
Enthalpy Wheel	$1.59	$0.96	$0.55	$0.59
Enthalpy Wheel w/VAV	$1.95	$1.19	$0.82	$1.00
Heat pipe	$0.86	$0.56	$0.41	$0.27
Run-around loop	$0.91	$0.52	$0.41	$0.32

Labs21® energy recovery study results indicating savings in terms of gas consumption (percent), peak electrical demand (W/sf), and total energy cost ($). *Image courtesy of NREL, Labs21®.*

elements listed above are filtration and coils. Supply air to laboratories should be relatively clean so that another variable is not introduced into the scientific results. This results in a requirement that the filters in air handling units supplying laboratories should have a high efficiency—they should capture a high percentage of incident particles. Filters may be selected at a lower velocity so that the air pressure drop is reduced.

Air handling units for office buildings are often sized at a velocity of 500 fpm—a general limitation is that face velocities greater than that will cause moisture carryover from the coil into the air stream. For lab facilities, air handling units process 100 percent outside air, so the cooling coil sees a higher wet-bulb temperature and the probability of carryover is greater. Therefore, the face velocity is often 450 fpm. The pressure drop is a function of the face velocity to the power of 1.65, which results in a significant fan energy savings if the air handling unit face velocity was decreased to 300 fpm. Although the capital expense of this approach is higher (the air handling units are larger), the economics are driven by the continuous operation of these units (compared to an office system which is generally off during unoccupied periods).

Ductwork is often sized for a constant friction loss—a common rule of thumb is 0.1 inches water per 100 feet of duct length. If this criteria is relaxed to 0.05 inches water per 100 feet of duct length (with minimum and maximum velocity constraints), then the pressure drop due to friction through the air distribution path may be decreased.

Demand-Controlled Ventilation

Office buildings commonly employ demand-based ventilation to reduce airflow. In high-density spaces such as conference rooms, carbon dioxide concentrations may be measured as an indicator of occupancy level. If the carbon dioxide concentration in a conference room is low, indicating a lower-than-design occupancy, the supply airflow to that room may be reset downward during low load conditions. This concept may be utilized in a laboratory if total volatile organic compounds (TVOCs) and particulates are measured as indicators of cleanliness.

Gordon Sharp conducted a study concerning the relationship between TVOC concentration, particulate count, and dilution (air change rate) in 18 geographically diverse North American laboratories, including 300 lab rooms that were intended to represent a wide cross-section of lab environments (primarily life science research spaces as well as a few smaller chemistry and physical-science labs). The majority of the study involved spaces with a low to medium fume hood density. Approximately 1.5 million operating hours of data between fall 2006 and winter 2009 were acquired from these spaces. This resulted in the analysis of more than 20 million sensor values, including data on TVOCs, particulates (with a size range of 0.3 to 2.5 micrometers), carbon dioxide, and dew point temperature. For both TVOCs and particles, measurements were taken to determine the difference between the measured concentrations in the room and in the supply air to reduce potential effects of sensor drift as well as to remove the effect of outdoor conditions on the measured room conditions. Since room and supply air concentrations were measured by the same sensor, this process ensured the accuracy of the study findings.

The TVOC sensor data was organized by the number of times that nine threshold values were exceeded. The data was then analyzed to determine the percentage of time the data exceeded these thresholds.

When these values are graphed, they form a cumulative summary indicating the percent of time that each bin value was exceeded. Generally, the typical minimum dilution rate in the labs studied was between two and six air changes per hour. When significant levels of TVOCs or particulates were sensed, the airflow rate was commanded to between 12 and 16 air changes per hour. Airflow rates higher than the minimum may have also occurred due to the opening of fume hoods or instances of high heat gains.

The results of the study showed that the labs have very low (less than 0.2 ppm) TVOC concentrations for 99.5 percent of the time, indicating the potential for energy savings by operating at reduced minimum dilution rates for the vast majority of the time. However, another parameter that can increase the dilution rate is an increase in particulates in the lab. This may be caused by an unusual reaction or acid spill that generates smoke or aerosol. Typically a level of 1 million particles per cubic foot (pcf) is used as the threshold for increasing the minimum dilution airflow rate. The study demonstrated that the average lab

room environment is above the 1 million pcf threshold almost 0.4 percent of the time, or about 30 minutes per week on average. Therefore, the amount of time that either TVOCs or particulate levels are above the control threshold is only 1.0 percent of the total time.

When 1.5 million hours of operating data were assessed, the lab indoor environmental quality conditions permitted substantial reductions in dilution (air change) rates taking into account both TVOC and particle contaminants and assuming average conditions. Energy consumption was then reduced approximately 99 percent of the time. The average lab experienced only 1.5 hours per week in which environmental conditions drove an increase in the air change rate. The data was also compared to demonstrate variations in the data among different sites. Data analysis showed that a demand-control ventilation concept can operate and thus save energy about 98 percent of the time. Even at the worst-case site with the greatest amount of TVOC and particle activity, it was found that the minimum room dilution rate would only be increased to respond to TVOC events for 3.5 hours per week (Sharp 2009, 21–27).

Increase Return Air from Labs

For systems that are supplied from a central air handling system, air is returned from each room to the air handling units to be reprocessed and supplied to the rooms again. If air was returned from labs, a spill in one lab would be returned to the central air handling units and supplied to all other labs served by those units. This causes a spill in one lab to become an event in many other areas. This is the driver for using 100 percent outside air (no return air) in labs, although it is more energy-intensive. However, labs should be examined on an individual basis to determine if air can be safely returned, which would repre-

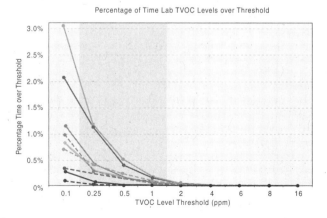

Average TVOC concentrations at multiple lab sites during 1.5 million recorded hours. *Image courtesy of Gordon P. Sharp, Aircuity, Inc.*

sent an energy savings. For example, air could be returned from packaging labs in which strength testing is conducted on potential materials, since no chemicals are used. This concept is further discussed later in the chapter.

Passive-Evaporative Downdraft Cooling

As outside air enters a stack, water is sprayed into the air stream. Introduction of water into the air stream increases the air density, which causes the higher-density air to fall into the space below. As water evaporates into the air stream, energy to cause the evaporation process comes from the air itself, and the loss of energy causes the air temperature to drop. The higher-density air is cooled and falls into the open space below and out of the building after it

cools the room through an opening in the envelope (e.g., a window).

This technology is termed passive-evaporative downdraft cooling (PEDC) and is optimally applied in climates with a high wet-bulb depression (dry-bulb temperature minus wet-bulb temperature); these geographic areas have the most capacity to evaporate water into the air stream. In more humid climates, the air cannot accept as much water.

Biowall

A biowall, first introduced in Canada by Diamond & Schmitt Architects, uses plants' natural respiratory properties to cool the indoor air in summer, and functions like a humidifier in the winter. This technology is being applied at the Drexel University Integrated Science Center in Philadelphia, Pennsylvania. Operating in conjunction with the building mechanical system, air will be circulated throughout the volume of the atrium, across all floors and through the plant wall biofilter. The plant wall removes carbon dioxide (CO_2) and volatile organic compounds (VOC's) from the air.

Radiant Heating Systems

Decoupling the heating load from the ventilation load offers savings in cold climates, since the supply air system would not be sized for the peak demand. This concept is limited to facilities in cold climates with low internal heat gains and a low density of fume hoods. If the internal heat gain was high or if the fume hood density was high, then the supply air system would be sized for those demands, which reduces the available savings. For example, the Tahoe Center for Environmental Sciences previously discussed used a radiant floor heating system to achieve savings based on this technology.

Rumsey Engineers applied PEDC technology at the Carnegie Institution for Science, Department of Global Ecology, on the grounds of Stanford University in Palo Alto, California. The stack containing the water-injection system is visible on the left. *Image courtesy of D. Esch.*

Cephalon, Building 200 Renovation, West Chester, Pennsylvania

During a laboratory renovation project for a biopharmaceutical company, implementation of large numbers of microisolator equipment in a common room posed a number of challenges in the design of the room's air distribution system and controls. The challenge was compounded when existing available area produced a nonrectangular room shape (a departure from the current lay-out paradigm, but a trend which fosters a more collaborative research environment and utilizes expensive research building square footage more efficiently. Multiple air terminal types, arrangements, and throw patterns were tested using Computational Fluid Dynamics (CFD) modeling to evaluate their performance in terms of temperature uniformity and local air

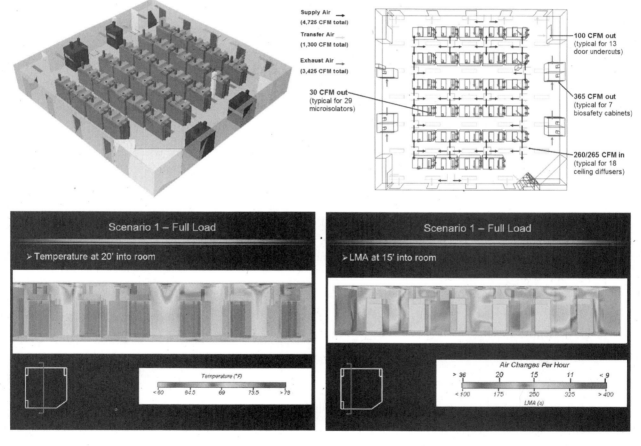

CFD modeling of Cephalon's Building 200 laboratory renovation in West Chester, Pennsylvania, helped to optimize its air distribution and control system. *Image courtesy of KlingStubbins.*

continued

change rate across the equipment aisles. Separate modeling was performed to derive a library of validated diffuser models before the different types tested were implemented and studied in the main room model. One scheme that includes mixing-type diffusers was chosen as the most appropriate and cost-effective for this particular facility, with the lay-out consisting of air diffusers placed around the perimeter of the room with throws away from the biosafety cabinets. Multiple microisolator utilization schemes were also simulated to ensure proper airflow performance under reduced room dilution rates to achieve energy savings during partial thermal load conditions. The model helped predict how the room could be used effectively with the building HVAC air measurement and temperature controls. These results helped to form conclusions and optimize the final air distribution system design before construction—representing a significant cost savings over "trial and error" adjustment of the room once it was constructed and occupied that would have disrupted valuable laboratory research and increased operating costs.

Internal Ventilation Requirements and Design Considerations

RWDI Consulting Engineers & Scientists
Guelph, Ontario, Canada

As mentioned earlier in the chapter, air changes per hour is a common measure of design ventilation rates in laboratories. Historically, the ventilation rate in a typical laboratory has been set to a minimum value of between 6 and 12 air changes per hour (ACH) in an effort to maintain acceptable indoor air quality, meet desired fresh air requirements, and maintain temperature within the space. These high ventilation rates, combined with the need to exhaust all ventilation air without recirculation, lead to high energy usage and costs. Although laboratory designers are aware that, in most cases, the ventilation systems may be overdesigned, there is reluctance to reduce ventilation rates due to the perceived risk involved. Part of the risk is associated with the potential to compromise the safety within the laboratory when a chemical spill or leak occurs outside of a fume hood. In these cases, the hope is that the ventilation rate will provide enough air changes to recover from the spill and provide some

protection to the occupants of the lab. However, even for minor chemical releases within the room itself, a ventilation rate between 6 and 12 ACH is not nearly enough to maintain safety, as evaluated in the context of odor thresholds and occupational health limits. As an example, considering a database of commonly used liquid laboratory chemicals, the accompanying figure illustrates the percentage of commonly used chemicals adequately ventilated in the case of a spill by a given air change rate. For reference, consider that for a room 3 meters high by 6 meters by 9 meters (10 feet high by 20 feet by 30 feet), 10 ACH represents 0.45 m3/s (1,000 cfm). This data involves several assumptions including complete mixing of chemicals within the room, room supply

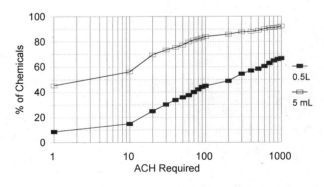

Chemicals controlled by ACH for two liquid spill volumes (500 mL and 5 mL).
Image courtesy of RWDI Consulting Engineers and Scientists.

and exhaust locations are ignored as are any related chemical density effects, the exposed surface area of the spill is based on a 0.5-mm spill depth, and the emission rate calculation ignores the effect of evaporative cooling.

To determine the required ACH for each chemical in the database, the most restrictive published limit was applied—the worst-case of the odor threshold or occupational health limit. Two spill sizes are represented in the accompanying figure. The 5 ml spill size is representative of a very minor spill, and would also be indicative of normal operating conditions within a laboratory where some analyses and procedures may take place on the bench itself, rather than within a fume hood.

Based on the high number of ACH required for most chemicals, it is not possible to maintain safety by simply relying on the ACH. The design of the laboratory to recover from a spill or to address emissions from activities performed outside of the fume hoods should instead be focused on other ventilation strategies or evacuation protocols, including the use of targeted source controls and laboratory-specific exhaust grill and diffuser design.

Space cooling within the laboratory is also a concern for designers. In some laboratories with a low number of fume hoods and a high density of equipment, high ventilation rates are used just to cool the space. Rather than providing an air change rate to meet the space cooling goals of the laboratory, a better approach is to use systems that recirculate the air within the individual labs, such as chilled beams or fan coil units which were discussed earlier in this chapter.

In an effort to reduce the high number of air changes typically seen in a laboratory setting, the primary reason for providing air changes in a laboratory needs to be reevaluated by the design community. It is not practical to address safety issues related to chemical use, and thermal comfort through air change rate. Aside from these, the only requirement for air change is to provide a sufficient amount of fresh air to the occupants and to ensure that there is enough air provided to support any local source control equipment. Thus, the approach for establishing the air change rate for a laboratory setting should be similar to that applied for an office space (i.e., ASHRAE Standard 62.1), and the goals of safety and thermal comfort should be addressed through other ventilation design and end-user initiatives.

Even moderate source control is more effective than increased air changes for the purpose of controlling indoor air quality for normal laboratory operations. This applies to scenarios where there may be some procedures taking place outside of the fume hood. As examples, this could include cleaning of glassware with solvents, handling small amounts of relatively benign chemicals (between 50 and 100 mL), and dispensing chemicals. The emissions from these applications should ideally be captured through the use of local source control measures such as snorkels, bench wall vents, and possibly grilled "downdraft" benches. The accompanying figure shows a concentration of acetone at nose level for a scenario of four air changes per hour and no source control. The lower concentration levels shown are a direct result of the local source control applied. Some reduction in concentration from the baseline is indicated with a doubling of air changes and no controls. However, the reduction is not as significant as shown with local source control. Thus, under normal laboratory operations where some procedures may take place outside of the fume hoods, the best approach is to provide moderate source control, rather than provide increased air changes for the purpose of controlling indoor air quality.

When a laboratory ventilation system recovers from a chemical spill outside of the fume hood, the ventilation strategy and gas density will have far more influence on the recovery from this type of release than the ACH. A clear understanding of the potential spill location and types of chemicals that could be released will have an influence on the optimal air supply diffuser and return

continued

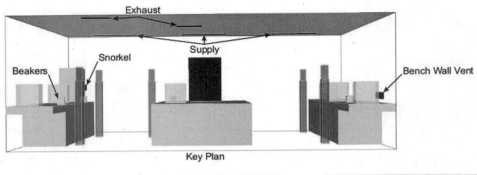

Key Plan

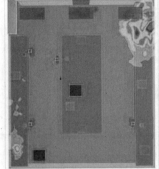

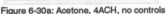

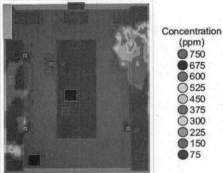

Concentration
(ppm)
- 750
- 675
- 600
- 525
- 450
- 375
- 300
- 225
- 150
- 75

Figure 6-30a: Acetone, 4ACH, no controls   Figure 6-30b: Acetone, 4ACH, with controls   Figure 6-30c: Acetone, 8ACH, no controls

Simulation of ventilation performance illustrating the effectiveness of local source control when compared to an increased air change rate without controls. The plan images represent a slice in section showing the concentration of chemical at nose level from two different chemical sources within the room. Lighter tones represent higher concentrations. *Image courtesy of RWDI Consulting Engineers and Scientists.*

grill design. For example, if there is a potential to spill or release a chemical that has a vapor density that is heavier than air, the best location for the return grill will be at a low elevation (i.e., at floor level).

Numerical fluid dynamics modeling tools commonly referred to as computational fluid dynamics (CFD) can be used to refine the ventilation design. This approach will allow designers to more efficiently ventilate a room so that design considerations associated with thermal comfort and chemical releases are addressed through means other than ACH. The accompanying figure shows an example of CFD modeling output for the spread of a vapor plume from a heavy gas spill for a number of configurations. This figure illustrates a case where a floor-level exhaust grill was shown to evacuate the chemical emissions more effectively than increased ACH.

As long as the minimum requirement for outdoor air is satisfied, the air from offices, hallways, and any other nonlaboratory areas can be used to supply the laboratory to reduce energy costs associated with conditioning outdoor air. However, it is difficult to define a set of criteria or circumstances when it might be acceptable to recirculate the air from within the laboratory itself to other spaces. As an example, the ANSI/AIHA Z9.5 Laboratory Ventilation Standard discusses specific criteria that should be met in order to recirculate air from laboratories. Specifically, there is reference to demonstrating that the concentrations in the laboratory are within acceptable levels for a credible chemical spill scenario, or that the air will be treated to ensure that the concentrations

20 ACH, High Exhaust

328.2 s after spill starts

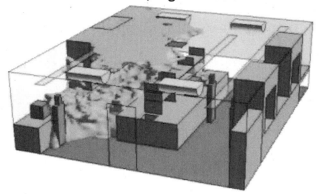

Concentration Plume
Defined by 403 ppm criterion (NOAEL)

10 ACH, High Exhaust

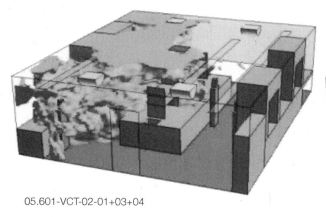

20 ACH, Low Exhaust

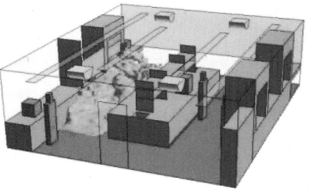

05.601-VCT-02-01+03+04

CFD simulation results for a heavy gas spill in a laboratory. *Image courtesy of RWDI Consulting Engineers and Scientists.*

are within these levels. There is also discussion that an emergency system should be provided that can supply 100 percent outside air in the event that the air from the laboratory cannot be recirculated.

The discussion in the ANSI/AIHA standard clearly illustrates the complications and design challenges associated with attempting to recirculate laboratory air to other spaces. Historically, there has been a large opportunity for energy savings associated with this initiative because of the potential to reduce the high amount of 100 percent outdoor air. However, if the approach for establishing air change rates discussed above is adopted, the need to recirculate laboratory air to other spaces to reduce energy costs will be substantially reduced. From a practical perspective, this would mean designers should focus efforts on methods of controlling air quality and thermal comfort levels without using high air change rates, rather than using high air change rates and subsequently devising complicated schemes to reuse laboratory air. In other words, design the laboratory to avoid high air change rates in the first place, rather than try to compensate by reusing the air.

Air Exhaust and Intake Design Considerations

RWDI Consulting Engineers & Scientists
Guelph, Ontario, Canada

In parallel with the building systems operation and internal ventilation requirements, the level of dispersion achieved between the laboratory exhaust and air intake points needs to be considered. Without sufficient dispersion, excess chemical concentrations could occur throughout a large area served by the affected air intakes. Likewise, health limits could be exceeded, or sensitive populations at neighboring locations could be affected. Through evaluation of parameters such as exhaust and intake location, stack height and stack exit velocity, these systems can be designed to maintain acceptable air quality levels at the air intakes. This step is important to allow designers to capitalize upon opportunities for energy savings through laboratory design, while maintaining safety for the building occupants.

Many heat recovery systems require outside air intakes to be located close to the laboratory exhaust stacks. To maintain acceptable air quality levels within the laboratory, the design of the exhaust stacks is critical, and the potential for the exhaust to reenter the air intakes needs to be considered as part of the design process. Although air intakes are the most obvious concern, other building openings also need to be considered for potential emissions infiltration. For a sustainable laboratory, these openings may include features such as operable windows for natural ventilation.

Exhaust Stack Design

Design suggestions for laboratory exhaust stacks are provided and discussed below.

• Avoid placement of exhaust stacks within circulation, or building wake zones.

Winds approaching a building can create several separation and wake zones that can affect the trajectory of laboratory exhausts after being emitted from the building. The ASHRAE Applications Handbook illustrates several of these zones. In particular, separation zones tend to form on the building sides, roof, and leeward side, as shown in the accompanying figure.

Exhaust released within the recirculation zone may fumigate the roof area and travel both upwind and downwind of the exhaust release point. This phenomenon could be particularly problematic for the heat recovery design configuration previously described. The accompanying figure illustrates the roof recirculation zone using flow visualization within a wind tunnel.

Exhaust discharge within these regions can be avoided through stack placement, and other design details such as plume rise and stack height. Stack exhausts with large momentum, through a combination of large flow rates and exit velocities, can sometimes overcome the effects of the roof recirculation region.

• Provide sufficient momentum directed away from the building, including a high exit velocity.

The exhaust plume should be able to resist the high turbulence that is likely to be encountered, and should not be discharged in a horizontal direction. As general guidance, exit velocities should be at least 10 m/s (2,000 fpm) (ASHRAE 2007, 44.1). Higher

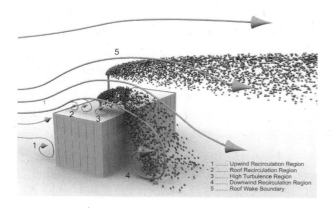

Recirculation regions and wake zones around buildings. In this figure, wind approaches from the left, strikes the building, and travels over the roof edge, creating a recirculation zone on the roof. *Image courtesy of RWDI Consulting Engineers and Scientists.*

Roof recirculation zone on building roof is illustrated using flow visualization within a wind tunnel. *Image courtesy of RWDI Consulting Engineers and Scientists.*

exit velocities up to 20 m/s (4,000 fpm) may be useful for improving exhaust dispersion. The ANSI/AIHA Z9.5 standard calls for a minimum 15 m/s (3,000 fpm) value.

To reduce energy consumption, there may be opportunities to reduce the discharge velocity and/or volume flow rate from the exhaust stacks under specific operating conditions. These conditions might include specific ambient wind conditions (i.e., speed and direction), periods of low building occupancy and low laboratory fume hood use where chemical emissions are not expected. Turndown based on ambient wind conditions needs to be evaluated through an exhaust dispersion analysis to define a matrix of wind conditions under which these exhaust parameters can be altered without compromising safety.

• Manifold fume hood exhaust.

Manifolding laboratory fume hood exhausts will, in most cases, provide additional dilution of chemical emissions prior to discharge from the building. This is based on the assumption that for most research laboratory applications, a high emission of one chemical would only come from one fume hood at any given time. This would mean that all of the air coming from the other fume hoods would dilute the emission before discharge. For example, there may be a high emission of hydrochloric acid due to a spill coming from one fume hood and an emission of acetone from another, but the probability of having more than one fume hood with simultaneous high emissions of hydrochloric acid is most likely very low. Of course, a clear understanding of the intended laboratory chemical use and operations is important to account for the internal dilution benefit appropriately at the design stage. Manifolding the fume hood exhaust with the general laboratory ventilation air will also provide this internal dilution benefit.

Manifolded systems will also have greater exhaust momentum so that the exhaust plume will travel up and away from the building, rather than reentering through outside air intakes or other ventilation openings on the roof or side of the building. The combined benefits of internal dilution and increased exhaust momentum can provide an exhaust system that facilitates the

continued

implementation of a heat recovery system, while maintaining the desired air quality levels at the air intakes. Some concern has been raised in the industry regarding manifolding of exhausts and increased explosivity due to interaction of chemicals. There is no evidence of explosive mixtures resulting from interaction of exhausts from two or more hoods. Typical exhaust concentrations are too low to support reactions or flammability concerns (AIHA 2002, 5).

• Place the exhaust stack as high as possible on the roof.

A location high on the building increases the likelihood that the exhaust will travel above and away from the building. This strategic placement of exhausts will allow for lower required exhaust momentum (i.e., volume flow rate and exit velocity) and stack heights to maintain adequate levels at the air intakes. The accompanying figure illustrates the benefit of this design concept using flow visualization within a wind tunnel.

Flow testing and visualization of exhaust stack plume dispersion for a University of Colorado, Denver research building. *Image courtesy of RWDI Consulting Engineers and Scientists.*

Exhaust Treatment and Emission Reduction

There may be cases where there are design limitations or other circumstances that will present a challenge for optimal stack design. In these cases, alternatives to tall stacks may include exhaust treatment or protocol for emission reduction from the fume hoods. In some cases, it may be desirable to combine these strategies with exhaust stack design to achieve the sustainable design goals while maintaining safety.

The concept of exhaust treatment can likely only be applied to an exhaust stream from a dedicated use fume hood or other laboratory procedure. As an example, acid gas scrubbers for clean room laboratories can be effective in reducing the amount of acid gas emissions in the exhaust stream, allowing for reduced stack height. However, exhaust treatment has not been effective for general laboratory fume hood applications because it is not possible to find a single control mechanism to target the wide range of compounds typically present. For this reason, stack design coupled with intake placement to provide adequate exhaust dispersion levels is the preferred approach for general use laboratory fume hood exhausts.

From an operational perspective, it is also possible to reduce the magnitude of chemical emissions from the laboratory exhausts through handling protocols and procedures at the point of use. The goal would be to establish procedures that would reduce the potential for a large release or spill of a chemical within the fume hood, and to promote efficient clean-up protocols to control emissions in the event of a spill. Examples of these procedures include spill trays to contain chemicals and limit available surface area for evaporative emissions, absorbent working surfaces to reduce available volume of liquid for evaporation, spill recovery or "clean-up" kits strategically located throughout the laboratory, and protocols for dispensing from, and storage of larger containers to restrict chemical volumes handled/stored within fume hoods. The sustainable benefits of these operational control strategies could range from lower exhaust momentum requirements at the roof to a lower number of fume hoods required within the laboratory itself.

Low-Energy Cooling and Heating

Along with the building-level systems, central heating and cooling systems should be selected and/or optimized. Some technologies to minimize heating and cooling plant energy use are discussed in this section.

Heat Pump Systems

Heat pumps operate as a reverse vapor-compression refrigeration cycle. In a conventional four-step vapor-compression refrigeration cycle, refrigerant is compressed to a superheated (high-pressure, high-temperature) vapor, then routed through a condenser, which cools the refrigerant to a saturated liquid. The condenser could be a refrigerant-to-air heat exchanger (similar to a residential system) or a refrigerant-to-water heat exchanger, which uses water generated by a cooling tower. A cooling tower is an evaporative cooling device, and can therefore create water temperatures lower than the outside air-dry bulb temperature. Using this water in a refrigerant-to-water condenser is more energy-efficient. The saturated liquid refrigerant then undergoes a throttling process—as the pressure is reduced, some refrigerant evaporates and some remains a liquid. Since the throttling process is adiabatic (no heat transfer), the remaining liquid refrigerant supplies the energy to cause the phase change and is consequently cooled. The cooled two-phase refrigerant proceeds through an evaporator, which cools the load. The refrigerant is heated to a saturated vapor in the evaporator and returns to the compressor to restart the cycle.

A heat pump cycle imposes a reversing valve into the vapor-compression refrigeration cycle so that refrigerant flows from the compressor to the indoor coil in the winter. This means that the coil (the evaporator in the summer) is the condenser in the winter and rejects heat to the building in the winter. The outdoor coil (which is the condenser in the summer) is then the evaporator in the winter.

One limitation of air-to-air heat pumps is that the available temperature at the evaporator decreases in the winter, when the building heat load is higher. A balance-point temperature exists at which the building heat loss exceeds the air-to-air heat pump capacity. For residential applications, supplemental heating—typically electric resistance—is required. The low temperature in the heat pump cycle is referred to as the "source," and the high temperature in the heat pump cycle is referred to as the "sink."

The HVAC industry uses "coefficient of performance" (COP) as an indicator of heat pump cycle efficiency—the COP is the beneficial effect divided by the work input and is dimensionless. For a heat pump, the beneficial effect is the heat rejected to the building and the work input is the electrical demand of the compressor. In the United States, heat transfer and work are expressed in different units, so the energy-efficiency ratio (EER) has been defined as the ratio of the beneficial effect (in Btu/hour) divided by the work input (in watts).

Different heat pump concepts have been used in laboratory facilities to increase system COP. In a water-source heat pump (WSHP) system, a heat pump is dedicated to one zone, and the compressor cycles on and off in response to the room thermostat. A closed-loop water system runs to each heat pump to act as either a source or sink. If the heat pump is in cooling mode, the water loop acts as a sink; if the heat pump is in heating mode, the water loop acts as a source. The water loop modulates between 60°F and 90°F. If the water loop temperature falls below the lower setpoint, a boiler adds heat to the water loop. If the water loop temperature rises

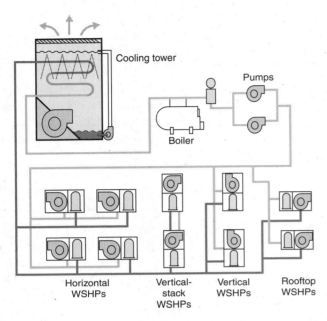

Water-source heat pump (WSHP) system flow diagram. *Image courtesy of KlingStubbins.*

above the upper setpoint, the loop rejects heat to a cooling tower.

This decentralized system can be cost-effective because the ductwork quantity is reduced for two reasons. The supply air ductwork quantity is reduced, since the cooling system is relatively close to the cooling load. Outside air is ducted to each heat pump for ventilation purposes, but this ductwork is typically only sized for ventilation duty (an airside economizer mode is not available). This concept has been applied to labs with relatively low cooling loads and few fume hoods. Heat pumps local to each lab offset the heat gain to maintain room temperature. If the fume hood density is low, the outside airflow rate can be reduced to the quantity needed for dilution.

One limitation of applying WSHPs to laboratories is that the heat gains have to be relatively low. If the

equipment heat gains exceed about 3 watts per square foot, the number of heat pumps required to offset the heat gain increases to the point where room sound pressure level targets are exceeded. Also, the count of fume hoods and other exhaust elements has to be low. If the exhaust air (and therefore makeup air) requirement for a lab is high, then the outside air ductwork to the heat pumps will be sized for that requirement and the capital expense increases.

A more passive and energy-efficient WSHP strategy is to have the water loop transfer heat to water in a lake or river. This system demonstrates energy savings because natural gas or electricity input to the boiler and cooling tower may not be required as a source to the heat pumps. For example, DePuy International (a surgical supplies business unit of Johnson & Johnson) moved its operations to Saint Priest (Lyon), France in 2000 (World Resources Institute 2006, 1–2). An underground lake 425 feet below the facility provides all heating energy and most cooling energy for the 75,000-square-foot facility. Taking advantage of the natural and relatively constant temperature of the underground lake, the system circulates water between the lake and a plate heat exchanger. Winter supply and return water temperatures from the well are 44°F and 55°F, respectively.

A secondary loop routes water between the plate heat exchanger and heat pumps in the building. Winter supply and return water temperatures leaving the plate heat exchanger are 43°F and 54°F, respectively. The secondary loop functions as the closed-loop water system described above—it is used as either a source or sink to each heat pump. However, the COP is increased because the source temperature is higher and the sink temperature is lower.

The heat pumps are "water-to-water"—the source and sink media are water. The heat pump discharge winter water supply and return temperatures are 122°F and 111°F, respectively. Hot water generated by the heat pumps in the winter, and chilled water generated in the summer, are circulated to fan coil units, air handling units, and radiant ceiling panels. With capacities of 1.8 million Btu/hr (heating) and 170 tons (cooling), the system produces a 66°F indoor temperature at the 14°F winter design outdoor temperature, and a 77°F indoor temperature at the 90°F summer design outdoor temperature.

DePuy's business case for using this system instead of a more conventional natural-gas heating system and electric cooling system is that the system eliminates natural gas cost and significantly reduces electricity cost. The payback period for the system was three years. Electricity is the only energy source for the building. Since there is no fossil-fuel combustion and a large percentage of power is generated by nuclear generation in France, the building's carbon footprint is small. The system also insulates the site from price fluctuations and potential supply disruptions associated with natural gas. Based on the success of the DePuy heat pump system, Johnson & Johnson is developing a similar installation at its Limerick, Ireland facility.

In the WSHP concept described above, the water loop transfers heat to a lake. If such a water source is unavailable, an alternative in terms of energy savings is to transfer heat with the earth via a geothermal heat exchange system. The geothermal exchange system either contains distributed heat pumps throughout the facility (the water-to-air type) or uses central heat pumps (the water-to-water type) to generate chilled water during the summer or hot water in the winter, which is then pumped to air handling units. The system circulates water between the heat pumps and a series of underground wells or boreholes on closed-loop geothermal systems,

The WSHP loop secondary pump house at DePuy International's Saint Priest, France site. *Image courtesy of Johnson & Johnson.*

which reject heat to the earth (winter) or accept heat input from the earth (summer). Because the mean earth temperature is more temperate than the outside air temperature, the source and sink temperatures allow a higher COP. A limitation is that room temperature tolerances and therefore supply air temperature tolerances are tighter in a laboratory. Chilled water flow through cooling coils in air handling units can be controlled effectively with modulating control valves to closely maintain a supply air temperature setpoint (and therefore the room temperature setpoint). Refrigerant cannot be modulated as effectively as water, which can make the water-to-water heat pump the preferred model for laboratory applications.

Howard Alderson, PE and Neal Babcock of Alderson Engineering, Inc. provided details of the geothermal heat exchange system applied at the new Weld Hill Research and Administration Building for the Arnold

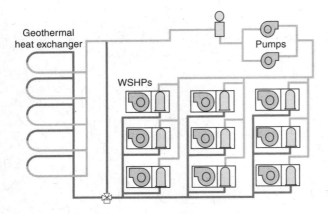

Cooling water flow diagram of a geothermal WSHP system at the Weld Hill Research and Administration Building of the Arnold Arboretum at Harvard University in Jamaica Plain, Massachusetts. *Image courtesy of Alderson Engineering.*

Arboretum at Harvard University in Jamaica Plain, Massachusetts. The facility is a 45,000-square-foot plant-science research facility with a program of greenhouses, growth chambers, bench laboratories, offices, and support areas.

One criteria for successful application of geothermal exchange heat pump systems is that the cooling and heating loads have to be "balanced" on an annual basis—if the building exhibited a high cooling load consistently throughout the year (e.g., a data center), the earth temperature would increase over time and the COP would be compromised, since the system would be rejecting heat to a higher-temperature sink. The Harvard lab met the criteria, since the large amount of 100 percent outside air systems causes a high heating requirement in the winter and a high cooling requirement in the summer.

Alderson Engineering used proprietary software to size the bore field based on peak demand, lifecycle loading, local mean earth temperature, and soil thermal conductivity to minimize the effects of earth-temperature shifts discussed above. The bore field consisted of 88 closed-loop boreholes.

The dominant feature of the site is a 65-foot-high hill. The preferred well location is at the low point of the

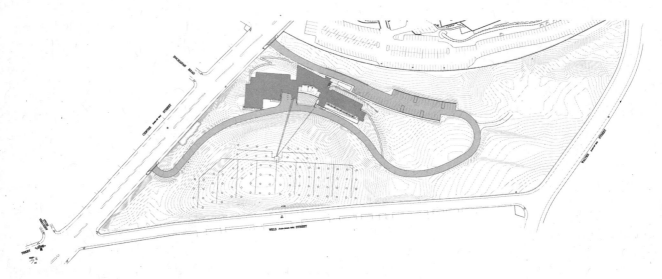

Site plan of Weld Hill Research and Administration Building including WSHP bore field. *Image courtesy of Alderson Engineering.*

site, with water pumped to the higher-elevation building. This allows entrapped air to be driven to the building, where it can be vented. However, site logistics (crane locations and laydown areas) required the wells to be located at a higher elevation than the building with water piping sloped to a vault with air vents.

Because the lab facility imposed a relatively high cooling load (400 tons), Alderson Engineering recommended a "hybrid" system to balance heat rejection on an annual basis—instead of rejecting heat solely to the earth, about 20 percent of the water flow is diverted to a dry cooler at certain times of the year, which then rejects heat to the atmosphere. A dry cooler is a water-to-air heat exchanger which transfers heat from the water loop to the atmosphere. An alternative is to use an evaporative cooler such as a cooling tower. In an evaporative cooler, the building condenser water travels through tubes. Water is sprayed on the outside of the tubes, which enhances heat transfer due to evaporative cooling. If cooling from evaporative cooling is inadequate, then a fan is sequenced on. Water-spraying makes this equipment more efficient from a heat transfer perspective, but increases the maintenance burden because the system has to be chemically treated.

During the summer, heat is rejected to the earth, storing energy underground to be used in the following winter and early spring. On late spring nights, when the dry-bulb temperature is depressed, the dry cooler cools the water (instead of all water being routed to the wells). This reduces the underground heat-rejection burden and reduces the ground temperature before the peak cooling season begins. The earth is effectively "subcooled" to accept heat rejection in the upcoming cooling season.

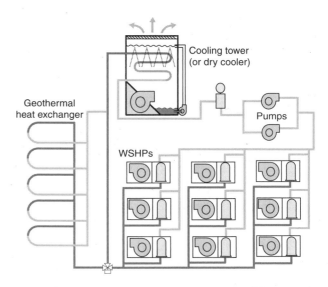

Hybrid WSHP geothermal system implemented at Weld Hill Research and Administration Building. *Image courtesy of Alderson Engineering.*

Chilled Water Distribution

Labs on a geographically large campus with central chilled water generation can achieve savings by reducing the power required to circulate chilled water from the central plant to the lab buildings. Several strategies can enhance distribution efficiencies. First, select the temperature difference between the supply and return chilled water temperatures to be as high as possible (e.g., 20°F). Because the flow rate is inversely proportional to this temperature difference, increasing the temperature difference decreases the water flow rate. Chillers producing low chilled water supply temperatures demand more power, which limits the low end of the supply temperature. For labs that use 100 percent outside air in relatively humid outside air environments, the chilled water temperature must be low enough to create a dew point that removes moisture from the air stream. This limits the high end of the supply temperature.

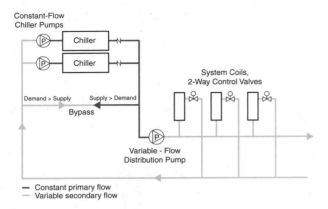

Schematic flow diagram of primary-secondary chilled water pumping. *Image courtesy of KlingStubbins.*

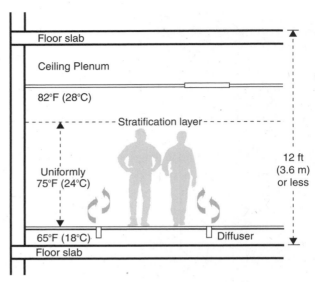

Schematic flow diagram of variable primary flow (VPF) chilled water pumping. *Image courtesy of KlingStubbins.*

Next, variable primary flow (VPF) distribution should be considered since it offers additional savings over more conventional constant-speed primary/variable-speed secondary chilled water distribution. This technology allows the chilled water flow through the entire system to be reduced as the demand decreases away from peak. Secondary pumps are not required, and the chilled water flow varies with the cooling load. The primary/secondary distribution concept was developed so that a minimum water velocity in the evaporator tube could be maintained to prevent freezing. The primary/secondary system staged chillers and pumps on and off, so that the velocity was well in excess of the minimum requirement. As control systems have become more accurate, the VPF distribution concept was developed to allow the chilled water flow to float above the minimum velocity. Additional pumping energy savings are available because the primary loop is variable-flow in this model.

Ice Storage and Nonelectric Cooling Technologies

Electricity is most often used to power the compressor in the vapor-compression refrigeration cycle to cool buildings, which causes electrical demand in most commercial buildings to peak at around the same time—in the late afternoon in the summer. Electric utilities must have enough power generation capacity to meet this aggregate peak demand, driven by the air conditioning systems. Since the early 1980s, significant additions to power generation capacity in the United States have not been made due to increased power plant construction cost and environmental hurdles. If electric utilities are in a geographic area that experiences economic development, then the power demand increases incrementally each year. Therefore, the aggregate power demand will meet or even surpass the installed power generating capacity. Electric utilities have introduced an approach called demand-side management (DSM) which emphasizes a decrease in customers' power demand, rather than increasing power generating capacity. The DSM goal is to flatten the demand peak—instead of peaking in the late afternoon, the peak demand is reduced or shifted. This is sometimes referred to as "peak shaving."

Commercial buildings' electricity tariffs are separated into two major components, consumption and demand. The consumption component is virtually the same as that of a residential customer—it reflects the amount of energy used over a monthly billing period and is measured in kilowatt-hours (kWh). The demand component reflects the highest peak demand sustained by a building for some interval and is measured in kilowatts (kW). The demand component is sometimes adjusted by electric utilities to motivate customers to implement DSM strategies.

Because air conditioning loads are the largest demand component for commercial buildings, several technologies have emerged to meet this goal: nonelectric compressors, steam absorption technologies, chilled water or ice thermal storage, and hybrid central plants.

Most typically, the compressor in the vapor-compression refrigeration cycle is driven by electricity. However, the compressor shaft can also be driven by a natural gas-driven engine or a steam turbine. Steam enters a turbine at high pressure, expands through

the turbine and causes the turbine shaft to rotate. Although most often, the turbine shaft is coupled to a generator shaft to generate electricity, the turbine shaft can also be coupled to a compressor shaft to operate a compressor in a vapor-compression refrigeration cycle. This avoids using electricity generated by an electric utility to power the air conditioning system. Merck Research Laboratories in Boston, Massachusetts, uses a steam turbine-driven compressor. To see additional information on this project, see color images C-60 through C-65.

Another strategy uses the absorption refrigeration cycle, which does not use a compressor to circulate refrigerant. Instead, a lithium bromide solution is used to circulate refrigerant within the chiller. The lithium bromide solution is concentrated as part of the cycle by a heat source. This cycle could be indicated for a site with a low-cost heat source (e.g., hot water from a co-generation system or steam from a boiler using a low-cost fuel source). Because a compressor is not used, the peak power demand is reduced relative to a more conventional vapor-compression refrigeration cycle. The U.S. Food and Drug Administration Research Headquarters Consolidation uses this technology to generate cooling on their White Oak, Maryland, campus. An alternative is to use parabolic concentrating-type solar collectors to create hot water to be used in the absorption refrigeration cycle.

Chilled water storage uses an electricity-powered vapor-compression refrigeration cycle to generate chilled water to be used in the building's cooling coils. However, the chillers produce chilled water at night and the chilled water is stored and then reused the following day. One benefit of operating chillers at night is that the wet-bulb temperature is depressed at that time, which in turn allows the condenser water temperature to be decreased, resulting in more efficient chiller operation. In this application, 44°F chilled water

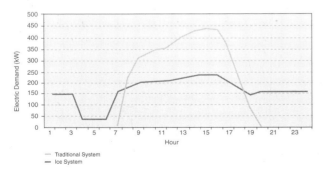

Hourly electric demand savings with an ice thermal storage system. *Image courtesy of KlingStubbins.*

is stored in its liquid phase in tanks, then used the following day. This system shifts the individual building power peak from late afternoon to the night, which in turn reduces the electric utility's aggregate peak demand. The Tahoe Center for Environmental Sciences mentioned earlier charges a 50,000-gallon chilled water thermal storage tank at night, and uses the cooling energy the following day, which eliminates all electric compressor-driven cooling during the day.

An alternate thermal storage medium is to store the cooling energy in ice form. Under this model, chillers operate at night to generate low-temperature (20°F) chilled water. This creates the same benefits as described above (more efficient chiller operation and shifted peak power demand). This chilled water is then pumped to a tank, where the subfreezing chilled water freezes a separate water volume inside a tank at night—the two water systems (chilled water and ice) do not mix, but merely exchange heat. The cooling energy is discharged the following day by melting the ice and using the latent enthalpy associated with the solid-to-water phase change to cool chilled water. Ice storage is more volumetrically efficient, since the cooling energy is stored as latent enthalpy. Since the system operates at lower chilled water temperatures than a conventional plant, supply air temperature can be depressed. Because the supply airflow to load-driven labs is inversely proportional to the supply air temperature, the availability of low-temperature supply air reduces the airflow rate and associated fan power. Ice-storage chilled water economics is often a function of the demand charge. Drexel University (Bossone Research Center) and the University of Pennsylvania (Module 7 central plant) applied ice-storage technology.

Lastly, hybrid central plants incorporate several of these technologies into one central plant. This hybrid

Thermal ice storage tanks. *Image courtesy of KlingStubbins.*

strategy is sometimes implemented in order to diversify energy sources. Since electricity is only used for a fraction of the chilled water production, the central plant is less reliant on one utility.

Optimum Chiller Configuration

Chilled water is generated by using the vapor-compression or absorption refrigeration cycles previously described. Chillers may be configured in detail to enhance system efficiency by using different application concepts.

Incrementally sized chillers are combined to form a central chilled water plant in order to improve reliability and off-peak performance. Often, the chillers are piped in parallel with each other. A more efficient alternative may be to pipe the chillers in series with each other. For example, Chiller #1 reduces the chilled water temperature from 60 to 52°F and Chiller #2 reduces the chilled water temperature from 52 to 44°F. Condenser water is piped in reverse order; Chiller #2 receives condenser water at 100°F, cools refrigerant and is then piped to Chiller #1. This piping configuration minimizes the compressor "lift" for each chiller and therefore increases each chiller's efficiency, while reducing distribution energy due to the higher supply-to-return temperature difference.

Evaporative Cooling of Condensers is another system concept. Typical chiller condensers are shell-and-tube refrigerant-to-water heat exchangers. If condenser water was sprayed over tubes containing refrigerant, the condenser's heat transfer coefficient would increase, since spraying causes some water to evaporate. The tubes could not contain fins due to the concern of condenser water forming scale around the closely spaced fins. The net effect, however, is the heat transfer process—therefore chiller efficiency is increased.

The Alza Corporation site in Vacaville, California installed variable-speed drives on chillers and achieved a 17 percent internal rate of return on the $115,000 investment. *Image courtesy of Johnson & Johnson.*

Part-Load Operation of chillers also should be investigated using the energy modeling techniques discussed previously. As chillers unload to support off-peak cooling loads, the compressor power is reduced by either modulating inlet vanes or by decelerating the compressor motor by a variable-speed drive. The variable-speed drive more faithfully tracks power used by motor-to-chiller load. Further, power consumption is a function of the cube of the speed. Variable-speed drives availability for 4 kV chillers is an issue, but generally the payback period is attractive. Also, as the outside air wet-bulb temperature decreases, cooling towers can generate lower-temperature condenser water, which in turn drives an increase in chiller COP. Allowing the condenser water temperature to drop to a lower limit is termed "condenser water temperature relief."

Another efficiency option is condenser water heat recovery. Instead of heat from the refrigerant cycle being rejected to the atmosphere, condenser heat can be recovered to heat water, which then can be used in the lab. This technology typically uses a refrigerant-to-water condenser, which condenses the refrigerant and heats water to 95°F. This 95°F water is routed to a plate-and-frame heat exchanger, which heats a secondary closed-loop water circuit to around 90°F. This secondary water is then pumped to coils in the air handling units, where it preheats outside air. Water cooled by a cooling tower is typically not used at reheat or preheat coils since it contains solids which would clog heat transfer tubes. Since the cooling load peaks in the summer, the secondary water loop also can be used for summer reheat loads.

The Janssen Pharmaceutica site in Gurabo, Puerto Rico, applied this chiller heat recovery technology to provide reheat for its air change-driven facility. The $5.2 million project generated a 19 percent internal rate of return. *Image courtesy of Johnson & Johnson.*

Ethicon installed a condenser water heat recovery system on a 280-ton chiller in 2008 at their San Lorenzo site in Puerto Rico, which showed a 16 percent internal rate of return on the investment. *Image courtesy of Johnson & Johnson.*

Lake Source Cooling Water

Deep lakes, often of glacial origin, maintain low water temperatures year-round. If low-temperature lake water is available, then chilled water can be generated by heat exchange with the deep lake source. This is a minimum-energy option for cooling, since it displaces the vapor-compression refrigeration cycle.

Cornell University uses this technology to cool buildings on the Ithaca, New York, campus. Lake Cayuga is a glacial lake two miles from the campus. Cornell takes water from two miles out in the lake and 250 feet deep (only 10 feet above the bottom), where the water is 39°F year-round. This water is pumped through heat exchangers, which cools chilled water, which is then pumped to the campus. Because aquatic life is cold-blooded and cannot adapt to external changes in temperature, this technology carries a concern that a change in the water temperature will cause damage to the lake ecosystem. Cornell resolved this issue by separating the intake and discharge points, diffusing discharge water into the lake at a low velocity through small openings, and installing fine screens and low-wattage lights at the water intake location.

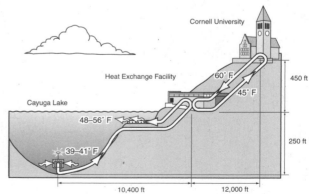

Cornell University lake-source cooling project. *Image courtesy of © ASHRAE Journal, February 2008.*

High-Efficiency Condensing Boilers

Fuel combustion creates water as a reaction product. If water in flue gases is a vapor, then some energy has been expended to cause that phase change. If this water is condensed into the liquid phase, then the latent energy associated with the phase change could be utilized. This concept forms the basis for condensing-boiler technology, which achieves boiler efficiency in the 90 percent range. Boiler efficiency is a strong function of the hot water temperatures—a boiler producing 110°F hot water is more efficient than a boiler producing 140°F hot water. The condenser heat exchanger uses hot water to cool the flue gases, and more water can be condensed with a lower hot water temperature, which corresponds to a higher efficiency.

Condensing boilers were installed at a pharmaceutical research and development facility in Arizona to produce 110°F hot water to reheat air. Because the preheat load is minimal in that climate, there was no need to produce higher-temperature water for preheat service.

Heat Recovery from Boilers

Laboratory facilities typically use steam or hot water to meet heating and process loads. Steam or hot water is most often generated by combustion of natural gas or oil to heat flue gases to a high temperature. A boiler transfers heat from the flue gases to either boil water (a steam boiler) or to sensibly heat water (hot water boiler). The flue gases are discharged from the boiler into the atmosphere through a stack at approximately 350°F. A heat exchanger (economizer) can be inserted into the stack to recover heat from the discharged 350°F flue gases to preheat makeup water entering the boiler.

The Janssen Pharmaceutica site in Beerse, Belgium, implemented a $1.8 million project in 2006 to install boiler economizers, which resulted in cost savings during the first year. *Image courtesy of Johnson & Johnson.*

Selection of the boiler economizer should assure that the flue gas temperature will not be cooled below the sulfuric acid (H_2SO_4) dew point temperature, which is a function of the sulfur content of the fuel. Flue gases generated from combustion of high-sulfur oil will have a higher dew point than flue gases generated by combustion of low-sulfur natural gas. Sulfuric acid condensation causes corrosion of the breeching and stack downstream of the economizer and should be prevented.

Active Solar Heating and Cooling

Solar energy collection can produce domestic hot water or heating hot water, and is a newer technology that is starting to be implemented in commercial building projects. The solar collectors can be either stationary or tracking types, or either flat-plate or parabolic shapes. Arrangements also exist with solar arrays generating hot water that powers absorption chillers, effectively creating a solar-powered cooling system.

Refrigerant Selection

Refrigerant types used in lab building HVAC systems also need to be assessed. Chlorine was found in the 1980s to erode the stratospheric ozone layer, which protects the Earth from incoming ultraviolet-wavelength radiation. Refrigerants in use at that time were chlorofluorocarbons (CFCs) and contributed to this effect, since the chlorine atom in the compound did not react until it reached the stratosphere and reacted with ozone. CFCs were phased out by the 1988 Montreal Protocol. Some replacement refrigerants are Hydrochlorofluorocarbons (HCFCs) such as R-22 and R-123, which still contain chlorine, but have a much lower ozone depletion potential (ODP) than CFCs. For example, the ODP of R-123a is 0.02. These compounds are also being phased out—starting in 2010, new HVAC equipment cannot be charged with an HCFC refrigerant. Other types include Hydrofluorocarbon (HFC) refrigerants, such as R-134a, which are chlorine-free and therefore have an ODP of zero. However, HFCs act as greenhouse gases and have relatively high global warming potential (GWP). Ammonia (NH_3) is chlorine-free (zero ODP) and does not contribute to global warming (zero GWP). Its use has been limited by its toxicity in certain concentrations—its permissible exposure limit in the United States is 50 ppm. Also, ammonia chiller applications have historically been perceived as unconventional technology and less efficient than other refrigerants. However, the absorption chillers in the efficient CHP applications previously described may utilize ammonia in their process, making them attractive as a method to eliminate refrigerants with GWP in HVAC systems.

Power Generation and Renewable Energy

After the internal building system, cooling and heating plant, and refrigerant options are explored, alternatives to generate power or harvest renewable energy in the lab building should be evaluated. Some primary candidate technologies are described next.

Photovoltaic Arrays

Incident solar radiation can be converted directly into electricity by photovoltaic (PV) cells. This technology uses photodiodes to cause photons to change electrons to a higher state of energy, thereby generating electricity. Electricity is generated in direct current (DC) mode and an inverter is required to change electricity into alternating current (AC) mode. PV cells can be building-integrated (e.g., mounted on a building surface such as a window), roof-mounted, mounted

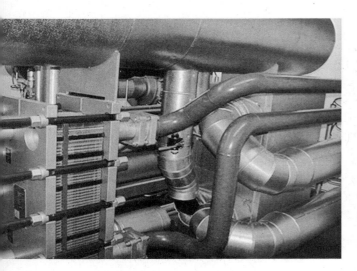

Janssen Pharmaceutica installed ammonia chillers at its Geel, Belgium site at a cost of $2.7 million to avoid greenhouse gas emissions and ozone depletion issues. The site has avoided the equivalent of 1,400 metric tons of carbon dioxide by using this natural refrigerant. *Image courtesy of Johnson & Johnson.*

Johnson & Johnson incorporated a 235-kW sun-tracking photovoltaic array on the parking garage of its world headquarters in New Brunswick, New Jersey. The system cost was $675,000, but the first-year cost savings was $50,000 and 165 metric tons of CO_2 was avoided. *Image courtesy of Johnson & Johnson.*

Johnson & Johnson completed a 246-kW roof-mounted photovoltaic system at its research facility in La Jolla, California, in 2007. The system cost was $1,486,000 and an IRR of 11% is being achieved. *Image courtesy of Johnson & Johnson.*

on a parking garage, or situated adjacent to the building on grade.

Wind Turbines

Wind energy can be used to generate power by rotating wind turbines. However, this technology is relatively expensive at a small scale, so its application to individual building sites has been limited. Electric utilities can generate wind power through an economy of scale and offer wind energy credits for sale to lab facilities—this model encourages the development of large-scale wind turbine farms. One simple investigation technique is to assess wind power class and resource potential for the site (often expressed in watts per square meter of swept area) from wind resource maps which may be obtained from the U.S. Department of Energy.

Biomass-Fueled Power Generation

Biomass is a fuel source derived from biological material, such as wood or biowaste, which undergoes a combustion process to generate steam or hot water. Centocor Biologics in Cork, Ireland installed a 2.1-MW biomass-fueled boiler that uses wood chips. The boiler replaces half the natural gas used at the facility and reduces its carbon dioxide emissions by 22 percent. The wood chips that fuel the boiler are byproducts from logging operations in sustainable forests near Cork. Completed in September 2008, the installation uses hook bins, essentially converted trailers designed with moving floors to handle wood chips in a contained fashion. Wood chips are transferred into the boiler, where they are burned to heat water. The resulting steam satisfies the heating and process needs of the facility, and ash produced in the combustion process is collected and used to fertilize new trees.

The Cilag CH Schaff Operation in Schaffhausen, Switzerland, installed a 350-kW boiler in 2006 which burns wood chips sustainably harvested in the area. The system avoids 200 metric tons of carbon dioxide per year. *Image courtesy of Johnson & Johnson.*

Landfill-Derived Methane-Fueled Generation

Methane (CH_4) is the main constituent of natural gas, which can be burned to generate steam. Although most often extracted from wells, processed, and sold to end users, methane can also be derived from landfills. Solid waste decomposition in a landfill creates landfill gas (LFG), which consists of about 50 percent methane and 50 percent carbon dioxide. Since these two gases are greenhouse gases, escape of LFG into the atmosphere contributes to climate change, but also represents a lost economic opportunity in terms of energy. As of 2009, around 500 LFG projects were operational in the United States, and the Environmental Protection Agency (EPA) has identified approximately 500 additional landfills that present attractive opportunities for LFG project development.

Johnson & Johnson (J&J) has committed to reducing its greenhouse gas emissions by 7 percent below its 1990 levels by 2010 (Climate Northeast 2006, 1–3). Each of the company's business units has an emissions target whose progress is tracked annually. Alza Pharmaceuticals, a J&J company, had a target greenhouse gas emission reduction and implemented an LFG project to meet their objective. Alza's research and development facilities in Mountain View, California, are adjacent to the Shoreline Landfill, which was closed in 1993 and redeveloped as a public recreation center. The 150-acre facility is next to San Francisco Bay and contains a golf course, clubhouse, and the Shoreline Amphitheater. LFG produced in the Shoreline Landfill by decaying waste was captured and flared in accordance with EPA regulations for large landfills. Although the flaring protected recreational visitors from offensive fumes, it wasted a valuable source of clean energy. Accordingly, Alza contacted the City of Mountain View to propose a project that would use the landfill gas at three of its nearby research and development facilities. The city was interested in a clean energy project and accepted Alza's proposal in February 2004.

Alza and the City of Mountain View signed a 15-year contract for the sale of the gas, which Alza uses to power three 970-kW generators at each of its lab buildings. The generators are configured for combined heat and power operation, with electric output used to power the buildings, and waste heat from exhaust gases recovered and used to provide hot water. The gas purchase agreement sets a fixed price with cost-of-living adjustments over the term of the contract, which Alza may extend for an additional five years.

Alza takes possession of the gas before the existing flare and processes it onsite using a standard moisture-elimination system. Three 60-hp blowers maintain the gas pressure at 6 pounds per square inch as it passes through a chiller. The chiller sensibly cools 1,300 standard cubic feet per minute of gas

from its inlet temperature of 70°F and also removes 90 percent of the moisture.

Alza located the clean-up station at the landfill so it could send waste liquids directly back into the landfill. To provide safe operation of this system, a very small portion of LFG is still flared. This will protect the environment if there is a sudden interruption in LFG consumption. The processed gas is injected into a 1.25-mile-high-density polyethylene (HDPE) pipeline, which is flexible yet strong enough to withstand forces created by landfill settlement. The pipeline is also maintained at 6 psi and has sections of 6-, 8-, and 10-inch diameters with fused-seal connections. Four isolation valves enable operators to close sections of the pipeline, either in a planned or unplanned scenario. Alza had to secure the pipeline right-of-way from the City of Mountain View and a private landowner. The pipeline delivers gas to three GE-Jenbacher generators located in three separate buildings. The generators are rated for 970 kW when burning LFG, for a total net capacity of 2.9 MW. The system is expected to generate 24 GWh of electricity annually and displace 150 million Btu per hour of natural gas consumption.

The $11 million project was approved with an annual pretax savings of $900,000 and a 15 percent internal rate of return (IRR), based on expected natural gas and electricity cost inflation. Higher-than-expected energy prices have since driven the IRR above 20 percent. The project will save an equivalent of 7,250 metric tons/year of CO_2 emissions through avoided electricity and natural gas consumption, representing 71 percent of Alza's greenhouse gas emission reduction target.

Alza addressed several challenges during the execution of this project. The project was delayed because of difficulties meeting emissions limits for carbon monoxide (CO), and GE-Jenbacher replaced the pistons and sleeves for each unit with a product designed specifically for low emissions. Alza also needed to educate its landlord about risks and rewards of LFG projects in order to obtain approval to use the generator onsite.

Alza also discovered some keys to a successful LFG project. Developing a relationship with the City of Mountain View was critical to the success of the project. Because the City Council agreed that the project had a high priority, city employees and regulators were responsive and flexible throughout the project, and the environmental approval process, right-of-way negotiations, and building appraisal proceeded without major interruption. Alza secured internal project approval in less than five weeks, largely because it had sought buy-in from stakeholders within J&J, particularly the finance and energy management groups. Assistance was also sought from the EPA Landfill Methane Outreach Program (LMOP) when negotiating the gas contract with the City. This was the City's first LFG project, and the LMOP team was able to provide price benchmarks from other California projects. Finally, securing a guarantee from the generator manufacturer proved to be an important factor in meeting CO emissions targets. GE-Jenbacher assessed the issue and replaced the pistons and sleeves with the low-emission components at no charge.

Fuel Cells

A fuel cell electrochemically separates electrons and protons of a fuel and forces the electrons through a circuit to generate electricity. The electrochemical reaction is enhanced by a platinum-based catalyst. Waste products from the process are water and car-bon dioxide, making the process environmentally friendly. However, fuel cell technology has not yet attained significant market penetration within laboratory facilities.

Co-Generation

Co-generation is the simultaneous generation of power, heating, and sometimes cooling, and is occasionally referred to as combined heat and power (CHP). As mentioned at the beginning of this chapter, power generation efficiency is limited to relatively low values. Co-generation technology recovers the otherwise-wasted energy and beneficially uses it. Lab facilities have significant simultaneous power and heating demands and are therefore attractive applications for this technology. Several CHP technologies are available and are outlined below.

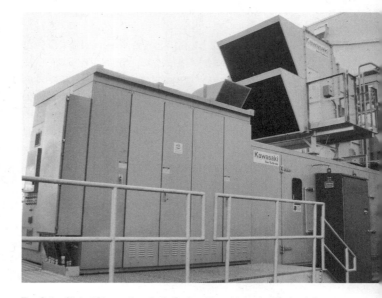

The Ortho Clinical Diagnostics site in Raritan, New Jersey, installed a 1.6-MW gas turbine with a heat recovery steam generator in November 2007. The project showed a 15 percent internal rate of return on its initial investment of $5 million. *Image courtesy of Johnson & Johnson.*

With gas turbine cycle CHP, an air/natural gas mixture undergoes a combustion process to form high-temperature flue gases that rotate a gas turbine to generate electricity. The flue gases exiting the gas turbine are still approximately 350°F and are routed to a heat exchanger, which creates either steam or hot water, which is used by the facility. Heating needs of the facility can be partially met by the recovered hot water, or the hot water may be used by an absorption chiller to create chilled water.

In the reciprocating-engine cycle, an air/natural gas mixture burns in an internal-combustion engine to generate electricity. Water used to cool the engine jacket and radiator is routed to a heat exchanger, which can generate either low-pressure (10 psig) steam or hot water. Steam or hot water is then used for heating or cooling demands as described above.

The Johnson & Johnson PRD facility in Lexington, Massachusetts, installed a 250 kW co-generation system which generates power, hot water, and chilled water and also uses solar energy for supplemental hot water heating. Shown in the image is the flue gas heat recovery in the CHP system. *Image courtesy of Johnson & Johnson.*

Carbon Neutral Laboratory Buildings

As previously mentioned in the energy modeling portion of this chapter, calculating the carbon footprint of a building requires accounting of the site heating, cooling, and process energy end uses, the source energy use, and then the site and source-related carbon emissions. A carbon neutral building achieves a "net-zero" carbon footprint in terms of emissions by balancing a measured amount of carbon released

The Johnson & Johnson PRD site in La Jolla, California, uses CHP technology to recover heat in a plate-and-frame heat exchanger (shown here) and produce hot water. *Image courtesy of Johnson & Johnson.*

with an equivalent amount sequestered or offset. This is complicated by the gridded nature of utility power—the fuel source for generating electricity varies by region.

Carbon Footprint Reduction

As a simple example, consider a pharmaceutical discovery lab in Massachusetts that recently proposed implementing a glycol runaround heat recovery system. The proposal increased the net annual electricity use by 31,000 kWh (106 million Btu) because savings in the summer are offset by an increase in fan energy. However, the proposal decreased annual natural gas use by 2,445 million Btu because of the heating savings in the winter. This opportunity can be judged in several ways. First, there is a net savings of 2,339 million Btu, or about 9 percent of the total energy use. Second, the forecasted cost savings is $29,000, and with the installed cost of $250,000 a simple payback period of 8.6 years is generated. And finally, using some assumptions about the regional mix of fuels needed to generate electricity, the increase in carbon dioxide emissions due to the increase in electricity use is 31 metric tons of CO_2. However, the corresponding decrease because less natural gas is burned in the winter is 143 metric tons of CO_2. The net decrease in carbon dioxide emissions is therefore 112 metric tons of CO_2. If the project were located in a region where power was generated using less carbon, the numbers would vary. For example, if the power for the building was generated by carbon-neutral means, the carbon footprint reduction would be greater—143 tons.

Research laboratory operators, such as pharmaceutical manufacturers and universities, have recognized the need to reduce carbon emissions in order to minimize global climate change. Many colleges and universities have become signatory to the American College and University Presidents' Climate Commitment, which involves first completing an emissions inventory. Within two years, a target date and interim milestones for becoming climate neutral must be set. Immediate steps are then taken to reduce greenhouse gas emissions by choosing from a list of short-term actions. Sustainability topics must be integrated into the curriculum to make it part of the educational experience. Lastly, the action plan as well as inventory and progress reports must be made publicly available.

Corporate Carbon Emission Initiatives

In 1999, J&J set a goal to reduce greenhouse gas (GHG) emissions from its facilities worldwide. This goal became the basis for the Climate-Friendly Energy Policy, which was approved by the Executive Committee in 2003. The goal for 2010 is to be 7 percent below 1990 levels in absolute terms (Climate Northeast 2006, 1–3). This is aggressive in a growing company, and achieving it requires actions on a number of fronts. It begins with implementing engineering changes and equipment changes to reduce energy consumption. Next, J&J looks for opportunities to install co-generation systems on its sites, where heat from electricity generation is recovered to maximize overall efficiency. The company also has installed onsite systems that make use of solar, geothermal, biomass, landfill gas, and other forms of renewable energy. Another way J&J achieves this goal is by purchasing electricity generated from renewable energy and by purchasing Renewable Energy Certificates (RECs) and carbon offsets.

The major challenge is attaining CO_2 reduction while the business continues to grow. To avoid the most damaging effects of climate change, experts believe that global GHG emissions must be reduced by 60 to 90 percent by 2050. Therefore, as J&J sales increase, GHG emissions must move in the other direction— and eventually without the help of RECs and carbon offsets. Another challenge is to account for GHG emissions from the supply chain, as well as from the use and disposal of different products. J&J hopes to begin to influence suppliers, contract manufacturers, and carriers to measure, report, and reduce their GHG emissions.

Although J&J has completed many cost-effective projects to improve efficiency and use renewable energy, it is admittedly not at the pace and scale needed to meet its absolute GHG reduction goal. RECs and carbon offsets provide a mechanism to support renewable energy projects on a scale that is impractical on J&J sites, such as large wind farms and biomass projects. This strategy is consistent with a market-based, "cap and trade" system that is a fundamental part of most regional and international agreements in place to address climate change. In 2007, J&J spent about $1.5 million on RECs, offsets, and green power premiums. All are verified by a third party as being attributable to credible projects. For instance, all RECs purchased in the United States are "green-E certified" by the Center for Resource Solutions.

According to the United Nations Intergovernmental Panel on Climate Change, global GHG emissions from human activity were 49 billion metric tons in 2004. In 2007, J&J emitted less than 1 million metric tons of CO_2 from the use of fuel and electricity at facilities worldwide. While the J&J emissions are a relatively small part of the world total, it will take the collective action of many such organizations to prevent the adverse consequences and costs of climate change. J&J believes it has a responsibility in this

area, even if the impact of the company's efforts alone may seem insignificant compared to the magnitude of the challenge. In addition to fulfilling a social responsibility, the investments J&J has made to reduce CO_2 emissions have returned good value to the company. From 2004 through 2007, through the CO_2 Reduction Projects Funding Process, J&J committed $97 million for the construction of 49 projects. In addition to reducing CO_2 emissions by 88,000 tons per year, these projects will collectively provide a 16.3 percent internal rate of return (IRR).

However, traditional IRR comparisons did not often incorporate the full value of GHG-reduction projects or an adequate means of comparing investment options and allocating capital. Most proposed GHG reduction projects were relatively low risk and offered operating cost savings, GHG reductions, and other business value or community benefits. According to J&J, what was lacking was both flexibility and incentive to pursue clean energy and efficiency upgrades coupled with the certainty that these investments would not restrict the business units' capital budgeting. With strong support from J&J's Chief Financial Officer, a capital relief strategy was implemented to overcome the barriers to approval for GHG-reduction projects. Up to $40 million was allocated annually to business units to cover the capital costs for investments in GHG projects if projects meet certain criteria such as IRR, with the intent of increasing available funding for large-scale projects ($500,000 or more). To provide flexibility, J&J generally approves upgrades with an IRR of 10 percent or higher if they demonstrate additional benefits to the company and its stakeholders. Thus capital relief funds are made available to those facility upgrades that perhaps do not quite reach the target IRR, but offer substantial GHG reductions or benefits to the business, such as energy reliability and building performance. For example, solar projects expecting IRRs of approximately 11 to 14 percent received funding because they helped build knowledge in an important emerging technology and also support strong community interest in clean energy sources. Overall, the capital relief funds serve to supplement business units' capital budgets, and with project approval from the corporate committee, business units make the final decision on which investments ultimately move forward.

Laboratory Water Conservation

Another significant component of reducing the environmental impact of buildings is water consumption and efficiency. In many parts of the world, potable water is not an abundant resource and minimizing usage should always be a primary goal when designing or operating a laboratory. When feasible, a sustainable laboratory should control site surface runoff, use water efficiently, and recycle nonindustrial wastewater.

Laboratory Water Demand and Consumption

Similar to energy usage, water demand and consumption in a modern laboratory differ from other commercial facilities. Percentage of daily peak instantaneous water demand classified by end use is illustrated below for an example laboratory building. The sanitary domestic water demand component (37 percent) primarily represents the population-based requirements for toilet room fixtures and freshwater drinking. The irrigation component (5 percent) is related to exterior building landscaping. HVAC equipment water (19 percent) is primarily fed to evaporative cooling towers for heat rejection from water chillers used for environmental dehumidification and cooling during summer months. Deionized or other high-

purity water systems are common in most laboratories, and in this example account for about 2 percent of the peak instantaneous demand. Lastly, the laboratory domestic water component (37 percent) includes lab sinks, glasswash systems, and other lab equipment. Peak instantaneous demand figures are primarily useful only for sizing of system components. An analysis of daily water consumption by end use, such as the accompanying illustration, or annual consumption is more useful for targeting and quantifying water efficiency measures. It is evident by comparing these two summaries for the example building that while there may be many fixtures and other equipment that use domestic laboratory water, its consumption is not a major component of overall building consumption when compared to other end uses such as HVAC, irrigation, and sanitary domestic water consumption—therefore these are key systems to which water conservation measures should be applied.

For each water end use in a typical laboratory facility, there are specific design opportunities that can be exploited to reduce overall water usage and dependence on municipal water. Synergies between the sustainable HVAC strategies discussed earlier and building water usage frequently exist. Cooling load reduction or efficient system selection can lower cooling tower makeup water consumption, sometimes dramatically, and certain low-energy HVAC concepts such as evaporative cooling can actually increase water usage.

Sustainable Water Systems

There are several sustainable central water systems that should be considered for new laboratory facilities. Two major concepts are recycled "gray water" systems and rainwater collection systems. "Black water" systems, which involve reuse of biologically or chemi-

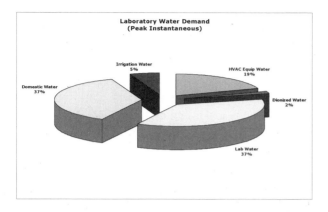

Peak instantaneous water demand by end use for a mixed-science laboratory in the United States. *Image courtesy of KlingStubbins.*

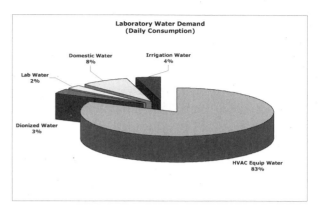

Daily water consumption by end use corresponding to the previous building example. *Image courtesy of KlingStubbins.*

cally contaminated sanitary and industrial waste, are currently considered unsuitable for modern laboratory facilities. This includes recycling water from water closets, urinals, HVAC equipment (including boiler and cooling tower blow down), and lab sinks.

Gray water in laboratories typically consists of water recycled from handwashing sinks, showers, washing machines, and other equipment, as well as any other sources that are not considered black-water uses as described above. Depending on the project, gray-water sources may also include water used for rinsing of equipment, testing of fire protection sprinkler systems, water condensation from air conditioning cooling coils, and water rejected from water purification processes. Some purified water pretreatment systems use chemicals, and can generate a constant wastewater stream of 25 to 30 percent of the purified water flow. Gray water is most immediately suitable for landscape irrigation and can often be used to offset 100 percent of that demand if proper storage, filtration, and distribution systems are employed. In some parts of the United States (subject to local plumbing codes), gray water also can be used to

supply water to toilets and urinals. Another possible use of gray water is cooling tower makeup, depending on overall total dissolved solid (TDS) and phosphate levels in the water collected. Collecting cooling coil condensate can be particularly effective in humid climates due to the large volumes of outdoor air that laboratory HVAC designs typically dehumidify.

Rainwater can be collected from roofs and other hardscape areas of the site. It is common to locate rainwater storage tanks and distribution equipment below grade, such as in basement areas in laboratory buildings. The architectural design of the building also can be enhanced to maximize the harvesting capabilities of the collection surfaces. Rainwater is typically cleaner than gray water, but under normal conditions can be contaminated by organic materials such as pollen, leaves, and dust. Flushing controls are typically incorporated into rainwater recycling systems to allow the initial volume of rainwater to pass through the system and eliminate the majority of impurities. In the United States, rainwater is largely used for irrigation and toilet flushing, similar to gray water systems. With proper filtration, however, other options for supplying rainwater to domestic, HVAC, and laboratory end uses may be considered. Unlike gray water, rainwater is not a regular water source, so the storage volumes required to meet daily system demands are higher and more sophisticated controls are necessary. Rainwater storage requirements should be analyzed using tools such as a site water balance, which was mentioned earlier in this chapter.

Below is a summary of conservation opportunities that may be considered for each laboratory water end use component.

Domestic Water (General Use)

- Flush valves with lowest available flow for toilets and urinals
- Dual-flush water closets, waterless urinals, and other high-efficiency sanitary fixtures
- Aerators for handwashing sink faucets
- Shower water flow control devices
- Gray water or rainwater for toilet and urinal water supply
- Filtered rainwater used for specific domestic supply water needs

Irrigation

- Landscape plant types that are climate-tolerant and can survive on natural rainfall volumes after they are established
- Gray water and/or rainwater for irrigation

HVAC

- Gray water, rainwater, and collected cooling coil condensate for cooling tower makeup

- Inspection and repair of leaks in closed system hydronic systems
- Maximization of design criteria for total dissolved solids (TDS) concentrations in open cooling tower systems to minimize blow down water flow and required chemical treatment
- Collected rainwater as a source for humidifier makeup
- Recycling all steam condensate back to boiler in lieu of dumping to sanitary drain

Purified Water Systems

- Maximization of efficiency of reverse osmosis (RO) units and other equipment to minimize water rejected
- Capture of reject water into gray-water collection system
- Minimization of number of supply outlets in facility
- Installation of water flow control devices at all use points

Domestic Water (Laboratory Use)

- Minimization of number of use points in facility
- Installation of water flow control devices at all use points
- Use of water-efficient equipment
- If available, use of rainwater for sinks and other fixtures
- Low-flow lab and handwashing sink faucets with aerators
- Elimination of cup sinks in fume hoods to discourage using domestic water for local cooling (this also

helps to prevent potential environmental issues if there is a chemical spill)

Purified Water

• Use of equipment that aligns to user criteria for water quality but maintains the lowest water quality that meets the requirements of relevant guidelines such as ASTM ratings, ISO (International Organization for Standardization), NCCLS (National Committee for Clinical Lab Standards), or U.S. Pharmacopeia

• Encouragement of users to rely on central water purification equipment instead of local purification systems to minimize disposal and maintenance

• Use of RO membranes with high recovery rates

• Selection of RO equipment that does not have a high frequency of flush cycles

• Utilization of looped distribution systems to avoid stagnant sections that require flushing periodically

• Limiting of distribution system pressures to reduce pump horsepower

• Utilization of pretreatment equipment that is self-cleaning to reduce the amount of disposable filtration components

Water Supply Concepts

When planning a sustainable laboratory building, there are numerous design techniques that can be considered for plumbing/process services that will meet the minimum quality required by most users and also are considerate of global environmental concerns. The design focus for piped laboratory utilities should be centered on specifying piping materials that have the least environmental impact and orienting systems so that the length of piping distribution is minimized. In addition, system pressures for pumped utilities should be minimized. Another key element of piping distribution systems is insulation. Specification of insulation thickness should be based upon water service temperatures and the surrounding climate of the project site. More temperate climates may not require insulation since groundwater temperatures are higher and the ambient air temperatures and moisture levels are not extreme.

Piping materials considered for service distribution should be examined for their sustainable aspects. Pipe material quantities can be significant in a laboratory building—a typical three-story, 150,000-square-foot laboratory can contain over 10,000 linear feet of piping for laboratory supply services such as compressed air, vacuum, nitrogen, purified water, cylinder gasses, process cooling, steam, condensate, domestic water, laboratory water, and tempered water for eye wash and safety showers. The same building can also have over 4,000 linear feet of laboratory drainage piping from laboratory sinks, cup sinks, and fume hoods. There are several different pipe material choices, including copper, PVC, CPVC, PVDF, polypropylene, glass, steel, and cast iron. There is a service lifespan and carbon footprint of manufacturing for each type of pipe material, and various fitting options also affect the lifecycle cost of the piping system. Plastic materials have emerged as good candidates for sustainable designs. Plastics are cost effective, energy-conscious building materials and have a manufacturing process that requires less energy than metallic pipe. However, pipe material selection is highly dependent on the size and type of project. Other considerations may include recyclability and the installation procedure. Metallic piping is generally recyclable, while not all plastics may be recycled. Plastic piping with glued joints tends to be less labor intensive than metals, which reduces construction costs and energy during the installation process.

Most large lab facilities require booster pumps for both domestic and laboratory water to meet the pressure requirements of safety showers and other equipment. The pumps can be selected in a triplex split-unit skid and each rated at one-third of the total required capacity. In this configuration the "lead" pump operates continuously and the second and third pumps start when there is a demand increase. On average during 75 percent of operating hours, only 25 percent of the maximum demand will be needed. This configuration allows the lead pump to handle the diversified load the majority of the operating hours, and results in more efficient operating points and longer service lifespan for the lag pumps. Another key element in a booster system is the integration of a bladder tank to regulate the water pressure and allow the pumps to shut down during periods of low or zero demand, resulting in reduced energy consumption and pump wear.

Depending on the geographic location and function of a lab building, the incoming municipal water service may need treatment before it can be used for domestic cold water purposes. The required treatment will vary depending on the water quality levels determined by a local authority water test. Systems such as water softeners may also be required to treat mineral salts, and recycling the water rejected from this process may also be possible.

In addition to specifying efficient plumbing fixtures, toilet room devices such as auto-sensor faucets and flush valves with disposable battery packs have permeated the building industry. These devices provide water conservation by using less than one-quarter of a gallon of water per cycle and disabling water flow immediately after the hands are pulled away from the faucet. There are also self-powered sensor faucets available with a small hydroelectric turbine that charges the power supply during usage, eliminating the need to replace batteries or use external electricity.

Another component for consideration is hot water production for the domestic and laboratory water systems. Numerous energy source options exist for hot water heating, including natural gas, electricity, and steam utility services. These systems may then be supplemented by a solar thermal system, which has proven to be cost-effective in many applications. A recent laboratory project in Tucson, Arizona, implemented a solar thermal system, and 32 percent of the domestic hot water heating demand was offset. Specifying instantaneous water heaters may also be a suitable option for minimizing spatial requirements and storage losses of the equipment. There are also alternatives to recover low-grade heat from wastewater and use the energy to preheat incoming services. One example is utilizing heat rejected from the HVAC system (chiller or condenser water heat recovery mentioned earlier) to preheat domestic water, which may normally enter facilities below 60°F. Each laboratory building has different functions and design criteria, and certain options may or may not be feasible. For example, if a building is located in a climate where there is significant solar insolation, then solar thermal heating panels might prove to be effective—the technique is to find an application that is matched to the building location and requirements. This process of developing specific options is critical in creating a unique sustainable solution and should be commenced early in a project.

Waste System Concepts

The design of the gravity laboratory waste system is important when minimizing required plumbing piping materials. The sanitary waste system in a laboratory building will typically serve the toilet rooms, janitors' closets, and mechanical room floor drains. Stacking the toilet cores vertically in a building reduces the amount of pipe required, since common risers can be used to serve the toilets and the amount of transitional fittings will be lower. This concept can be applied to the laboratory waste piping system design by incorporating vertical stacks for the main collection associated with each laboratory module. A vertical gravity stack allows larger water volumes when compared to horizontal piping of the same size, so horizontal drains should be limited to connecting each lab bench to a vertical riser for each lab module. These risers may then be connected to larger horizontal pipe mains on one level only.

The vent piping for both sanitary and laboratory waste should utilize a combined waste and vent design whenever allowed by local plumbing codes. Dedicated vents for each fixture should be avoided, if possible. In some cases, system concepts should be reviewed with local code officials early in the design process, and if necessary consider applying for a variance.

System Cleaning and Testing

Due to the precise nature of tests and experiments conducted using laboratory gases and liquids, cleaning and testing of laboratory plumbing and process piping distribution systems can be extensive and the sustainability of various methods should be considered. These processes should be scrutinized and tailored for each separate piping system. For example, consider deleting the oxygen-grade service cleaning requirement for certain gas and specialty gas systems. Cleaning requirements as defined by NFPA 99: Standard for Health Care Facilities for gas systems

such as compressed air, nitrogen, and carbon dioxide have been removed in several projects and nitrogen purges used instead. Also, packaging waste will be reduced if piping and components are not bagged for shipment. Labor and energy savings along the delivery chain (when the material is fabricated, boxed, shipped, and installed) will also be realized during construction.

In addition, reducing the flushing requirements for recirculating-type HVAC piping systems can improve environmental impact. Consider eliminating the final flush from the specified cleaning and flushing process to reduce freshwater consumption during construction. Some building owners have opted to allow the final chemical treatment used in the cleaning process to remain in the piping system. This decision greatly reduces the volume of chemically treated water that must be treated offsite. After flushing and cleaning, the initial start-up of domestic water piping systems can lead to chemicals entering the sanitary system. Instead, an alternate sanitization process as opposed to chemical treatment may be considered. Other options for sanitization include hot water flushing, which is referenced in ASHRAE standards. A more aggressive technique is to find a use for the wastewater from starting systems so that it does not become discharged waste.

It is suggested that during the design process each plumbing and process system and the sustainable strategies that apply to each be listed. For each item indicate the benefits—does it reduce material, reduce energy, reduce water consumption, and/or reduce carbon footprint? Possible disadvantages, such as increased material or labor costs, availability, durability, and adherence to the function and criteria of the laboratory should also be weighed. Then the preferred concepts can be selected and coordinated to optimize the laboratory lay-out and their interaction with other engineered systems.

Conclusion

Since ventilation requirements in laboratories are more significant than other commercial buildings, thermal load is driven predominantly by either internal load, dilution rate, or exhausted equipment such as fume hoods. Minimization of these loads and process energy end uses is a vital first step in energy conservation efforts for laboratory environments. There are many options for air and waterside systems, and selection should be based on analysis conducted using the interactive energy and lifecycle cost models discussed in Chapter 5, as well as tradeoffs with other components of the building design. These system options, in addition to the design alternatives for heating and cooling, power generation, renewable energy, and laboratory water systems also presented in this chapter, are not intended to form an exhaustive list, but rather a framework of relevant ideas. The laboratory designer or building owner will clearly have a constantly evolving palette of different options to consider during sustainability efforts, and while there are many variables which will influence the performance of a building and its systems, achieving a suitable balance between safety, comfort and convenience, and resource efficiency is possible.

Key Concepts

- Laboratory HVAC loads are primarily related to three characteristics—internal load, dilution rate,

and equipment exhaust—and should be minimized to the extent feasible as a first step in energy conservation.

- Energy-efficient air and waterside system designs should be explored and an optimal solution chosen based on factors such as HVAC loads, climate, complexity, and lifecycle cost.

- Control of laboratory systems, especially energy-intensive components such as fume hood exhaust, is critical in reducing building energy consumption.

- Both internal and external building airflow characteristics should be considered during sustainable system design so that environmental safety is not compromised.

- Many options exist for low-energy heating and cooling, power generation, and renewable energy, and they should be analyzed in parallel with the air and waterside system design.

- The carbon footprint of a laboratory can be estimated and the relationship between building carbon emissions and site energy use should be understood.

- Laboratory building water usage is significant and sustainable design requires implementation of strategies that reduce potable domestic and HVAC equipment water consumption.

REFERENCES

American Industrial Hygiene Association. 2002. Position Paper. Hazardous Exhaust Systems in Research Laboratories That Involve "Laboratory Scale" Use of Chemicals.

ASHRAE. 2007. *ASHRAE Handbook-HVAC Applications*. American Society of Heating, Refrigerating and Air-Conditioning Engineers, Inc.

Climate Northeast, a project of the World Resources Institute. 2006. GHG Project Case Study. Heat and Power from Landfill Gas: Johnson & Johnson's Experience.

Johnson & Johnson. 2008. 2007 Sustainability Report.

Rumsey, Peter, and John Weale. 2007. Chilled Beams in Labs. *ASHRAE Journal*, January.

Sharp, Gordon P. 2009. A Comprehensive Review of the IEQ and Energy Savings Impact of Dynamically Varying Air Change Rates in Labs and Vivariums. *ALN Magazine*, March.

U.S. Environmental Protection Agency (EPA) in partnership with the U.S. Department of Energy. 2003. Energy Recovery for Ventilation Air in Laboratories. Laboratories for the 21st Century: Best Practices.

World Resources Institute, in collaboration with The Climate Group. 2006. Corporate Case Studies. DePuy (Johnson & Johnson): Using Geothermal Energy for Heating and Cooling.

chapter **7**

Indoor Environment
The Health and Happiness of Building Occupants

Courtesy of Croxton Collaborative / KlingStubbins
Photography by © Woodruff / Brown Architectural Photography.

Introduction

A significant amount of the discussion of sustainability has centered on energy, carbon, and water use, and rightly so—as mentioned above, buildings use a significant percentage of these resources throughout society. Efforts to reduce carbon emissions, energy use, and dependence on fossil fuel for energy production are a vital part of our ongoing effort to create and operate high-performance facilities. It's important to keep in mind that the primary reason for buildings is to provide enclosed interior spaces for people to occupy. Possibly the most important part of sustainable facility design is focusing on the satisfaction and human health issues associated with the indoor environment. Since people spend an average of 90 percent of each day inside buildings,[1] the different factors of the indoor environment play a big part in people's everyday health and satisfaction. Studies have shown that strategies associated with human factors can have a significant impact on self-reported satisfaction, measured human

This chapter focuses on several of the sustainability categories discussed in Chapter 1. See page 18 for more information.

health indicators, and on overall productivity. In some cases, indoor environmental strategies require using more energy, so a balance must be maintained between energy use and human factors. In laboratory buildings, there are several strategies that need to be carefully considered, because the human satisfaction must be balanced with scientific requirements. For example, although daylight has been correlated with occupant satisfaction, some experimental setups are not possible in the presence of uncontrolled daylight. Attention to both the occupants and the scientific mission is required for a successful outcome. In addition, there are many ways in which laboratory planners and owners can learn from newer workplace strategies that are being implemented in office buildings and other nonlab spaces—in many cases lab design can benefit from the accumulated wisdom of these strategies moving forward.

This chapter discusses a number of factors that shape the indoor environment. Beginning with broad investigations of how laboratories function as workplaces, we'll examine how issues of organization and flexibility can contribute to successful laboratory designs. Corporate workplace strategies are often applicable to laboratory facilities. Also included is an investigation of several general types of indoor strategies—indoor air quality, daylighting, occupant control—and how they can contribute to increased productivity and human health. Finally, we will delve into detail about laboratory lighting and acoustics and how they impact the interior environment of laboratory facilities.

Learning from Corporate Workplace Trends

Before delving into specific strategies, it is important to think about broad issues of how people work in

laboratories, and how to make safe, healthy, and productive places for researchers to work. Many recent strategies for workplace organization can offer lessons for laboratory planning. There are a number of trends that contribute to workplace efficiency and productivity, and many of these, proven in corporate interiors, are beginning to be implemented in labs.

In many ways, workplace trends have always informed lab planning decisions. In the past, corporate office lay-outs and labs were both similarly fixed and static—a conventional relationship of fixed offices to workstations is paralleled with conventional fixed lab lay-outs. In the recent past, corporate workspace strategies have evolved to recognize the value of flexibility and adaptability, as we have recognized the

For AstraZeneca's R&D Expansion project in Waltham, Massachuetts, fixed fume hoods and sink cabinets are placed near the service corridor, leaving the majority of the lab space open for movable tables with overhead service carriers. This allows for significant modular flexibility which should significantly reduce time and materials used for reconfiguration. Flexible systems also allow for individual researchers to adjust their spaces to specific needs and to address individual ergonomics. *Image courtesy of KlingStubbins. Photography © Robert Benson Photography.*

value of dynamic, flexible solutions. It is not surprising that labs, because of the speed of scientific change, have even more need for flexibility and adaptability, to be able to reconfigure lay-outs without significant renovation time or cost. Many of the solutions in lab casework flexibility grew out of the success of flexible office systems furniture in the late 1980s. A concern for ergonomics and the realization that workers come in all sizes and their tasks require different accommodations, all helped the growth of flexible systems furniture and this, in turn, influenced the design of flexible casework systems as well.

Conventional fixed peninsulas casework with centrally located services often becomes cumbersome

By placing journals, microfilm, and computer technology in this key corner location, and by including a communicating stair, research teams can meet and interact informally in this break room/reading room at the Johnson & Johnson PRD Drug Discovery Laboratory, Phase II facility in La Jolla, California. *Image courtesy of KlingStubbins. Photography by © Tom Bonner 2007.*

to users needing space for newer and larger free-standing equipment. Walk through an older lab configured with such an arrangement and any open floor space is usually suddenly home to the newest equipment, with support spaces fit in wherever possible. For new lab spaces, flexible lab casework, modular utilities and demountable partitions can provide solutions. As in corporate workplace planning, it is critical to weigh the first costs for flexibility with a projection of how frequently the spaces will be reconfigured. Current statistics indicate that distributed work accounts for 10 percent of all work, with a projected growth by year-end of 2010 to be upwards of 25 percent.[2] With this significant increase in such a short timeframe, one can only assume that this percentage will continually increase as continental boundaries become blurred with the global industrial development. Distributed work is made possible only through the advancements of computer connectivity.

The corporate workplace approach toward teaming and collaboration and its successes are being recognized by the scientific community as similar accommodations are being requested and implemented within the lab environment. As such, the physical space may vary but the goal of supporting individual project teams locally or globally, supplemented through technology, remains the same—connecting people with people.

Teaming accommodations vary from the formal, closed, more conventional conference room configurations, to the random seating accommodations in a common corridor or secluded nook. Recent experience has shown that the most frequent population for meetings is four or fewer—this has led in corporate planning to more informal, smaller teaming areas, "touchdown" spaces or "cafe" spaces. Although many lab planners would find it problematic

204

to place a beverage service within a floor's reach of a laboratory, it is more and more frequently done. It is possible to create informal teaming areas and cafe areas close to the labs, but clearly delineated to maintain safety procedures for the labs themselves. Frequently they are contained within a zone outside of a lab and centrally located to other general support services such as copy, mail, and restrooms. These informal spaces offer a casual atmosphere where employees can grab a cappuccino and discuss the latest project details with colleagues. Cafes can be

as simple as offering the basic accommodations to elaborate settings including a variety of seating options, wireless technologies, and conferencing tools, such as writable and tackable surfaces.

Although there are many common workplace trends seen in both the corporate and scientific environments, there remain some specific applications where the scientific culture and work patterns are different. Evidence is showing that these differences are decreasing.

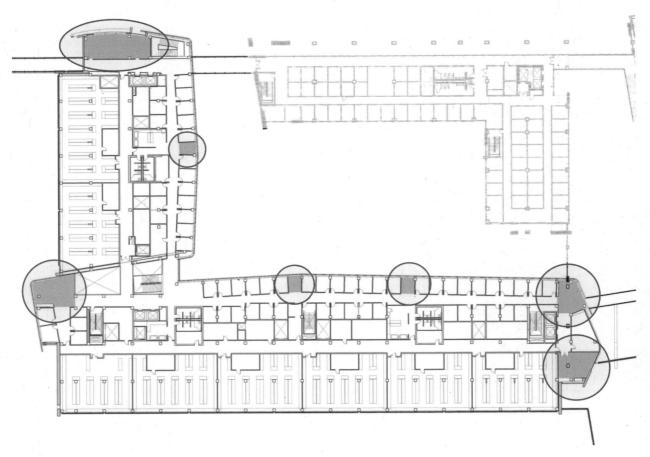

At the U.S. Food and Drug Administration's White Oak, Maryland, campus, the new facility blocking and stacking plan shows a distribution of interaction areas ranging from informal cafes and break rooms to conference and meeting rooms. *Image courtesy of KlingStubbins.*

At University of Colorado Denver Research 2 in Aurora, Colorado, a dual-height interaction space connects teams and allows for casual collaboration. Amenities and computer connectivity makes this space effective for informal seminars and team study. *Image courtesy of KlingStubbins. Photography © Ron Johnson Photography.*

Traditional scientific research relies on physical analysis of concrete elements and compounds, yielding data that is analyzed and interpreted. While much of corporate workflow is completely digital at this point, there is still a significant majority of scientific research that is physically based. From a practical standpoint, this difference is negligible—there is still in both corporate and research institutions the need for some of the work to be physically collocated, and the ability for much of the work to be connected electronically. When it comes to facility lay-out, the concept of "hotelling," setting up generic workspaces that do not permanently belong to one employee, can work for both, but for the lab spaces themselves this is less true. In an effort to attract and retain the best and brightest talent, many scientific organizations have traditionally provided researchers private offices, and shared offices for junior researchers. Recently, corporate office projects have been migrating from mostly closed offices to majority open-office environments, and in the recent years scientific projects are starting to follow suit. Recent projects illustrate a trend toward accommodating just 40 percent of the scientific staff in private offices, which is a great leap in advancement as just ten years ago the metric was far greater—closer to 70 to 80 percent.[3] In addition, space planners have found that the preference for closed offices has a generational component—as the baby boomers begin to retire to make room for the younger generations, the trend for heavy private-office utilization in labs may mirror the streamlined corporate approach, including the integration of collaboration and teaming spaces throughout.

Of course for many "dry" lab spaces, the differences between laboratory and office space is less distinct, and the similarities to corporate office planning are greater.

Costs and Returns

To effectively evaluate sustainable design strategies and how they can be implemented, it is important to understand the impacts on cost relative to return. While there have been several studies showing different cost for "green buildings," one of the key recent studies on LEED Certified Buildings concluded that "there is no significant difference in average cost for green buildings as compared to non-green buildings."[4] This means that in looking at a range of different projects, including laboratories, the variation in costs based on other factors was more significant than the variation in costs based on conventional versus "green." On a single project basis, it is definitely true that some strategies cost more than their con-

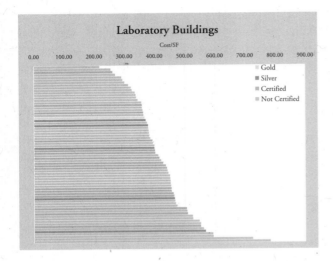

Laboratory Buildings
Cost/SF

Gold
Silver
Certified
Not Certified

This graph indicates costs per square foot for various different laboratory projects studied in 2007. The variation in costs based on research standards is greater than any variation due to incorporation of sustainable strategies. *Courtesy of Peter Morris and Lisa Matthiessen.*

that help keep employees healthier, satisfied, and more productive are going to have more economic impact on operations. The Center for Building Performance and Diagnostics at Carnegie Mellon University has estimated, based on over 20 different research studies, that buildings that include these strategies can increase productivity and satisfaction by 8 to 20 percent overall.[6] The strategies primarily break down into the following categories: Indoor Air Quality, Thermal Comfort, Occupant Control, Access to Outdoor Environment, and Acoustical Performance.

ventional alternatives—for example, a dimmable light fixture ballast costs more than a standard nondimmable model. These costs can be offset by energy savings (payback) or satisfaction. Energy savings are relatively easy to calculate—if the dimming ballast costs $100 more to purchase, and it saves $25 per year in energy use, it will pay for itself in four years of operation. Analyzing the returns based on productivity is more difficult to quantify, but potentially much more powerful, because the vast majority of operating costs of a typical building is the salaries and benefits of the employees who work there. One study for office buildings showed that 86 percent was employee costs (see the following figure). In that study, energy made up about 5 percent, and maintenance made up another 5 percent.[5] Although for laboratories these numbers would be different—higher energy cost, but also higher salaries—the main point is that a 1 percent increase in productivity will cover the cost of rent, utilities, and maintenance! Strategies

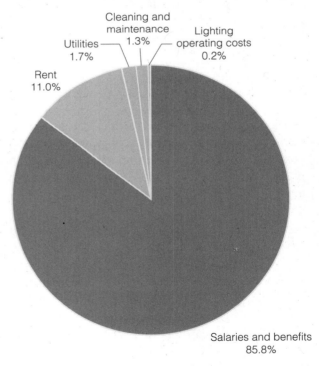

Cleaning and maintenance 1.3%
Utilities 1.7%
Lighting operating costs 0.2%
Rent 11.0%
Salaries and benefits 85.8%

The relative costs for operation of a typical office building, per square foot. Since the employee salaries and benefits make up such a large majority of the costs, strategies that decrease absenteeism or increase productivity have a large impact on overall operating costs. *Image courtesy of Energy Star website (www.energystar.gov/index.cfm?c=business).*

Figures C1-C5: This project adds 55,000 square feet of office facilities and 72,500 square feet of research space to AstraZeneca's research campus outside of Boston. The new facility was carefully sited to preserve natural features, wetlands, and other habitat. The landscaping plan features local vegetation, for low-impact and low-maintenance plantings. The native plant species contribute both aesthetically and functionally, working to help manage stormwater and restore wetlands through natural means. The office and lab wings are connected via a one-story bridge spanning the existing wetlands.

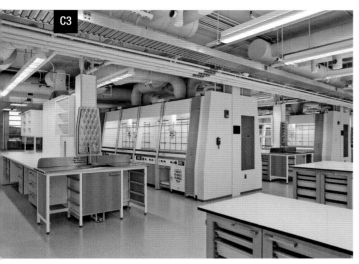

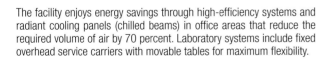
The facility enjoys energy savings through high-efficiency systems and radiant cooling panels (chilled beams) in office areas that reduce the required volume of air by 70 percent. Laboratory systems include fixed overhead service carriers with movable tables for maximum flexibility.

C6

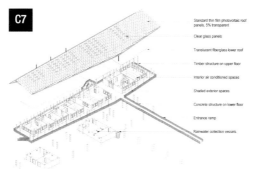

C7

Standard thin film photovoltaic roof panels, 5% transparent

Clear glass panels

Translucent fiberglass lower roof

Timber structure on upper floor

Interior air conditioned spaces

Shaded exterior spaces

Concrete structure on lower floor

Entrance ramp

Rainwater collection vessels

Figures C6-C10: Located in a sensitive environment in Panama, with challenging climate and rainfall, this project incorporates a number of different sustainable strategies simultaneously. Set on piers, bridging existing wetlands, and sited to avoid key trees and landscape features, the project sits lightly on the site. Rainwater collection and onsite waste treatment are key components of this project's relationship to the site.

The large roof is two-layered; the top layer is a photovoltaic (PV) array that generates up to 75% of the base building energy use. This is possible because the PV and inner roof layers allow daylight to penetrate to interior spaces, reducing electrical lighting needs. Space conditioning is limited to research critical areas only. Open air circulation areas are covered to protect from the local rainfall, but naturally ventilated, as shown above. See chapter 2 for additional information about this project.

Image Credits: Kiss+Cathcart, Architects

Smithsonian Tropical Research Institute—Mobile Labs

Panama, Various Locations

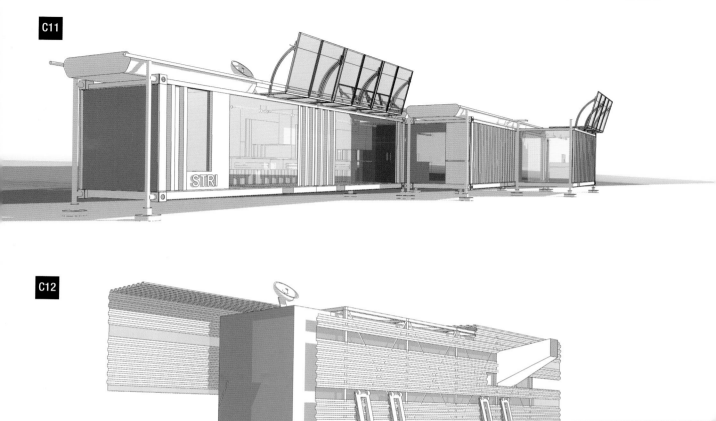

C11

C12

Figures C11-C14: Environmental science and environmental design function in unison for the Smithsonian Tropical Research Institute. KlingStubbins completed a Comprehensive Master Plan for STRI, whose facilities span over a dozen sites throughout the diverse tropical environments of Panama. The demands of tropical field research require swift deployment of support spaces, while the stewardship of the natural

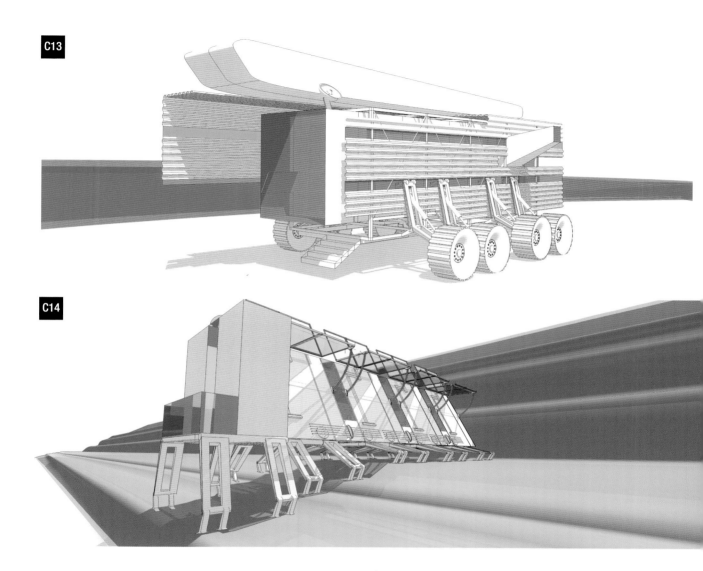

C13

C14

environment requires that those support spaces leave a minimal footprint. The master plan investigated an approach to this paradox with the development of reusable and movable field research facilities—lightweight structures that can support research activities and safe residence for researchers.

Image Credits: KlingStubbins

St. Lawrence University Johnson Hall of Science

Canton, NY

Figures C15-C19: This facility houses academic biology and chemistry departments at St. Lawrence University. Materials selection and arrangement provided significant opportunities for community collaboration and project synergies. Working with local Amish farmers who used discarded wood, over 78 percent of construction waste was diverted from landfills. Nearly 50 percent of building materials were manufactured within 500 miles of project site, the project's materials were made from 19 percent recycled content, and 95 percent of wood was FSC certified.

C35

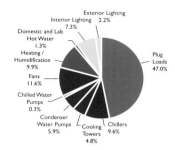

C36

Laboratory / Office Building

Exterior Lighting 2.2%
Interior Lighting 7.3%
Domestic and Lab Hot Water 1.3%
Heating / Humidification 9.9%
Fans 11.6%
Chilled Water Pumps 0.3%
Condenser Water Pumps 5.9%
Cooling Towers 4.8%
Chillers 9.6%
Plug Loads 47.0%

Office Building

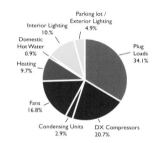

Parking lot / Exterior Lighting 4.9%
Interior Lighting 10.%
Domestic Hot Water 0.9%
Heating 9.7%
Fans 16.8%
Condensing Units 2.9%
DX Compressors 20.7%
Plug Loads 34.1%

Laboratory Building

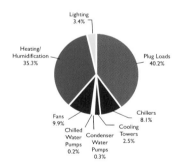

Lighting 3.4%
Heating/ Humidification 35.3%
Fans 9.9%
Chilled Water Pumps 0.2%
Condenser Water Pumps 0.3%
Cooling Towers 2.5%
Chillers 8.1%
Plug Loads 40.2%

Simulation and energy modeling during design ensures that sustainability strategies are being met. Building Information Modeling allows for design coordination of architectural, structural, and MEP engineering systems before construction starts.

C37

Figures C37-C40: A research partnership between the Sierra Nevada College and University of California, Davis, this 47,000-square-foot facility fits into a campus fabric near the alpine lakes and streams that the researchers study.

Within the vocabulary of traditional exterior detailing are carefully designed shading devices and skylights modeled and evaluated using simulation tools as well as physical models on a heliodon at the PG&E Energy Center in San Francisco. Inside the building are high-tech laboratories with flexibility to meet future research needs. Use of daylighting,

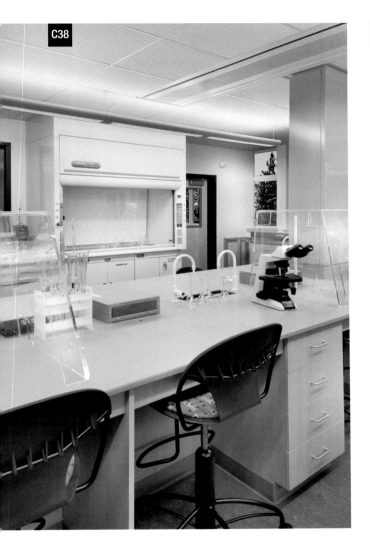

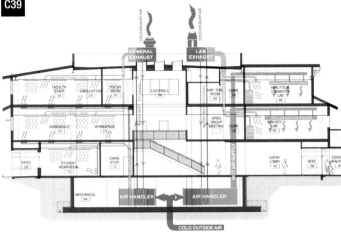

selective natural ventilation and chilled beams for cooling and a high-efficiency hydronic heating system contributes to an estimated 63 percent energy savings over ASHRAE 90.1 standards.

The configuration around a central atrium for daylight, a water reclamation system, as well as sensitive landscaping contribute to this LEED Platinum design. The 30-kW photovoltaic system covers approximately 10 percent of the electricity demand of the building. For more information, please refer to Chapter 6.

Image Credits: *Collaborative Design Studio, Architects*

Figures C41-C45: This project was conceived as a catalyst for interdisciplinary science. The complex's sustainable design features include; automatic light sensors and an integrated lighting system that conserves energy by adjusting for ambient light levels in interior spaces; an energy wheel that utilizes already cooled exhaust air to condition incoming fresh air; extensive exterior glazing and sunshading to maximize interior daylight while minimizing heat gain; and an energy monitor in the building's lobby to encourage conservation by demonstrating the building's energy load. The facility should use approximately two-thirds the amount of energy normally used by science buildings of similar size.

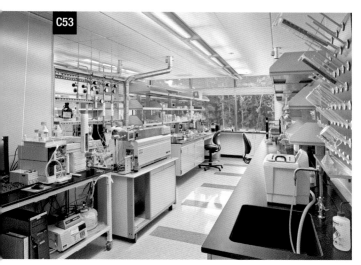

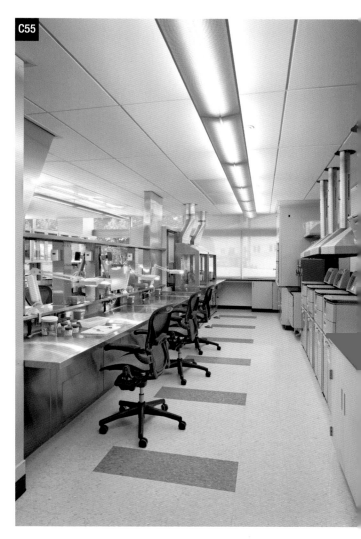

lab spaces, and all lab and office spaces were designed as VAV air systems. Due to the prominent view of a significant portion of the roof by the laboratory/office spaces, that portion of the roof was designed to be free from MEP equipment, ductwork, and appurtenances. The structure was sized to allow for a future vegetated "green" roof to be installed.

Figures C56-C59: Transformed from producing NECCO wafers, Sky Bars, and Sweetheart Conversation Hearts, the landmark NECCO candy factory in Cambridge, Massachusetts was converted to research laboratories for Novartis. The factory's robust structural frame, along with high floor-to-floor heights allowed for a minimum of modification to convert to laboratory planning modules. Cutting into the existing structure to create a dynamic and light-filled atrium creates a dynamic space for

the new occupants. The revitalization of this landmark building had positive impacts on the environment, the local community, and because of the dense urban nature of the site, ties into existing infrastructure as well. In addition, the design and construction schedule was compressed since the existing structure could be preserved.

Merck Research Laboratories (MRL) Boston

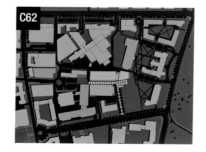

Figures C60-C65: MRL Boston is a 614,000-square-foot research complex located in the Longwood Medical Area of Boston, a highly active educational, cultural, and historical environment. By designing such a facility in a dense urban fabric, the project was successful in maximizing land use and minimizing larger-scale infrastructure improvements usually required in more typical suburban environments.

Throughout the facility, the provision of daylight has been a fundamental driver. The east wall along which the offices are located consists of a

combination of clear and silk-screened glass, behind which a sloping 12-foot-high ceiling and expansive clerestories afford significant light into corridors and interior offices. As a high-rise lab building in an urban area, one of the major challenges facing the team was that lab configurations and mechanical areas needed to be located differently than in buildings located on more spacious campuses. Instead of a single, 20-foot mechanical penthouse on the roof, mechanical areas in the building are located in basement and subgrade areas, on a mid-level floor, and at the penthouse level.

Figures C66-C73: From a canyon-edge site in coastal southern California, Johnson & Johnson's goal was to expand their existing facility to maximize the use of their site, while augmenting the experience of the site for the existing and expanding scientific community. In addition, the objective was to facilitate personnel movement between and through buildings, and enhance the entrance to the site and building complex.

A combination of exterior landscaping irrigated with nonpotable water, high-efficiency indoor fixtures, and cooling coil condensate recycling saves well over 1,000,000 gallons of water per year. A high-performing envelope and shading devices allow for maximum daylighting with minimal solar gain and glare. An existing parking lot was transformed into a landscaped courtyard usable for outdoor meetings and informal gatherings for most of the year given San Diego's mild climate.

C71

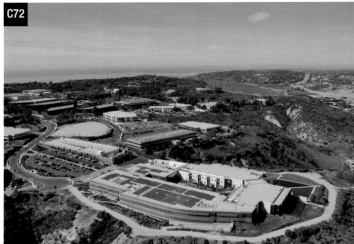

C72

C73

The project applied two strategies to source energy from an efficient source. By using an onsite Combined Heat and Power system (CHP), power is generated onsite, and the waste heat is used for hot water heating and absorption chiller operation. The facility's 2.2 MW system provides 360,000 therms of heat and 1,600,000 ton-hr/yr of chilled water, providing more than 90 percent of the facility's electric power and much of its heating and cooling needs. The co-generation system along with the aggregated energy saving strategies will reduce the emissions of over 3 million pounds of CO_2 per year. A 225 kWH roof-mounted solar array provides renewable energy to the facility.

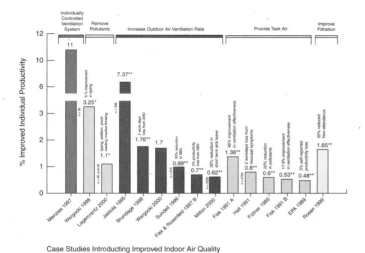

Case Studies Introducting Improved Indoor Air Quality
* Performance improvements for specific tasks multiplied by estimated time at tasks)
** Improved ventilation effectiveness calculated relative to productivity gains from other studies)

There have been a number of studies that correlate improved indoor air quality with increased individual productivity. This chart shows a range of productivity increases based on several different methods of improving IAQ. *Courtesy of Vivian Loftness, Carnegie-Mellon University Center for Building Performance and Diagnostics (CMU/CBPD/ABSIC BIDS™)*

Protecting ductwork, keeping construction materials dry, and minimizing dust and contaminants during construction contributes to higher air quality at occupancy. This requires a careful Construction IAQ management plan, specified by the design professional and implemented by the construction manager or contractors. It also helps protect the mechanical equipment from debris that can impact performance, such as at MEDRAD's project site in Saxonburg, Pennsylvania. *Image courtesy of KlingStubbins. Photography by MEDRAD.*

Indoor Air Quality

In a typical building, indoor air can have two to five times the pollutant levels of the outdoor air.[7] This is based on several factors—contaminants that are captured inside the building during construction, contaminants that are formed during the operation of the building, contaminants inherent in finish materials that are emitted or offgassed into the air over time, and contaminants that are brought into the building during occupancy.

Contaminants During Construction

The construction process creates a significant amount of dust, fumes, and other contaminants, and unless care is taken, these contaminants can be trapped in the building systems when they are closed in. Welding, drywall construction, painting, and other activities leave residues and dust which will end up in ductwork and be absorbed into finish materials. Developing an indoor air quality plan to protect the systems, the ductwork, and the indoor environment from these contaminants is crucial for all buildings, especially for laboratory buildings. A successful plan will include four main features: protecting the ductwork and HVAC system from airborne dust; segregating and ventilating any processes that give off airborne contaminants (such as welding or painting); protecting any absorptive finish materials such as drywall or carpet from dust or moisture; and instituting an overall policy of consistent cleaning and maintenance during the construction process once spaces are closed in. The final step after construction is completed is changing out any filtration media after construction is complete—otherwise they will distribute the most contaminants when the occupants are moving in!

Contaminants from Material Offgassing

Many conventional materials contain solvents and volatile organic compounds (VOCs) that are emitted over time once installed. Carpet, flooring, and construction adhesives contribute to indoor air quality issues, as can paints, fabrics, furniture, and floor and wall coatings. Millwork substrates such as plywood and medium density fiberboard are conventionally manufactured with binders that contain Urea-formaldehyde. A study in a residential setting in 1996 found a 60 percent reduction in asthma symptoms and 63 percent reduction in the presence of allergies among children whose homes had been constructed using formaldehyde-free wood products and furnishings. [8]

Specifically in laboratories, the effects of VOC offgassing can be mitigated in several ways. If high chemical resistivity is required, epoxy paints and flooring are often specified. Formulations of these materials can be selected with low VOC levels. Paints, adhesives for sheet flooring, and casework materials can meet aggressive low VOC targets. Part of the strategy should include setting material criteria commensurate with the real resistivity required. For example, if the cleaning regimen calls for scrubdown of walls, extensive epoxy wall systems may be called for. If, however, the walls are likely to be repainted when needed rather than scrubbed down, conventional zero or low VOC latex paints can be durable enough with fewer potential environmental issues.

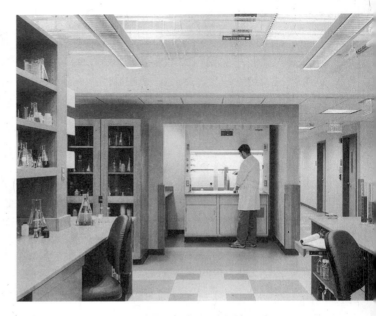

For Boston University Medical Center's BioSquare II in Massachusetts, projected research operations did not warrant use of finish coatings that could be hosed down or scrubbed down—standard latex-based low VOC paints were used for most painted wall surfaces. *Courtesy of © Trustees of Boston University and KlingStubbins. Photography © Robert Benson Photography.*

In addition, for many labs, the indoor air quality challenges are mitigated by the laboratory ventilation system—100 percent outside air ventilation systems will safely remove contaminants and dilute the effects of offgassing.

Contaminants from Occupancy

Once the building is occupied, contaminant levels rise due to systems operation, chemical use, and equipment use. Copiers and printers emit particulate matter, and other contaminants are tracked in by building occupants. The main way to handle these contaminants is through adequate ventilation and separation, eliminating sources of vapors and dust that migrate from one space to another. This is part of good laboratory design—ventilation for occupant safety is a primary driver for many laboratories. Taking a holistic view of all of the different spaces, all kinds of potential contaminants are important parts of maintaining good indoor air quality. One major source of contaminants is office copiers and printers—studies have shown that the process of fusing the toner to the paper can give off ozone and other contaminants, and a recent study showed that even the small copiers and printers used throughout offices can cause significant emissions. For laboratories, the critical part of this specific factor is care in storage and use of chemicals, and minimizing the amount of "open" chemical systems.

Chemical Safety/Chemical Dispensing

Part of laboratory design focuses on the materials that will be used during the operation of the lab, including gases, chemicals, and biological and other consumables. Many features of typical labs include safety procedures and equipment to protect laboratory workers from these materials. Building codes are set up to limit quantities of potentially hazardous materials in any one building, and much of the design of labs is involved in this management. There are several different ways to manage this challenge.

Separation/Compartmentalization

For safety reasons mostly having to do with fire control, most building codes have included some categorization and limitation on the amount of flammable chemicals that can be used in buildings. The general philosophy around chemical control is to keep certain quantities of materials in different locations, and separate those locations with fire-resistant construction. The purpose of this strategy is to make sure that

chemicals that can accelerate fire spread are kept in relatively small quantities. Many of these same materials also pose health and safety risks, so by creating protected areas for chemical storage, the building occupants will have some measure of safety as well.

Limited Quantity Usage— Dispensing/Centralized Storage

Another method of maintaining occupant safety is to minimize the quantities of chemicals being stored in each lab. By providing a dispensing station that can deliver small quantities of solvents or other chemical

Instead of distributing larger quantities of solvents throughout the building, Johnson & Johnson PRD Drug Discovery Laboratory, Phase II in La Jolla, California, uses a self-contained dispensing system. Researchers can come to these highly protected storage spaces and dispense small amounts of solvents as needed for research, and the overall quantities of flammable solvents can be minimized without hindering the research goals of the facility. *Image courtesy of KlingStubbins.*

Yes	?	No			
0	0	0	**Materials & Resources**		**14 Points**
Y			Prereq 1	**Storage & Collection of Recyclables**	Required
Y			Prereq 2	*Hazardous Material Handling*	Required
			Credit 1.1	**Building Reuse**, Maintain 75% of Existing Walls, Floors & Roof	1
			Credit 1.2	**Building Reuse**, Maintain 100% of Existing Walls, Floors & Roof	1
			Credit 1.3	**Building Reuse**, Maintain 50% of Interior Non-Structural Elements	1
			Credit 2.1	**Construction Waste Management**, Divert 50% from Disposal	1
			Credit 2.2	**Construction Waste Management**, Divert 75% from Disposal	1
			Credit 3.1	**Materials Reuse**, 5%	1
			Credit 3.2	**Materials Reuse**, 10%	1
			Credit 4.1	**Recycled Content**, 10% (post-consumer + ½ pre-consumer)	1
			Credit 4.2	**Recycled Content**, 20% (post-consumer + ½ pre-consumer)	1
			Credit 5.1	**Regional Materials**, 10% Extracted, Processed & Manufactured Regionally	1
			Credit 5.2	**Regional Materials**, 20% Extracted, Processed & Manufactured Regionally	1
			Credit 6	**Rapidly Renewable Materials**	1
			Credit 7	**Certified Wood**	1
			Credit 8	*Chemical Resource Management*	1

Using the same format as the LEED rating system, the Labs21® Environmental Performance Criteria (EPC) checklist includes laboratory-specific strategies not included in LEED, as well as refined definitions of some credits common to both rating systems. *Image courtesy of NREL, Labs 21®. (www.labs21century.gov/toolkit/epc.htm).*

compounds, the individual labs can be kept safer—the scientists can dispense the amounts needed for a particular study or procedure, and the rest can stay safely in a controlled closed-loop system, and the scientists minimize their exposure to the chemicals. The Labs21® Environmental Performance Criteria (EPC) have developed a separate strategy, called "Chemical Resource Management." This strategy encourages an overall resource management plan to reduce the quantities and exposure of occupants to the risks of chemical use. The best practice includes the following recommendations:

- Clear material flow design and material handling as part of building design

- Clear space designated in each lab for receipt, return, and disposal of hazardous materials

- Decanting procedures to minimize waste or recycling of waste streams

- Material transport strategy to encourage "just-in-time" delivery

- Equipment and research apparatus that uses smaller quantities of hazardous materials—efficient equipment, automated equipment, or other ways to reduce demand. [9]

Thermal Comfort/Occupant Control

Studies have shown that the largest determinant of occupant satisfaction and productivity is tied to thermal comfort—facilities operators note that their number one complaint is that the building is too cold, and their number two complaint is that the building is too hot. Maintaining temperatures and humidity levels in an acceptable range is a significant determinant of thermal comfort, but there are a number of other factors that play a strong role in this strategy. ASHRAE 55, the compliance standard for thermal comfort, includes factors for activity level, amount of clothing typically worn, air speed and radiant temperature, in addition to air temperature and humidity. Recognizing the variation in people's perceived comfort, ASHRAE 55 lists as "acceptable" any condition where up to 20 percent of people report dissatisfaction! In addition, the ASHRAE 55 standard is based on "steady state" or comfort in a single environment—people moving from one space to another may not be comfortable until they adjust. [10] For laboratories, where occupants often move from offices to labs, adding or removing lab coats and personal protective equipment (PPE), the temperature levels need to be carefully calibrated to accommodate these clothing levels. According to the standard, prior environment or activity levels can impact comfort for about an hour—if you are moving back and forth from lab to office over the course of a day, it can have a significant impact on occupant comfort. Researchers at the Center for the Built Environment at University of California, Berkeley (CBE), have seen through research several additional determinants of thermal comfort.[11] One recently identified determinant is Adaptive Comfort. Studies showed that occupants will be satisfied with the thermal conditions in a much wider range of temperatures when they work in spaces with operable windows or other naturally ventilated spaces.[12] Operable windows or other natural ventilation strategies are possible in some lab spaces, depending on the local climate. For many labs where temperature and humidity swings are antithetical to research goals, segregating lab spaces from other functions such as office and support areas is an option. Other lab buildings can incorporate natural ventilation or operable windows only during part of the year, based on weather conditions. This can be accomplished through BAS control of the windows, locking them when outdoor conditions are not amenable to effective ventilation, or by incorporating automated systems that alert occupants when conditions are appropriate to open windows. In either case, care must be taken to maintain building pressurization differentials for lab safety.

The CBE has also pursued research on thermal comfort factors that indicated that separate from overall space conditions of temperature, humidity, radiant heat and cooling, occupants are more productive, more comfortable, and report better air quality when specific areas of their bodies received conditioning— "task-ambient" conditioning systems that use low-power systems to provide heat to hands and feet, and cooling to hands and face. Similar to lighting design strategies of having a lower ambient light level with specific task-related lighting, this showed how having specific task-related conditioning equipment could save energy at the same time as increasing occupant satisfaction and productivity.[13] While this research is not yet directly applicable to laboratory settings, it represents an interesting set of questions

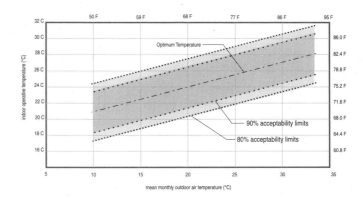

ASHRAE Standard 55–2004 includes the concept of Adaptive Comfort, illustrating that occupants will report satisfactory thermal comfort in a wider range of temperatures in naturally ventilated spaces, compared with mechanically conditioned spaces. This helps with occupant satisfaction and productivity as well as energy use. *Courtesy of © ASHRAE Standard 55–2004.*

about how we will address comfort in lab occupants. Although these task-ambient systems are not now commercially available, they offer an interesting potential for giving lab occupants added thermal comfort and individual control in settings where typical systems would not allow for other methods of flexibility—where the scientific needs of the spaces may be different than the occupant preferences. This is important, because studies have shown a significant increase in occupant productivity—up to 3 percent—for spaces where occupants have individual temperature control (Carnegie Mellon University BIDS™ database).[14]

Access to Exterior Environment/Daylight

Another major factor in occupant health and satisfaction is the visual connection to the exterior environment. One study showed that building occupants in close proximity to exterior windows had markedly lower health complaints than those sitting at the center areas of buildings, near the building cores. A study done at Montefiore Hospital in 2005 indicated that postoperative patients in a brightly sunlit surgical ward requested 22 percent less analgesia than patients on a dimly lit ward.[15] Another study showed that employees at a call center with access to views had a 6 to 7 percent increase in productivity over employees without a view to the exterior.[16] Employees with a view were also much less likely to report health complaints and fatigue than those without a view.

Daylighting in Buildings

Buildings that have significant daylight contribution have been correlated with both health benefits and increased productivity, as well as energy savings. Studies have shown that buildings that are daylit can mean more productive employees, better test scores for students in schools, more sales in retail areas, and reduced health complaints.[17] However, designing a building with access to daylight is more complicated than just providing all glass exterior walls. Too much glazing can lead to excessive heat gain and glare. Effective daylighting is a multistep, multidisciplinary process that takes advantage of true design integration. Starting with site selection and building massing, the project team has a number of ways to help facilitate successful daylighting strategies. The first and main determinant of whether a building can effectively be daylit is geometric—the depth of the floor plate and the height of the top of glass will dictate generally how much of a given floor will be able to receive natural light. The building orientation will dictate how well the direct solar glare can be controlled. Once that is determined, the configuration of the floor plan can facilitate daylighting or make it more of a challenge—a lay-out where the perimeter is lined with enclosed offices can reduce the depth of daylight penetration, unless the office enclosures are

highly glazed. In addition, the amount and height of glazing, while increasing daylight penetration, also will increase the potential for excessive heat gain or loss and glare. Effective daylighting design is based on the concept that direct sunlight hitting work surfaces are to be prevented—the contrast between the areas of sunlight and the adjacent areas results in visual discomfort. During design phases, physical models can be constructed, or computer daylight simulations can be generated to analyze what types of shading devices will be most effective in allowing the most daylight in while minimizing visual glare.

Daylighting Process

Why Do It?

There are a number of reasons to implement daylighting in a building, primarily characterized by three main categories: Design/Aesthetics: Use of natural light in common and public spaces can be dramatic and transformative—it can make a conventional space seem extraordinary. Energy Efficiency: Use of natural daylight instead of electrical light, if done correctly, can save energy. Health/Productivity: As noted above, studies have shown that naturally lit spaces are better for the people occupying them. For laboratory projects, where typically the lighting energy is a smaller part of the overall facility energy usage, it is a combination of all three of these categories that makes the case for implementing daylighting in the building design. Below are a number of steps involved in the process of daylighting design.

First Things First

Arguably the most important thing about daylight is what it is not: It is not direct sunlight coming into a building and hitting the bench top or work surface.

This results in glare, and in some cases it is strong enough to hinder the occupants' ability to work. At its extreme, this is called disability glare. Good daylighting is not dependent on direct beam sunlight, the best light is diffuse—light reflected from the sky dome provides a clear and unshadowed source of light. The calculation method devised in LEED for versions 1 and 2 encouraged significant glazing in rela-

tion to the occupied space. This resulted in many overlit and glare-conditioned spaces. LEED version 3, issued in 2009, includes an upper limit of 500 foot candles for daylight, which should serve to reduce this tendency.[18]

Evaluation

The first step in a daylight design study is evaluation—the integrated team must evaluate and make conclusions about what factors will influence the daylighting goals. These factors include external and internal factors. External factors include geographic location, weather/climate data, context, and adjacent buildings and obstructions—what is the potential for accepting daylight into the building, and are there times of year where the weather extremes make it disadvantageous to admit or lose heat through the envelope? Internal factors include programmatic requirements and criteria—are there functions in the building that make it less amenable to the natural swings of light levels that will come with natural daylighting?

KEY
1 South Walkway
2 Wet Bench Labs
3 Special Procedure
4 Equipment Corridor

For the Leichtag Biomedical Research Building at the University of California, San Diego, the building organization and massing was adjusted to maximize the amount of daylight penetration into the space. Ceilings slope upwards to a higher window head height at the perimeter, and exterior shading devices mitigate glare and gain potential from the additional glazing. Natural light at the perimeter means that the electric lighting can be dimmed or turned off. *Image courtesy of ZGF Architects LLP. Photography © Anne Garrison.*

Goals/Parameters

The next step of the design process is defining goals and parameters for daylighting. For lab spaces, it often means confirming which labs can function with natural light penetration and which cannot. For some buildings, the goals would be to provide daylight to a certain percentage of spaces, or certain types of spaces. It is also important to determine whether there are spaces where glare control is less critical—certain transitional and circulation spaces may have less stringent glare control criteria. Depending on the climate, it may also be possible to allow direct solar penetration during heating months, with the assumption that blinds will be closed during those months,

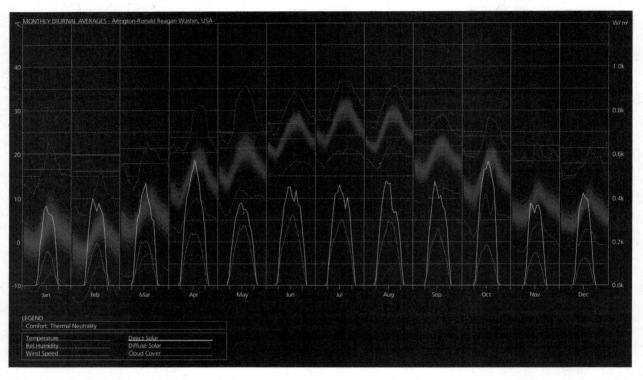

Evaluating the potential for different strategies is a critical part of early design study. Using databases of weather data and evaluating solar and typical sky conditions ensures that the building can be effectively lit by natural daylight without glare. U.S. Department of Energy weather data presented graphically using Autodesk Ecotect.

allowing the heat to be "collected" by perimeter blinds.

Rules of Thumb

There are a number of "rules of thumb" related to lighting penetration, but the most commonly quoted rule is that daylight will penetrate approximately two times the height of the window head into a space. This rule helps designers understand how much of a floor plate will be able to be daylit before more detailed simulations can be done. However, researchers have found that by adding a factor for obstruction objects makes this rule of thumb much more effective. Of course the rule of thumb does not take into account orientation or geographic location. For that, simulation or modeling is required.

Massing/Orientation

Early massing models help the team evaluate where sunlight will penetrate and what areas of buildings will be shaded by others. Although there are tools that allow for very detailed simulation of energy and lighting impacts on buildings, the design team can learn a great deal with simple shadow studies showing what

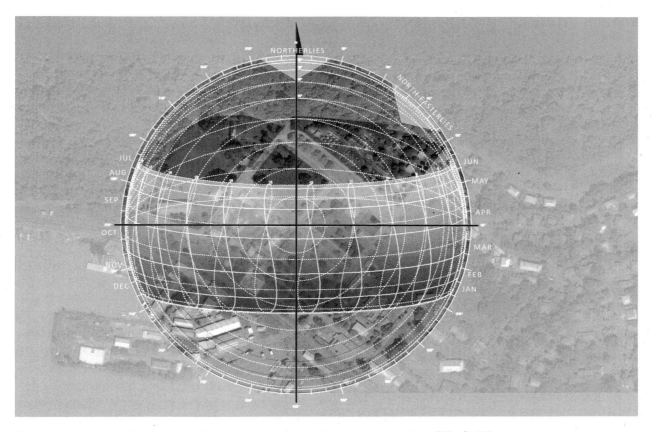

Site analysis diagram for Smithsonian Tropical Research Institute in Gamboa, Panama. *Image courtesy of KlingStubbins.*

portions of the building will receive direct solar gain through different times of year.

Shading Devices—Glare and Thermal Control

The simple massing studies can also be used to focus the design efforts on areas of the building that will need more detailed window and shading device design. It is critical to attend to this portion of the process, because for most climates, the energy saved through daylighting would more than offset increased cooling loads from unprotected glazed areas. For some build-

ings, shading devices can be provided to reduce thermal loads significantly, but if the orientation is not optimal, glare control will need to be achieved through a combination of exterior and interior shading devices.

Dynamic Daylight Analysis

Many of the tools used for daylight simulation are geared toward giving static solutions—evaluating the conditions on a single time and day. By simulating the conditions at key points during the year—the solstice and equinox—and at different times of day, decisions

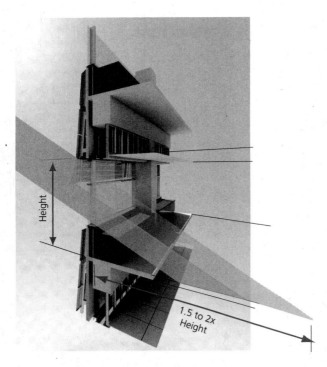

Even before detailed simulation models are created, designers can use rules of thumb to evaluate how far daylight will penetrate into a building interior. For the U.S. Food and Drug Administration Life Sciences Laboratory in White Oak, Maryland, rules of thumb were used to create shading device options, which could later be tested with more detailed simulations. *Image courtesy of KlingStubbins.*

can be made about how much daylight will be brought in, and how effectively glare can be controlled. In addition, new tools have been developed that allow for annualized simulation of lighting and energy conditions. In some cases this is a graph of conditions, which is essentially an automated series of single-static simulations. In other tools there are some specific metrics for calculating what percentage of the year a given area of the building will receive a certain amount of light. The one illustrated here is Useful Daylight Index, or UDI. It measures both lower and upper limits of lighting levels produced by a perimeter glazing solution.

Detailed Material Specification

As the building design progresses, detailed study of the lighting and energy effects of different materials can make a big difference in the final resulting space. By using a higher performing glazing, the amount of light that is allowed in can be maximized while the amount of solar heat gain admitted is reduced. In addition, the light reflectance values of the finish materials can have a big impact on the overall light levels—the lighter colored materials will diffuse and reflect light throughout the space, increasing the overall light levels, and reducing the need for electric lighting.

Control Strategies

For the majority of spaces, the goal is to harness the natural daylight and use it instead of electrical lighting. This requires a careful coordination between the building configuration, design, and lighting system design. Implementing daylight sensors that will turn off or dim the electric lighting in response to natural light is a relatively simple concept. The lights need to be laid out and circuited such that when the system dims the lighting, the overall space remains uniformly lit—this means zones of lighting that are parallel to the daylight glazing areas. The more carefully the zones are coordinated with expected daylight penetration, the more uniform the overall lighting will be. Of course the zoning and control system used will also impact the overall system cost, so it is important to balance number of zones with expected need for flexibility. In addition, the use of perimeter shades or blinds can significantly impact the daylight— depending on who is controlling them, they can cut down on actual energy savings or daylight harvesting. Studies have shown that individually controlled manual blinds are often lowered to handle a worst-case glare condition and often remain in a lowered

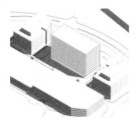

Base Case
250' x 110'
Area = 306,821 SF
Skin Area = 110,000 SF
Basis for comparisons

Rotated
Increases east/west faces
Cooling Load = **4.7% over**
Skin Area = same as base
Conclusion: Orientation is important. East/West exposure drives cooling loads.

Double Bar / Atrium
Increases daylight/views
Cooling Load = **1.6% over**
Skin Area = 8% more
Daylight Penetration +12%
Conclusion: Surface area of atrium increases heat gain, but with a significant advantage for daylight and views.

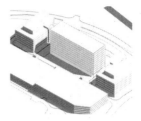

Thinner
Increases daylight/views
Cooling Load = **0.3% over**
Skin Area = 9% more
Daylight Penetration +12%
Conclusion: Despite greater surface area, performs pretty well.

Square
Reduces Surface Area
Cooling Load = **1.0% over**
Skin Area = 7% less
Less Daylight Penetration
Conclusion: Despite smaller surface area, greater east/west exposure drives up heat gain.

Round Plan
Reduces surface area
Cooling Load = **11.8% under**
Skin Area = 18% less
Daylight Penetration is Worse
Conclusion: Extreme reduction in surface area = less heat gain.

Bent Bar
Alters north/south facades
Cooling Load = **1.0% over**
Skin Area = same as base
Conclusion: Minimal change. South face kink appears to increase heat gain.

Pinched Ends
Reduces east/west exposure
Cooling Load = **7.4% under**
Skin Area = 3% more
Daylight Penetration slightly better than base
Conclusion: Pinching down the east/west exposure reduces heat gain dramatically.

For this project in Northern Virginia, early studies were done to compare different massing options relative to envelope loads. The study was used to balance increased daylighting potential with increased thermal load from added envelope area. *Image courtesy of KlingStubbins.*

position semi-permanently. Some projects have implemented automated shades that raise and lower based on external conditions; others use a semi-automated system that retracts to full open each morning.

Energy Model Integration

As noted above, although it is true that green buildings are not statistically more expensive than non-green buildings, it is still true that the components described here—automated blinds, dimming ballasts,

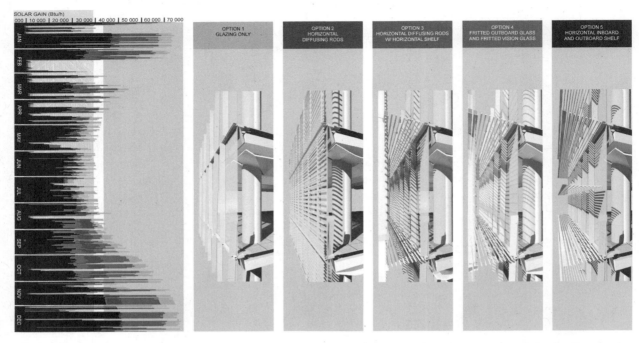

For the Pearl River Towers in Guangzhou, China, different shading device options were modeled, and thermal simulations were done to quickly analyze how much solar gain was reduced off the facade with each option. Overlaid on the left side of the image is the resulting graph. *Image courtesy of KlingStubbins.*

Daysim is a tool that allows for a dynamic simulation of lighting conditions; this shaded grid at the working plane shows the percentage of time that the lighting level will be between 200 and 2000 lux. Generated using Autodesk Ecotect and Daysim.

Lighting control zones were adjusted to allow for perimeter lighting to be dimmed or turned off, while still providing some artificial lighting at the interior zones of St. Lawrence University's Johnson Hall of Science in Canton, New York. *Courtesy of Croxton Collaborative / KlingStubbins. Photography © Woodruff/Brown Architectural Photography.*

These images of U.S. Food and Drug Administration Life Sciences Laboratory in White Oak, Maryland, show simulation results for a laboratory space with blinds opened and closed. For many projects, exterior sun-shading devices are not feasible, and in these cases an automated blinds system can be set to close when glare conditions exist. *Images courtesy of KlingStubbins.*

daylight dimming systems, and shading devices—add cost to a project. The major method that these systems are justified is through health and productivity benefits, but the energy savings are also a part of the equation. Energy simulation tools need to include information about these items to calculate what impact they will have on overall energy use. In some cases, the energy simulation software includes modules where data about lighting dimming, shading devices, and automated blinds can be added in. In many cases, however, it is up to the design team to use simulation tools to figure out how many hours per week, month, or year the systems will contribute to energy use. Most energy simulation tools allow for calculation and scheduling of loads and systems, and if the particular light harvesting system is not directly included in the energy model, it can easily be created through a customized schedule. This can be done on an annual basis, or in some cases it is done on a quarterly basis—separating the amount of time when daylight will contribute between summer months, winter months, and the equinoxes.

Shaping the Building for Daylighting—Conclusions

Many studies have shown the positive impact of natural daylight on building occupants, and many designers have worked to implement daylighting strategies in recent designs. Successful daylight strategies pay attention to light quality, glare reduction, and occupant control. Strategies that allow the occupants to lower blinds but still let in daylight are especially challenging but rewarding. Laboratory designs must start by classifying any spaces that need particularly tight control of light and glare, and make sure they are laid out and organized appropriately. As the design is developed, more detailed lighting design strategies are required, and they are discussed in more detail below.

Lighting Design for Laboratories

The most important factor in designing lighting for laboratories is providing enough light to allow for a

CIE Clear Sky - sensor 16 feet from glass, WP height (fc)

	1:	2:	3:	4:	5:	6:	7:	8:	9:	10:00	11:00	12:00	13:00	14:00	15:00	16:00	17:00	18:00	19:00	20:00	21:00	22:00	23:00	24:00	hours
Jan	-	-	-	-	-	-	8	23	38	57	81	102	107	109	92	61	28	-	-	-	-	-	-	-	9
Feb	-	-	-	-	-	-	14	27	40	55	72	89	99	113	112	89	49	14	-	-	-	-	-	-	10
Mar	-	-	-	-	-	9	22	33	43	52	63	74	86	101	112	103	74	34	-	-	-	-	-	-	11
Apr	-	-	-	-	6	20	30	37	42	47	54	62	71	83	97	104	113	62	15	-	-	-	-	-	12
May	-	-	-	2	15	26	33	37	40	43	49	57	63	73	85	98	105	79	28	2	-	-	-	-	14
Jun	-	-	-	6	18	27	34	37	39	42	47	57	61	67	78	91	99	79	36	10	-	-	-	-	14
Jul	-	-	-	3	15	26	33	37	39	42	47	56	61	68	79	92	101	85	38	9	-	-	-	-	14
Aug	-	-	-	-	9	22	31	37	41	45	50	57	66	76	89	101	111	82	26	-	-	-	-	-	13
Sep	-	-	-	-	2	16	28	37	44	51	60	69	81	94	106	103	85	39	1	-	-	-	-	-	12
Oct	-	-	-	-	-	9	23	35	47	60	76	88	100	114	117	103	43	7	-	-	-	-	-	-	10
Nov	-	-	-	-	-	2	16	31	46	66	88	103	108	116	88	53	20	-	-	-	-	-	-	-	9
Dec	-	-	-	-	-	-	10	25	41	62	89	108	107	103	79	47	16	-	-	-	-	-	-	-	9

CIE Clear sky - sensor 21 feet from glass, WP height (fc)

	1:	2:	3:	4:	5:	6:	7:	8:	9:	10:00	11:00	12:00	13:00	14:00	15:00	16:00	17:00	18:00	19:00	20:00	21:00	22:00	23:00	24:00	hours
Jan	-	-	-	-	-	-	2	6	12	21	31	33	25	16	10	6	2	-	-	-	-	-	-	-	3
Feb	-	-	-	-	-	-	2	7	12	18	25	26	22	16	11	7	4	1	-	-	-	-	-	-	2
Mar	-	-	-	-	-	1	4	7	11	15	18	19	16	13	10	7	4	2	-	-	-	-	-	-	0
Apr	-	-	-	-	1	3	5	8	10	12	13	13	12	10	8	7	5	3	1	-	-	-	-	-	0
May	-	-	-	-	2	4	6	7	9	10	11	11	10	9	8	7	5	4	2	-	-	-	-	-	0
Jun	-	-	-	1	3	4	6	7	8	9	10	11	10	8	7	7	6	4	3	1	-	-	-	-	0
Jul	-	-	-	2	4	6	7	8	9	10	11	10	8	7	7	6	4	3	1	-	-	-	-	-	0
Aug	-	-	-	-	1	3	5	7	9	11	12	12	11	9	8	7	5	4	2	-	-	-	-	-	0
Sep	-	-	-	-	-	2	5	8	11	14	16	16	14	11	9	6	4	2	-	-	-	-	-	-	0
Oct	-	-	-	-	-	1	5	9	14	20	23	22	17	12	9	5	3	-	-	-	-	-	-	-	0
Nov	-	-	-	-	-	-	4	9	15	24	31	28	20	13	8	4	1	-	-	-	-	-	-	-	2
Dec	-	-	-	-	-	-	2	7	14	24	35	33	23	15	9	4	1	-	-	-	-	-	-	-	2

Simulation tools allow for the designer to model how effectively a daylighting strategy will work. This output shows the lighting level for two different sensor locations in a proposed building design. The output is shown with time of day (horizontal axis) and months of the year (vertical axis), so the full year's performance can be evaluated. *Image courtesy of KlingStubbins.*

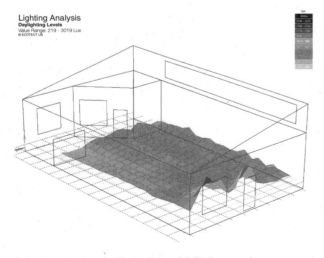

Lighting Analysis
Daylighting Levels
Value Range: 219 - 3019 Lux
© ECOTECT US

At the Hawaii Institute for Marine Biology (HIMB), Ecotect software was used to refine and confirm the effectiveness of the daylight design for the New Dry Labs Complex at Coconut Island. Similar software was used to model and verify thermal comfort and ventilation effectiveness. *Image courtesy of Ferraro Choi and Associates.*

Rendered interior view of the high-ceiling portion in a typical modular laboratory at the HIMB New Dry Labs Complex. This image conveys how the height and volume of this portion of the lab are driven by daylight design including the north-facing clerestory, and the curved, light-colored ceiling which functions as a daylight diffuser. Ventilation enters low and exhausts high (note exhaust diffusers in upper-right-hand side of rendering. *Image courtesy of Ferraro Choi and Associates.*

high level of visual acuity and unstrained sight. To do so sustainably requires using the least amount of electricity to achieve this goal.

Luminaire and System Component Selection

Not only must selected luminaires suit the design of the laboratory and produce the correct quality of light for tasks conducted within, but they must also be the most efficient option available. Research the materials used in each component. Look for lead content in the ballast or the wiring and mercury in the fluorescent lamp. New options available reduce or even eliminate these environmental toxins. System components must be efficient; internal electronics should be specified properly to achieve that goal. Identify ballasts built into the luminaire that are the most appropriate for the desired light level and lighting control method, and that do not waste electricity by unnecessarily producing heat.

Integrated Approach to Lighting Design

Turning the lights off manually or with occupancy sensors when the space is unoccupied is an obvious energy saver; dimming the lighting when the sun is contributing enough good-quality light not only saves energy but also creates an interior atmosphere that reduces employee sick time and increases productivity. Designing sustainably involves the lighting designer in aspects of the building design traditionally under the purview of others. For instance, photocell-activated window shades allow for the change of days and seasons to be experienced while eliminating harsh and glary direct sunlight or extreme shadows that will interfere with visual accuracy. Previously, shades were selected by the interior designer or architect and often the decision to raise or lower them was left to the occupant, resulting in shades

that were lowered to eliminate glare but not raised again for long periods of time. As appreciation of the importance of automation and daylight quality increases, the lighting designer is involved more often in specifying and programming these systems as part of an integrated sustainable lighting strategy.

According to the Labs21® Energy Benchmarking database, lighting is responsible for between 8 and 25 percent of most laboratory facilities' total energy usage. Significant energy savings are realized when lab bench light level requirements are relaxed and beneficial daylight contribution is maximized. These savings are enhanced when synchronized with a properly commissioned lighting control system that automatically shuts off the lights when a space is unoccupied, or dims the lighting when and where there is enough daylight contribution.

Lighting Levels

Clients, from management to scientists and facilities personnel, are finding that sustainable lighting design is beneficial. Energy costs are rising drastically. The general population is realizing that energy resources are becoming more limited while demand grows. Rolling blackouts are more common during peak load periods, and mandatory load-shedding is becoming a reality. The struggle to create an efficient and profitable renewable energy source is proving to be slower and more difficult than hoped. Reports have been published with the gloomy news that even when renewable resource energy generators are functioning at their maximum capacity, they will not be able to reach a level of energy production to meet increasing energy consumption. Finding where we as a society can reduce our lighting energy consumption is imperative, and research shows that we can do it in part through evaluating our real lighting needs and designing for the human eye rather than for the light meter.

Light levels are measured in foot candles (fc), the amount of light from a single candle, striking a surface that is one foot wide square and held one foot away from that candle, the metric equivalent is lux.[19] Requests for 100 foot candles average or more, based on ageing standards, were not uncommon a few years ago. More commonly now, recommendations for lower light levels, the use of task lighting, and automatic daylight harvesting are not only accepted but rather embraced. In the early to mid-1900s the Illuminating Engineering Society of North America (IESNA) made office lighting recommendations of an average of 125 foot candles. At the same time research began to focus on how humans see, and how different lighting styles would affect vision and perception. Research showed that many of these early standards were extremely conservative; these recommendations have been lowering ever since.

Prior to electricity, kerosene or natural gas was burned for nighttime lighting. Unfortunately, burning fuel converts most of its energy into heat and only a little into light. When electric lighting became accessible, electricity was cheap. People rebelled against the darkness and relished excessive brightness. During that time, interior luminaires were typically an incandescent lamp in a socket with a protective piece of glass. Better lighting design consisted of a Holophane-type prismatic diffusing lens around the lamp to make the light somewhat more comfortable. These lamps were high wattage and created a great deal of glare.

As the more efficient fluorescent lamp became viable, designers for commercial and industrial applications

LABORATORY MAINTAINED ILLUMINANCE CHART		
Area	Footcandles	
Specimen collecting	*50-75-100	**50 Horizontal 10 Vertical
Laboratories		
Tissue laboratories	*100-150-200	**50 Horizontal 30 Vertical
Microscopic reading room	*20-30-50	
Gross specimen review	*100-150-200	
Chemistry rooms	*50-75-100	
Bacteriology rooms		
General	*50-75-100	
Reading culture plates	*100-150-200	
Hematology	*50-75-100	
*Footcandles taken from IESNA handbook 8th Edition 1993 **Footcandles taken from IESNA handbook 9th Edition 2000		

The Illuminating Engineering Society of North America (IESNA) publishes recommendations for lighting levels based on space type and activities performed. *Image courtesy of KlingStubbins.*

found they could use the same amount of energy but have an even brighter environment. Obviously, saving energy and sustainability had not yet become part of the lexicon. The conventional method for providing visual clarity was to increase light levels to offset the glare of the lamp, utilizing more energy. More recently, designers have started to focus on minimizing contrast ratios as a method for increasing visual clarity without added energy use. This strategy, relatively new to lighting designers, has been used effectively by photographers throughout history.

Like a camera, human eyes only see details within a limited contrast ratio. This means the brightest object in view determines how bright the darkest object in view needs to be in order for it to be easily seen. In the laboratory environment, keeping well within the maximum contrast ratio is very important, since measurement and identification tasks are crucial to an experiment's success.

If too great a contrast ratio exists in the lab, important details are lost in silhouette. Newer lighting fixtures are designed to eliminate direct glare, thereby minimizing contrast ratios and enabling designers to provide visual clarity without increasing lighting levels, as had been required in the past.

Top photo: Maximum foot-candle level on these rocks was 900 fc with a minimum of 400 fc between them at mid-afternoon. Bottom photo: Maximum foot-candle level on these rocks was 40 fc with a minimum of 15 fc between them at the beginning of dusk. A camera as well as our eyes can adjust to different light levels but the contrast ratio will always restrict our ability to see comparatively darker objects. *Images courtesy of KlingStubbins.*

Lamp Efficiency and Related Selection Considerations

Efficiency is "the ratio of the effective or useful output to the total input in any system."[20] Particularly for lighting, efficiency usually refers to luminaire efficiency. This is a percentage of total available light output from the working lamps divided by the total light output of the luminaire. As an example, for a luminaire with a single 2,900-lumen output lamp and total light output of 1,624 lumens, the luminaire is 56 percent efficient. Efficacy in lighting describes the ability of a particular lamp/ballast combination to convert electricity to light, or more specifically, lumens created per watts consumed. This is the calculation of a system's efficiency in converting electricity into light. For instance, the amount of light that a nominal 32-watt linear fluorescent T8 will emit is reported to be 2,900 lumens. The ballast input wattage is published at 29 input watts. Dividing 2,900 by 29 results in 100 lumens per watt for that lamp/ballast configuration. When every watt counts, it is a good idea to figure the energy calculations using the published ballast input watts provided by the specified ballast manufacturer, and the lamp manufacturer's published initial lumen output.

All lamps, over the course of their life, will reduce in lumen output from the first time they are energized. Lumens are listed by the lamp manufacturers as initial lamp lumens—the rated output the first time the lamp is used. Manufacturers also list "design" or "mean" lumens. Design/mean lumens are the average depreciated light output at 40 percent of lamp life based on the lamp's lumen depreciation curve. Mean lumens are most suited to help determine normal lamp light loss for illuminance calculations but should not be used for calculating efficiency or efficacy.

A linear fluorescent 4-foot, 32-watt T8 lamp with a standard electronic ballast is the most energy-efficient lamp/ballast configuration available today. This system offers efficacies of 100 lumens per watt or more and comes with the widest variety of ballast options. The major lamp manufacturers also offer energy saving versions of the 4-foot lamp in 30, 28, and 25 nominal watts. These lamps are useful in a renovation where the existing lighting system is known to provide too much light and the facility is looking for easily realized energy savings. These "energy savings" lamps use less energy than their 32-watt counterparts, but just as a dimming control system works, fewer watts also means less light produced. Due to the electronics of a standard ballast being tuned to the 32-watt lamp, there will be inefficiencies in the system reducing lamp efficacy while using the lower wattage lamp. This makes them a poor option when designing a lab with new lighting equipment. Lamp efficacy diminishes with these lamps since no ballasts are made to specifically operate these lamps at maximum efficiency.

During the design of a lab space where the lighting power density will remain close to the applicable ASHRAE/IESNA 90.1 standard, every watt becomes precious. Overlighting a space results in not meeting the energy code requirements, which could in turn impact a facility's voluntary sustainability accreditation or even the certificate of occupancy. Light levels can be carefully moderated with the use of specially designed ballasts that increase or decrease a lamp's light output compared to the standard ballast, without using a dimming system. These ballasts are designed with alternate ballast factors. Lowering a system's ballast factor equally reduces a luminaire's wattage consumption and the lamp's light output. A ballast factor of 0.88 is considered the standard for T8 linear fluorescent technology. Also available are

ballast factors ranging from 0.71 to 1.41. The reduction of ballast factor not only lowers the light level but also reduces energy consumption. In other words, if tweaking light levels up or down is required, but adding or removing a full lamp's worth of output would result in the addition or subtraction of too much light, then changing ballast factors allows accurate altering of a luminaire's total output.

T5 fluorescent lamps have increased in popularity recently due to their stated efficiency. However, when deciding on an appropriate light source all factors must be considered. Ballast/lamp system comparisons for T5 and T5HO (high output) are not as efficient as for the older and more developed T8 systems. T5 lamps are very sensitive to temperatures outside their optimum temperature range. If the ambient temperature around the lamp dips below 30°C or reaches above 40°C, the lamp's light output is reduced considerably, but the consumed wattage

LAMP CHART					
LAMP TYPE	Abbreviation	Watts	Lumens	Lumens/ Watt	Avg. Life
T5 Fluorescent	T5	28	2,600	93	20,000hr
T5 High-Output Fluorescent	T5HO	54	4,450	82	25,000hr
T8 Fluorescent	T8	32	3,100	94	36,000hr
Compact Fluorescent	CF	32	2,400	75	12,000hr
Compact Fluorescent	CF	26	1,800	69	12,000hr
Compact Fluorescent	CF	18	1,200	67	12,000hr
Ceramic Metal Halide	CMH	70	6,300	90	12,000hr
Ceramic Metal Halide	CMH	150	15,500	103	12,000hr
Ceramic Metal Halide	CMH	250	24,500	98	12,000hr
Standard Metal Halide	SMH	175	14,400(V) 12,800(H)	82	10,000hr (V) 7,500hr (H)
Standard Metal Halide	SMH	250	22,000(V) 20,000(H)	88	10,000hr (V) 7,500hr (H)
High-Pressure Sodium	HPS	70	6,300	90	30,000hr
High-Pressure Sodium	HPS	150	16,000	107	30,000hr
High-Pressure Sodium	HPS	250	29,000	116	30,000hr
Light-Emitting Diode	LED	3	139 max	46	50,000hr
Lamp information from OSRAM SYLVANIA; LED information from CREE					

Selecting the appropriate lamp type includes both efficacy—how many lumens are produced per watt of energy—as well as the average lifespan of the lamp. *Image courtesy of KlingStubbins.*

remains the same. When the light output becomes compromised, the lamp efficacy drops to a level below that of a T8 lamp system with the same environmental factors. The early premise for the smaller T5 lamp diameter was that a luminaire's optical system could be designed to be more efficient, since the lamp itself would not interfere with as much light coming off of the reflector. Unfortunately, for the most part, luminaire manufacturers have responded to the smaller lamp by producing smaller fixtures with smaller reflector chambers. Smaller reflector chambers make them equal to or less efficient than a larger T8 luminaire. For the time being, T5 ballasts are only available in ballast factors from 0.95 to 1.15, and T5HO ballast factors range from 0.99 to 1.02, although more options are likely in the near future. The current limited options may lead to a situation with too much or too little light and very little recourse to tweak these levels, since the lab module often limits options for lighting spacing.

Although compact fluorescent lamps are not as efficacious as linear fluorescent lamps are, they are still an excellent alternative to incandescent. The compact fluorescent lamp produces a light quality very similar to a standard incandescent with significantly better efficacy. An efficient incandescent lamp can achieve up to 20 lumens per watt, whereas a compact fluorescent yields 60 or more lumens per watt. Compact fluorescent lamps work well anywhere a relatively small lamp is needed. These lamps can be found in recessed downlights or "low bay"-type luminaires for a loading dock. Because of their size and shape compact fluorescent lamps cannot be used to replace a strong directional light source.

Light-emitting diodes, or LEDs, are gaining in popularity as possible replacements for many available light sources. The efficacy for a single-color diode is exceptionally high. If using colored light for accent or effect, there is no longer a reason to use any other light source, although there are few applications for this in the lab itself; they might be incorporated into the design of break spaces, corridors, interaction areas, and other parts of the research building. For a number of reasons, white light remains a different story, and as such, the use of LEDs in the laboratory is still a developing science. See the *sidebar* for further discussion. Compared to incandescent and halogen lamps, LEDs are very efficient point sources, and even when compared to compact fluorescent and standard metal halide, operating efficacies are close. LEDs on the research bench have been tested up to 150 lumens per watt under ideal conditions; it is only a matter of time before the science develops and LEDs become the light source of choice even in laboratories.

Lighting

The natural state of existence for an LED is as a red, amber, green, blue, or yellow light source. LED colors are not completely predictable but are within varying degrees of each other. Luminaire manufacturers put the LEDs through a time-consuming and expensive process of comparing all of the same color LEDs and matching or binning them with the others that are within the same small color range, so when viewed as a luminaire there will be no distracting variations. The problem occurs when these tiny, energy-efficient, vibrantly colored dynamos are expected to perform like white light. Since white light is not, and does not

continued

look like it will ever be, an LED's natural state, LEDs must be coerced into producing white light. This coercion takes the form of a blue LED, which has very high emissions in the ultraviolet (UV) range. The blue LED is coated with phosphors that react to the UV. The phosphors produce white light when bombarded by the UV photons. (This is similar to the production of white light from a fluorescent lamp. The same phosphors are used; both are excited by UV emissions from a different source.) Unfortunately, the phosphors that balance the blue light and contribute enough other colors to the light in order that the light be perceived as white also absorb and block a great deal of the LED's initial emission, making them less efficacious than an LED in its unfiltered state.

Lighting Design Strategies

The nature of the lab environment is conservative and deliberate in order to maintain unquestionably repeatable and accurate results. Thus, lab lighting design concepts are slow to change. However, sustainability has become a more popular concept. Rising energy costs have created demand for saving energy. Local codes and voluntary "green" certifications are changing the minds of both the scientists and the lab planners and lower light levels are now not only being accepted but embraced by all involved. Lighting levels of 70 foot candles average are now accepted by most laboratory planners and users. This metric will continue to drop as modern automated scientific practice is considered and lower general light levels are tested. Since many measurements and application procedures are now automated, visual inspection can be confined to designated high-light-level zones; more and more, documentation, modeling, and research are done with a computer, and these higher general light levels for the entire laboratory are becoming obsolete.

It is more energy-efficient to provide lower general lighting and augment only where necessary with task lighting than to provide a higher overall maintained light level throughout the lab, and the added benefit is that individual researchers can control their own workspaces.

When the majority of lab tasks required visual inspection, typical lighting levels provided were much higher. Current best practice is to use lower general lighting with increased lighting to suit specific tasks.

Seventy foot candles on the lab bench is the highest average light level that can be achieved using only overhead lighting that still meets the most stringent energy standard. Even at 70 foot candles, the lighting level in ancillary spaces around the bench might have to be reduced for the overall laboratory to comply with the energy standards. For scientists with compromised vision due to age or other factors, these lower levels in the ancillary spaces are inadequate. If task lighting is unacceptable, an overhead direct lighting system is the most efficient.

Since a portion of light is absorbed every time a beam of light is reflected off of a surface, it is important to design the lighting so that it is reflected by as few surfaces as possible before arriving at the task area. This is referred to as direct lighting, since light rays emitted from the luminaire travel in the direction directly toward the task instead of being intentionally reflected off of an architectural surface such as the ceiling or the wall before striking the task plane.

Location of these luminaires in the ceiling is critical to having the system function properly. Because of the eye's sensitivity to brightness, keeping the typically bright and glary luminaire lens out of the scientists' line of sight is of utmost importance for this to be a comfortable working environment. Reducing glare from the luminaire lens also minimizes errors due to compromised vision. Keeping the luminaires directly above the lab bench has three benefits. First, this location allows for the most direct route between the luminaire and the task. Second, if the luminaire is directly overhead and there are shelves that block views of the adjacent lighting, direct glare is eliminated because the luminaires are not within the field of view. Third, this location eliminates shadows on the task surface. If the light originates from the center of an aisle, scientists are likely to create their own shadows that reduce light levels at their work area.

Using uplight-only pendants, or indirect lighting, can make the visual environment much more comfortable to work in. Indirect lighting works by reflecting the luminaires' distributed light off of a diffuse surface before it reaches the task plane. This produces a very soft light, and few shadows. Where there are shadows, they will be soft-edged and low-contrast. Indirect lighting also eliminates glare that causes visual disability by spreading out the brightness on the ceiling and effectively reducing it to an acceptable level.

In order for indirect lighting schemes to work, portable or under-shelf-mounted task lights must be used. This allows for lower ambient or general light levels in the room; the task lighting raises the bench top levels as necessary. Indirect pendants without task lighting are not able to both reach 70 foot candles and comply with IESNA/ASHRAE standard 90.1. The indirect pendants should be centered within the bench aisles so they reflect light off of the ceiling that then falls onto the bench on either side of the aisle. Indirect pendants must hang a minimum of 2 feet-0 inches below the ceiling for correct light distribution. There should not be any obstructions, such as cable trays or lab service carriers between the ceiling and the task plane. Obstructions in the path of the light will lower the overall light level at the task plane and create unwanted shadows.

An indirect lighting system works best with a highly reflective white, flat finish ceiling. The use of off-white or darker ceiling colors reduces the reflectance and the effectiveness of indirect lighting. Also, black bench tops completely absorb any light that strikes them,

 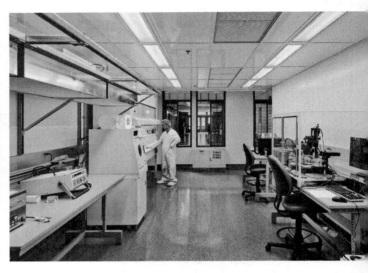

Simulation tools allow the designer to calculate lighting levels using different luminaires. This view simulates recessed direct lighting fixtures. *Left image courtesy of KlingStubbins. Right image courtesy of ZGF Architects LLP. Photography by Robert Canfield.*

thereby reducing overall room light levels. If the lab has no ceiling, lighting designers should pay particular attention to coordinating ductwork and piping loca-

tions with fixture location, since these obstructions will reflect light unevenly, even if painted. Ductwork interference reduces the amount of light on the bench and the overall average lighting level in the laboratory.

Another laboratory lighting design style is a hybrid system that uses direct/indirect distribution luminaires. These pendant-mounted luminaires uplight the ceiling just like an indirect luminaire, but there is an additional aperture at the bottom of the pendant that allows downlight to be distributed below as with a direct luminaire.

A hybrid system offers the benefits of an evenly illuminated ceiling and higher light levels at the task location (depending on design). A hybrid system requires a ceiling high enough to allow the pendant to be hung above the bench in order to achieve the direct light benefits without seeming uncomfortably low to the scientist. There must be enough room above the luminaire so that there is adequate space for proper

Computer simulation of pendant direct light fixtures. *Image courtesy of KlingStubbins.*

 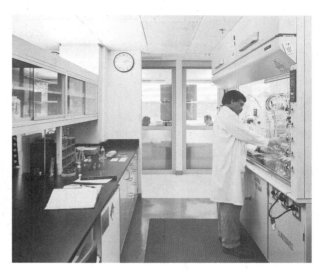

Simulation and example of pendant fixtures with indirect lighting distribution. *Images courtesy of KlingStubbins. Photography ©Tom Bonner 2007.*

light distribution at the ceiling too. Because of the direct downlight source, there is no need for supplemental task lighting. Correctly designed, a laboratory lit by a hybrid system is the most comfortable. This system works best with benches that do not have

shelving. Not having shelving allows the pendant to be mounted centered on the bench and not looming over the scientist, and it allows the reflected light from the ceiling to come from the front and the back of the scientist, so that shadows are filled in.

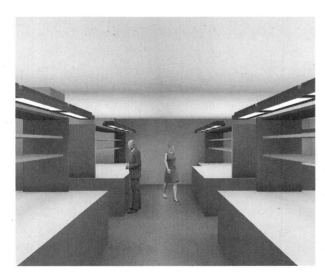 

Fixtures modeled here are direct/indirect fixtures, where a portion of the light is reflected toward the ceiling (indirect) and the balance of the light is directed toward the work surface (direct). *Image courtesy of KlingStubbins. Photography © ChristopherBarnes.com.*

Design Impacts on Lighting

As light travels over a distance its intensity is reduced by the inverse of the distance traveled, squared.

It makes sense then, when using direct lighting in the lab, that it is more efficient to have a lower ceiling bringing the light source closer to the task plane. This also has the added benefit of keeping the horizontal reflective surfaces closer together; less light is lost through the distance it travels between reflections. When an indirect or a direct/indirect source is used, the luminaire has a required pendant distance from the ceiling for distributing light properly, maximizing luminaire efficiency, and reducing hot spots on the ceiling. Generally the distance is a minimum of 2 feet-0 inches, but for some specialized luminaires that distance varies. Distance off the floor is critical also. Even if luminaires are high enough so that they are not obstacles, heights below 8 feet-0 inches create a sense of a very low false ceiling. Direct light pendants over the bench don't create a false ceiling or act as a

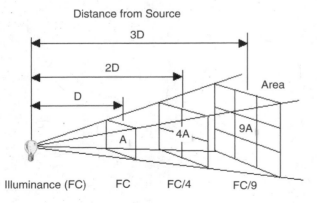

Distance from Source

The diagram illustrates the inverse square law. As light from a point source radiates out into space, the area illuminated increases as the square of the distance and the intensity of the light decreases as the square of the instance. *Image courtesy of KlingStubbins.*

physical barrier, but they also have mounting height restrictions primarily driven by bench top shelving. If these pendants are mounted lower than the top shelf, there is a good chance that they will become visual barriers to items on the shelf, or act as physical barriers to opening upper cabinet doors. From a lighting perspective, a 10- to 11-foot ceiling works the most efficiently allowing enough distance for proper light distribution and reflected bounce to occur without wasting light through excessive distance traveled.

The color and reflectance of all room surfaces play a very important role in allowing light to reflect around the room to increase the overall levels. Surface colors, whether natural or chemically dyed, absorb all the light colors not reflected. That seems obvious enough but the order of magnitude is not commonly understood. Assume in a hypothetical situation there is a light source that creates all colors within the visual spectrum evenly (although none actually exist). While observing a medium blue wall, the reflected light that is predominantly within the blue side of the spectrum and perhaps a small amount of the other colors that give it personality are perceived. The blue light reflected may well be limited to 20 percent of the total light energy hitting the wall. The additional colors reflected by the wall finish—a little of everything else left—could be an additional 20 to 25 percent of the total light started with, for a maximum reflectance of 45 percent. Then, there is another reduction of reflected light due to the surface sheen. The duller the sheen or more "flat" the finish, the more light gets trapped within the texture of the finish. This reduces the reflected light by 5 to 10 percent. The wall texture also impacts the reflected light, possibly reducing the light another 5 percent. The reflected light from this medium blue wall is around 30 percent of the total light striking it. The rest is absorbed by the wall, never to be seen again.

A case study illustrates how much energy can be reclaimed just by choosing finishes that have higher reflectivity. In this instance, the black bench top with no reflective value was switched for a gray bench top with a 70 percent reflectance value. Dark casework and shelving was changed to a lighter material that has a 50 percent reflectance. As the calculated levels show there was a 7 foot candle increase in the lab average and almost a 10 foot candle increase on the bench top itself. This represents approximately 10 percent higher lighting levels, using the same amount of energy!

Task Lighting

Task lighting options are increasing in number and decreasing in size. Historically, linear fluorescent sources have been the lamp of choice for efficient task lighting and continue to be an efficient option. The drawback of the T5 or T8 lamp is that they often produce too much light on the bench top creating an uncomfortable work surface. The excess of light also creates a source of glare if the luminaire's lens is not adequately shielded from sight. This problem is often dealt with by shielding the lamp with a diffuser that inherently absorbs a lot of the light produced, but that makes the luminaire inefficient by design. LED

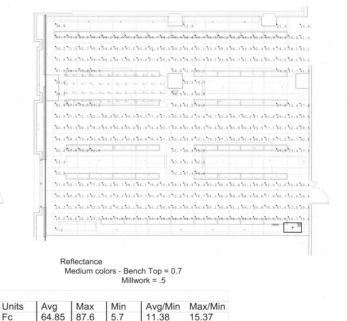

Reflectance
Dark colors - Bench Top = 0.0
Millwork = 0.38

Reflectance
Medium colors - Bench Top = 0.7
Millwork = .5

Calculation Summary							
Label	CalcType	Units	Avg	Max	Min	Avg/Min	Max/Min
Lab with dark surfaces	Illuminance	Fc	64.85	87.6	5.7	11.38	15.37
Bench with dark surface	Illuminance	Fc	69.37	91.2	7.3	9.50	12.49
Lab with medium surfaces	Illuminance	Fc	72.33	97.0	7.2	10.05	13.47
Bench with medium surface	Illuminance	Fc	78.77	105	28.2	2.79	3.71

Changing the reflectance of the finish materials can have a significant effect on the amount of general light provided through the space. Lighter finishes can mean higher light levels with the same amount of energy expended. Lighting simulation software models predicted light levels (in Foot-candles or Lux) on a grid throughout the space; summary results are in the table above. *Image Courtesy of KlingStubbins.*

task light luminaires are being produced in a way that optimizes the balance between light level and energy used. The light-emitting diode is a very efficient light source that can be grouped with other diodes to create more or less light as needed. Manufacturers have recognized this and are creating task lights that effectively eliminate the possibility of glare, deliver the correct amount of light on the bench top, and reduce energy consumption compared to other available task light sources. LEDs have advanced greatly in their color quality and light output per energy used ratio; continued advancements are likely.

Daylighting and Daylight Harvesting

Daylighting is often thought of as an excellent energy saving device, but that is not automatically the case. Unless the system is well thought out, electronic components tested and proven for compatibility, and supported through complementary architectural details, it is not likely that any expected energy savings will be realized. A poorly thought out design adds more complicated programming and systems to the project with marginal benefit. The control system components add 25 to 50 percent to the luminaire's cost and an additional 100 to 200 percent over a basic, code-compliant lighting control system. Most likely, this extra expenditure will have been spent in vain as a poorly designed system's return on investment rarely reaches its potential. If the system is thought of as daylight harvesting and intentionally designed there is a much better chance of realizing some payback.

Daylight harvesting must be planned for from the beginning. A building's siting must be correctly coordinated with the sun's path and angles of longitude and latitude considered. Buildings or trees might block detrimental low-angle direct sun, or these same buildings or trees might block beneficial daylight contribution most of the day. Through thoughtful design of the building and an automated dimming system, daylight has a positive energy saving contribution. Architecturally, the system requires an opening, of course, that allows daylight to pass through.

Examples range from a complicated sunlight collection panel with an array of focusing lenses and a fiber optic delivery system, to a sun-tracking light tube or roof-mounted light well, all the way to a simple window that is at least as tall as the interior ceiling. A window shading system is necessary to keep direct sunlight from causing disabling glare and reducing excessive heat load during low-angle exposure. The most important hardware consideration is an automatic light sensing system that has been properly located in order to correctly respond to adequate daylight contribution and instruct the electric lighting system to dim accordingly.

Similarly to electric lighting, the quality of daylighting is what makes for a successful daylighting project.

Light redirecting technologies offer the possibility of natural light penetration into core areas and basement spaces. *Image courtesy of Parans.*

The dimming system might be impeccably designed and perfectly implemented and saving 50 percent of the building's energy consumption, but if the light is glare-filled and makes for an uncomfortable work environment, the design cannot be considered successful. Softer light will create fewer and softer shadows and will be more useful for general tasks than direct light from a single source. High contrast ratios are a distinct pitfall of allowing in too much daylight. Glare from the sun is a product of sun angle and fenestration and is highly variable depending on time of day and time of the year. Left untreated direct sunlight on a task surface creates harsh shadows with very high brightness levels that make fine visual tasks difficult.

As low-angle morning or late afternoon sunlight begins to stream through a window striking a task surface, the foot-candle level jumps significantly as direct sunlight can reach 10,000 foot candles and might only be regulated by the glazing's light absorption factor. Window treatments such as manual shades or blinds are often added in an attempt to control the negative effects of direct sunlight, but these often lead occupants to lower the blinds on a cloudless winter morning when the glare is particularly harsh and never open them again; the building's electric lighting then illuminates their space undimmed all the time. This reduces the energy savings as well as the pleasure of inhabiting a daylit space.

A building manager's best defense available against permanently lowered blinds or shades is an automatic system that works in conjunction with the lighting dimming system. These shade systems can be tied into the daylight dimming system and lower the shades based on time clock events or a photocell that reports when the light level is too

high. This photocell should be dedicated to the function of the shades and should be placed "looking" outside the building so that it recognizes when it is being struck by direct sunlight and when it is not. This photocell should not be able to see the action of the shade since this creates a feedback loop of shade control, lowering the shades to eliminate direct sunlight, and then raising them when the direct sun is blocked by the shade, only to lower them again when the direct sun is again revealed. Placing the photo sensor outside, or facing out of a portion of window that is always visible to the outside above the shade roller, allows the sensor to react to the actual amount of daylight available, so that it does not raise the shade until it no longer senses direct sunlight.

Reflected daylight provides the most functional quality for an office or lab environment. Commonly, this includes sunlight that has been reflected off of the atmosphere, light shelves, a ceiling, and the ground outside the building. Like its electric counterpart, reflected or indirect daylight will produce soft shadows and has an overall more even appearance on the task surface. A clear and unobstructed window or light well serves as easy and excellent delivery systems for daylight. Adding horizontal architectural features such as exterior or interior light shelves allows for more comfortable, usable light to be harvested during times that would normally be too glary for occupants near the windows. There is a common misconception though that light shelves will extend the distance that daylight travels into a space. This has not been proven except for the case of interior light shelves that have a highly specular metalized finish. These are able to redirect low-angle sunlight deep into a room since they do not diffuse the light after reflection. The benefit of this specular surface is minimal at best, since there is only a short period of time during the day where the sun is in a geometric relationship that allows for the reflection to reach deep into the space. Also, the higher the sun angle, the shorter the throw into the room. Without a long throw, the specular reflector causes an extreme hot spot that is distracting or glary to occupants who have a clear view of the perimeter ceiling.

Laboratory Lighting Controls

Lighting controls offer a significant opportunity for energy savings. There are long periods of the day when a lab bench may be unattended. During these times lighting may be able to be dimmed to 25 to 50 percent of its normal output and task lighting turned off completely. Dimming can be controlled by room occupants or automatically controlled with the use of a time clock or occupancy sensors. A dimming system also has the possibility to control and maintain an even light level throughout the life of the lamp.[21] A discussion of the points that must be considered and their associated technologies follows.

It's an obvious fact that the best way to conserve lighting energy is to turn lights off when they are not in use. However, despite people's increased awareness of the importance of saving energy and even their increased desire to do so, individuals frequently leave lights on when exiting spaces; the same people who would never leave water running because it is wasteful will still leave lights burning. This may be due to human nature, force of habit, or perhaps natural familiarity with diurnal light cycles of day and night. That is to say, people are used to light filling the world during the day and the absence of light during the evening hours. Scientists are no exception to this behavior. Lighting controls address the need for a more sustainable and operationally cost-effective means of controlling lighted environments.

For quite a while now, controls have had the ability to turn on and off automatically based on time of day schedules, by electronically sensing the presence of an occupant, and then even tuning the lighting system's light levels in response to external light entering through glazed portions of a space. However, costs associated with these technologies were initially high and outweighed the savings which could be captured; high front-end costs made any hope of achieving a short-period return on investment (ROI) difficult. However, as with many new technologies, economical means of producing lighting control system packages have been developed, thus lowering their initial front-end costs.

Lower system costs combined with the industry's demand for sustainable design have fueled the development of sophisticated lighting controls. Today it is not unheard of for many laboratory lighting controls to be fully automated with user overrides. Increasingly, facility design criteria require computer terminal control interfacing and monitoring from a single point, and sometimes connection to a building management system (BMS) is a requirement as well. A scientist enters the lab where an occupancy sensor sends a command signal to the BMS to actuate a motorized breaker to energize the lab's lighting.

While detailed lighting control systems such as automatic shut-off controls and specific control zones used to be a key strategy in sustainable lighting design, current energy codes including the International Building Code (IBC) and California Energy Code Title 24 require many of these strategies to comply with the code. Currently, designers must include compliant control strategies for the particular space(s) they are designing. In addition to designing a compliant control strategy, one must document the design strategy in a regimented format for the reviewing official having jurisdiction over the project. Individual states have adopted either ASHRAE 90.1 or IECC as their mandatory energy design criteria; knowing which path should be followed to meet code is critical.

In the following examination of several different types of common lighting controls employed in modern laboratories, the assumption is that the lighting system is entirely fluorescent. Control systems discussed include use of dual switching, occupancy sensors, daylight sensors, dimming ballasts, and Digital Addressable Lighting Interface (DALI) ballasts.

Dual switching is a very simple means of reducing energy consumption. Two switches are placed on the wall and each switch controls a portion of the lighting. This can be on a fixture-by-fixture basis—turning some fixtures off, or within a single fixture it can turn individual lamps off. This allows the researchers to lower the lighting levels (reducing energy use) without requiring dimmable fixtures. While actual energy savings will be dependent on specific information about the fixtures, lamping, ballast configuration, quantity, and types, a frequently used configuration is a three-lamp luminaire, where the outer two lamps are controlled by one switch, the inner lamp is controlled by another, and this will use nominally 30 or 70 or 100 percent of the connected power depending on the switch location. This gives the researchers four different light settings depending on what they need—all on, two lamps on, one lamp on or off.

Occupancy sensors are ceiling- or wall-mounted electronic devices that are wired back to a power module. These are wired in line with a lighting control circuit. Someone entering the space creates a read-back signal that tells the power pack to either open or close the circuit. When a person exits the space

the lack of the read-back signal for a predetermined set time calls open the lighting circuit thus turning the lights off.

Occupancy sensors are typically available in three types of operational technologies: passive infrared (PIR), ultrasonic (US), and dual technology (DT) sensors that combine both PIR and US readings. PIR type sensors are typically used in spaces such as corridors or open offices where there is a large range of motion such as people walking around. US sensors are more finely tuned to small range of motion such as people sitting at computers typing or filing papers. Dual technology sensors combine PIR and US and are used in locations such as toilet rooms where line of sight may be limited. For laboratory spaces, where the work patterns include some static work—researchers sitting at benches; as well as some transitory work, for example, moving from one setup to another—the DT sensors are usually the best application. They must be carefully tuned for each lab environment.

Daylight sensing controls (DS) are used when ambient fenestration allows entry of solar lighting through windows or skylights to light the space. Daylight sensors are typically adjustable to cycle on or off based on an adjustable foot-candle level. Daylight sensors are typically used in conjunction with 0–10 volt electronic dimming ballasts or DALI ballasts. They read ambient light within the space being illuminated. When the ambient light from outdoors reaches a high enough level the sensor reads this ambient light and sends a control signal to the ballast to either dim or shut off the lights in the brighter region near the window or skylight.[22]

Dimming ballasts are available in several different ranges. Some dimming ballasts dim down to 10 percent light output while others dim down to 5 or even 1 percent light output. Light output is relative to power consumption. The lower the light output, the less power is consumed. When tied into a daylight sensor reading light from ambient fenestration, the light output is lowered and less energy is consumed.

While conventional ballasts received control signals through the same circuits that power them, there are newer systems employing something called a Digital Addressable Lighting Interface (DALI). The DALI ballast is an intelligent ballast that has the ability to store a programmed digital address and communicate with other DALI ballasts. It can be controlled either separately or in tandem with a group or zone. Some DALI control systems allow programming by means of software packages at a central point, such as a computer in a facility director's office or in a mobile fashion, with a personal digital device. Many manufacturers offer personal remote control devices or PC application-based individual control for more visually

ergonomic environments for individual users. This means that changes to lighting control strategies can be accomplished without any change to the electrical infrastructure itself.

The laboratory planner, the lighting designer, and the controls engineer should coordinate on the controls design of the laboratory. Failing to consider details of a laboratory space results in generic designs with functional problems. For instance, mechanical diffusers (of which there are many in a laboratory) actually make a low noise when air is passing through the louvers. This may create a false start for lighting. Similarly, lab equipment such as centrifuges and shakers that make low-level noise when in use also create false starts if US sensors are used. Throw patterns of sensors are frequently blocked by wall-mounted casework that controls designers might not have considered if only evaluating the space in plan; different sensors might be required that offer a more elongated rectilinear distribution for the lab.

Occupant Controls

Hawaii Institute of Marine Biology, Dry Labs Complex, Coconut Island, Hawaii
Ferraro Choi and Associates
Engineering Solutions, Inc.

For more information about this project, refer to Chapter 4, Site Design.

Giving occupants reasonable control over their working environment is a basic principle of good practice. In a laboratory setting, occupant control is elevated in importance as environmental conditions are basic to many types of research, as well as an occupant's health and safety.

The underlying design concept of the new dry labs complex is to provide individually controllable and environmentally independent laboratories. This approach provides maximum flexibility for accommodating various types of research and meeting the individual comfort preferences of the researchers themselves. Both factors combine to contribute toward increased productivity and comfort.

The types of occupant control provided at the new dry labs complex include the following:

- Thermal comfort is achieved by standalone air conditioning units and humidity control for each lab. The researcher controls temperature to his or her needs.

- In the event of a noxious spill, a highly visible "panic button" is provided adjacent to the lab exit which increases the hood ventilation rate to its maximum setting.

- Hood ventilation rates are typically set to six air changes per hour when the room is occupied but can be set to three air changes per hour when the room is unoccupied.

- Ambient and task lighting is manually driven in accordance with the perceived need by the researcher. If daylight is adequate, the lights are left off. If lights are accidentally left on when the room is unoccupied, occupancy sensors turn them off following a preset default period.

- Views to the outdoors are available in each lab, but may be closed off at the researcher's discretion. Affording outdoor views to occupants has been shown to be beneficial to the human psyche, and a positive influence on productivity.

Photo montage rendered view of the east face of the modular dry labs complex for Hawaii Institute of Marine Biology at Coconut Island, Hawaii, incorporating existing landscape features from the actual site. The Koolau mountain range of Oahu appears in the distance. This public side of the complex features individual entrance walkways to each lab space, from a main pedestrian circulation path through a central lawn. Predominant in this view are the north-facing clerestories. *Image courtesy of Ferraro Choi and Associates*.

Connections Between Acoustical Considerations and Sustainable Design for Laboratories

Douglas H. Sturz and the Acentech Staff

Noise Control

There are compelling connections between energy savings for HVAC systems serving laboratory buildings and minimizing or avoiding noise-reduction treatments. This impacts both noise conditions due to HVAC systems inside buildings and noise emissions to outdoors. In noise control there is the axiom that it is best to control noise at the source or not to generate the noise in the first place. This axiom carries over to energy and resource conservation which are fundamental to LEED.

Outdoor Noise

LEED objectives address a variety of environmental pollution issues such as for light (SSc8) and other emissions, but they do not expressly address noise pollution, at least as this directly relates to determining LEED credits toward project certification. But

continued

clearly, there is an environmental benefit to reducing noise emissions outdoors either in attaining desirably low noise levels or reducing the treatments necessary to achieve a particular noise goal.

Favorable site planning of significant noise sources can be very helpful for controlling noise. These are very low- or no-cost strategies to minimize the required noise-control treatments for mechanical systems. Locate noisy equipment far from sensitive receivers to take advantage of the dissipation that naturally occurs with increasing distance. Where sources have a directional aspect to their noise emissions, orient them away from nearby receivers. Use the building itself as a barrier to shield sensitive receiver locations from noise sources.

To the extent that highly energy-efficient fans can be used, these typically produce less noise than fans with only nominal efficiency. To the extent that the air-flow requirements for the building can be reduced through other means that are LEED friendly, this directly reduces the work (and noise) that the fan systems produce in doing their job. To the extent that the system pressures can be lowered, this also directly reduces the noise that the fan systems produce. These approaches can favorably reduce the noise emission to outdoors from air handling unit intakes and from exhaust discharges, which are major building systems that emit noise outdoors. The degree of potential concerns for noise emissions from the inlets of air handling systems serving labs can vary widely depending upon how close receivers are and what sort of environment is desired. For typically acceptable campus noise conditions and where neighbors are not particularly close to the building or acoustically sensitive, the concern for exterior noise emissions is often modest. With good fan selections, lower system flow, and reduced system pressure, it can be possible to avoid attenuation treatment altogether on the exterior sides of such systems. This can further reduce the overall flow resistance of the system which, in turn, can allow the system to operate at lower pressure and still lower noise emission levels.

There are a number of environmental issues that must be addressed for laboratory exhaust discharges, and there may also be an aesthetic concern regarding the appearance and scale of the exhaust stacks. If the stacks need to be particularly short for visual reasons, this tends to push designers toward the use of silencers in the discharges of exhaust fan systems which introduce extra flow resistance that the fans must overcome. Extra flow resistance involves extra energy consumption. The silencers for such applications are applied to relatively large air flow quantities and at relatively high flow velocities. If the attenuation treatments needed for the exhaust stacks can be minimized or avoided altogether, this can save energy. Most LEED initiatives that translate to lower energy consumption (flow reduction, minimum system pressure, and favorable fan selections) translate into lower noise emissions, which can lead to less restrictive attenuation treatments or even the elimination of stack attenuation. Given the magnitude of air flow typically involved in laboratory exhaust systems, the silencers can be rather large in physical size and require substantial material. Elimination of the silencers avoids the need for them to be made in the first place.

Stack silencers can often produce a pressure loss on the order of 0.25 inches. Over the life of the facility, the energy consumed to overcome this flow resistance can be very substantial. (In Chapter 6 there is more detailed discussion of reducing pressure losses as an energy saving strategy.) In

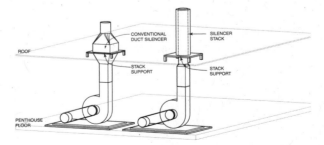

Exhaust stack options: silencer in the exhaust stack versus an attenuating stack. *Image courtesy of KlingStubbins.*

project designs where there is ample stack length available, the desired attenuation can often be provided with an attenuating stack (lined stack) rather than having a discrete silencer in the stack. This approach still requires material to make the double-wall stack, but it eliminates the extra resistance of a silencer in the exhaust discharge path and makes a more appealing aesthetic for the stacks. The accompanying is an illustration of the differences between having a silencer in the exhaust stack and having an attenuating stack.

Cooling towers are another significant source that emits noise outdoors. Cooling towers are relatively energy-efficient because they involve both sensible and latent heat rejection. With a given amount of air movement, they reject more heat than dry coolers, and this allows less fan energy to be expended for rejection of a given amount of heat. In turn, cooling tower fans produce less noise for a given amount of heat rejection compared to many methods of heat rejection. Cooling towers can be available with low-noise fans (compared with standard fan selections). Because low-noise fan designs have especially good aerodynamics, they are more energy-efficient than standard fans. Cooling towers are also available with variable speed drives which reduce their energy consumption and noise emissions in accordance with the heat they need to reject. The noise reduction achieved at reduced load and speed can be dramatic. When multiple tower cells are used, all the available cells should turn on at some low speed before their speeds all ramp up and down together in response to demand to achieve significant noise reduction with variable speed drives. For multiple cell towers this may not be the absolute lowest energy consumption approach to tower operation because more motors are operating at less-than-peak efficiency, but it is a very powerful approach for noise reduction.

When roof screens are used to visually hide rooftop equipment, use the screens as effective noise barriers by designing them to be solid and extend down close to the roof. If the screen allows air to transfer through it or if there is a significant gap under the bottom, the acoustical benefit for reducing noise to the nearby community will essentially be defeated.

The mitigation of noise pollution to the environment using strategies discussed here may be grounds for an Innovation in Design credit (IDc1). Strategies to reduce noise pollution can also lead to more efficient building energy performance, which contributes toward achievement of LEED points under credit EAC1, "Optimize Energy Performance."

Indoor Noise

Inside laboratory buildings there is typically a need to attenuate the noise of the main supply and exhaust fans that are emitted to the duct systems, and there is need to control the noise produced by terminal boxes that provide the final control of air flow to the various spaces. Anything that can be done to lower the flow quantity and pressure loss of the system will reduce the work the fans need to do, and this will lower the noise the fans generate in doing the necessary work. With less noise from the fans, the need for attenuation treatment in the duct system is minimized. This further reduces the work that the system needs to do compared to more conventional system designs, while still satisfying the system performance requirement.

Lowering the external duct system flow resistance not only reduces the work and noise of the main fans, but also reduces the throttling that the terminal boxes need to do to control the flow to and from the various spaces. The energy dissipated in throttling the flow is simply lost, and if a system design can be conceived which minimizes the throttling need, this will save the throttling energy and avoid the need for attenuation on the building side of the terminal box. Ideally, all the terminal boxes would operate

continued

at the minimum pressure that is needed for them to control flow, but it is seldom practical to achieve this perfectly in real buildings; some boxes will naturally see higher pressure than other boxes. How can the duct system be conceived to minimize pressure? Certainly the velocities at which systems are designed are a major component in how much energy is needed to move air through the duct systems. The velocities should be particularly low and the air-flow path should have good aerodynamics. However, if the velocities are pushed to very low levels, this can cause the need for very large space in which to run the ducts, which translates into more building construction to contain the ducts. Clearly there is a reasonable and practical limit to how low the velocities can be. Typically it is the sizes of the major ducts near the air handling units and fans that control how much building construction is needed to house them. The smaller distribution duct runs typically do not impact the size of the building envelope. However, it is the pressure that is required to push the air to the extremes of the system in the final distribution ducts that controls how much pressure the system requires. If the system can be designed with progressively lower flow resistance in ducts moving toward the extremes of the system, this will lower the overall system pressure, which will lower the noise of the main fans and reduce the throttling that has to be done by the terminal boxes. This design strategy can typically be implemented without adversely impacting the building envelope. The shorter the runs to the extremes of the duct systems, the lower the pressure will need to be. Avoiding one (or a few) long duct runs that control the system pressure will lower the overall system pressure. The accompanying schematic portrays a highly desirable system concept.

Designers of low-energy consuming systems should not only compute the pressure required to serve the ends of the system, they should also optimize the design to require as little pressure as possible by avoiding a small number of branches which limit how low the system pressure can be. Another strategy that can help produce low-resistance duct distribution systems in laboratories is to have a constant size duct/manifold in the mechanical room (with little pressure differential throughout), and then use numerous risers to serve the various floors of the building so each riser will serve a smaller floor area. The ducts to serve the floor area will thus handle less air and extend less far compared to other system concepts. Such a design has low flow resistance without ducts that are so large that they adversely impact the floor-to-floor heights of the building.

For quiet operating conditions in buildings, designs should take steps to ensure that there is minimal duct leakage. Duct leakage makes the system work harder to deliver the required flow; it boosts the pressure the system needs to develop to get air flow to the ends of the runs and this means the pressure arriving at boxes near the beginning of the system will be high. This added pressure requires unnecessary energy consumption and generates unnecessary noise. Quiet and energy-efficient systems have very little leakage. Typically there is little cost associated with this system feature and it does not add to the space required for mechanical systems; this simply enables the planned system to work at peak efficiency.

The above features are important for design of buildings to create systems that can operate at very low pressures and will operate quietly with minimal added attenuation treatments. For any building, the systems need to be set up and operated at the lowest pressures that will satisfy the flow requirements. Building systems cannot be left to operate with

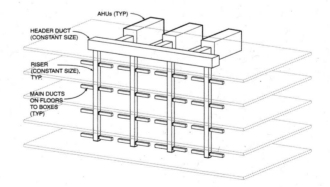

System design schematic: Balancing acoustical requirements with pressure drop penalties is important to system design. *Image courtesy of KlingStubbins.*

more pressure than necessary simply because it makes them easy to set up and balance. Various computer control systems and algorithms are available today to help operate HVAC systems at the lowest pressure point needed to maintain proper system function. Use of such control systems ensures system operation at low pressures, and this can help further reduce the need to add attenuation treatments.

Silencer Applications

Although LEED does not specifically address the energy required to overcome attenuation devices in the system, even a well-conceived silencer scheme for laboratory systems can add about an inch of pressure loss (for both inlet and discharge of the supply and exhaust systems). Silencers must be located to avoid excess system-effect losses due to poor aerodynamic conditions. Some silencer applications are arranged so poorly that the project can actually be better off without them. Systems need to be conceived from the outset with good locations for silencers rather than squeezed into poor flow locations. Providing appropriate space for attenuation treatments may require more space than a lesser quality design, but this can translate into a great deal of energy savings over the life of the building. Elbow silencers are also available, and although they cost more than straight silencers, it is better to use such devices than to have poorly applied straight silencers.

Architectural Acoustics Design

There typically is not much need for special sound isolating constructions in laboratory spaces. The most typical acoustical design issue is to address room acoustics treatment to improve laboratory comfort and to help control mechanical system and lab equipment noise. Sound absorptive treatment at the ceiling is often the desired design approach because this can be practical, effective, and inexpensive. A good rule of thumb is to develop an area of acoustical treatment approaching the area of the ceiling. In LEED building design there are often additional design parameters that can impact the ability to implement simple, basic treatments such as a conventional acoustical panel ceiling. The use of heavy floors to increase the thermal mass and the storage effect of the building often result in exposed structures to optimize the radiation efficiency of the floor masses. Conventional acoustical ceilings or surface-applied materials that are sound-absorptive tend to be thermal insulators, working against the desire to maximize the thermal radiation of the heavy slabs. This design approach forces the incorporation of room acoustics treatment into other schemes, such as space absorbers (e.g., vertically suspended baffles), and these can present other substantial design implications. It is typically difficult (and expensive) to develop the desired magnitude of treatment by working with surfaces other than the ceiling.

When radiant floor structures are used, sometimes a compromise solution can be found with a partial ceiling which allows for sufficient radiant effect from the slab through openings in the ceiling, especially openings at the most important locations for the radiation effect. Such an open ceiling can be acoustically effective beyond the area of treatment that is exposed at the underside to the occupied zone because some of the sound that goes through the open areas between treatment zones is absorbed by the back side of the ceiling panels.

Another common LEED directed design is to have light reflecting surfaces near external windows to reflect natural light deeper into buildings (see LEED credit EQc8.1). Light-colored acoustical ceilings can work very well with this objective, and if such

continued

ceiling treatment is acceptable, the LEED and acoustical objectives can mesh very easily. If ceiling treatment is used, it can be acceptable to have a modest zone of mirrored ceiling surface near the windows if this is desired for lighting purposes. When a light-reflecting surface near the exterior walls is combined with a radiant slab, design incorporating sound-absorptive treatments can become very complex; there can be significant design challenges here.

Some laboratory projects include training, large conference, and classroom spaces. Such spaces will generally benefit from following the fundamental features for sound isolation, room acoustic design, and background noise that are found in LEED for Schools guidelines.

Acoustical Materials for Laboratories

The most common acoustical treatments in laboratory buildings are ceiling treatments and in the ceiling treatment realm for labs, the commonly used materials are either mineral fiber or glass fiber panels.

Both glass fiber and mineral fiber ceiling panels can have a substantial recycled material content and they can be recycled when the building is decommissioned. The use of sound-absorbing material with high recycled content can contribute to the achievement of LEED points under credit MRc4.

Attenuation treatments used in silencers and for lining of ducts are typically a fibrous, porous, sound-dissipating material such as glass fiber. The sheet metal that is used for facings over linings and for construction of the baffles in silencers is all recyclable and the glass fiber is recyclable, as well. There are also cotton-based sound-dissipative materials for use in silencers that have a very high recycled material content, and these can again be recycled at the end of service.

Conclusion

Laboratory research is not a linear process—often innovation and scientific breakthroughs happen at irregular and unpredictable intervals—but it remains true that the many factors of the indoor environment can contribute to a setting that is conducive to creative and productive research. Certainly health and human safety is a critical part of this process, but access to daylight, thermal comfort, and individual control are important as well. Informal and flexible lay-outs and spatial relationships allow the research teams to adjust and react to new concepts and methods of investigation. Attention to acoustical treatment, and a focus on lighting quality over quantity is an important part of making a highly effective sustainable research environment.

Key Concepts

- Sustainable strategies focused on indoor factors are critically important to achieving occupant health, satisfaction, and productivity.

- There are several ways that laboratory facility organization can take cues from recent trends in corporate workplace planning:

- Increased flexible space;

- Decreased individual offices, increased shared/open offices; and

- More amenity spaces/teaming spaces/collaboration spaces.

- Evaluating operating costs of typical buildings, employees make up to 86 percent of annual costs, so strategies that increase productivity can potentially save more cost than energy savings.

- General strategies that improve occupant health and productivity include the following:

  - Indoor air quality improvement leads to health and productivity gains.

- In laboratories, chemical use management leads to improved health and safety for employees.

- Thermal comfort is correlated with increased productivity and decreased absenteeism.

- Occupant control can lead to satisfaction and productivity.

- Daylight or access to views has been shown to have multiple positive effects.

- Designing for daylighting is an integrated process requiring architecture/engineering and interior design cooperation and coordination.

- Lighting design is a critical part of sustainable laboratory design, which involves several different tasks:

  - Setting appropriate criteria and lighting levels is critical.

  - Selecting different types of lighting approaches—direct versus indirect, ambient versus task lighting, general lighting and accent lighting—is good practice.

- Light fixture selection and lay-out impacts both lighting levels and lighting quality.

- Selection of finish materials can have a significant impact on required energy to achieve certain lighting levels.

- Attention to sensors, daylight harvesting, and lighting control systems is important to allow for lighting to meet needs while still conserving energy.

- Laboratory acoustics are an important part of creating a successful facility:

  - Exterior noise should be mitigated to minimize transmission into the facility.

  - Laboratory projects often require sound mitigation to reduce sound transmission from the facility to the neighboring properties.

  - There are several different methods of reducing indoor noise from a laboratory facility; care must be taken to pursue strategies that do not have a heavy energy penalty.

REFERENCES

1. U.S. Environmental Protection Agency. Healthy Buildings, Healthy People: A vision for the 21st Century 2001 www.epa.gov/iaq/hbhp/hbhp-toc.html, as cited in LEED Building Design + Construction Reference Guide, USGBC, 2009, p. 401.
2. KlingStubbins Interior Design Benchmark Data, 2009.
3. KlingStubbins Interior Design Benchmark Data, 2009.
4. Davis Langdon, "The Cost of Green Revisited: Re-examining the Feasibility and Cost Impact of Sustainable Design in Light of Increased Market

Adoption," July 2007, p. 2 www.davislangdon.com/USA/Research/ResearchFinder/2007-The-Cost-of-Green-Revisited/.

5. The Costs and Financial Benefits of Green Buildings, A Report to California's Sustainable Building Task Force, October 2003 Principal Author: Greg Kats, Capital E, p. 55, table VIII-1.

6. The Center for Building Performance and Diagnostics at Carnegie Mellon University

7. U.S. EPA, "Healthy Buildings, Healthy People . . ." cited in LEED Reference Guide, p. 401.

8. Garrett, M.H., M.A. Hooper, and B.M. Hooper (1996), Low levels of formaldehyde in residential homes and correlation with asthma and allergy in children. Proceedings of Indoor Air 96. Vol 1, cited by Vivian Loftness, Sustainable Design for Health & Productivity, Keynote Address, GreenCities 08, Feb. 2008.

9. *Labs21 Environmental Performance Criteria*, version 2.1, Credit MR 8, www.epa.gov/lab21gov/pdf/epc21_printable_508.pdf, accessed 9/2009.

10. *ASHRAE Standard 55–2004: Thermal Environmental Conditions for Human Occupancy*, American Society of Heating, Refrigerating and Air-Conditioning Engineers, Inc., Atlanta GA, 2004.

11. There are a number of research institutions that have been pursuing studies relative to energy, comfort, and productivity, and many more studies than there is space here to discuss. See www.cbe.berkeley.edu/research/publications.htm for a listing of some of the recent studies at CBE.

12. Brager, G.S., and R. de Dear, "Climate, Comfort, & Natural Ventilation: A new adaptive comfort standard for ASHRAE Standard 55," Center for the Built Environment, U.C. Berkeley, 2001, http://repositories.cdlib.org/cedr/cbe/ieq/Brager 2001 Windsor AdaptiveComfort.

13. Zhang, H., D. Kim, E. Arens, E. Buchberger, F. Bauman, and C. Huizenga, "Comfort, Perceived Air Quality, and Work Performance in a Low-Power Task-Ambient Conditioning System," Center for the Built Environment (CBE), University of California, Berkeley, 2008.

14. Summary of eight different international case studies, Loftness, "Sustainable Design for Health & Productivity, 2/08.

15. Walch, reference study, cited by Loftness, 2/08.

16. Heschong Mahone Group, cited by Loftness, 2/08.

17. Heschong Mahone Group, Multiple studies on behalf of California Energy Commission's Public Interest Energy Research (PIER) program, available at www.h-m-g.com/projects/daylighting/projects-PIER.htm, 1999, 2001, 2003.

18. USGBC, LEED Rating System, www.usgbc.org.

19. Lux is defined as 1 square meter, 1 meter away, where fc is 1 square foot, 1 foot away. 1 lux is approximately 10.76 fc, for rough comparisons 1:10 is usually an acceptable conversion factor (and easier to calculate in your head). For more detailed study, accurate conversion is preferable.

20. Dictionary.com. *The American Heritage® Dictionary of the English Language, Fourth Edition*. Houghton Mifflin Company, 2004. http://dictionary.reference.com/browse/efficiency (accessed: June 19, 2009).

21. Rundquist, R.A., T.G. McDougall, and J. Benya. 1996. *Lighting Controls: Patterns for Design.* Palo Alto: Electric Power Research Institute and Empire State Electric Energy Research Corporation.

22. For further in-depth design considerations refer to the Illumination Engineering Society of North America's RP-5–99, Recommended Practice of Daylighting.

chapter **8** # Materials
What Is the Sustainable Lab Made Of?

Courtesy of KlingStubbins.
Photography by © ChristopherBarnes.com.

Introduction: What Makes Materials Sustainable?

Generally speaking, selecting materials for sustainability means evaluating how it impacts the overall environment through the life of the material. It means taking a look at how the material is extracted from the earth, harvested, or synthesized from raw materials. It means thinking about where those raw materials come from, how far they need to be shipped, and what the byproducts of harvest and manufacture will do to their local environments. It also means considering the energy needed to fabricate, refine, finish, and make the material ready for installation, transporting it to the project site, and any energy that will be used to maintain or refinish the material during its useful life in the building. Included is the length of useful life, and any embodied energy associated with removal and reuse or disposal of the material. The ideal material, from an environmental point of view, would be made from raw materials that are nontoxic

This chapter focuses on all five of the sustainability categories discussed in Chapter 1. See page 18 for more information.

and plentiful, that are easily and gently harvested or collected, are available very close to the project site so as to minimize transportation energy required, are very durable and easy to maintain, and can be reused.

The challenge is that this ideal material described above doesn't really exist—there are always some competing factors to be weighed, and it is often very difficult for designers to determine which material has the least impact on the environment. The

Sample Characteristics of Environmentally Preferable Materials	
Category	*Characteristic*
Material Cost	Relative ocost to equivalent products that do not possess sustainable characteristics
Life Cycle Cost Impact (LCI)	Relative impact on the life cycle cost of buidling operators (not to be confused with environmental life cycle assessment, which measures environmental burden s, not financial impacts).
Energy Efficiency (EE)	Construction materials that directly influence building energy use
Water Efficiency (WE	Construction materials that directly influence building water use
Locally Manufactured (LM)	Construction materials that are manufactured within a defined radius (500 miles for the LEED rating system) of the project site. LANL strongly encourages the use of construction materials manufactured in northern New Mexico
Material Reduction (MR)	Products or materials that served a defined function using less material than is typically used.
Locally Derived Raw Materials (LRM)	Construction materials that are locally manufactured using raw materials within a defined radius of the project site. LANL strongly encourages the use of construction materials manufactured using raw materials derived from northern New Mexico
Non-Toxic (NT)	Construction materials that release relatively low levels of emissions of odorous, irritating, toxic or hazardous substances. Volatile organic compounds (VOCs), formaldehydes, and particulates and fibers are examples of substances emitted from construction materials that can adversely impact human health (allergens, carcinogens, irritants).
Recycled Content (RC)	Amount of reprocessed materials contained within a construction product that originated from post-consumer use and / or post-industrial processes that would otherwise have been disposed of in a landfill.
Salvaged (S)	Construction materials that are reused as-is (or with minor refurbishing) without having undergone any type of reprocessing to change the intended use. This includes the reuse of existing building structures, equipment, and furnishings at LANL
Rapidly Renewable (RR)	Construction materials that replenish thenselves faster (within 10 years) than traditional exraction demand; and do not result in adverse environmental impacts
Certified Wood (CW)	Construction materials manufactured all or in part from wood that has been certified to the standards of the Forest Stewardship Council as originating from a well-managed forest.

This table highlights a number of different ways to evaluate how materials impact the environment. Developing a list of Environmentally Preferable Materials is an important part of a sustainable design project. *Courtesy of Los Alamos National Laboratory.*

other factor involved is that manufacturers developing "greener" alternatives to their conventional offerings are adjusting formulations and manufacturing processes, and specifiers are often reluctant to have their project be a test case for a new material. In addition, the market for new materials must be balanced with the time required to develop and bring them to market. Because there is no single process for determining the most appropriate material for a given use, there are a number of different strategies and metrics that have been developed.

Material Reuse/Refurbishment/Downcycling

The first, and perhaps best-known strategy is to decrease the amount of new raw materials needed to generate finish materials. This can be done in a couple of ways. Using existing materials, refurbished and reused for their original purpose, is often the least energy-intensive method. Retooling existing furniture, doors, flooring, and ceiling materials is feasible and can be done for many projects. Taking existing materials and reworking them for new uses is another method—remilling large timber frame construction and repurposing them as flooring, shading devices, or millwork items is a way to reduce the amount of new material that needs to be harvested. Neither of these strategies are a major portion of laboratory building design, but they often can be implemented in specialty areas or public spaces.

Recycled Content and Recyclability of Materials

A step down from reuse and refurbished materials, recycled content materials are formulated such that a portion of the raw material base comes from a re-

For the Robert Mondavi Institute for Wine and Food Science in Napa, California at University of California, Davis, the palette of sustainable materials included locally reclaimed olive barrel redwood for finish materials. The project also employed stained concrete and traditional lime plaster, taking advantage of the passive benefits of thermal mass in this Northern California climate. *Courtesy of ZGF Architects LLP. Photography by Robert Canfield.*

cycled source, that is to say, that it would otherwise be a waste product. This is usually defined either as postindustrial, or waste from manufacturing, or postconsumer, waste from individual use. An example of post-industrial-based (also referred to as pre-consumer-based) material is synthetic gypsum, which is a byproduct of manufacturing—largely by collecting the gypsum from flue-gas-desulfurization processes, frequently at power generating plants. This product both uses the waste product, as well

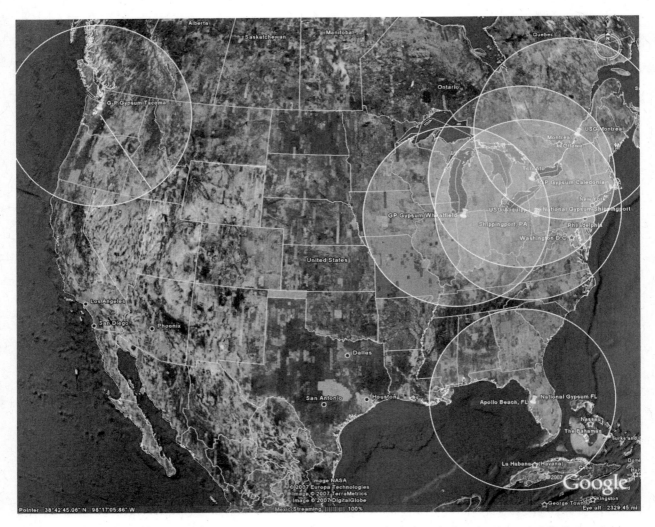

Using data available from gypsum manufacturers, the project team can develop a map to clearly determine how close to a project site these materials are being manufactured. Google Earth image, information derived from USG, National Gypsum, G-P, and other manufacturers' websites. *Image courtesy of KlingStubbins.*

as reducing the need to mine for virgin gypsum. This synthetic gypsum is used in approximately 7 percent of the gypsum wallboard manufactured in the United States. An example of postconsumer recycled content is the paper facing on gypsum wallboard, which is generated from recycled newspaper.[1] Other materials such as interior glass, steel, and aluminum have both recycled content in their makeup, and are also formulated to be able to be recycled again at the end of their use.

Harvesting Practices and Transportation

Another factor in the environmental impact of materials is how they are harvested or manufactured, and how much energy is used to transport materials to the jobsite. This strategy can be pursued if care is taken to use local and indigenous materials whenever possible. Selecting stone, brick, or wood from locally grown areas means that less energy is spent on transit. Of course this strategy has a very different impact on the project depending on where the project is—some lab-specific materials are not made everywhere in the country or world, so some remote

Nearly 50 percent of the building materials on St. Lawrence University's Johnson Hall of Science in Canton, New York, were manufactured within 500 miles of the site. Using locally sourced stone, brick, and gypsum board, as well as masonry and concrete contributed to reduce drastically the energy expended on transporting the building materials to the site. *Courtesy of Croxton Collaborative / KlingStubbins. Photography © Woodruff/Brown Architectural Photography.*

project sites will preclude achieving high percentages of local materials in the overall palette.

Healthy Materials, VOCs, and Low Toxicity

Another factor in selecting materials is the effect they will have on building occupants. Materials with solvent-based ingredients will offgas volatile organic compounds over time, with the majority emitted soon after construction. Part of this issue can be resolved with care toward selecting materials with zero or low VOC content, and it can also be mitigated through careful ventilation to dilute the effects of VOC emission on building occupants. For most laboratory spaces, low VOC materials work well, but in a few specialized applications high-performing epoxies and other materials are called for, and these can have high VOC content.

Sustainable Material Sources

Finish materials or raw materials that are mined, harvested, and extracted can have a big impact on the regional environment, and for each category of materials to be selected there are options that have a lower environmental footprint than conventional "business as usual" materials. This includes materials made from agricultural waste—wheatboards and strawboards that are often as strong as or stronger than conventional wood-based fiberboard substrates, as well as wood products that have been certified to be harvested in a way to promote long-term forest viability. Some materials conventionally manufactured from petrochemical sources have been reformulated to use soy-based or other plant-based oils as feedstock—materials including vegetable-based phenolic resins and insulation products made from soy or cotton.

Certifications

To try to help design teams get some comparative data, there are a number of organizations that have worked to analyze and compile lists of materials that meet certain criteria. For each different category, there are often several lists to consult. The accompanying table shows a listing of most of the major certifications and evaluation groups, with a description of each of the major characteristics of each sys-

	Program	Managing Organization	Product Range	Levels	Used in LEED*	Type of Standard or Certification	Comments (see article text for details)
Sustainable Forestry	Forest Stewardship Council	Forest Stewardship Council (FSC)	Forest Products	Variety of labels for pure and percentage content	Y	Third-party certification to regionally specific standards	Only forestry program in LEED; roots in the environmental movement. More prescriptive than SFI
	Sustainable Forestry Initiative	Sustainable Forestry Initiative (SFI)	Forest Products	Variety of labels for pure and percentage content	N	Third-party certification	Thorough system but less prescriptive than FSC. Historically close to the forest industry.
	American Tree Farm System	American Forest Foundation	Forest Products	Single standard for small U.S. landowners	N	Third-party certification	Very non-prescriptive standard. Does not label products itself, but the SFI label applies.
	CSA Sustainable Forest Management System	Candadian Standards Association	Forest Products	Single standard applied to specific forest areas	N	Third-party certification	Industry-and government-backed standard used in Canada
Emissions Certifications	California Section 01350	California Department of Health Services	Wide range of interiors products	n/a	Y	Specification guidance on which other certifications are based	Designed to reduce pollutant concentrations in classrooms and offices.
	Greenguard	Greenguard Environmental Institute	Wide range of interiors products	Greenguard Indoor Air Quality, Greenguard for Children and Schools	Y	Third-party certification	Uses ASTM test methods
	FloorScore	Scientific Certification Systems, Resilient Floor Coverings Institute	Non-textile flooring	FloorScore	Y	Third-party certification	Based on California Section 01350 specification. Equivalent to Indoor Advantage Gold
	Indoor Advantage	Scientifc Certification Systems (SCS)	Wide range of interiors products	Indoor Advantage, Indoor Advantage Gold	Y	Third-party certification based on a variety of standards	Indoor Advantage meets LEED requirements; Indoor Advantage Gold also meets stricter California Section 01350 limits
	Green Label	Carpet & Rug Institute (CRI)	Carpet, pad, adhesive	Green Label, Green Label Plus	Y	Second-party certification	Green Label Plus meets California Section 01350 limits.
Energy	Energy Star	U.S. EPA and U.S. Department of Energy	Range of products	n/a	Y	Government label based on manufacturer data	Popular program with wide impact. Moderate standards capture wide market share
Multi-Attribute Standards and Certifications	Sustainable Choice	Scientific Certification Systems (SCS)	Carpet, others expected	Silver, Gold, Platinum	ID	Third-party certification based on both consensus and proprietary standards	Similar to SCS's EPP standard but with social considerations. Respected as a leader in the field.
	Cradle to Cradle (C2C)	McDonough Braungart Design Chemistry (MBDC)	Wide range of products	Biological, Technical, Nutrients, Silver, Gold, Platinum	ID	Second-party certification, based on a proprietary standard	Developed by respected industry leaders, but key pieces are not transparent.
	SMaRT Consensus Sustainable Product Standards	Institute for Market Transformation to Sustainability (MTS)	Wide range of products	Sustainable, Silver, Gold, Platinum	ID	Third-party certification	Works with outside auditors to verify performance
	NSF-140 Sustainable Carpet Assessment	NSF International	Carpet	Bronze, Silver, Gold, Platinum	ID	Standard, requiring third-party certification	California Gold Sustainable Carpet Standard has merged with NSF-140 Platinum
	Sustainable Furniture Standard	Business and Institutional Furniture Manufacturer's Association (BIFMA)	Furniture	Silver, Gold, Platinum	N	Standard, to which first, second or third-party certification is possible	Draft standard being developed, no certification program available yet.
	Green Seal	Green Seal	Wide range	n/a	Y	Third-party certification	Uses various ASTM standards depending on product type
	EcoLogo / Environmental Choice	TerraChoice Environmental Marketing	Wide range of products	n/a	Y	Third-party certification	Backed by the Canadian government

Product Certification Summary Table courtesy of Environmental Building News *www.BuildingGreen.com*, reprinted with permission from the article *Behind the Logos: Understanding Green Product Certifications.*

tem or list. These certifications are invaluable for project design and specification—it makes it possible to write performance metrics into a specification, so that the owner can be assured of certain criteria, without having to write a proprietary or sole-source specification.

What Is Different about Laboratory Materials?

For many of the materials in a laboratory, there are no differences between conventional building materials, but for certain finish materials within the research spaces themselves, there are a number of other factors that must be considered. For most lab spaces, the first criterion is chemical resistance—depending on the type of research being done, there may be specific chemical resistivity required. For some labs, the chemical resistance is not based on the research, but based on the maintenance/cleaning procedure. For biological labs, there may be harsh antibacterial cleaning regimens that are most critical to the durability of the materials. Knowing at the outset whether a lab will be cleaned using a wipe-down procedure, as opposed to a scrub-down or hose-down procedure, has a big impact on the detailing and possible finish materials for that lab. For labs where a specific level of particulate classification is needed, there are other factors in the design to allow for cleanability and low particulate accumulation. For labs where radioactive media are used, there are different requirements for finishes where these media might come in contact with bench tops, casework, walls, and flooring. For each of these different types of criteria, there are materials that are effective, and they are not necessarily the same materials for each type. Key to effective design and specification is a clear understanding of what might happen in each lab, so it can be detailed accordingly. Since sustainable

For a facility where scrub-down cleaning is required, finishes must be higher-performing and more chemical-resistant, such as this research facility for MEDRAD in Saxonburg, Pennsylvania. *Image courtesy of KlingStubbins. Photography by MEDRAD.*

For this academic laboratory for the University of California at Berkeley's Stanley Hall, the finishes are primarily the same as typical commercial office finishes. *Courtesy of ZGF Architects LLP. Photography by Robert Canfield.*

materials are a subset of general lab materials, it is often the case that the more sustainable choice will be possible with a realistic "rightsized" determination of what will happen in that lab. For example, standard acoustical ceiling tiles are often made with significant recycled content, and can easily be recycled. If a lab is not going to be wiped down or scrubbed down, it is not necessary to provide vinyl-faced ACT, which is usually made up of less recycled content and is less easy to recycle at the end of its useful life. It is the right material if wipe-down is a projected part of the research regimen. It is a critical part of the planning and programming process to clearly denote, space by space, what the material finish criteria are, and then select materials accordingly.

Casework

Casework is a significant part of the overall lab environment, and changes to lab casework to make them more environmentally friendly play a big role in greening the lab environment. With the advent of LEED and other rating systems, most lab casework manufacturers have responded by calculating their own environmental statistics, and in many cases reformulating or changing the process to make them more sustainable in nature.

Casework manufacturers have worked to make their products more sustainable by addressing the materials themselves, the construction process, and even methods of shipping supplies and the finished products. Sustainable options now exist for plastic laminate, metal, and wood casework.

Work Surfaces

Similar to other lab material selections, casework bench tops can be made of several different materials, with different levels of durability, chemical resistiv-

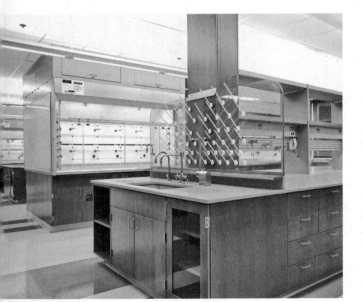

Wood Casework

Thermo Scientific Hamilton standard wood furniture contains hardwoods, veneers, and plywoods which originate from managed forests. Glues used contain no added urea formaldehyde. In addition, agrifiber cores and veneers made from rapidly renewable materials are offered as options. Sustainable initiatives practiced by the company in the production of wood casework include:

• Being certified by SmartWood/Rainforest Alliance as a Forestry Stewardship Council Chain of Custody manufacturer and adhering to the standards established by the FSC including rapid regeneration following a timber harvest and protection of soil and site productivity

• Developing a highly chemical-resistant waterborne wood finish with no HAPs and minimal VOCs and developing and using adhesives and glues with low VOCs

• Applying finish in custom spray booths to reduce airborne emissions and boost total finish transfer

• Maximizing natural resources with advanced robotic equipment that minimizes waste, and using wood waste to heat manufacturing facilities

• Expanding the product line to include wheatboard core and bamboo

Text credits: Text courtesy of Thermo Fisher Scientific.
Image Credits: Featured project: Merck Research Laboratories Boston. Courtesy of KlingStubbins. Photography © ChristopherBarnes.com.

Metal Casework

Through the utilization of state-of-the-art manufacturing equipment and robotics, Bedcolab, a manufacturer of laboratory casework, adaptable furniture systems, and fume hoods, is able to produce a high volume of metal casework in minimal time. The robotics equipment optimizes material usage by minimizing scrap, and it consumes less energy than the last generation of equipment. The metal casework is made from cold rolled steel that contains between 25 to 50 percent recycled content. As part of a recycling program, all generated steel scrap is returned to its point of origin. Bedcolab uses a powder coating system that allows the capture and reuse of overspray.

Text courtesy of Bedcolab

Featured project: University of Colorado Denver Research 2 in Aurora, Colorado. Courtesy of KlingStubbins. Photography © Ron Johnson Photography. For more information on this project see color images C-20 through C-28.

ity, and cleanability. For specialty laboratories where biological cleaning agents can damage conventional work surfaces, seamless stainless steel countertops are an (expensive) option. Traditional labs have used epoxy resin or phenolic resin tops for many years, and there are several manufacturers that are incorporating some preconsumer recycled content into their formulations. Plastic laminate countertops are also used in many lab environments where harsh chemicals are not being used. The other issue to keep in mind with work-surface selection is color. As discussed further in Chapter 7, the color of the bench top can have a significant impact on lighting levels and energy use—lighter-colored countertop materials will reflect the ambient light and will mean less energy is needed to achieve the same overall lighting levels.

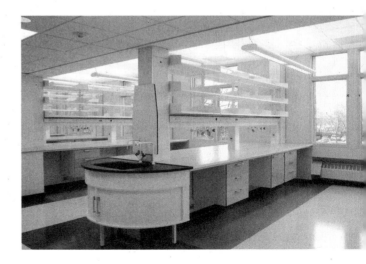

Plastic Laminate Casework

As featured in this image of Wyeth Building 87 in Pearl River, New York, a number of casework manufacturers offer laboratory casework fabricated from high-performing plastic laminate finishes over a millwork substrate of medium-density fiberboard or high-density fiberboard. The embodied energy of these products makes them a sustainable choice when the research activities and cleaning regimens do not require high chemical resistance from the laboratory casework surfaces. The substrates for these products can be specified with high preconsumer recycled content, and they can be made with Forest Stewardship Council (FSC) certified wood products for a significant percentage of the overall material.

Featured project: Wyeth Building 87 in Pearl River, New York.
Image courtesy of KlingStubbins.

Material Selection Metrics

There have been a number of performance metrics developed to evaluate different materials, and they follow one of a couple of methods. They are balancing the desire to have a calculable result for each material that can be compared with the practical nature of the task of calculating impacts consistently among a huge number of different materials. The rating systems, including LEED, have taken the approach that they should divide up the categorization into different characteristics—comparing materials by

recycled content separate from local materials, separate from materials that have been certified by a testing agency for VOC content or sustainable harvesting. By separating the characteristics, it is possible to easily get a result for each material—manufacturers can easily report on each of these characteristics, and project teams can collect this information. The theory is that you need to have a method that can be widespread in order for it to be adopted. The problem with this approach is that it leaves to the designer the hierarchy of which categories are more important, and it can lead to selections that are good on one charac-

						Primary Energy (MMBtu)	GWP (tons)	Weighted Resource Use (tons)	Air Pollution Index	H2O Pollution Index
			TOTAL IMPACTS BY BUILDING COMPONENT			TOTAL	TOTAL	TOTAL	TOTAL	TOTAL
			COLUMNS & BEAMS			11074	543	1540	71280	1457.99
			INTERMEDIATE FLOORS			17943	695	3391	303755	718.75
			EXTERIOR WALLS			143521	9565	20981	2073003	4170.14
			WINDOWS			160926	10125	22986	2531221	250.00
			INTERIOR WALLS			8736	471	1358	116820	720.83
			ROOF			16256	846	1243	199964	1102.34
			WHOLE BUILDING			358456	22246	51498	5296043	8420.05

ATHENA® EcoCalculator for assemblies

B. INTERMEDIATE FLOORS

ATHENA ASSEMBLY EVALUATION TOOL v2.3—Pittsburgh low-rise building

IN THE YELLOW CELLS BELOW, ENTER THE AMOUNT OF SQUARE FOOTAGE THAT EACH ASSEMBLY IS USED IN YOUR BUILDING

	Floor Structure *Assemblies in red forthcoming*	Interior Ceiling Finish	Square footage	Percentage of total	Primary Energy per SF (MMBtu)	GWP per SF (lbs)	Weighted Resource Use per SF (lbs)	Air Pollution Index per SF	H2O Pollution Index per SF
Average:					0.06	8.00	49.02	0.97	0.0052
1	CONCRETE FLAT PLATE AND SLAB COLUMN SYSTEM 25% flyash	gypsum board; latex paint	200000	67%	0.06	4.97	23.92	1.07	0.0024
2	CONCRETE FLAT PLATE AND SLAB COLUMN SYSTEM 25% flyash	none	100000	33%	0.05	3.95	19.98	0.89	0.0024
3	PRECAST DOUBLE T CONCRETE SYSTEM	gypsum board; latex paint	0		0.08	17.72	103.08	1.43	0.0006
4	PRECAST DOUBLE T CONCRETE SYSTEM	none	0		0.07	16.69	99.15	1.24	0.0006
5	CONCRETE HOLLOW CORE SLAB	none	0		0.06	14.15	91.38	1.29	0.0025
6	GLULAM JOIST AND PLANK DECKING	gypsum board; latex paint	0		0.07	6.23	61.48	0.75	0.0019
7	GLULAM JOIST AND PLANK DECKING	none	0		0.06	5.20	57.55	0.57	0.0019
8	WOOD CHORD AND STEEL WEB TRUSS SYSTEM	gypsum board; latex paint	0		0.06	6.46	30.64	0.91	0.0099
9	WOOD I-JOIST AND OSB DECKING SYSTEM	gypsum board; latex paint	0		0.05	3.72	26.34	1.40	0.0047
10	WOOD JOIST AND OSB DECKING SYSTEM	gypsum board; latex paint	0		0.04	2.18	30.79	0.33	0.0001
11	OPEN WEB STEEL JOIST W/ STEEL DECKING SYSTEM AND CONCRETE TOPPING	gypsum board; latex paint	0		0.09	12.65	70.15	1.01	0.0139
12	OPEN WEB STEEL JOIST W/ STEEL DECKING SYSTEM AND CONCRETE TOPPING	none	0		0.07	11.63	66.22	0.82	0.0139
13	STEEL STUD JOIST AND OSB FLOORING SYSTEM	none	0		0.06	9.24	27.70	0.77	0.0217
14	WOOD TRUSS AND OSB DECKING SYSTEM	gypsum board; latex paint	0		0.06	4.36	32.06	1.12	0.0024

WELCOME & HOW-TO | COLUMNS AND BEAMS | INTERMEDIATE FLOORS | EXTERIOR WALLS | WINDOWS | INTERIOR WALLS | ROOFS

EcoCalculator: By entering information about the quantities of different materials on a project, the design team can see conclusions about relative impacts of different material options *(www.athenasmi.org/tools/ecoCalculator/)*. ATHENA® *is a registered trademark of the Athena Sustainable Materials Institute.*

teristic but are lacking on others. There are a number of systems that have tried to put together overall life-cycle analyses of different materials, so that designers can assess overall impact through the life of the material. The challenge is that this is only useful if there is significant volume of different choices included in the material databases, so that specifiers can compare different options for their projects. This is especially challenging for laboratory buildings because, as noted, the materials often have some extra performance criteria to meet.

Athena Institute

The Athena Institute has developed a couple of tools for doing lifecycle analysis. The first is a free downloadable tool, the "EcoCalculator," where the project team enters in the different material selections across a broad grouping of material categories, and the calculator generates reporting on five different categories of impacts: Primary Energy Use, Global Warming Potential, Weighted Resource Use, Air Pollution Index, and Water Pollution Index. Each material in their database has a weighting according to how its manufacture, use, and disposal impacts these five categories. This tool is useful for comparative studies of different options. The challenge is that there are options that are not included in the database, and it is difficult to know with some selections how to number the closest fit material to the ones being selected. This organization also has a tool called the Impact Estimator where they will take materials and do an assessment on a consultancy basis for what the overall environmental impact of that material would be.

There are several other tools that are similar to this tool. BEES (Building for Environmental and Economic Sustainability, developed by the National Institute of Standards and Technology (NIST), uses a different calculation methodology but comes up with a similar set of comparative tools for evaluating materials options. A new database being developed by the Healthy Building Network is called "Pharos," and is distinguished by a graphic reporting format that organizes the material's characteristics in a highly legible polar coordinates scorecard. Called a "lens," it is quickly notable how competing products compare.

Cradle to Cradle

In early 2002, William McDonough and Michael Braungart published a book called *Cradle to Cradle*,

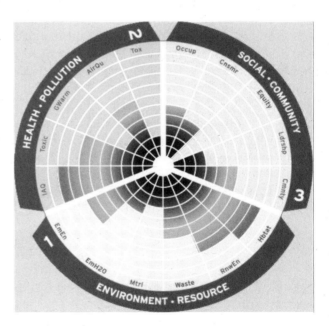

PharosLens: Using a graphic format that is easy to read and compare, materials can be compared for a project. As with any database, its success will be dependent on how many materials can be incorporated into the system, to allow teams to weigh options during design (*www.pharoslens.net*). *Used by permission. Healthy Building Network, © 2006–2009.*

which posed a challenge to conventional material evaluation. It compiled a set of concepts that Braungart, a chemist, and McDonough, an architect, had been working on for over a decade. Rather than looking at a lifecycle analysis, or "cradle to grave" analysis, the authors asked why we are not looking at materials that can be recycled into new materials indefinitely. Using natural systems as an inspiration, they pointed out that traditional recycling was really down-cycling—each successive reuse was delaying but not avoiding the end-of-life waste disposal issues. They developed a methodology and a description of a closed cycle: materials that could be broken down and reused as feedstock for materials or plants to be "food either for nature's ecosystems or for humans' industrial systems—perpetually circulating in closed systems that create value and are inherently healthy and safe."[2] To follow up these concepts, Braungart and McDonough formed a company called MBDC (McDonough Braungart Design Chemistry) and developed a methodology in 2005 to allow manufacturers to certify their own materials. It is a system that evaluates the materials and the manufacturing process against these principles, which were distilled into three main concepts:

- *Waste equals food:* Make products that can be continuously recycled

- *Use current solar income:* Use renewable energy sources for manufacturing

- *Respect diversity:* Evaluate the impact of manufacturing on natural systems[3]

The system grants three levels of certification: Silver, Gold, and Platinum. Silver and Gold certification are focused on identifying the components of the material and having a clear implementation plan to change the product for the better; Platinum rating is reserved for products that achieve the changes. At this writing, there are no Platinum-rated products, and time will tell if this system will evolve into the comprehensive system that meets the inspirational goals of its authors.

Living Building Challenge

As an add-on to the LEED rating system, the Cascadia chapter of the U.S. Green Building Council developed a system called the "Living Building Challenge" which has another approach to materials. The premise of the challenge is to push project teams beyond LEED certification to a higher level of

Prerequisite Five – Materials Red List

The project cannot contain any of the following Red List materials or chemicals.

- Cadmium
- Chlorinated Polyethylene and Chlorosulfonated Polyethlene
- Chlorofluorocarbons (CFCs)
- Chloroprene (Neoprene)
- Formaldehyde (added)
- Halogenated Flame Retardants
- Hydrochlorofluorocarbons (HCFCs)
- Lead
- Mercury
- Petrochemical Fertilizers and Pesticides
- Phthalates
- Polyvinyl Chloride (PVC)
- Wood treatments containing Creosote, Arsenic or Pentachlorophenol

The Living Building Challenge includes a Red List—a list of materials that cannot be in any of the materials in the project. Many design firms are employing this methodology, even on projects that are not enrolled in the Living Building Challenge. *Image courtesy of the International Living Buildings Institute (www.ilbi.org). © 2006, 2008 Cascadia Region Green Building Council.*

Prerequisite Eight – Appropriate Materials/Services Radius

Source locations for Materials and Services must adhere to the following restrictions :

Weight/Distance List

ZONE	MATERIAL OR SERVICE	MAXIMUM DISTANCE
7	Ideas	12,429.91 miles
6	Renewable Energy Technologies	9000 miles
5	Assemblies that actively contribute to building performance once installed	3000 miles
4	Consultant Travel	1500 miles
3	Light, low density materials	1000 miles
2	Medium Weight and density materials	500 miles
1	Heavy, high density materials	250 miles

Materials radius determined by shipping weight.

The Living Building Challenge includes a graduated set of limits for material transportation, as shown in this list. It is relatively easy for project teams to develop a map illustrating these distances relative to the project site. *Table courtesy of International Living Buildings Institute www.ilbi.org. Google Earth image superimposed with graphics by the author.*

sustainability—there is a set of 16 prerequisites, no optional points. Though achieving all 16 prerequisites is a difficult task, it is still interesting to consider how the materials prerequisites are organized. Two of the materials strategies in specific are particularly interesting. The first, (Prerequisite Five) is a "Red List," a list of components that cannot be in any of the materials in the project. These have been selected because of concerns about their health impacts or toxicity. The second (Prerequisite Eight) asks for teams to put together a materials plan categorizing materials by type and distance: Heavier materials must come from closer to the project site, lighter materials and materials that contribute to performance can come from farther away. Unlike LEED, this requirement is for all materials, not for a percentage of the materials. Being able to comply with these requirements is challenging—it is likely to be

applicable to a select few projects at this point—but it still offers a compelling way to organize and plan material selections.[4]

BRE Green Guide to Specifications

The Buildings Research Establishment, the organization that developed the BREEAM rating system, publishes a directory (both as an annual book and as an online database) called the "Green Guide to Specifications," which organizes materials by category and ranks them according to environmental and carbon impact over the lifespan of the material, using a proprietary LCA methodology called "the BRE Environmental Profiles Methodology." Although focused on materials in the United Kingdom, it is still interesting as comparative descriptions of basic building materials. It does not focus on lab materials, but has chap-

breglobal   THE GREEN GUIDE TO SPECIFICATION

< Back to BRE
Home
Introduction to The Green Guide
Sponsors
Publications, Reports and Tools
How the Green Guide was compiled
How to use the Green Guide to Specification
Register
Login
Green Guide 2008 Ratings
Search by element number
FAQs - The Green Guide
Presentations from Events
Scheme Documents

Green Guide 2008 ratings

Building type > Health
Category > Floor Finishes
Element type > Soft Floor Finishes

	Element number	Summary rating
Heterogeneous polyvinyl chloride floor coverings (EN 649). FCSS 33, 34.	821570039	A+
Homogeneous and heterogeneous profiled surfaced rubber floor coverings (EN 12199). FCSS 34.	821570057	A+
Homogeneous and heterogeneous smooth surfaced rubber floor coverings (EN 1817). FCSS 34.	821570056	A+
Homogeneous polyvinyl chloride floor coverings (EN 649). FCSS 33, 34.	821570038	A+
Plain and decorative linoleum (EN 548). FCSS 34/43.	821570058	A+
Polyvinyl chloride floor coverings with enhanced slip resistance (Safety Flooring) (EN 13845). FCSS 34.	821570055	A+
Polyvinyl chloride floor coverings with foam layer (EN 651). FCSS 34.	821570053	A+
Printed Laminate polyvinyl chloride floor coverings (EN 649). FCSS 34.	821570054	A+
Semi Flexible Polyvinyl chloride tiles (VCT) (EN 654). FCSS 34.	821570092	A+
Synthetic Thermoplastic (EN 14565). FCSS 33, 34.	821570060	A+

© Copyright BRE 2008 | Terms, Conditions and Privacy policy

The BRE Green Guide to Specifications categorizes different building materials according to their environmental impact over the lifespan of the products. Currently, these products are UK-focused—the impact is based on transportation to UK project sites, but broader categorization will be possible in the future. Reproduced by permission of the BRE Group. For further information on the Green Guide, go to *www.thegreenguide.org.uk*.

ters on exterior enclosure materials, interior wall construction, windows, insulation, and floor finishes. Each material is graded from A+ (best) through E (worst) according to a number of different categories. The material has a summary grade, and then has subcategories graded as well, so that project teams can determine its own hierarchies if some of the categories are more important to that project's specific region or culture.

ASHRAE 189

As noted in the introduction, ASHRAE/IESNA/USGBC standard 189.1P is a performance stan-

dard for green building that was initially issued in 2010. The idea behind this standard is that by creating a consensus-based standard using conventional methodologies and language, building codes could more effectively start to require sustainable building techniques. It has been difficult to codify requirements in LEED or other single-source type standards, but by going through the methodology of ASHRAE standards development, the same performance values could be codified and referenced in local and national building codes. The goals are typically in line with base LEED certification. Rick Fedrizzi from the USGBC has stated that if it is adopted, LEED may phase out the base LEED certification [building green article]. Standard 189 has several ways that it handles materials. The first is prescriptive—requiring thresholds be met for several different characteristics from LEED, with a few added strategies:

• Construction Waste Management—50 percent diversion

• Recycled Content—10 percent

• Certified Wood—60 percent

• Regional Materials—15 percent

The system has an exception that allows for materials shipped by water or rail to have a larger possible radius, to recognize the efficiency of shipping by these methods (as opposed to truck transport)

• In addition, the system has a requirement of 5 percent "bio-based" products.

As with other performance standards, there is also an option for a lifecycle analysis showing 5 percent improvement over baseline alternatives for two different impact categories. The categories listed are: land use (or habitat alteration), resource use, climate change, ozone layer depletion, human health effects, eco-toxicity, smog, acidification, and eutrophication.[5]

Material Classification

Listed below is a matrix of different materials, organized by material type. These are focused on finish materials used in laboratories, with different factors associated with each one. Also included are some technical comments about each one to assist in product review.

Flooring

Traditionally, laboratory flooring has been developed to minimize or eliminate seams—trowelled on or broadcast epoxy flooring was traditional, as was heat-welded seams at sheet vinyl. There are a number of new formulations that meet the requirements of minimal seaming while reducing the environmental impact of the materials. For many labs, depending on the criteria, sheet goods can be replaced with rubber, vinyl, or linoleum tile which is much more affordable and can be replaced, tile by tile, if necessary.

Wall Finishes

Depending on the work that is going on in the labs, the wall finishes can range from a reinforced fiberglass wall system that is installed on the walls to conventional latex wall paint. There are a range of different options available that address both chemical resistivity as well as environmental factors.

FRP and PVC Panels

For some applications, an adhered panel is installed to protect the facility walls from strong chemicals and cleaning regimens.

Reinforced Epoxy Wall Coatings

A number of manufacturers make a system where a fiberglass reinforcing mesh is mixed in with a roll-on or trowel-on system. This provides a strong barrier, but can be difficult to repair or replace.

High-Performance Coatings

The next step down in enhanced coatings are high-performance coatings and epoxy systems. These are applied similar to conventional paint systems but they can stand up to increased abuse and harsh cleaning treatments. Care must be taken in selecting systems that are compatible with the substrates, and that comply with the requirements of the project.

Wall Paint

For many projects conventional paint performs well. If the regimen includes repainting as opposed to

For St. Lawrence University's Johnson Hall of Science in Canton, New York, the laboratory flooring is polished concrete. Using a low-VOC sealer over a polished structural concrete slab saves on materials and is seamless by definition. *Courtesy of Croxton Collaborative / KlingStubbins. Photography © Woodruff/Brown Architectural Photography.*

Flooring Materials

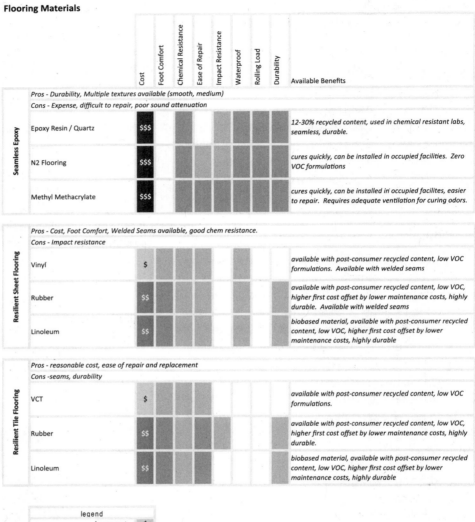

Flooring material matrix. *Courtesy of KlingStubbins.*

Wall Finish Materials

		Cost	Chemical Resistance	Ease of Repair	Impact Resistance	Waterproof	Scrubdown	Durability	Available Benefits
FRP and PVC Panels	*Pros - Durability, Multiple textures available (smooth, medium)*								
	Cons - Expense, difficult to repair, poor sound attenuation								
	Standard FRP	$$$							Baseline panel product, no green attributes
	Phenolic Panels	$$$							Low VOC formulations biobased substrate, durable
	PVC-free panels	$$$							Low VOC formulations, durable
Specialty Coatings	*Pros - Durability, cleanability*								
	Cons - cost								
	Fiberglass reinforced epoxy	$$$							available with low or zero VOC content. Seamless system, ties in with epoxy flooring systems with integral coved base
	N2 wall coating	$$$							zero VOC formulation. Quick cure process means that it can be installed in occupied facilities. Integrates with N2 flooring system
	Roll-on Epoxy	$$$							low VOC formulations available. Less durability than reinforced system, a step up from epoxy paint.
High Performance Coatings (Epoxy)	*Pros - durable, higher peformance than baseline latex*								
	Cons - maintenance and touch up are more complicated than baseline latex								
	Waterborne Epoxy	$$							low VOC formulations possible. Coordinate topcoats with compatible primer for each substrate.
	Metal Primers	$$							low VOC formulations possible
Latex Paints	*Pros - Cost, ease of maintenance and touch up*								
	Cons -durability, life, cleanability								
	Flat Paints	$							low and zero VOC formulations available. Ideal for ceilings
	Eggshell Paints	$							low and zero VOC formulations available. Eggshell finish means light scrub down is possible
	Semigloss	$							low and zero VOC formulations available. Semigloss finish allows for more cleanability.

legend
lower cost — $
median cost — $$
higher cost — $$$

neutral performance
good performance
better performance

Wall finish material matrix. *Image courtesy of KlingStubbins.*

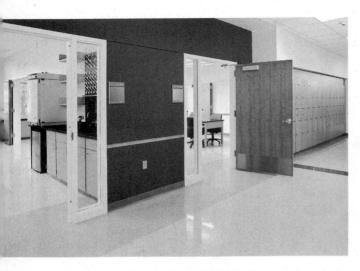

At the University of Colorado Denver's Research 1 in Aurora, Colorado, the maintenance protocols did not require industrial strength coatings and chemical cleaners. Conventional low-VOC latex paints were used and have been successful. *Courtesy of KlingStubbins. Photography © Ron Johnson Photography.*

labs do not have a process for wipe-down or scrub-down of ceilings, so standard acoustical ceiling tiles perform well, are more affordable, have more recycled content, and are easier to recycle. Both fiberglass and mineral fiber make good ceiling materials, often the difference is the acoustical performance of the different materials.

Conclusions

The ongoing challenge with material selection for laboratories is to balance the appropriate level of resistance to lab environmental impact with an assessment of what it takes to fabricate, transport, install, and eventually remove the product. This type of assessment is still very difficult because of the amount of time needed to investigate the different impacts a material

scrubbing down, conventional low-VOC latex paint should meet all the project's requirements.

Casework

As noted above, for laboratory casework, there are two main considerations—type of casework and the materials they're made of. The types to consider are movable, adjustable, and fixed casework, and most manufacturers have product lines in each of these types, allowing the project team to determine how much flexibility is needed for the project. For materials, most casework is made of metal, wood, or laminate.

Ceilings

Traditionally vinyl-wrapped and mylar-faced tiles have been used in laboratories, but as noted above, most

At Janssen Pharmaceutica's Drug Safety Evaluation Center in Beerse, Belgium, a fixed casework system was used. Undercounter cabinets are modular and can be changed out when necessary. Countertop materials are set based on the type of work to be done at the bench top. *Image courtesy of KlingStubbins.*

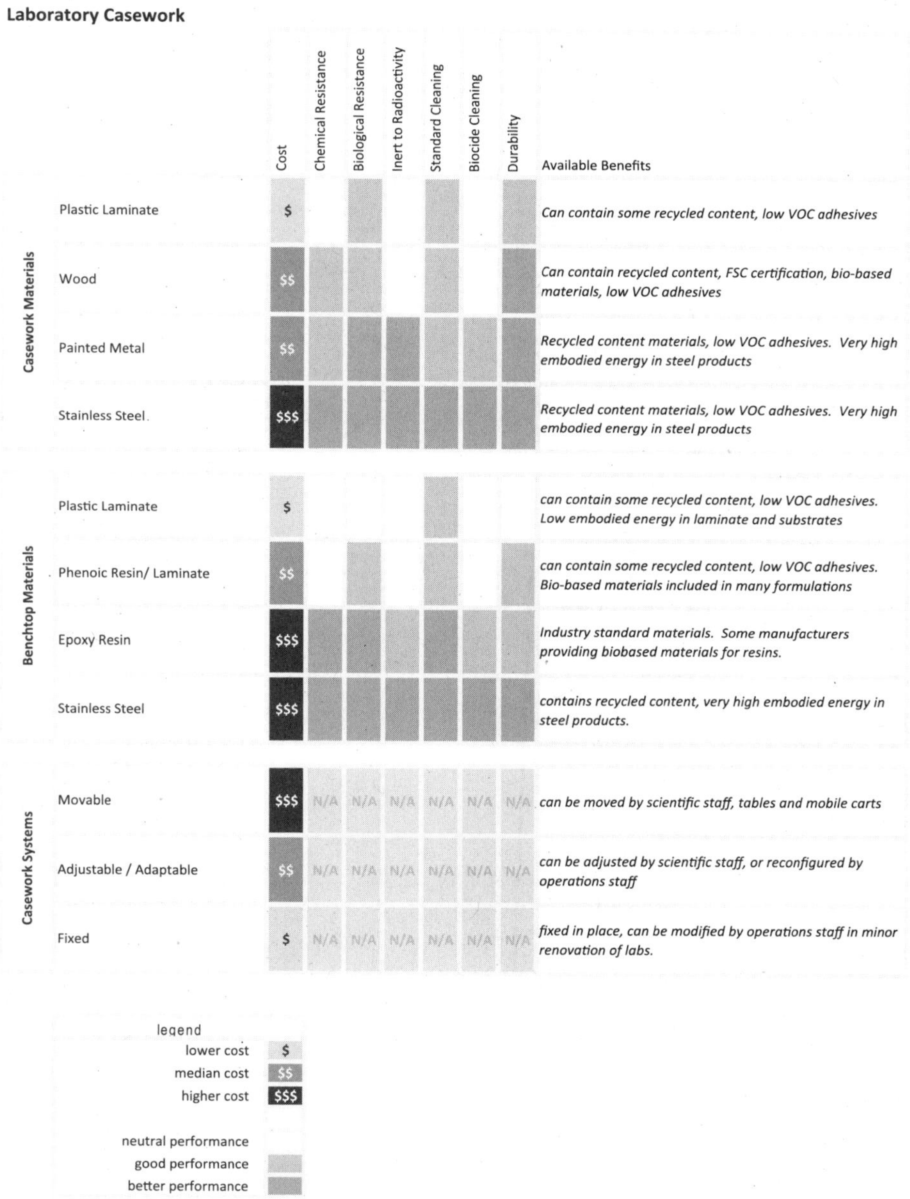

Laboratory Casework

		Cost	Chemical Resistance	Biological Resistance	Inert to Radioactivity	Standard Cleaning	Biocide Cleaning	Durability	Available Benefits
Casework Materials	Plastic Laminate	$							Can contain some recycled content, low VOC adhesives
	Wood	$$							Can contain recycled content, FSC certification, bio-based materials, low VOC adhesives
	Painted Metal	$$							Recycled content materials, low VOC adhesives. Very high embodied energy in steel products
	Stainless Steel	$$$							Recycled content materials, low VOC adhesives. Very high embodied energy in steel products
Benchtop Materials	Plastic Laminate	$							can contain some recycled content, low VOC adhesives. Low embodied energy in laminate and substrates
	Phenoic Resin/ Laminate	$$							can contain some recycled content, low VOC adhesives. Bio-based materials included in many formulations
	Epoxy Resin	$$$							Industry standard materials. Some manufacturers providing biobased materials for resins.
	Stainless Steel	$$$							contains recycled content, very high embodied energy in steel products.
Casework Systems	Movable	$$$	N/A	N/A	N/A	N/A	N/A	N/A	can be moved by scientific staff, tables and mobile carts
	Adjustable / Adaptable	$$	N/A	N/A	N/A	N/A	N/A	N/A	can be adjusted by scientific staff, or reconfigured by operations staff
	Fixed	$	N/A	N/A	N/A	N/A	N/A	N/A	fixed in place, can be modified by operations staff in minor renovation of labs.

legend
lower cost	$
median cost	$$
higher cost	$$$

neutral performance
good performance
better performance

Casework matrix. *Image courtesy of KlingStubbins.*

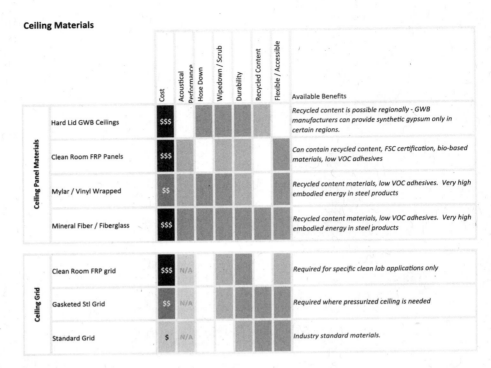

Ceiling Materials

		Cost	Acoustical Performance	Hose Down	Wipedown / Scrub	Durability	Recycled Content	Flexible / Accessible	Available Benefits
Ceiling Panel Materials	Hard Lid GWB Ceilings	$$$							*Recycled content is possible regionally - GWB manufacturers can provide synthetic gypsum only in certain regions.*
	Clean Room FRP Panels	$$$							*Can contain recycled content, FSC certification, bio-based materials, low VOC adhesives*
	Mylar / Vinyl Wrapped	$$							*Recycled content materials, low VOC adhesives. Very high embodied energy in steel products*
	Mineral Fiber / Fiberglass	$$$							*Recycled content materials, low VOC adhesives. Very high embodied energy in steel products*
Ceiling Grid	Clean Room FRP grid	$$$	N/A						*Required for specific clean lab applications only*
	Gasketed Stl Grid	$$	N/A						*Required where pressurized ceiling is needed*
	Standard Grid	$	N/A						*Industry standard materials.*

legend

lower cost	$
median cost	$$
higher cost	$$$
neutral performance	
good performance	
better performance	

Ceiling matrix. *Image courtesy of KlingStubbins.*

has over its useful life. At present there are a number of different databases and metrics to assist the design teams in material selection, but no one method is clearly best for all selection criteria. Most project teams now employ a set of guidelines for materials, with different ways of calculating different aspects of the material's environmental footprint. This subcategorization is imprecise, because materials that effectively minimize impact in one category will often have a larger impact in others. Over time, several of the methods mentioned in this chapter should develop further and become more broadly applicable to the selection process. It seems likely that it will include some sort of grading process equating the materials used to the lifecycle energy, so these results can be included in overall energy use calculations for the facility.

Key Concepts

- There are many different ways of classifying environmentally preferable materials:

  - Reuse/Refurbished/Down-cycled materials—reduce need for new materials.

Depending on what is being done in the space, some lab buildings are designed with no ceilings at all, as shown in Boston University Medical Center BioSquare II project in Boston, Massachusetts. This reduces the overall amount of materials going in to the building, and allows for more flexibility in postoccupancy modifications. *Courtesy of © Trustees of Boston University and KlingStubbins. Photography © Robert Benson Photography.*

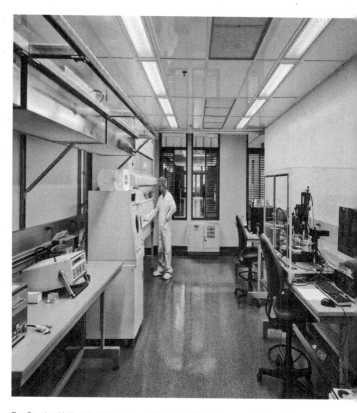

For Stanley Hall at the University of California, Berkeley, a sealed and cleanable ceiling system was used for specific research spaces. *Courtesy of ZGF Architects LLP. Photography by Robert Canfield.*

- Materials with recycled content or that can be recycled.

- Materials harvested responsibly to allow for future harvesting.

- Local materials—harvested and manufactured to minimize transportation to the building site.

- Low-VOC/Low-toxicity materials.

- There are a number of different organizations that provide databases and certification of material properties, to help design teams compare different options.

- Material selection for laboratories includes added criteria for chemical resistivity, research requirements, cleaning and disinfection regimens.

- Metrics for evaluating materials selections include databases, lifecycle analysis tools, and calculation tools for environmental impacts.

- A number of systems have been developed that evaluate material selection more broadly than LEED. These systems can help project teams develop material palette priorities.

REFERENCES

1. Technical papers of the Gypsum Association, www.gypsum.org/topical.html#synthetic.
2. Cradle to Cradle Design, referenced in www .c2ccertified.com/.
3. "Cradle to Cradle Certification: A Peek Inside MBDC's Black Box," Environmental Building News, 16:2, February 2007.
4. More information about the Living Building Challenge can be found at www.ilbi.org.
5. ASHRAE Standard 189.1, "Standard for the Design of High-Performance, Green Buildings Except Low-Rise Residential Buildings," Section 9.5, http://spc189.ashraepcs.org/, accessed 9/2009.

chapter 9

Renovation and Leasing
Alternative Approaches to New Construction

Courtesy of New England Confectionery Company (NECCO).

Introduction

For most research companies and institutions, a new research facility will involve ground-up construction. New ground-up construction comes with a significant environmental footprint including consumption of energy and raw materials, air/water/noise pollution, and generation of waste materials. To minimize this footprint, alternate building delivery strategies should be considered including:

- Converting existing buildings to laboratory use

- Leasing laboratory space in multitenant buildings

- Renovating previously occupied laboratory space

Each of these alternate laboratory building delivery strategies offers unique advantages and challenges, the evaluation both of which will vary depending on the specific circumstances of each project. Nonetheless, each deserves careful analysis in targeting the

This chapter focuses on several of the sustainability categories discussed in Chapter 1. See page 18 for more information.

minimal environmental footprint of a new laboratory project.

Converting Existing Buildings to Laboratory Use

Transformed from producing NECCO Wafers, Sky Bars, and Sweetheart Conversation Hearts, to life-saving medicine, the landmark NECCO candy factory in Cambridge, Massachusetts, was converted to research laboratories for the Novartis Institutes for Biomedical Research Global Research Headquarters (see color images C-56 through C-59). From tracking bar codes to tracking DNA codes, a Federal Express Processing Center in suburban Maryland was adapted to Bioinformatics Research Facilities for GeneLogic. Bringing new life to an historic campus building, the University of Delaware upgraded the Brown Laboratory Building to a chemistry research and teaching facility. A former Ford automobile assembly plant in Cambridge, Massachusetts, was converted to a speculative multitenant research laboratory building for an institutional developer.

These are just four examples of successful conversions of existing buildings to laboratory use. Why did these projects convert an existing building to laboratory use rather than build a new purpose-built building from the ground up?

The environmental, as well as economic, benefits of converting existing buildings to new uses including laboratory uses, range from avoiding the energy, material, and pollution impacts of building a new building; avoiding the energy, waste, pollution, and landfill contribution of demolishing a functioning existing building; and preserving historic cultural resources. In addition, renovating an existing building

may be easier to permit than new ground-up construction. As real estate cycles see demand shift from office to laboratory use, as is the current situation in many urban areas, building owners attempt to reposition their buildings for a different type of tenant. In dense urban locations, sites for new laboratory buildings are rare and often just not available, but the desired proximity to hospitals, universities, and a skilled workforce convince research companies and institutions to consider converting existing buildings. Lastly, grant programs and tax credits are often available for preserving and adapting historical buildings.

While many buildings can easily and economically adapt to laboratory use, others do not. This chapter explores some of the desirable characteristics to consider in evaluating the suitability of a building for conversion to laboratory use and the environmental considerations and benefits of such a conversion as compared to the construction of a new purpose-built building.

Benefits of Converting an Existing Building to Laboratory Use Compared to New Construction

Laboratory buildings are usually thought of as specifically designed purpose-built high-tech buildings. Like all new buildings, construction of a new laboratory building consumes great resources including raw materials and the energy and related pollution resulting from the extraction, refinement, manufacturing, transportation, and erection of new construction materials. Often, the construction of a new building on a desirable site requires the demolition of older and sometimes historically significant buildings reduced to waste materials and trucked to a landfill for disposal. Furthermore, a new building construction site is disruptive to neighbors, with noise and air pollution from construction activities and deliveries.

Converting an existing building to laboratory use can offer many advantages over constructing a new building. These advantages include reduced capital cost, faster schedule to occupancy, revitalizing an historically significant landmark, finding an opportunity to build laboratory space in a context such as a heavily developed urban center or university campus that cannot easily accommodate new construction, and a reduced impact on the local and global environment.

The design, permitting and approval, and construction of a new laboratory will require an investment of several years, while the demand for facilities is often immediate. Converting an existing building can offer a significant schedule advantage over new construction, delivering a new facility in months rather than years. Costs vary depending on the suitability of the existing building and the requirements of the laboratory program, but are often less than new construction.

Desirable locations for new laboratory facilities, such as densely developed urban centers adjacent to hospitals, or an historic university campus, often cannot easily accommodate new buildings. In these situations, adapting an existing building may be the only option for a new laboratory facility. These situations also offer the opportunity to add new life into an existing historic landmark, resulting in an interesting new space and capturing the identity of an historic icon.

For organizations with an interest in green buildings and environmental sustainability, reusing, or in essence recycling, an underutilized existing building is good for the local and global environment. The materials for a new building require the consumption of raw materials, energy to refine those materials into manufactured building products, and then their transportation to the building site. The environmental value of construction materials is often referred to as embodied energy. Adapting an existing building to a new use not only saves that building from a wasteful end as material dumped into a landfill, but also conserves the embodied energy contained in that reused construction material, resulting in less waste, less raw material and energy consumption, and less pollution. For building owners pursuing certification under the U.S. Green Building Council's LEED v3 Green Building Rating System, adaptive reuse of an existing building directly earns up to four of the required forty points, and indirectly contributes to earning several more through the LEED certification process.

Conserving Embodied Energy and Reducing Waste

The extraction, refinement, manufacturing, transport, and erection of construction materials consume energy and create pollution. This investment of energy, called embodied energy, or the energy "embodied" in building material in place is wasted when functional, useful building materials are demolished and sent to a landfill. Following is a good example.

A six-story, 250,000-square-foot former Ford automobile assembly factory in Cambridge, Massachusetts, is being evaluated for adaptive reuse as a modern core and shell laboratory by a developer. This will preserve a recognized cultural icon for another building lifetime, set a path for an easier permitting process, and save construction cost compared to building new. Consider the environmental impact this adaptive reuse will have:

- Approximately 13,221 cubic yards of concrete columns and floor slabs will be reused. Production of a cubic yard of concrete consumes, on average, 1.7 million BTUs of energy. Therefore, approximately

22 billion BTUs would have been consumed in the production of the equivalent floors and columns in new construction.

- Approximately 165,000 bricks will be reused. Production of one standard brick consumes, on average, 14,000 BTUs of energy. Therefore, approximately 2.3 billion BTUs would have been consumed in the production of the equivalent quantity of bricks in new construction.

- Approximately 371 cubic yards of concrete foundations will be reused. Production of a cubic yard of concrete consumes, on average, 1.7 million BTUs of energy. Therefore, approximately 630 million BTUs would have been consumed in the production of the equivalent new foundations.

- In total, the production of the equivalent new construction of floor slabs, columns, bricks, and foundations would have consumed approximately 25 billion BTUs of energy.

- In addition, on average, trucking one ton of new materials to the site or one ton of construction/demolition waste away from a construction site, on average, consumes approximately 594,000 BTUs. This existing building includes approximately 4,050 tons of brick. To demolish the building, haul these materials away, and transport an equivalent quantity of materials would have consumed an additional 4 billion BTUs of energy.

According to the energy model prepared of the renovation, the baseline annual energy use for this building is predicted to be 66 billion BTUs.

- The energy required to produce the equivalent new construction of floor slabs, columns, foundations, and brick walls (equal to the amount that will be reused) would equal approximately 45 percent

(30 million BTUs) of the baseline energy use of the building for one year.

- In addition, demolition of the existing building would have created 4,050 tons, or 15,000 cubic yards, of waste material, or a volume 75 feet by 75 feet by 75 feet deposited in a landfill. That would require 500 30-yard dumpsters to transport the demolition debris from the site to a landfill.

This analysis is admittedly imperfect, in that it approximates only some of the energy and waste required to build a new building. For example, it does not account for waste and energy during manufacturing or hauling the normal construction and demolition waste from the construction of a new building. It does illustrate, however, how much energy is embodied in construction materials, the environmental benefit of conserving existing materials in place, and the environmental cost of new materials.

Adaptive Reuse and LEED

LEED certification applies not only to new ground-up construction but also to existing buildings. Depending on the specific circumstances, one of the LEED v3 Green Building Rating Systems is appropriate for use in measuring the sustainable design success of the project.

Both LEED for New Construction (LEED-NC) and LEED for Core & Shell Development (LEED-CS) recognize the environmental benefits of reusing existing buildings as an alternate to building new. Specific point examples include:

- Up to four points (MRc1.1 and 1.2) are awarded for increasing percentages of Building Reuse. These points recognize the environmental benefits of reusing existing buildings as an alternate to building new.

- One point (SSc1) is awarded for many previously developed building sites.

- One point (SSc3) is awarded for soils cleanup of many previously developed sites.

- Up to 19 points (EAc1) are awarded for energy efficiency. There is a lower percentage threshold to earn these points for an existing building renovation.

Adaptive reuse of an existing building offers a great advantage to a project team pursuing LEED certification. On the other hand, adaptive reuse of an existing building presents certain challenges for certain LEED credits. For example, the existing geometry building envelope may not readily accommodate good daylighting design.

There are multiple versions of the LEED v3 Green Building Rating System that could be applied to renovations of existing buildings to laboratory use. The LEED for Existing Buildings Operations and Maintenance (LEED-EBOM) rating system is most appropriate for ongoing building upgrades of renovations while a majority of the building occupants remain in the building during the renovation. The LEED for New Construction rating system is most appropriate for complete renovations and additions. LEED for Core & Shell Construction is most appropriate for building shell upgrades where tenants can independently complete interior fit-out construction under the LEED for Commercial Interiors (LEED-CI) ratings systems. All systems share the same goal of encouraging sustainable construction, which starts with maximizing the potential to reuse current resources before using new material and energy resources.

Characteristics of a Suitable Existing Building for Conversion to Laboratory Use

Buildings suitable for conversion to laboratory use should ideally have:

- A column bay spacing compatible with laboratory module planning (typically, a 10- to 12-foot module)

- A floor-to-floor height tall enough to accommodate the distribution of building systems above the ceiling (typically, at least 12 foot-0 inches clear)

- A floor plate size that can accommodate laboratory modules and shared support spaces (typically at least 20,000 square feet)

- Adequate structural capacity (typically, 100 to 150 pounds per square foot) and vibration characteristics

- Building systems that can support laboratory demand

- A building exterior envelope suitable to the specific demands of laboratory use

A typical module of laboratory case work, with two parallel rows of 3-foot-deep benches and a 4- to 5-foot-wide aisle is between 10 and 11 feet wide. Ideally, the column bay spacing of a laboratory building will be a multiple of this planning module. Therefore, a 20- to 22-foot-wide structural bay is ideal. Wider bays can work, but less efficiently, as the extra width results in wider aisles. Laboratory modules can be planned independently of the column grid, but this approach often results in columns that compromise ideal laboratory planning.

Laboratory spaces require higher floor-to-floor heights as compared to other building uses. A 9-foot-tall ceiling, 3 feet or more of horizontal mechanical, plumbing, and electrical service distribution, and 2 feet of beams and other structures are not uncommon. For most conventional laboratory types, a 14-foot floor-to-floor height is adequate, and greater floor-to-floor heights offer taller ceilings, more flexibility in design and future modifications, and increased energy efficiency. Laboratory space can fit into lower floor-to-floor heights with certain compromises, including more local vertical shafts or lower ceilings. In addition to these practical concerns, laboratory buildings tend to have deep floor plates, with interior spaces far removed from windows. Taller ceiling heights allow natural daylight to penetrate more deeply into the building and accommodate more energy-efficient and comfortable indirect lighting.

Laboratory spaces typically require a structural floor loading capacity of 100 to 150 pounds per square foot and certain large pieces of equipment may require even heavier loading. In addition, the seismic requirements of most building codes have become more restrictive, so significant building renovations often require additional lateral bracing to meet current building code requirements for resistance to wind and earthquake forces. Other structural concerns to consider in converting a building to laboratory use include the added weight of new roof-top mechanical equipment and the insertion of floor openings for new service shafts.

In addition to enhanced floor loading, laboratory buildings may also require certain vibration characteristics, for microscopy or other vibration-sensitive equipment. Modifying the vibration characteristics of an existing building can be challenging. It is often more practical to locate vibration-sensitive programs in the areas of the structure that are less prone to vibration. For example, a ground floor or basement floor on grade or floor area adjacent to columns

and lateral bracing are less likely to exhibit problematic vibration. In addition, localized structural reinforcement, dampening, or even specialized isolation tables can reduce vibration in a specific area.

Laboratory functions require larger and more sophisticated building systems than other uses. Unlike office buildings, where a majority of the interior air is conditioned and recirculated with a small percentage of fresh air intake and used air exhaust, most laboratory buildings require 100 percent of the inside air to be exhausted at a rate appropriate to the laboratory use. As a result, cooling and heating demands and air distribution ducts in laboratory buildings are all larger and more sophisticated than in other building types. Additionally, certain chemical and biological uses may require dedicated exhaust ducts.

In addition to domestic plumbing demands, including bathrooms and kitchen areas, laboratory buildings require specialized plumbing systems such as laboratory gases, high-purity water distribution, and acid neutralization. While these plumbing systems are relatively easy to distribute through a building, all require equipment and storage space. Finally, specialized laboratory functions can impose additional building system demands, such as a dedicated and secure loading area and service elevators. Electrical demands for a laboratory program include not only increased watts per square foot but also standby power to protect experiments and equipment in the event of a power failure.

Many of the requirements and concerns with the laboratory building exterior envelope are similar to any other building types. Older windows and other exterior envelope materials must be evaluated for their age, condition, and thermal and moisture performance. Window replacement is often recommended, either to increase energy performance or to allow more daylight into laboratory spaces.

Evaluation of an Existing Building for Conversion to Laboratory Use

A feasibility study can quickly identify major considerations for converting a specific existing building for laboratory use. The team for this study should include:

- An owner representative who can describe the priorities and intended uses for the new facility

- An architect and lab planner to develop and evaluate planning options

- Engineers to evaluate the building structure and systems

- A contractor to evaluate construction logistics

- A cost estimator to identify the cost of each option relative to benchmark data for similar renovated and new facilities

Particular challenges to consider:

- What historical as-built documentation is available, and/or what investigation is required to confirm visible and concealed construction?

- What are the existing structural capacities and fire rated assemblies? Is it possible and/or feasible to upgrade?

- Is there structural capacity and will the local zoning code allow the addition of a new mechanical penthouse or new roof-top equipment?

- Are there environmental considerations? (i.e., soil contamination, lead paint, asbestos, etc.)

- What existing construction can be saved and reused, what must be replaced?

- What are the cultural and historical preservation concerns?

Case Study Examples

The following are case studies to illustrate some of the points discussed related to adapting buildings to laboratory use.

Novartis Institutes for Biomedical Research, Global Research Headquarters, Cambridge, Massachusetts

The Novartis Institutes for Biomedical Research (NIBRI) in Cambridge, Massachusetts, recently converted the landmark 500,000-square-foot former NECCO candy factory to research

Historical photograph of the exterior of the landmark 500,000-square-foot NECCO candy factory in Cambridge, Massachusetts, prior to conversion to research laboratories for the Novartis Institutes for Biomedical Research. *Image courtesy of New England Confectionery Company.*

Historical photograph of an interior space in the landmark 500,000-square-foot NECCO candy factory prior to conversion to research laboratories for the Novartis Institutes for Biomedical Research. Note the mushroom-shaped column capitols and exterior windows retained and featured as part of the renovation. *Image courtesy of New England Confectionery Company.*

View of the new six-story central atrium added as part of the renovation of the former 500,000-square-foot NECCO candy factory to research laboratories for the Novartis Institutes for Biomedical Research Global Research Headquarters. *Courtesy of KlingStubbins. Photography © Jeff Goldberg/Esto. All rights reserved.*

laboratories. NIBRI was looking for an opportunity to develop a large facility in the densely developed Kendall Square area. The aggressive project schedule did not allow for the time necessary to design, permit, and construct a new building. By choosing to adapt this existing building, NIBRI not only met the aggressive project schedule, but also found a suitable location in a densely developed area with limited opportunities for new

development, and realized a design that was enhanced by the historic character of this landmark building.

The former candy factory was built with a robust concrete structural frame with tall floor-to-floor heights and a 20-foot column bay spacing that, while slightly narrower than ideal, could be adapted to a laboratory planning module by slightly reducing the casework depths. The building required extensive building systems upgrades, including a new mechanical penthouse, various service shafts, and elevators. In addition to large windows, which were replaced with historically accurate modern glazing, the character of the original structure enhanced the design of the new facility through exposed concrete slabs and columns at the new eight-story atrium and the conversion of the former power plant to a large and open cafeteria and conference space.

View of a typical laboratory space added as part of the renovation of the former 500,000-square-foot NECCO candy factory to research laboratories for the Novartis Institutes for Biomedical Research. *Courtesy of KlingStubbins. Photography © Jeff Goldberg/Esto. All rights reserved.*

Specific benefits realized by converting this existing building:

1. Embodied energy in existing construction materials was conserved.

2. Landfill disposal of demolition debris was avoided.
3. An historical and cultural resource was preserved.
4. Permitting was easier and the construction schedule was accelerated compared to new ground-up construction.
5. Tax credits offset construction costs.

University of Delaware, Brown Laboratory Renovation, Newark, Delaware

The Brown Laboratory at the University of Delaware was originally built in 1937, but changes in codes and standards over the past 60 years drove the need for a complete renovation. The 90,000-square-foot project includes new chemistry and biology labs and a complete update of the MEP systems, as well as a new NMR hall which was inserted in an existing courtyard area. The resulting project preserved the historic character of the building's exterior while creating new state-of-the-art labs for faculty and students.

Preconstruction view of the new NMR hall which was inserted in an existing courtyard area between existing building wings of Brown Laboratory. *Image courtesy of KlingStubbins.*

View of the 90,000-square-foot Brown Laboratory at the University of Delaware in Newark, Delaware, demonstrating the historic character of the 1937 building exterior. *Image courtesy of KlingStubbins.*

Postoccupancy view of the Brown Laboratory's new NMR hall which was inserted in an existing courtyard area between existing building wings. *Image courtesy of KlingStubbins.*

Specific sustainable design features realized by converting this existing building include:

1. Embodied energy in existing construction materials was conserved.
2. Landfill disposal of demolition debris was avoided.
3. An historical campus building was preserved.
4. A new building in the same location would have been detrimental to the historical campus context.
5. Permitting was easier and the construction schedule was accelerated compared to new ground-up construction.

GeneLogic, Bioinformatics Research Facility, Gaithersburg, Maryland

In converting a 60,000-square-foot former FedEx Processing Center to a new bioinformatics research laboratory, GeneLogic encountered its own challenges and opportunities. The large, open, one-story warehouse structure, with few columns and a

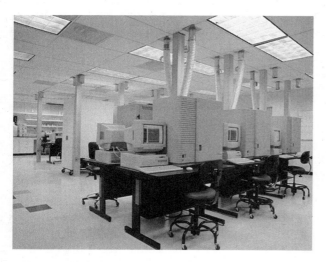

Typical laboratory fit-out at GeneLogic's Bioinformatics Research Facility in Gaithersburg, Maryland, demonstrating the flexibility available from the existing high-bay structure. *Image courtesy of KlingStubbins.*

Typical office fit-out at GeneLogic demonstrating the tall ceilings available from the existing high-bay structure. Note the interior windows visually connecting laboratory and office spaces. *Image courtesy of KlingStubbins.*

tall ceiling, allowed great flexibility in planning. The design team faced a challenge, however, in bringing daylight into such a deep space. In addition, the lightweight roof structure only allowed limited new roof-top equipment.

Large new windows that replaced loading dock doors combined with carefully configured circulation spaces, tall ceilings, and new skylights allowed natural daylight to penetrate deep into the building. New equipment was located on grade adjacent to the building. Most importantly, the large open plan allowed for greater flexibility and the ability to plan for ongoing future growth.

Specific benefits realized by converting this existing building:

1. Embodied energy in existing construction materials was conserved.
2. Landfill disposal of demolition debris was avoided.
3. The construction schedule was accelerated compared to new ground-up construction.

640 Memorial Drive, Multitenant Research Laboratories, Cambridge, Massachusetts

The MIT Investment Management Company is evaluating options to renovate a former Ford automobile assembly plant in Cambridge, Massachusetts. One option is to convert the building to a speculative multitenant research laboratory build-

Exterior photograph of the landmark 640 Memorial Drive, a former Ford automobile assembly plant in Cambridge, Massachusetts. One option is to convert the building to a speculative multitenant research laboratory building. *Image courtesy of KlingStubbins.*

ing. The landmark building is located in a highly visible river-front site. City regulatory agencies have been appreciative of the efforts to preserve and find a new life for this culturally significant landmark building.

The former automobile assembly plant was built with a robust concrete structural frame with large, flexible, open floor plates and tall floor-to-floor heights and a 22-foot column bay spacing, ideal for laboratory planning. The building would require extensive building systems upgrades, including a new historical facade renovation, a mechanical penthouse, various service shafts, and elevators.

Specific benefits that would be realized by renovating this existing building:

1. Embodied energy in existing construction materials would be conserved.
2. Landfill disposal of demolition debris would be avoided.
3. An historical and cultural resource would be preserved.
4. Permitting would be less complicated compared to new ground-up construction.
5. The construction schedule would be accelerated compared to new ground-up construction.

Adaptive reuse involves challenges related to the characteristics of the building construction that can change and the characteristics that cannot change. The floor plate size and shape, column bay spacing, floor-to-floor height, and the roof site area for new services and equipment are, generally speaking, fixed and difficult, if not physically impossible or cost prohibitive, to change. On the other hand, the perimeter envelope, service shafts, mechanical, electrical, and plumbing systems, and even the structural capacity of the building can all be modified to accommodate a laboratory program.

In conclusion, converting existing buildings to laboratory use can offer significant benefits over new construction. However, not all buildings are suitable for conversion. Consider the suitability of the building characteristics that cannot easily change and the cost and logistics of modifying those that can change as an alternative to an entirely new laboratory building. In all cases, renovating an existing building to laboratory use offers significant local and global environmental benefits compared to demolishing existing buildings and then building anew.

Leasing Laboratory Space in Multitenant Buildings

In many parts of the country, particularly in urban areas where high development costs demand large and complex buildings, laboratory clients are turning to developers as an alternative to building new purpose-built laboratory buildings. Leasing, as an alternative to owning laboratory space offers certain advantages and presents different challenges to both conventional laboratory design and operational issues and to implementing sustainable design measures. To realize sustainable design with this laboratory development model, it is important to understand the business relationship between tenant and landlord and what motivates each to build laboratory-ready shell space or a laboratory fit-out with sustainable design features.

Examples of developers building laboratory buildings include large real estate investment trusts such as BioMed Realty Trust and Alexandria Real Estate Equities, to national developers such as Forest City Enterprises and Boston Properties, to smaller local developers and landlords who may own only one or a few buildings. Tenants in these buildings include start-up ventures and large established companies, biotech and pharmaceutical companies, academic institutions, and hospitals. Often these tenants own other purpose-built research buildings, but for various reasons also lease research space.

There are many development models for these buildings. Examples range from build-to-suit, where a developer builds a purpose-built laboratory building customized to the needs of a specific tenant and then leases the building back to the tenant, to a more conventional tenant/landlord arrangement where a tenant rents all or part of a multitenant laboratory building. Some developers are offering built-out space and providing common services such as glasswash centralized lab gas distribution, while others only offer lab-ready shell space that is built-out and then individually operated by a tenant.

Increasingly, developers are building multitenant, core and shell lab buildings in certain growing urban markets where government, research institutions, health-care institutions, and pharmaceutical companies have historically built purpose-built lab buildings. In this market, developers are interested in sustainable design and construction for many reasons. These include fulfilling a corporate mission to create sustainable buildings, easing permitting of an otherwise unbuildable or challenging site; state and local incentives; energy conservation, reducing building operating costs, and enhancing the marketability of their project.

There is just as much interest in the general topic of sustainable design with this delivery model as there is with purpose-built laboratory buildings. Both building types share similar programmatic and technical challenges and opportunities. However, unlike a company or institution building their own building, in this development model there are two independent parties involved—landlord and tenant—each with their own interests and motivations. For each party, the rewards for implementing sustainable design features are quite different. There is a specific business transaction involved with this building type—developing a building for a given cost and with pro forma anticipating a specific return on investment, and renting space for a given rate with anticipated operating expenses. To understand how sustainable design applies to this building type it is important to understand how sustainable design impacts the financial interest of each party.

Landlords are challenged to target sustainable design features that will enhance their business. For example, sustainable site design practices can help in permitting negotiations or in appealing to neighborhood objections. Similarly, sustainable design features, and LEED certification in particular, can be imperative in marketing premium space to potential tenants.

Tenants also are challenged to target sustainable design features that will help their business. For example, sustainable design features help companies to reduce operating costs, attract and retain talent, improve worker productivity, and to demonstrate corporate values.

At a high level it would seem like an ideal match— landlords offering sustainable design features to tenants looking to fit out sustainably designed spaces. However, it is not always that easy as currently many lease structures and real estate marketing approaches do not connect the investment costs and benefits returns of each party. A successful sustainable design approach for a multitenant laboratory building must address the specific issues relevant to this unique building type and then must connect the motivations of the landlord and tenant.

Sustainability Issues Unique to Multitenant Buildings

While a leased space may feel like home to a tenant, the building is an investment for the building owner, and as such, must perform financially. There are many factors that increase or challenge the financial performance of a real estate investment. It is important to consider how sustainable design features impact the financial performance of the building, and how investment in sustainable design features reward both landlord and tenant. For example, in some lease agreements the landlord pays utility costs and that is considered in establishing the rent rate. In this case, the landlord will benefit from reduced operating costs from energy-efficiency investments. In other lease agreements, the tenants pay utility cost directly. The challenge comes when one party pays for construction and the other for utility costs because the investment and resulting consequences are not connected.

Another sustainable design challenge for multitenant speculative development is that the tenant needs are often unknown at the time of the core and shell construction, and will likely change over the life of the building. As a result, it is difficult to rightsize building systems to optimize systems performance.

Advances in metering technology and building management systems allow both landlord and tenants to accurately measure what is consumed by whom. Installing this metering requires an up-front investment and ongoing effort to monitor the metering and to assign the resulting utility costs. However, without metering, it is more challenging to encourage conservation in a multitenant building unless conservation by one tenant is recognized in reduced operating costs. By comprehensively and accurately metering utility costs, landlords encourage tenants to responsibly manage their utility consumption.

Beyond initial building construction and tenant fit-out, landlords in multitenant buildings are also responsible for ongoing building operations and maintenance activities that also greatly impact environmental considerations. In negotiating a lease in a sustainably managed building, ongoing building management practices should include continual proactive maintenance to ensure optimal performance of building systems, a recycling program, and a green housekeeping program.

The Landlord's Motivation

Sustainable design motivations for a commercial real estate developer or landlord begin with the permitting process and project schedule. Sustainable design features such as stormwater management, reduced light pollution, connections to public transportation, and energy and water efficiency, and reduced emissions decrease the burden of new construction on municipal infrastructure and can appease the concerns of the surrounding neighbors. By reducing these concerns, a sustainably designed building is often easier, less risky, and quicker to permit, resulting in a faster process from initial investment occupancy to rent collection.

Sustainable design features can reduce first costs, for example, in rebates for energy-efficient investment from utility companies, and also operating costs such as reduced power and water costs and reduced insurance premiums.

Recent market data is suggesting that sustainably designed buildings have greater value than typical conventional buildings. This value is partially a function of reduced operating costs but also of increased market demand and higher occupancy rates. Some real estate appraisers even consider the intangible benefits of a green building as an indication of quality and therefore as a reduced investment risk.

While there is little data to suggest that a sustainably designed building can command higher rents, there is recent consensus that sustainable design features, and LEED certification in particular, are an important market differentiator in appealing to potential tenants. Even without higher rents, higher occupancy and faster leasing will improve the financial performance of a commercial real estate investment.

The Tenant's Motivation

Sustainable design motivations for a commercial real estate developer or landlord begin with evaluating the advantages of potential building candidates. The lease terms of a specific building often dictate much of the sustainable design potential of a tenant fit-out. For example, if a tenant invests in an energy-efficient lighting system, will the tenant realize the reduced operating cost? As another example, the major base building tenant systems are already in place before tenant fit-out construction. Do these systems allow for an energy-efficient design? A successful lease arrangement will allow the party that invests in operating efficiency to realize the return benefits. Ultimately, a tenant must work with the benefits and compromises of the base building. Studies make the connection between workplace quality (i.e., daylighting, indoor air quality) and worker productivity. (See Chapter 7 for more discussion on the health and happiness of laboratory building occupants.) The best justification for investment in the quality of the workplace is the return on improved productivity considering the cost of people and time, and not just rent and hard construction.

Identifying Grants and Rebates

If ease of permitting, energy conservation, and reducing building operating costs and tenant demand are not enough incentive to incorporate sustainable features into new multitenant, core and shell lab buildings, then available financial incentives from utility companies and local and state agencies may be. For example, NYSERDA (New York State Energy Research and Development Authority) and the Massachusetts Technology Collaborative (Massachusetts) offer incentive programs to help defray the added cost of alternative energy and energy-efficiency measures, including design studies and energy modeling. Other programs offered by local utility companies help to offset some or all of the additional cost of energy-efficient investments.

The LEED Green Building Rating System

The U.S. Green Building Council (USGBC) was quick to recognize how sustainable design practices, as measured by the LEED Green Building Rating System, could readily be applied to commercial real estate development delivery models—core and shell development and tenant fit-out. The original LEED Rating System, LEED v1 for New Construction (LEED-NC), was not easy to apply to this new core-shell/tenant fit-out development model. Many credit calculations in the original LEED-NC v1 Rating System did not apply to core and shell development without the interior fit-out in place. It was even more difficult to organize the effort of multiple tenants, each

fitting out their respective space with their own motivations and interests.

In response, the USGBC published two new and intentionally complementary versions of the LEED Rating System, LEED for Core & Shell Development v2 (LEED-CS), and LEED for Commercial Interiors v2 (LEED-CI). Both of these rating systems continued to evolve in the latest LEED v3 revisions. In theory, a building certified under the LEED-CS program with tenant spaces certified under the LEED-CI program, would be comparable to a building certified by one party under the LEED-NC program. However, each rating system, LEED-CS and LEED-CI, applies to the specific interests and responsibilities of landlord and tenant.

It is important to note that LEED-CI certification, while easier in a LEED-CS certified building, is not limited to only LEED-CS certified buildings and can, theoretically, be achieved in any building. In addition, the LEED for Existing Buildings Program, or LEED-EB, provides a LEED path for older existing buildings similar to the opportunity offered to new buildings with the LEED-CS program.

The LEED Green Building Rating System has become a powerful force in commercial real estate development. For developers, LEED certification can aid in permitting and marketing to potential tenants. For tenants, LEED certification offers differentiating criteria in evaluating options for quality space with lower operating costs.

Case Study Examples

The following are case studies that illustrate some of the considerations discussed related to leasing laboratory space in multitenant buildings.

670 Albany Street at BioSquare, Boston, Massachusetts

670 Albany Street at BioSquare, designed by KlingStubbins and developed by Jones Lang LaSalle, was awarded LEED certification under the USGBC LEED Core & Shell (LEED-CS) v1 Pilot Program. 670 Albany Street is a multitenant, core and shell laboratory building currently occupied by six different user groups from Boston University and Boston Medical Center and is fully leased. The 176,000-square-foot, eight-story facility is the third state-of-the-art laboratory and research building at BioSquare, Boston's largest research park.

The sustainable design features of 670 Albany Street include a 20 percent reduction in energy consumption; a 40 percent reduction in domestic water usage; cleanup of a former industrial site in a dense, urban neighborhood with connections to public transportation; use of low-emitting and recycled construction materials; purchase of green power; sustainable landscaping; and floor plates designed for views to the outside

Exterior view of 670 Albany Street at BioSquare, a LEED-CS certified 176,000-square-foot, multitenant, core and shell laboratory building currently occupied by six different user groups from Boston University and Boston Medical Center. *Courtesy of © Trustees of Boston University and KlingStubbins. Photography © Robert Benson Photography.*

Typical tenant laboratory fit-out at 670 Albany Street demonstrating the flexibility available to individual tenants. *Courtesy of © Trustees of Boston University and KlingStubbins. Photography © Robert Benson Photography.*

and daylight penetration. Additional benefit to the investment in energy efficiency was realized through a comprehensive rebate program from the local utility company.

Rising energy costs, coupled with the growing volume of data on the financial paybacks associated with high-performance buildings, make a strong business case for owner-occupants to invest in sustainable design and construction. It is often more difficult, however, but still possible, for commercial developer-landlords, who must structure a lease agreement that will be both profitable for investors and attractive to tenants, to justify the same investments.

The owner's business strategy for 670 Albany Street was to enhance the project's marketability with the draw of LEED certification, but also specifically with the potential for reduced tenant operating costs. The reduced operating costs are accounted for in two categories. The first category of reduced operating costs is from the efficiency of the shared building equipment and services. The second category of reduced operating costs come from individual tenant accountability as measured through a submetering strategy.

The potential for reduced operating costs is connected to the tenants through triple-net lease agreements offering lower pass-through operating expenses than competing lab product in the marketplace. The owner and designers determined that operating expenses could be accurately calculated and apportioned using an innovative utility submetering strategy supported by measurement and verification—so that each tenant was paying for actual utility usage, not an estimated share of the totals—providing the economic incentive for tenants to conserve energy and water.

For 670 Albany Street, the owner and designers determined that operating expenses could be accurately calculated and apportioned using an innovative utility submetering strategy supported by measurement and verification. As a result, each tenant would only be paying for actual utility usage, not an estimated share of the totals. This strategy directly rewards the tenants who reduce their individual energy use.

Because 670 Albany Street is intended for occupancy by several individual tenants, it is important to understand the relationship between the landlord who owns the building and the tenants who occupy the building. This relationship, including the details of how each tenant shares in, and is held accountable for, their participation in overall energy and water efficiency of the shared building is defined with the lease that each tenant signs. The terms of the lease can do much to encourage energy and water efficiency for each individual tenant.

Laboratory building tenant leases are typically triple-net leases, meaning that the tenant is required to pay (in addition to rent on a square-foot basis) all real estate taxes, building insurance, and building operations such as maintenance, energy, and water costs. Triple-net lease agreements are more common for laboratory buildings than office buildings because the operating costs are so much higher for laboratory buildings. Compared to a single-net lease agreement, where energy and water just come with the rent, a triple-net lease directly encourages each tenant to conserve energy and water because the tenant receives itemized energy and water bills based on actual usage.

For a triple-net lease to work fairly, individual tenant submeters are required for accurate accounting of consumption. In some laboratory buildings, the landlord will attempt to avoid the cost of installing and monitoring individual tenant submeters and just divide the monthly building operating costs pro rata based on the size of each tenant space. However, this strategy will not fairly incentivize tenants to incorporate efficiency measures, because they will not realize a direct connection between their investment and the reward of reduced operating costs.

This strategy requires metering the load of each utility for the building as a whole, and submetering of the loads at the points where the associated risers branch off into each tenant's space. For each utility, the load is metered where it enters the building in order to determine a total amount, and branch meters are used for each tenant; individual tenants pay for their actual usage of utilities—electricity, autoclave or process steam—in their own spaces. In public areas, which are considered rentable space, utilities—including exterior lighting, interior lighting, and elevator operation—are also passed to tenants through the triple-net lease. These costs, however, are minor compared to the actual demand from the tenant.

The most significant engineering challenge was accurate measurement, apportionment, and recovery of the cost of electricity and district steam to run the HVAC's central plant system. The project engineers devised an innovative solution: airflow meters installed in the distribution branches at each tenant's space measure their actual usage in cubic feet per minute (CFM), and associated costs are calculated and apportioned per CFM of use.

The measurement of airflow is not yet standard; in fact, the ability to identify, measure, and verify what each space is using for HVAC is unusual in the market today. Most building owners pass through utility costs using estimates based on the leased area in square feet. Measurement of electricity, gas, and steam use, per se, is fairly straightforward. But it is a challenge for most owners to apportion the cost of HVAC use, which is such a large component in lab buildings, particularly because they are single-pass systems comprising several different utilities.

The strategy also required the addition of approximately 20 percent more control points on the automated building management system than might have been required on a typical building, which incurred additional expense for the technology. There were also consulting expenses associated with designing the system and writing the measurement and verification plan. However, most of these additional capital costs were offset through utility company rebates.

The building owners are in the process of conducting the first verification analysis, which will be used to verify the energy savings projected using design-phase energy modeling. While digital technology has made it possible to perform complex energy modeling studies, these simulations remain somewhat suspect in the minds of many designers and owners, who wonder to what extent they accurately predict real life building operations.

Multitenant, core and shell buildings with later interior fit-out by individual tenants are the standard in the commercial office development market. More recently, developers are applying this model to the development of laboratory building. The new LEED for Core & Shell Development rating system offers developers significant advantages in building and leasing sustainably designed core and shell lab buildings. The strategies that help a building owner to earn LEED-CS certification also can ease permitting, reduce construction and operating costs, and demonstrate a differentiating quality expectation that will help to attract and retain the best tenants.

Sustainable design is a relatively new factor in commercial real estate development. Similarly, developing research space for rent in the model now familiar for office space is also a new force in developing research space. As a result, there is not yet enough data to offer conclusive guidance to developers building new buildings and tenants negotiating new leases. Still, anecdotal evidence suggests emerging trends—that developers believe sustainable design features improve the financial performance of their real estate investments and tenants believe that sustainable design features of their fit-out improve their operational efficiency and productivity.

Renovating Previously Occupied Laboratory Space

This chapter would be incomplete without consideration of the potential alternative of reusing an existing previously occupied laboratory space. Previous sections of this book have focused on ways to "reduce" the environmental impact of laboratory buildings. Previous sections of this chapter have focused on ways to "recycle" existing buildings to contemporary laboratory use. "Reuse" of an existing laboratory space, however, may actually yield the most minimal environmental footprint.

Reusing an existing previously occupied laboratory space can prove to be a complicated endeavor. Careful analysis will be required to determine if moving to a previously occupied lab space will result in a reduced environmental footprint compared to new construction. Issues to consider include:

1. Is a move to a new facility really necessary? Can a renovation of the existing facility modernize buildings systems or increase space utilization avoiding the environmental impact of new construction and/or a move?

2. Is the existing space truly useful as is? In certain cases, the previous occupant may have moved out for reasons other than facility obsolescence, and the space may be renovated with only minimal new construction. In other cases, the space may be unusable without major renovation.

3. Would the optimal design of a new space yield a lesser footprint than the compromises of reusing an existing previously occupied laboratory space? A new optimal design may be in a location with lesser transportation demands, better daylighting, and more efficient building systems.

Conclusion

Alternative strategies such as converting existing buildings to laboratory use, leasing laboratory space in multitenant buildings, and renovating previously occupied laboratory space should be considered to reduce the environmental footprint that comes with new laboratory building ground-up construction. Each of these alternate laboratory building delivery strategies offers unique advantages and challenges, the evaluation both of which will vary depending on the specific circumstances of each project. Nonetheless, each deserves careful analysis in targeting the minimal environmental footprint of a new laboratory project.

Key Concepts

- New ground-up construction comes with a significant environmental footprint including consumption of energy and raw materials, air/water/noise pollution, and generation of waste materials.

- To minimize this environmental footprint, alternate building delivery strategies should be considered including:

  - Converting existing buildings to laboratory use

  - Leasing laboratory space in multitenant buildings

  - Renovating previously occupied laboratory space

- Each of these alternate laboratory building delivery strategies offers unique advantages and challenges, deserving of careful analysis in targeting the minimal environmental footprint of a new laboratory project.

- The extraction, refinement, manufacturing, transport, and erection of construction materials consume energy and create pollution. This investment of energy, called embodied energy, or the energy "embodied" in building material in place is wasted when functional, useful building materials are demolished and sent to a landfill.

- Leasing, as an alternative to owning laboratory space, offers certain advantages and presents different challenges to both conventional laboratory design and operational issues and to implementing sustainable design measures.

- "Reuse" of an existing laboratory space may actually yield the most minimal environmental footprint.

chapter 10 Conclusion

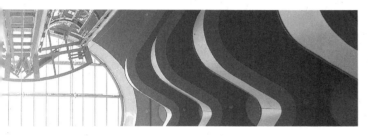

Courtesy of KlingStubbins.
Photography by © Jeff Goldberg / Esto.

Sustainable Design of Research Laboratories: Planning, Design, and Operation offers a comprehensive practical summary of concepts and technologies now available to those involved in the design and delivery of sustainable lab facilities. It's exciting to see how sustainable considerations can serve as a filter for virtually all planning and design decisions, whether projects simply provide improved operations, existing building system upgrades, facility renovations, or new research environments. Time will allow further advancements through research and analysis yielding yet-unthought-of technologies and strategies that enhance laboratory building performance. Research facilities historically have significant known and lasting implications on natural resources and the environment, making it imperative to utilize sustainable and energy-sensitive design solutions on all future building projects.

Competing with this are traditional design approaches, values, and standards that still shape decision-making for too many of today's laboratories. While it remains important to learn from prior generations of laboratory design, future research organizations and project delivery teams must have the will to advance yesterday's accepted practices into today's new energy-efficient and resource-conserving solutions for tomorrow's laboratories.

Past laboratory planning and design practices have been shaped by considerations ranging from safety practices pushing research environment toward zero risk, to the availability of relatively low-cost energy sources permitting the development of high-capacity and infrastructure-intense facilities. Prior research environments provided fume hood and supply air–intensive environments without pushing further to reduce air flows, limit sash openings, and conserve volumes of air. Tomorrow's laboratories must be far more aware of high operating costs and seek new technologies, design criteria, and direction, as well as operational methods, to offset these costs.

Prior high-cost and energy-consuming strategies such as installing high watts per square foot capability for laboratories powering anticipated instrumentation, high air change rates accommodating safety requirements as well as "building in" more system capacity than needed to guard against fear of running out of lab air, and once-through constant volume air systems must be challenged on future projects. Capital continues to be less available for research while heightened awareness concerning conserving resources exists. Tomorrow's laboratories' designs must challenge prior design criteria and "rightsize" systems, and give building occupants and operators monitoring and dashboard tools to modulate and manage building systems.

Prior practices utilizing space, and therefore resource-intensive service corridor and interstitial space for routing ductwork and piping, are giving way to higher net (and assignable) square foot to gross square foot planning strategies, enabling higher space utilization for science. Linear equipment rooms and in-lab ghost

corridors are now used to accommodate material movement and service distribution while yielding much higher space utilization. Individualized and customized laboratory spaces, unless driven by specific research methods, have given way to open and generic laboratory lay-outs.

Prior designs pre-invested in an array of lab bench service utilities, regardless of how uncertain their future use will be. Today's designs must consider distributing services only where needed while providing the flexibility for future run-outs.

Improvements to building design will continue to evolve over time. Building and scientific equipment vendors must push current boundaries for energy-efficient equipment; educational systems at all levels must continue to promote and expand environmental awareness. Now is the time to aggressively implement strategies to lessen future environmental impact and respond to new directions in research; we need to design tomorrow's laboratories today.

Tomorrow's laboratories will be characterized by new drivers including: codes and guidelines expanding regulations concerning the use of and creating penalties for high energy and chemical use; expanded application of "dry" laboratories that are instrumentation equipment–intensive; the drive to optimize the cost of research with discovery; and research approaches that are far more reliant on collaborative and networked science teams. On top of this, the laboratory workspace must have "humanistic" qualities providing social, ergonomic, communications, and interaction needs.

Future laboratory designs will be based on expanding collaboration within the research facility and the laboratory floor plate, throughout the research campus, and extending to linkages to external research sites. Tools such as telepresence, user interface technologies, and interactive white boards will be prevalent within the laboratory environment. Creating interaction and meeting spaces within the laboratory, organizing casework for visual contact, and integrating the office function more closely, if not within the laboratory environment, will be future features.

Further isolation of energy- and noise-intensive equipment and higher hazard functions into alcoves and support rooms will enable the concentration of building utility and air systems there while leaving the primary lab to function free from hazard (giving con-

sideration to once-through air), accommodating more instrumentation, and allowing the flexibility to reconfigure laboratories. Expanding daylighting strategies, chilled beams, heat recovery, consideration for underfloor air distribution, advancements in ductless fume hood technologies, and continuous monitoring of laboratory air for hazards will be routine design considerations for future laboratories.

Now is the time to merge sustainable design fully with new direction in how scientific research will be conducted. It is this book's sincere objective to generate continued discussion and document strategies to move sustainable design practices forward.

Index

WILEY BOOKS ON Sustainable Design

For these and other Wiley books on sustainable design, visit www.wiley.com/go/sustainabledesign